STRIKING BACK

Britain's Airborne and Commando Raids 1940–42

Niall Cherry

Helion & Company Ltd

This book is dedicated to all those who served their country in its hour of need 1939–1945.

Helion & Company Limited
26 Willow Road
Solihull
West Midlands
B91 1UE
England
Telephone 0121 705 3393
Fax 0121 711 4075
Email: publishing@helion.co.uk
Website: www.helion.co.uk

Published by Helion & Company 2009
Designed and typeset by Farr out Publications, Wokingham, Berkshire
Cover designed by Bookcraft Limited, Stroud, Gloucestershire
Printed in the UK by the MPG Books Group

Front cover image: A small group of commandos watching a burning oil tank during Operation Claymore, Lofoten Islands, March 1941. (IWM N396)
Rear cover image: A commando ready to go on operations, c 1941. (IWM H17461)

ISBN 978-1906033-25-5

British Library Cataloguing-in-Publication Data.

A catalogue record for this book is available from the British Library.

For details of other military history titles published by Helion & Company Limited contact the above address, or visit our website: http://www.helion.co.uk.

We always welcome receiving book proposals from prospective authors.

Contents

List of Photos

List of Maps

Maps drawn by a combination of Eugene Wijnhoud and Niall Cherry. Maps 6 and 9 courtesy of HMSO and Bob Peatling respectively. Maps 4 and 8 courtesy of the National Archives.

Glossary

ALC	Assault Landing Craft
BD	Battle Dress
Beehive	A shaped explosive charge which resembled a beehive
Clam	A small magnetic charge fired by a time delay fuse
CO	Commanding Officer or Combined Operations
Footprint 6"	A device fitted to normal Army issue boots to enable the wearer to walk easier on snow
FS	Field Service
GS	General Service
Hatbox	A term used to describe a container for storing Bren gun magazines
HEP	Hydro Electric Power
Housewife	A small linen pouch issued to every soldier containing a few needles, pins, cotton, darning wool, buttons and so to enable running repairs to be carried out on clothing
IWM	Imperial War Museum
LCS	Landing Craft Support
MI9	Military Intelligence 9, the Army Department specialising in escape and evasion in German held territory
MLC	Mechanised Vehicle Landing Craft
PHE	Plastic High Explosive
SAA	Small Arms Ammunition
SSRF	Small Scale Raiding Force

Foreword by Harry Pexton

I am highly delighted to have been asked by Niall Cherry to write a few words of introduction to his latest book. This deals with a new form of warfare of which I was proud to be a guinea pig. Perhaps a few words of explanation are due here. In 1940 I volunteered for Number 2 Commando and a few weeks later found myself being one of the first paratroopers in the British Army. Then early in 1941 I was selected to take part in Operation Colossus, the first time that airborne troops were used by us in the war. On February 10th 1941 I parachuted into an olive tree close to the Tragino Aqueduct in southern Italy with the intention of blowing it up. This we achieved within a few hours of landing.

It has slightly annoyed me over the years that our small involvement in the development of the airborne forces is frequently overlooked and that several books state that Bruneval was the first parachute raid of the war. I am therefore pleased to see that Niall has covered the role of X Troop in some detail and perhaps given us the credit that we deserve.

As well as our small part the actions of our fellow Army commandos is also included, and I hope this work is of interest as Niall tries to tell the story from the soldier's viewpoint.

I am delighted that someone has decided to pull all the early raids together in one work and hope that it achieves the success it deserves.

Preface

As the events of the Second World War fade into the distance I feel it is important that amongst the many activities and groups of men who fought in it a relatively small band of brothers are not overlooked. By this I mean the men who in the dark days after Dunkirk in 1940 volunteered for what in those days was known as 'Special Service'. Often given very little idea of what they were letting themselves in for, they all wanted to strike back at the enemy. Later, these SS units evolved into the airborne forces and commandos and went on to take a major part in operations such as Overlord, Market Garden and Varsity. However before this in the early years of the war they undertook a number of (compared to those just mentioned) small-scale raids. Indeed a friend of mine after reading part of my manuscript said to me, 'I've never even heard of half of these raids!'

Whilst some of the early raids such as St Nazaire and Dieppe have received quite a lot of coverage, in my view others such as Lofoten and Bruneval had not really appeared strongly on the radar and I hope this book will fill a gap that to me at least needed filling.

As usual I have received a lot of help and perhaps the most important group were that ever-dwindling group of veterans who allowed me to talk to them about their experiences. To each and every one of them my thanks, but a special word to Harry Pexton for writing the foreword.

However, given the passage of time a great deal of reliance has to be placed on 'desk research' and I would like to thank the staff at the National Archives and the Imperial War Museum for their help. Crown Copyright material in the National Archive is reproduced by permission of the Controller of Her Majesty's Stationery Office.

Book writing or research is hard enough on your own as I know from past experience and this time I decided to push the envelope outwards and pressgang some willing volunteers to help. My particular and deepest thanks go to my gang of research assistants for much valuable spadework, proofreading and 'eureka moments', particularly at the National Archives. In no particular order except alphabetically they fully deserve their 'Mention in Despatches' – Martin Bull, Steve Elsey, Keith Harris, John Howes and Stephen Sowerby.

Help especially with photos has been willingly given by the following people and I am happy also to say thank you here – Geoff Teece, Bill Penley of the Penley Radar archives, Howard Habron, Mark Bougourd from Guernsey, Silvio Tasselli from Italy and Kjell Sørensen and Odd-Arild Longstøyl from Norway.

The Dutch Airborne Mafia also assisted, namely Robert Voskuil for photos and Eugene Wijnhoud who helped with the maps. Also my long-standing friend Robert Sigmond, he knows that what he has done for me cannot be put into words.

My thanks also go to Karel Margry – the editor of *After The Battle* for permission to use extracts from various articles printed in their magnificent magazine. Major-General A Deane-Drummond, Graeme Deeley and Mrs. J Frost kindly gave permission for me to use extracts from *Return Ticket, Worst Fears Confirmed* and *A Drop Too Many* respectively.

A special mention also to Alan Brown and Andrew Blacklock at the Airborne Forces Museum for assistance and allowing me to plunder their files on several occasions.

Duncan Rogers of Helion willingly agreed to my choice of subject for my second book for them and I hope I have again repaid your faith in my ability. I have again been supported by my long-suffering wife Deborah and children Claire and Sarah by allowing me to escape to my study or to London on research trips for this, my fifth book. Both of the last two mentioned have been involved in some shape or form in this either by helping with the index or actually inputting words into the computer for the draft manuscript. Perhaps temporarily her husband and their father has returned from the shores of northern France and the ice and snow of Norway.

Chapter 1

The Seeds of Despair

The early years of the Second World War did not go well for Britain, the British Expeditionary Force (BEF) left for France in 1939 in similar heart as their predecessors had in 1914. However it is probably fair to say that they went with a similar mentality to the Tommies of 1914 and expected to fight a similar war. Our major ally the French certainly had a 'static' philosophy as they manned the Maginot Line. The only problem with this strategy was the opposition, the Germans certainly had no plans to fight a war dominated by trench fighting. Their philosophy envisaged 'Blitzkrieg' or lightning war, a war based on firepower and movement with heavy emphasis on armoured vehicles. However, hand in hand with this Blitzkrieg came the idea of airborne warfare by seizing key objectives and holding them until the land troops arrived.

Soon after arriving in France in September 1939 the BEF settled down to what came known as the 'Phoney War' with very little activity on either side. Indeed the winter of 1939/1940 was one of the worst on record. All of the inactivity changed in the early morning of 10th May 1940 when the German armed forces swung into action. As well as the Luftwaffe bombing airfields in France, German tanks and infantry unleashed a massive offensive through Belgium and Holland.

In May 1940 the BEF consisted of 10 divisions and was concentrated mainly in the northern part of France in areas that would have been familiar to the BEF of 1914. Together with French and Belgian troops the Allies were able to field 53 divisions. Arranged against them were 72 German divisions. In spite of these large numbers the fighting over the coming weeks was to be dominated by just 10 German armoured divisions. Indeed the coast of France was reached on 21st May by armoured troops.

Amongst all these operations on 10th May was the use of German airborne forces in several places notably against the Belgium fort at Eben-Emael. Perhaps it is worth mentioning here that also on this day Britain had a new Prime Minister- Winston Churchill. He had replaced Neville Chamberlain who resigned as he had lost the confidence of the majority of the House of Commons.

The main body of German airborne forces were to be used in Holland and to capture vital bridges at Rotterdam, Dordrecht and Moerdijk which carried the main road into the south of Holland over the lower Rhine. The remaining troops were to be used in Belgium by seizing bridges over the Albert Canal near Maastricht. A key point in the Belgian defences here was a modern fortress at Eben Emael. It was intended to land gliders on top of the fort and destroy the gun emplacements by using a new 'secret weapon'- a hollow charge. A hollow charge was a specially shaped explosive that looked like a small beehive that directed the explosive charge into a concentrated force. This meant it was able to blow a hole through concrete and steel up to 12 inches thick depending on the weight of explosives.

The fort at Eben Emael, situated on a plateau overlooking the Albert Canal, was manned by about 1200 Belgian soldiers and covered an area about half a mile wide by three-quarters of a mile long. There was a 50 yard drop on the canal side and wide anti-tank ditches had been dug on the others. The gun emplacements had a mixture of 75mm and 120mm guns together with many machine gun posts. In spite of these static defences, none of the gun casemates were protected by surface trenches, and no precautions had been placed on the large flat open top surface of the fort. Obviously no-one on the Belgian side thought an air assault was likely, indeed there was only one small anti-aircraft battery in the vicinity. The Germans had obviously spotted this weak link. Eleven gliders containing 86 men were to take part in the operation, which was timed to start at 0525, five minutes before German troops crossed the Belgian border. Other parties of German airborne forces were to capture three bridges over the Albert Canal, in all around 450 men. The planning had been greatly helped by aerial photographs of the fort, one of which showed Belgian soldiers playing football on top of the fort; this meant there should be no mines up there!

Although the fort held out in places for nearly 24 hours the majority of the casemates had been put out of action and didn't really hinder the German attack. This operation showed that a small group of determined men could attack a much larger objective and succeed. The German tactic of landing right on top of the target with the element of shock and surprise proved its worth, even if heavy casualties might result. The German casualties were six men killed and twenty wounded. The German High Command had estimated they would have taken 6000 casualties in a 'conventional' attack. Of the three bridges over the Albert Canal, two were captured intact, and within a few hours the Panzer divisions were pouring over them and into the heart of Belgium. Fewer than 500 troops in 42 gliders had opened the way for the defeat of the Belgian Army and led to the evacuation of the BEF.

The airborne landings opened the way for the armoured troops to move forward in numbers-the Germans used most of their tanks in one force, unlike the BEF who used them in 'penny packets'. Although in places giving the Germans a bloody nose, the superiority of the German Army was just too much and the situation became grim.

The BEF was in retreat and the decision was taken to evacuate it across the Channel. With Calais and Boulogne already under siege the only feasible option was the port and beaches of Dunkirk. An evacuation that started on 29th May managed to bring back around 330,000 men of varying nationalities. France signed an armistice with the Germans on the 22nd June 1940. Britain now stood alone with the Germans just across the Channel. Churchill realised that the Germans were not going to play this war by the rules of 1914-18. So perhaps recalling the exploits of the Boer Commandos in South Africa and the Eben Emael operation he decided that irregular operations were going to be a part of the struggle ahead. Perhaps almost as significant was the amount of publicity that around 4500 German airborne troops had been given in the British press.

Many articles had appeared and Britain was in the 'grip of parachutist fever' and preparing for a last-ditch fight against the German Army led by Hitler's airborne hordes. Panic, rumour and overheated imaginations had greatly inflated the modest number of airborne troops that Germany had at her disposal. It must be borne in mind that the Germans had dropped dummy parachutists in order to spread confusion and dupe their opponents into thinking that larger numbers had been dropped than actually were, but such was the extent of the exaggeration it seems that perhaps this was an easy excuse for the recent rout in France and Belgium.

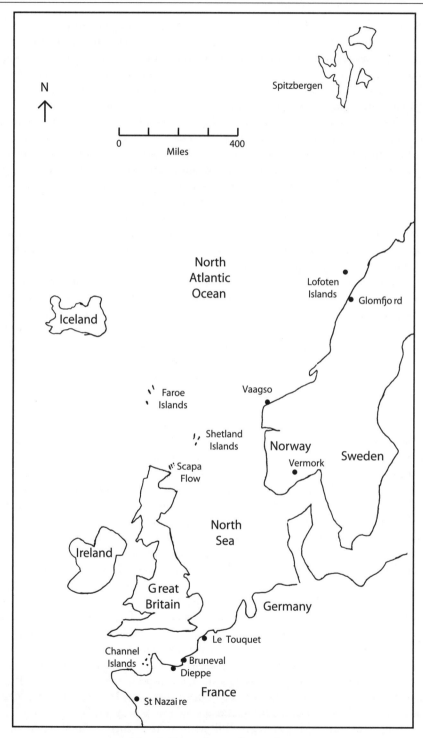

Map 1: General area of operations

Wild rumours went round of Germans landing in Holland dressed as anything from nuns to butchers-boys. Several books and pamphlets published at the time helped to add fuel to these flames. Perhaps one of the more popular was a sixpenny (2.5 pence in 'modern day' money) booklet called *The German Parachute Corps* by P.E.Popham- who on the cover claimed to have 'studied them for several years'. Amongst a great deal of accurate information about the aircraft used, uniforms worn and equipment carried, was also a great deal of untrue statements. He described how the German paratroopers often disguised themselves as vicars, nuns, butchers-boys and postmen. The clergymen carried machine guns under their garments and grenades in their trouser pockets, while the postmen had collapsible bicycles and weapons in their post bags. But the *pièce de résistance* was the butchers-boys outfit. As well as wearing a blue and white apron, Popham alluded to the meat basket on the front of a bicycle carrying a machine gun and grenades covered with a white cloth. Meanwhile in another booklet of the period, written by a Professor Low, it pointed out the disadvantages of such disguises for any but the occasional parachutist. He wrote: 'No one is likely to be deceived if he sees a nun, or even a postman, descending by parachute.'

However, it must be said that in spite of these fanciful comments, the British did take the threat very seriously. The almost immediate response was to issue to the nation a rallying-call to form a force to counter this expected airborne attack. This was the LDV or Local Defence Volunteers which was formed in the summer of 1940. They later changed their name to the Home Guard or as the famous TV show depicted 'Dad's Army'. Weapons to arm this new force were in short supply as much equipment had been left behind in France, and it was seriously considered issuing pikes to the LDV as these were seen as an ideal weapon to deal with descending paratroopers. The country in the summer of 1940 was certainly in the grip of 'invasion fever' and many people every day expected to see fleets of German transport aircraft disgorging large numbers of paratroopers over southern England. Fortunately for a variety of reasons this never happened, but in the interim Britain was intending to fight back.

In June 1940 Winston Churchill sent a memorandum to the Joint Chiefs of Staff in which he called for them to propose measures for 'a vigorous, enterprising and ceaseless offensive against the whole German occupied coastline'. He also in this memo called for the formation of a corps of 5000 parachute troops.

Also around this time an officer at the War Office – Lieutenant Colonel Dudley Clarke – wrote a paper on his ideas for a raiding force. Clarke was at this time Military Assistant to General Sir John Gill, the Chief of the Imperial General Staff. It is said that during the grim and black days of the Dunkirk evacuation he thought long and hard about how Britain could strike back. He thought back to the guerilla warfare against Napoleon's troops in Spain, and to the Arab Revolt in 1936 in Palestine, when he had been on the receiving end. A question he asked was 'Could desperate men, only armed with the weapons they could carry, disdaining artillery, baggage trains and all the normal paraphernalia of supply, carry on guerilla warfare against an enemy whose forces were stretched from Narvik in Norway to the Spanish border at the Pyrenees?' The easy answer is probably not; so on the evening of 4th June – which was actually the last day of the Dunkirk evacuation, he put together a single page plan.

It seems that also on this day Churchill wrote to the Chiefs of Staff as follows:

It is of the highest consequence to keep the largest number of German forces all along the coasts of the countries they have conquered, and we should immediately set to work to organise raiding forces on these coasts where the populations are friendly.

Desperate times call for desperate measures and what happened in the next few days must be some kind of record for the bureaucracy of the Civil Service and the Armed Forces. On the morning of the 5th June Dudley Clarke outlines his proposals to Dill, on the next day Dill briefed Churchill. Two days later on the 8th June 1940 Dill told Clarke that his plans had been approved and that afternoon Section MO9 (Military Operations 9) of the War Office had been created. Clarke was ordered to mount a raid across the Channel 'at the earliest possible moment.' However certain constraints were laid down by Churchill, firstly that no unit should be diverted from its most essential task, that of the defence of Britain, and secondly that the raiders would have to make do with the minimum quantity of weapons. But apart from these 'requests' Clarke was given a free hand. As was typical for Churchill with his 'Action This Day' stickers, he took an interest in the raising of these new units and wrote a minute to the Commander in Chief of the Home Forces – General Ironside on 18th June 1940. In this minute amongst other comments was the following:

What are the ideas of the C-in-C Home Forces, about 'Storm Troops' or 'Leopards' drawn from existing units, ready to spring at the throat of any small landings or descents? These officers and men should be armed with the latest equipment, tommy guns, grenades, etc....., and should be given great facilities in motorcycles and armoured cars.

But the next question was where to get the men to be trained or selected as these new troops? The Army who had been handed the task were unwilling to 'nominate' complete units in line with Churchill's previous request, so the only viable option left was to ask for volunteers. I'm sure most readers will be aware (especially if they are an ex-squaddie) of the old Army saying of 'never volunteer for anything'. In spite of this admirable piece of advice many soldiers did volunteer, smarting from the ignominy of the retreat in France. The decision was taken to form 'new' units not based on the traditional Army skeleton of sections, platoons, companies and battalions, but of semi-autonomous troops. A commando was to exist of a Headquarters and ten troops each of three officers and forty-seven men. The basic idea for this framework came from the ten 'Independent Companies' raised in the early part of 1940. These comprised mainly men from the Territorial Army who volunteered to go to Norway to raid the German lines of communications. As it turned out they did no raiding but a few Companies fought as 'normal' infantry, and now in June they were in the process of being disbanded. However enough of them escaped from being 'Returned to Unit' to form the basis of Number 1 and Number 2 Commandos. Men to fill up the gaps and provide some further Commandos were filled by calling for volunteers for special service. One of those who answered the call was a young Gunner Lieutenant by the name of Tony Hibbert. He had escaped from Dunkirk and recalls:

We waded out into the phosphorescent waters of Dunkirk where I and most of my half battery were picked up by a flotilla of launches which ferried us out to a Thames tug. We had been defeated, but they gave us a hero's welcome in Ramsgate. In due course, we reformed at Aberystwyth but since we had no weapons, there was little to do except march up and down the sea front. The only real compensation during this period was the arrival of the Chelsea School of Physical Training for Young Women which had been evacuated to Aberystwyth. These beautiful, healthy girls really kept us on our toes and sometimes even on our knees. But some of us were getting very fed up with being inactive and we started applying to join any unit that looked as if it might have some weapons, and might get us back into the fight again. I volunteered for Number 2 Commando.

The first of the many commando raids over the coming years was carried out on the night of 23rd/24th June 1940. The troops, around 120 in number, under the command of a Major R Tod and with Lieutenant Colonel Dudley Clarke in tow as an observer came ashore on the French coast between Boulogne and Le Touquet. This unit had been given the name of No 11 Independent Company. This small operation was one

1. Commandos in training evacuating a casualty using an aerial
ropeway and a Neil Robertson stretcher. (IWM H32113)

2. A typical WW2 Commando, Paddy Habron. (P Habron)

of the first really 'combined operations'. In the early days it seems the planning was all a bit off-the-cuff. Clarke had earlier pitched up at the Admiralty to see what could be scrounged and got an appointment with the Assistant Chief of the Naval Staff. Like many others in the Navy he was disappointed at what had happened a few weeks earlier and was enthusiastic when he heard the Army wanted to fight back and he promised Clarke 'Anything he'd like to ask for from the Navy.' So a Captain G Garnons-Williams was given the task of collecting suitable vessels and later set up his headquarters in a yacht on the Hamble estuary on the south coast. The armada collected owed more to the little ships of Dunkirk than proper landing craft, as all of them had been lost in Norway. Additionally Garnons-Williams had managed to borrow six rescue craft from the Royal Air Force. Although these were fast, reliable and eminently seaworthy, their bows were high out of the water, and so not the best vessel to be used as landing craft. Still needs must and the small flotilla set out from Newhaven, Folkestone and Dover. The raiders had additionally been loaned the use of half of the country's entire arsenal of Thompson submachine guns – 20 guns. This excursion had been given the name of Operation Collar.

A word or two here about the Thompson submachine gun. During the First World War the need arose for short weapons which could be used in trench fighting, which would have a high rate of fire and which could be fired both from the hip and shoulder. Regretfully the technology wasn't really around at the time to design and manufacture large numbers of weapons such as those envisaged. However the Italians designed the first 'submachine gun' the Villar Perosa. The Germans were as usual not far behind and in 1918 Hugo Schmeisser designed the first German weapon for the Bergmann Company. His weapon was the MP18 – which incidentally was the predecessor of the MP40 which acquired the name of Schmeisser during the Second World War. Britain of course, following on from the High Command's initial dislike of machine guns failed to develop or buy any such weapons for many years. Indeed when war broke out in 1939 nearly every British infantry soldier was armed with a bolt-action rifle. However, in the 1920's in America a Colonel Thompson designed a submachine gun which bore his name, first appearing on the market in 1928 manufactured by the Auto Ordnance Company. It used a calibre of bullet at .45 inch, which was also used in revolvers and automatic pistols. Normally the weapon which became known as the 'Tommy Gun' had a 20 round straight magazine but could also be fitted with a 50 or 100 round drum (circular) magazine. Initially the American military were not interested as it was a relatively expensive weapon, but found favour with gangsters. The British Government, finally waking up to the threat from Germany and realising that her soldiers were ill-equipped with automatic and semi-automatic weapons, placed an order in 1939 for 100,000 guns! Deliveries were at first slow and by 1940 only 40 had been delivered of which 20 were loaned out as described above. It must be said that the Thompson was a precision machined and high quality weapon but expensive, which led to the designers at the Royal Small Arms Factory at Enfield coming up with the Sten submachine gun. Comparing these two weapons is like comparing a Rolls-Royce with a Mini. The Sten was made as cheaply as possible using stamped parts where possible from the thinnest possible sheet metal.

On the coast of France on the night of 23rd/24th June 1940, due to a lack (at that time) of decent navigational aids, one party was on the verge of entering Boulogne harbour, before their error was realised. Swiftly turning round they headed off down the coast and managed to land in some apparently deserted sand dunes. Soon after landing they had a brush with a German patrol. The only British casualty was Dudley Clarke, who it is believed was grazed on the ear by a stray British bullet. Another party had more success, landing about four miles south of Le Touquet. They chanced upon a building surrounded by barbed wire and apparently being occupied by Germans. Two sentries outside a thick belt of barbed wire were swiftly dispatched, and because the commandos were unable to penetrate the thick belt of barbed wire, grenades were thrown through the windows. Exactly who was in this building or what its use was could not be ascertained but it is safe to assume these two unfortunate German sentries were the first kills by the embryonic commando forces. The commandos all safely returned to England and the War Office wasted no time in announcing that British troops had struck the first of many blows back at Hitler's Germany.

Tod's party had been split into four groups and one of them was led by Lieutenant R Swayne. His mission was to land in the area of Le Touquet and to attack the Merlimont Plage Hotel, which was believed to have been requisitioned by the German Army. Swayne and his men successfully made it ashore only to find the hotel boarded up and empty. Somewhat disappointed they patrolled the area but didn't find anything or anybody to attack before the time they were due to be picked up. They returned to their pick-up point, only to find that their boat was nowhere to be seen. Lieutenant Swayne later recalled:

> It was hanging around some distance offshore and we couldn't make contact with it. Some Germans turned up then whom we killed and that created a bit of noise. I'm afraid we bayoneted them. I was armed with a .38 revolver. I'm sorry to say that I forgot to load it in this occasion. So I hit one of the Germans on the head with the butt of my revolver. My batman bayoneted one, and I grappled with another and we killed them. It wasn't really very serious soldering, I'm sorry to say. And,

of course, because we were being rushed, we never got their identity papers, which was very inefficient of us. We also lost a lot of our weapons. Then some more Germans appeared in the sand-dunes and I needed to get the men away fast, so there was nothing else for it but to swim out to the boat.

In any case comments like weapons were left behind were not made public, and a press release was issued to acclaim the first commando raid. This said:

In co-operation with the Royal Air Force, naval and military units yesterday carried out a successful reconnaissance of the enemy coastline. Landings were effected at a number of points and contact made with German troops. Casualties were inflicted and some enemy dead fell into our hands. Much useful information was obtained. Our forces suffered no casualties.

3. A picture of part of a commando troop inside an ALC in those last few seconds before hitting the beach. Note that the fourth man back in the left-hand file has a Boyes anti-tank rifle. (IWM H17474)

MO9 were now busy thinking up the next raid and this was mounted on the night of 14th/15th July when Operation Ambassador was launched on the island of Guernsey in the German-occupied Channel Islands – the only part of the United Kingdom to be under German occupation in the Second World War. The Channel Islands had been occupied by the Germans beginning on 30th June and two days later Winston sent another of his famous minutes to General Ismay, the head of the Military Wing of the War Cabinet Secretariat. This said:

> If it be true that a few hundred German troops have been landed on Jersey or Guernsey by troop-carriers, plans should be studied to land secretly by night on the islands and kill or capture the invaders. This is exactly one of the exploits for which the commandos would be suited. There ought to be no difficulty in getting all the necessary information from the inhabitants and from those evacuated.

So over the next few days a Guernsey man who had escaped was landed on the island for a clandestine reconnaissance. H Nicolle was a previous member of the Royal Guernsey Militia but had been given a commission in the British Army and the plan was for him to stay on the island for two days. He successfully avoided capture and on his pick up, his place was taken by two other officers who were familiar with Guernsey and would guide the commandos in. They were Second Lieutenants P Martel of the Hampshire Regiment and D Mulholland from the Duke of Cornwall's Light Infantry. In a report written at the time it was said there were 469 Germans on the island. This number was found out by information from a Guernsey resident who had been told by a German the number of rations he had been required to provide daily. Additionally it was known that the majority of them were centred around St Peter Port with a few isolated positions away from here. This particular operation had been given to the relatively newly formed No 3 Commando, commanded by Lieutenant Colonel J Durnford-Slater. He had volunteered for special service when Adjutant of the 23rd Medium and Heavy Training Regiment Royal Artillery based at Plymouth. It can perhaps be said that he was probably somewhat surprised to be told on 5th July that he was now the Commanding Officer of No 3 Commando with the rank of Lieutenant Colonel. A reason for this may have been that Plymouth had been selected as the headquarters for this particular commando.

It was planned that these new units would not be based on the traditional infantry battalion structure of sections, platoons and so on. A commando was in theory to consist of 532 officers and men, this was subdivided into a headquarters element and ten troops of 50 men each commanded by a Captain with two subalterns. This number of 532 broke down into 250 men, 247 NCOs (122 Lance-Corporals, 81 Corporals, 42 Sergeants and 2 Warrant Officers), 24 subalterns, ten Captains and one Major or Lieutenant Colonel. The men were to be all volunteers and additionally had to be already trained soldiers. Whilst they were expected to act as infantry, the training given was to be tougher and greater emphasis placed on independence and initiative. One of the major perks was that the men were not accommodated in the normal barrack environment but had to find their own living quarters. For this they were given a daily allowance of 6 shillings and 8 pence (in today's money 38 pence).

4. A commando ready to go on operations. Note the assorted weaponry he is carrying which appears to include as well as the rifle, bayonet and Fairbairn-Sykes fighting knife, two other knives. Next to the fighting knife is a coiled toggle rope. (IWM H17461)

No 3 Commando was probably the first unit to be officially formed and given this number as the numbers 1 and 2 had been tentatively 'reserved' for two 'special airborne' commandos.

The first plan in Operation Ambassador was for 40 men from H Troop under the command of Captain V de Crespigny to land and create a diversion for the main aim of the operation. This was to be a raid on the aerodrome in the district called Forest, which is situated in the southern part of the island. The aerodrome raid was to be carried out by the (almost disbanded) No 11 Independent Company (later to form the basis of No 11 Commando). This group was split into two parties – 70 men commanded by Major Tod and 20 by Captain Goodwin. As well as the Army commandos, the other services were represented by two Royal Navy destroyers – HMS *Scimitar* and HMS *Saladin* and seven RAF air-sea rescue launches. The two destroyers were to transport the men and act as escort to the RAF launches, which would transport the troops from the ships to the beaches. Bad weather at the last minute delayed the operation by 24 hours, which must have been a worrying time for the two officers still on Guernsey, as there was no way of informing them of the delay. Another last minute problem then reared its head.

This description of the problem comes from Lieutenant Colonel Durnford-Slater:

Since we were to sail from Dartmouth, I had breakfast at the Royal Castle Hotel on the morning of the 14th. I was excited, naturally, at being on the verge of our first operation, a very secret affair of course, and it came as rather a shock when I saw my sister Helen sitting at the next table with her husband, Admiral Franklin. Helen saw me and smiled happily. "Hello, John! What on earth are you doing here?"

I replied that we had some troops training in the area and asked what she was doing. She said they were down to visit their son at the Royal Naval College. I felt uneasy but tried not to appear so. Fortunately, for the strain was growing, I was called out to the foyer of the hotel a few minutes later. An officer from Combined Operations Staff had just come off the night train from London. He said; "Colonel, the whole plan has been changed. Jerry is too strong. He's been reinforced at some of the places where we had intended to land."

We moved into a bedroom of the hotel and worked out a new plan on the spot. Now we were to land at Petit Port on the south side of the island, just west of the Jerbourg Peninsula and not on the north coast as originally decided. We were to sail at six o'clock that evening. Our role was still to create a diversion for the Independent Company which was to attack the airfield. We completed our preparations in the gymnasium of the Royal Naval College, Dartmouth. Many of the weapons had been specially brought from London, as Tommy guns and Brens were in very short supply and could only be issued for actual operations. We obtained the help of some cadets from the college who thoroughly enjoyed the

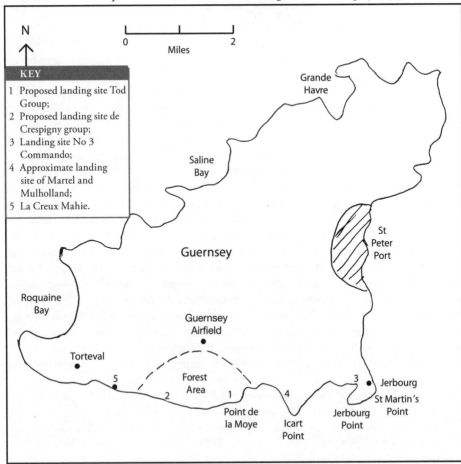

Map 2 – Operation Ambassador

work of loading the magazines and helping us in general. We planned the approach with the naval commanders and started to brief the men. Before we realised it, it was a quarter to six, and we had to embark hurriedly in the destroyer. It was a lovely summer evening and as we steamed out of the harbour most of the town was out walking on the quay. I wondered what they thought of our strange-looking convoy.

I went over the final details with my officers in the Captain's cabin of the *Scimitar* on the way across. We had been so busy all day, dealing with naval officers and obtaining and issuing our special weapons, that this was the first chance our officers had had to discuss it all together.

Lieutenant Joe Smale's party was to establish a road block on the road leading from the Jerbourg Peninsula to the rest of the island, so that we should not be interrupted by German reinforcements. My own party were to attack a machine gun post and put the telegraph cable hut out of action. Captain de Crespigny was to attack the barracks situated on the Peninsula. Second Lieutenant Peter Young was to guard the beach. Peter did not relish this job as he wanted more action. "All

5. A commando on a training exercise in England. Cliff climbing had to be second nature. (IWM H17500)

right," I told him, "if it's quiet, come forward and see what's going on." "You chaps satisfied with the arrangements?" I asked finally. They nodded. We synchronised our watches. The password for the operation was Desmond.

The official report compiled after the raid detailed another last second problem, it was found that two of the rescue craft were unserviceable and had to be left behind in port. So a revised plan was put together. The party (known as Number 1 landing) under Durnford-Slater was left undisturbed. The Number 2 party under Captain Goodwin was halved in size and now had only one rescue launch instead of two. Major Tod's party was allocated two launches and the surplus men being put into the whaler of HMS *Saladin*, which was being pressed into use as a landing craft.

The following is again taken from Durnford-Slater's account:

Owing to the trouble over the launches, certain stores had to be transferred to other boats and two of the other serviceable launches had to make extra trips to embark the men in the destroyers. The convoy started from Dartmouth harbour at 1845 and proceeded to sea at the speed ordered. For some reason (possibly an extra trip to collect life belts), launch 313 was delayed in starting, and at about 1950 she was five or six miles astern of the convoy. For a time she kept at this distance, so the speed of the convoy was reduced to 15 knots to allow her to catch up. 313 came up well for a time and then dropped astern again, so the speed of the convoy was still further reduced to 10 knots; 313 then came up into her correct position just before nightfall. Speed was then increased to 18 knots.

Landfall was made at about the time expected and the convoy then went to within about five miles of the shore in order to check its position. Visibility was poor, there was some mist and the moon was obscured. The high cliffs at the western end of the south shore of the island were easily distinguishable but it was extremely difficult to distinguish any points on the coast to the westward. Beyond the ending of the cliffs there appeared to be a number of rocky points protruding with misty spaces and low lying land in between.

HMS *Scimitar* and two of the rescue launches broke away and passed *Saladin* on the starboard side. Just as *Scimitar* was disappearing into the mist and slight drizzle ahead she appeared to be turning in towards the coast. When the Captain of Saladin was satisfied that he had reached position Y, he stopped, the rescue launches came alongside and the whaler was put into the water. The troops were then embarked in the boats, rescue launch commanders were shown the points on the shore by the Captain of *Saladin* and the boats had all left the ship by 0045.

The launches purred away from the mother ship. The naval officers in charge of the launches started off on the agreed course, watching their compasses carefully. My own eyes were on the cliffs and I was astonished to note that we were heading out to sea in the direction of Brittany. "This is no bloody good," I said to the skipper of our launch, "we're going right away from Guernsey." He looked up from his compass for the first time. Then he looked back and saw the cliff. "You're right! We are indeed. It must be this damn degaussing arrangement that's knocked the compass out of true. I ought to have had it checked."

We then headed straight for the beach, about a hundred yards from the beach a black silhouette seemed to approach from our port side. In undertones some of the men murmured, "U-boat." Momentarily my heart sank. What a mug's game this was! Why hadn't I stayed at home in warmth and comfort? Then I realised that the U-boat was only a rock which bore the exact shape of a submarine superstructure. At that moment the launches simultaneously and side by side, hit the bottom. As they had not been designed as landing craft, they drew several feet of water. Besides, as the plan had been postponed for forty-eight hours, the tide was not halfway out. It was high. The bottom instead of being smooth sand as has been calculated, was studded with boulders. I jumped in, armpit-deep. A wave hit me on the back of my neck and caused me to trip over a rock. All around me officers and men were scrambling for balance, falling, coming up and coughing salt water.

I doubt if there was a dry weapon amongst us. Once on shore, we loosened the straps of our battledress to let the sea pour out. Then, with a sergeant named Knight close behind me, I set off running up the long flight of concrete steps which led to the cliff top, 250 feet up. In my eagerness I went up too fast. By the time I reached the top I was absolutely done, but Knight was even worse, gasping for breath like an untrained miler at the tape. I was exhausted myself and my sodden battledress seemed to weigh a ton. My legs were leaden, my lungs bursting, I could hear the squeak and squelch of wet boots as the rest of the troop followed us up from the beach. Fortunately the night was warm.

The consequences of just one German soldier being at the top of the path for the future of the commando forces are relatively easy to imagine. Apart from re-embarking and attempting to land elsewhere there was no other way inland from the beach. The commandos coming up the steep path would have been easy targets and who knows what a disaster would have done for the fledging raiding force. Fortunately no Germans were in the area and it was an unopposed landing.

Durnford-Slater's account continues:

I had an idea we were already behind schedule and I led on between a few small houses. We had to be clear of Guernsey by 3.00 a.m. As we passed each house, a dog inside began to bark. Presently there was a chorus of barking dogs behind us. "For God's sake, come on." I panted to Knight, who seemed to be slowing down. "We haven't got all night." By then I had my second wind and didn't feel tired again during the operation. My headquarters party was close on my heels – Lieutenant Johnny Giles, CSM Beesley, Knight, two lance-bombardiers and a sapper. Another dog began to bark. "Shut up!" Johnny Giles yelled at it and the barking became louder. "This is going to alert the whole damn island." somebody remarked ruefully. One of the staff officers in London had suggested sending an aeroplane to circle over our operational area with a view to deadening any noise we might make and I had accepted this idea. At this moment I saw the aircraft, an Anson, circling above us about three hundred feet. He was plainly visible and his exhaust pipes were glowing red.

The machine gun post, which was the first objective of my little group, was at the tip of the Jerbourg Peninsula, eight hundred yards from the landing place. I went as far as the barracks with de Crespigny. Just before going into the barracks, de Crespigny broke into a house to get information from the householder. I went in with him through the back door. However, the man we found was so terrified that he had entirely lost the power of speech; all he could do was to let out a series of shrieks. We left de Crespigny and began climbing down the cliff. I sent Beesley, Knight and the others to the cable hut. Johnny Giles and I crawled up on either side of the little mound in which the machine gun nest was dug. I carried grenades and a .45 Webley; Giles, a giant of well over six feet, had a tommy gun.

We jumped to our feet and into the nest, a sandbagged circle. We were both ready to shoot, but I found myself face to face with Johnny's tommy gun, and he with my Webley. We then went down to where the others were cutting the cables leading from the hut. Knight asked me rather plaintively: "Please can I blow the place up, Sir?" He had a pack of demolition stores on his back and was aching to use it. I replied: "No. Apparently the Germans don't know yet that we've come. There's no point in announcing it. Just cut the cables."

We went back to see if we could help de Crespigny's party. It was pitch black and, as I approached, Corporal Gimbert burst through a hedge at me. The next thing I felt was a bayonet pushing insistently through my tunic. "Password!" Gimbert hissed.

6. A typical obstacle on a commando assault course- the rope bridge, made more interesting by the use of simulated artillery fire. (IWM H26620)

He was a big powerful man. It seemed a long time before I could say anything. There have been worse occasions since, when I've been less scared. At last I remembered the word and let it out with a sigh. "Desmond!" I said. Gimbert, recognising my voice, removed the bayonet quickly. "All right, Colonel." I thought he sounded disappointed.

When we rejoined de Crespigny, his men had finished searching the barracks. There, as in the case of our machine gun nest, no one was at home. It was now past the time for the fireworks at the airfield between the Germans and our Independent Company. I listened. The night was still. The dogs had stopped barking some time before. I looked at my watch and saw with surprise and some dismay that it was a quarter to three: time to go.

We formed up on the road between the barracks and the Doyle Column, a monument we had used as a landmark. [Author's note: the Doyle Monument was in 1940 a hundred foot column built to commemorate the work of a previous Governor of Guernsey – Lieutenant-General Sir John Doyle. It was later blown up by the Germans as it potentially obstructed a gun battery's field of fire]. It was easy to guess from the muttered curses that the others shared my disgust at our negative performance and at the fact we had met no Germans. George Herbert was particularly upset and begged me to give them a few minutes more to visit some houses nearby which he thought might contain Germans. In this atmosphere of complete anti-climax it was clear that none of us wanted to leave but I called the officers together. "We've got to be back on the beach in ten minutes." I said urgently.

They got their men going on the run. In short order I herded them like a sheepdog down the concrete steps. Still the enemy showed no sign that he knew of our visit. I was last down from the cliff top with Peter Young clattering just ahead of me. Near the bottom I accelerated and suddenly realised that my feet had lost the rhythm of the steps. I tripped and tumbled the rest of the way, head over heels.

7. Two commandos demonstrating how to cross barbed wire. (IWM H17509)

I had been carrying my cocked revolver at the ready. During my fall it went off, seeming tremendously loud and echoing against the cliffs. This, at last, brought the Germans to life. Almost at once there was a line of tracer machine gun fire from the top of the cliff on the other side of our cove. The tracers were going out to sea towards the spot where I thought our launches must be awaiting us. "You all right, Colonel?" It was Johnny Giles's anxious voice. I answered yes and told him to get on with forming the men up on the beach. I had landed hard on the rocks and was shaken and bruised but there was nothing seriously the matter. I never carried my pistol cocked again. Within five minutes my men were all formed up on the beach. I knew now that we were late for our rendezvous – it was ten past three- and that if the destroyers had obeyed instructions they were already steaming towards Britain. Then I saw the dim shapes of our launches about a hundred yards out.

I shouted "Come in and pick us up!" They replied "Too rough. We've already been bumping on the rocks. We'll stove our bottoms in if we come any nearer." So I shouted for them to send in a dinghy for the weapons. They did this. It was a tiny craft, no more than nine feet in length. With each load of weapons went two or three men. As it came in for the fifth run, a high sea picked it up and smashed it against a rock. The dinghy was a total loss and one trooper was reported drowned. I then ordered that we would all have to swim for it. Fortunately we were equipped with Mae Wests and we all started to blow them up. Some of the men began peeling off their uniforms and wading into the sea. Three men came up to me in the darkness. I recognised Corporal Dumper of Lieutenant Smale's road-block party. "Could we have a word with you, please Sir?", Dumper said. He seemed a little nervous. "What is it?" I replied. "I know we should have reported this in Plymouth, Sir, but the three of us are non-swimmers."

I was ready to explode. The original letter calling for commando volunteers had specifically mentioned that they must be able to swim. Then I calmed down. "I'm afraid there's nothing we can do for you except try to send a submarine to pick you up tomorrow night." "Thank you, Sir." Dumper said. "Sorry to be such a nuisance."

I removed my tunic and struck out in the water. Some of the men, with more wisdom than modesty, preferred to swim naked. I had the added handicap of sentiment. In my right hand I carried a silver cigarette case which my wife had given me; in my left a spirit flask which had been my father's. A rough sea had come up since our original landing. In these circumstances the hundred yards to the launches seemed endless. For the first fifty, breakers thundered and broke over my head. It took, I suppose, seven or eight minutes to swim out but it seemed hours and I was exhausted. As a sailor bent down from the launch to drag me aboard, the final effort of helping him, to my great annoyance, made me let go of the flask and case. I also noted that my wristwatch had stopped. I asked the time and was told it was half-past three. I was worried that we would have missed the destroyers completely. However, the discipline and bearing of the men during the difficult swim out to the boats was admirable. There was no shouting or panic; each man swam along quietly. The crews of the launches were continually diving in to help the most exhausted men over the last stages of their journey. Altogether, this most difficult re-embarkation was carried out quietly and efficiently. With dawn half an hour off, it looked as if we should have to head for home in the launches. This was not a prospect to bring delight. The crews of these boats were brave men, mostly yachtsmen with no service experience. At this point, they seemed unable to reach a decision for further action. The second launch had just broken down: ours threw it a line and had it in tow. There was a general discussion of the situation by all hands. Even the engine attendant left his recess to chip in. This was too much for me so I suggested they stop the talking and pull out to sea. They did as I suggested.

I was sure that by now the *Scimitar* had gone; a certainty shared by all aboard the launch. It now seemed doubtful that, towing the other launch, we could make it back to England, even if we were lucky enough to escape German fighters which could easily nip out from airfields on the French coast. I felt that only a piece of extraordinary luck could save us. I asked the captain if I could borrow a torch. He handed me one and I flashed it out to sea, knowing that this was a despairing hope. To my delight a series of answering flashes came back from just beyond the point. The *Scimitar's* Captain, I learned later had decided to take one last sweep around for us on his way home. He was exposing himself to a tremendous risk of air attack, as daylight was only a few minutes off and the Luftwaffe had many airfields within a few minutes flying time. Our own air cover could not be expected at this time to operate so near to the coast of France. After blowing up the ailing launch, we transferred to the destroyer. Captain de Crespigny noticing that I was shivering with cold, kindly lent me his tunic. I wore no shirt and put the tunic directly over my bare shoulders and arms. Just before getting to Dartmouth, de Crespigny said to me: "Oh, by the way, Colonel, I do hope everything will be all right." I replied

8. Two photos of the beach and cliffs that commandos landed on in Guernsey during Operation Ambassador (Mark Bougourd)

"What do you mean?" "I forgot to tell you that I've been suffering from scabies," he replied.

I rushed off for a hot bath in the Captain's cabin. Like the operation itself, nothing came of it. My own tunic, which had my name sewn into the collar, was picked up next morning by the Germans on the beach. Durnford is a well-known name in the Channel Islands and some of the Durnfords there were harried a good deal by the Germans who thought that I might still be lying up in the island, harboured by namesakes. As it was we arrived back in Dartmouth, safe but distinctly down in the mouth, at eight o'clock in the morning.

Just to go back a little here are few comments from Lieutenant J Smale about his part in Operation Ambassador:

When we made the landfall at the Jerbourg peninsula it seemed that we might get ashore with dry feet, but the boats soon beached and we had to wade ashore. As my task was to set up a road block we had brought coils of Dannert wire with us and it was fairly tough getting up those steps with it. Eventually we found the isolated bungalow that was the spot where we were ordered to set up the road block. I went inside and found one old man still living there. He looked at me and my men with black faces and armed to the teeth and was scared out of his life. In order to stop him interfering in any way, I got one of my men to put him in his toilet and stand outside the door. Outside we started to put up the wire and bolstered it by using the larger stones from the old man's rockery in his front garden. I had been told by the Colonel that anyone coming along this road would be German and I was to take the appropriate action. When we did hear people coming along the road we waited until they were really close before challenging them and they turned out to be other members of 3 Commando. So it is a good job I didn't get the men to open fire, if I had I've always wondered what effect that action may have done for the commandos as a whole. Perhaps it might even in those early days have led to our disbandment.

If this part of Operation Ambassador can be looked on as a bit of a damp squib, the other elements of the raid were little short of farcical. There were two other parties detailed to land on Guernsey. The first party, the so-called main party under Major Tod, had been allocated two of the launches and the whaler from HMS *Saladin* to get ashore in. The men (around 70 in number) got successfully into the boats, whilst the whaler was towed by the launches. The whaler's serviceability was probably not checked beforehand and soon started to leak and water was soon sloshing around the bottom of the boat. Attempts to pump and bail out the water proved ineffective. There was no option but to transfer the men in the whaler to the two launches. For reasons that could not be ascertained launch 303 now took over towing the whaler. Although I have never been in a boat towing a sinking one I can imagine that it was like trying to run through treacle and progress was slow. Then at 1.45 in the morning the decision was taken to return to HMS *Saladin* which was reached about 80 minutes later.

Meanwhile the remaining men including Major Tod (about 35 in number) struggled on until at about 2.00 a.m. he estimated they were still several miles off shore, and suggested they retrace their steps to HMS *Saladin*. They could not find the ship and had no option but to head for England independently. Luckily, they made it back to Devonport around 10.00 a.m. assisted by RAF fighters who had provided an aerial escort.

The last party under the command of Captain Goodwin (20 men) which again was to raid the airfield at Forest, left HMS *Saladin* around half past midnight in one of the launches. Again it seems this boat's compass was defective and ended up landing on an island which is believed to be Sark. Again they managed to retrace their steps to *Saladin* and successfully found the ship. However, it was nearly 3.00 a.m. before they arrived back – far too late to consider another attempt, so they remained on HMS *Saladin*.

Anyway there were still some men left behind on Guernsey. The official casualty figure for Operation Ambassador was four, although this does not include the two officers landed before the actual operation. Gunner J McGoldrick of the Royal Artillery was reported as 'missing believed drowned'. One of the party of three non-swimmers was, as Colonel Durnford-Slater recorded, Corporal D Dumper, he had originally been in the 1st Battalion East Surrey Regiment before volunteering for special service. The other two were Private A Ross (6th Black Watch) and Private F Drain (2nd Battalion Bedfordshire and Hertfordshire Regiment). These were all mentioned as 'missing, probably prisoners of war'. As it turned our Gunner McGoldrick hadn't drowned so the gang of three became one of four. Fred Drain survived the war and in an interview related his views of the raid. It turns out that he had been in the boat which capsized when ferrying weapons out to one of the launches, and he was only saved from drowning by his brother Pat who was also on the raid.

Fred added that he and his brother had joined the 2nd Battalion of the Bedfordshire and Hertfordshire's before the war and they had both volunteered for special service shortly after being evacuated from Dunkirk. They were both posted to H Troop of what he said was 'Special Service Troops' and claimed they received very little 'commando' training before the raid except a few days 'messing about in little boats'. His ability to swim was certainly never tested. On Guernsey he together with his brother had been given the job of cutting telephone wires near the Doyle Column. This was achieved by Fred climbing on Pat's shoulders to enable him to reach the foot brackets nailed to the telegraph pole.

Fred also stated that a submarine would appear at a bay a few miles away from midnight the following Wednesday (7th July) to pick up any stragglers. Having been given additional French money by the returning commandos the gang of four were in high hopes of also reaching England. However, they were not too well equipped for evading capture as all they possessed was a silk handkerchief escape map, collar stud compasses and a single .38 revolver. Anyway the four men retraced their way up the steps and started walking parallel to the road, but a distance away from it in case a German patrol came along. After a while they came across what appeared to be a disused small wooden shed on the way to a place called La Creux Mahie. In spite of its run down appearance some tins of food and fruit were found inside. The group stayed here all through Monday and Tuesday and the best part of Wednesday. To assist with rations two of the party foraged some tomatoes growing nearby.

Around ten o'clock on that Wednesday night they finished their journey again without meeting any Germans and ended up at the headland of La Creux Mahie. By now Gunner McGoldrick's torch had dried out and at midnight started sending three short flashes out to sea. But there was no answer nor any sign of a rescue, by two the following morning the batteries in the torch had run out of charge and spirits were plummeting. There was no submarine coming, apparently the Senior Naval Officer at Plymouth had refused to send one after hearing Durnford-Slater's report on the raid. The reason given being simply "for naval reasons the attempt to take the men off later was not possible".

The somewhat downhearted group of four went back to their shed to consider their options. It was decided to try and contact the locals to see if a boat could be found to get them back to England. They temporarily found shelter with a local family in the village of Torteval for a couple of days but all efforts to find a boat were frustrated, the main reason being the difficulty in getting petrol. The Germans, although not really actively searching for them (they probably didn't even know they were there), still carried out routine house searches. The gang of four realised that it was becoming too dangerous to the family (named Bourgaize) that was sheltering them to remain with them. The decision was taken to walk in daylight towards the airfield which they had been told was heavily guarded, perhaps deep down each of them realised the game was up and being taken prisoner was the only option. Before long they were picked up by a German patrol and eventually they were taken to the civil prison in St Peter Port, where they spent the night. The following morning they were taken back to the landing beach and questioned by a German officer about what had happened and what they were doing on Guernsey. Fred recalls that all four of them had no intention of revealing any information about the raid. Losing patience the group spent another night on Guernsey before being taken by a transport plane to Cherbourg and then into the German prisoner of war system. It would be five years before they would be released.

This just leaves the two officers, Second Lieutenants Martel and Mulholland on Guernsey. It had been planned for them to signal to the launches from Le Jaonnet beach by flashing the letter D in morse if it was safe to come in. As we have seen due to the last minute change of plan no-one landed at this bay. As they were both born in Guernsey they managed to find sanctuary with their families while they tried to find a way to escape. This again proved difficult and like the gang of four, they gave themselves up to the Germans.

A few days later back in London, Churchill, never one to mince words, was not best pleased when he received the post-operation report. He had expected great things from this new embryonic force and he sent a withering note which contained the unequivocal comment: 'Let there be no more silly fiascos like those perpetuated at Guernsey'. Whilst this comment is easy to understand, it is perhaps not that fair. The Navy did their best with inadequate landing craft and by waiting for longer than they should have, saved the operation from being a complete disaster. The Army too, lacking an enemy to shoot at, otherwise in parts achieved what they set out to do. There was the expectation they would do better next time. Indeed, just before Operation Ambassador a 'Combined Operations' department was set up to co-ordinate matters better. Perhaps as result of Churchill's memo two days after the abortive raid Admiral of the Fleet Sir Roger Keyes was brought in as the Director of Combined Operations. Keyes was probably a good man for this job as he had been present at the one of the early 'combined operations' at Gallipoli in 1915 and had masterminded Operation Dynamo the evacuation from Dunkirk.

Chapter 2

Airborne Initiatives

Having looked at the first two commando operations, it would be good to go back in time a few weeks to the early weeks of June 1940. As well as Winston Churchill suggesting commando troops he was looking for an 'airborne or parachute force'. The Royal Air Force had taken the decision in early June to set up a parachute training school at Ringway airfield near Manchester. This is now Manchester International Airport and I suspect few people travelling through there today realise its significant place in the history of the airborne forces nor its contribution to the war effort. They decided with typical RAF logic to call it the Central Landing School (CLS) and its first commander was Squadron Leader L Strange. Within a few days a Major J Rock from the Royal Engineers was sent there to implement 'the military organisation of British airborne forces'. It was decided that Physical Training Instructors would be ideal candidates to train men in parachuting and nine men from the Army Physical Training Corps and fourteen from the RAF Physical Education branch were posted in.

Then on 22nd June 1940 Churchill penned another memo to General Sir Hastings Ismail, head of the Military Wing of the War Cabinet Secretariat. This said:

> We ought to have a corps of at least 5,000 parachute troops, including a proportion of Australians, New Zealanders and Canadians, together with some trustworthy people from Norway and France. Advantage of the summer must be taken to train these troops, who can nonetheless play their part meanwhile as shock troops in home defence. Pray let me have a note from the War Office on the subject.

The real problem now was that the services were being asked to do in a few weeks what the Germans had for instance undertaken in several years. The RAF grudgingly 'gave' six virtually obsolete Whitley bombers and a thousand parachutes. The civil aerodrome at Ringway was chosen probably because it would be unlikely to suffer much from German interference. Then in late June/early July it was decided to send one of the newly formed commando units to be converted to the parachute role, and No 2 Commando was selected. So this unit was moved to Knutsford in Cheshire, not far from Ringway, and on 3rd July Lieutenant Colonel C Jackson from the Royal Tank Regiment arrived to take command of this unit.

The RAF were not exactly overjoyed at their new role and it is probably fair to say that they did not make the best use of the summer. Indeed in an Air Staff paper dated 12th August 1940 the following comment is contained: 'We are beginning to incline to the view that dropping troops from the air by parachute is a clumsy and obsolescent method and that there are far more important possibilities in gliders. The Germans made excellent use of their parachute troops in the Low Countries by exploiting surprise, and by virtue of the fact that they had practically no opposition. But it seems to us at least possible that this may be the last time that parachute troops are used on a serious scale in major operations.' The report continued by outlining the difficulties encountered since June in training the first five hundred let alone five thousand.

On 9th July 1940 B and C Troops of No 2 Commando started to arrive at Ringway. They must have looked to an RSM a strange bunch, nearly every Regiment and Corps was represented. They kept their parent formation's dress, so there was a mixture of berets, sidecaps, glengarries and tam o'shanters and a multiple of cap badges. However, there were several common bonds, every man was a volunteer, had a desire to hit back at Hitler, and guts. It appears that apart from an interview no other selection procedures took place. This would all change over the coming months. Before the training started a suitable drop zone had to be found – eventually Tatton Park just a few miles away was selected. Also all commanders in the area were told that friendly paratroopers would be landing in the area and were not to be shot at while descending. The threat of invasion was still a very present one and as previously explained the country was in the grip of parachutist fever.

The parachutes sent to Ringway were of a slightly bigger diameter (28 feet) than the normal aircrew one of 22 feet. This had been found to give a softer landing than the aircrew one. I suppose the logic being a smaller diameter was easier to fit either inside a cockpit or the fuselage of an aircraft. A paratrooper would be expected to go straight into action whereas aircrew would either be in captivity or go back to his base for tea. The CLS reported they were ready to carry out the first descents on 13th July by the instructors at Ringway. In these early days it was all a matter of trial and error. Pre-war stuntmen had carried out descents by climbing out onto the wing of biplane aircraft, and while holding on to a strut, had released the canopy. The canopy filled up with air from

9. A stick of paratroopers at Ringway waiting to board a Whitley. The men are wearing the third type of helmet known as a rubber bungee. (ABF Museum)

10. Two paratroopers boarding a Whitley, giving a nice view of the X type
parachute with the static line stowed in its pocket on the rear. (ABF Museum)

the aircraft's slipstream and they were then pulled off the wing. This became known as
the 'pull-off' method. One of the first volunteers at Ringway was Captain Lindsay who
was later sent out to India to raise and command the first parachute unit there. He gave
a graphic description of the basic method used at that time:

> We climbed into the aircraft and sat on the floor of the fuselage. The engines roared
> and we took off. It seemed an age, but it cannot have been more than ten minutes
> when the instructor beckoned to me. I began to make my way down the fuselage
> towards him, screwing myself up to do so. I crawled on my hands and knees
> into the rear gunner's turret, the back of which had been removed. I tried not to
> overbalance and fall out, nor to look at the landscape speeding across below me as
> I turned to face forward again.
>
> I now found myself on a small platform about a foot square, at the very back
> of the plane, hanging on like grim death to the bar under which I had had such
> difficulty in crawling. The two rudders were a few feet away on either side of me;
> behind me there was nothing whatsoever. As soon as I raised myself to full height,
> I found that I was to all purposes outside the plane, the slipstream of air in my
> face almost blowing me off. I quickly huddled up, my head bent down and pressed
> into the capacious bosom of the Flight Sergeant. I was about to make a "pull-
> off", opening my parachute which would not pull me off until fully developed – a
> procedure which was calculated to fill me with such confidence that I should be
> only too ready to leap smartly out of the aircraft on all subsequent occasions.
>
> The little light at the side changed from yellow to red. I was undeniably
> frightened, though at the same time filled with a fearful joy. The light changed

to green and down fell his hand. I put my right hand across to the D ring in front on my left side and pulled sharply. A pause of nearly a second and then a jerk on each shoulder. I was whisked off backwards and swung through nearly 180 degrees, beneath the canopy and up the other side. But I was quite oblivious to all this. I had something akin to a black-out. At any rate, the first thing I was conscious of after the jerk on my shoulders was to find myself, perhaps four seconds later, sitting up in my harness and floating down to earth. The only sensation I registered was one of utter astonishment at finding myself in this remarkable and ridiculous position.

I looked up and there was the silken canopy billowing in the air currents. I looked down, reflecting that this was certainly the second greatest thrill in a man's life. Suddenly I realised that the ground was coming up very rapidly. Before I knew what had happened I was sprawling on the ground, having taken a bump but not hurt. As I got to my feet, a feeling of exhilaration began to fill me.

However, this is not to say everything went well in the early days. The obvious disadvantage of the pull-off method was its slowness, only one man could jump at a time. One officer was waiting his turn to go and had to fly round while he watched the man who had jumped before him, RSM Mansie, being carried away from the DZ after a bad landing. Here are his recollections of the next few minutes:

Flight Sergeant Brereton said to me, "Take your time. We'll make a dummy run first; we are almost over the park now." With a great effort of will I dared to look down. To my horror I saw 500 feet below, a tiny stretcher with a dark, motionless figure. Brereton must have seen it too, for he looked hard at me and said: "There's nothing to worry about. If you like I'll pull the rip-cord for you myself." I replied that I'm all right; just tell me what to do. "Watch my hand then, and when you see

11. A stick of paratroopers receiving last minute instructions before boarding their Whitley. (ABF Museum)

it fall, pull the handle upward and outward." OK, I said. You mean like this? "Not now, you bloody fool!"

But it was too late. I'd gone. Three hours later the search party found me, six miles away from the dropping zone, hanging helplessly from the highest branches of a clump of trees.

12. Lieutenant Colonel C Jackson, the CO of 11th SAS Battalion, explaining the intricacies of the new paratrooper boot with crepe soles and side lacing to General Sir John Dill. Note also the somewhat primitive leather jumping helmets. Photograph taken during an inspection in December 1940. (ABF Museum)

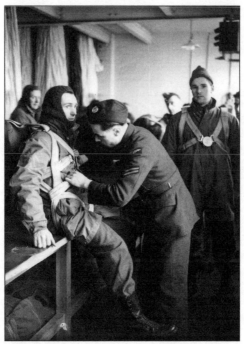

13. Early days at Ringway, a RAF Corporal checking a trainee's harness. Note at least three different types of protective headgear. (IWM CH2598)

14. Synthetic training using a dummy parachute harness at Ringway, in theory the trainee will shortly be demonstrating a parachute roll on the mat. (IWM CH2595)

It was planned for the trainee's first two jumps to use the pull-off method and then to graduate to what probably was an even worse experience! The Whitley used to have a mid under-turret so some boffin decided that with this removed a hole a couple of feet in diameter appeared but it was also a short three foot tunnel. The first two jumpers of a stick sat opposite each other with their feet dangling into the tunnel. On the word of command from the dispatcher the first man launched himself into this void whilst attempting to maintain a position of attention. This posture had to be adopted to avoid two potential pitfalls, too hard a jump forward often ended with the paratrooper smashing his face into the opposite side of the tunnel. Not enough push-off usually meant the parachute on the wearers back catching on the edge of the hole with the same result as before. To the trainees from No 2 Commando the expression 'ringing the bell' entered the vocabulary. In spite of these difficulties the first two men exited the aircraft very rapidly and the rest of their stick shuffled forward on their bottoms to follow them out as quickly as possible. The jumpers' parachutes were opened by having the rip-cord connected by a static line to a fixed point in the aircraft. This meant the jumper could concentrate on his exit. This somewhat undignified exit continued until 1942 when exiting in a more gentlemanly fashion was possible through a door in the side of the Dakota. This aircraft taking over from the Whitley.

Later in training it was possible to get a stick of ten out in reasonable time. Today if stretched Hercules aircraft are used it is possible to do 'Sim 45's', this is 90 men jumping in one pass – 45 from each of the offset side doors. Training in the early days continued at what today appears to be a slow pace but we must consider that virtually everything was new and there was no one to turn to for advice. Certain items of German parachutist equipment had been captured in France and Belgium in 1940 and the majority of

15. Some of the Army Top Brass meeting the glider wing of the 11th SAS Battalion in late 1940. The glider is a civilian one converted to military use. (IWM H6215)

these were handed over to Major Rock. He asked the clothing people to come up with similar items and it must be said that the early version gabardine jumping smock was closely modelled on the German paratroop smock. Also crepe-soled jumping boots were introduced but these were later found to be unnecessary and normal leather soled boots with metal studs were worn. As well as Whitley aircraft somehow Major Rock managed to convince the RAF to release some Bombay transport aircraft to help at Ringway. One officer, Lieutenant A Deane-Drummond, after having done a pull-off descent, found himself in a Bombay for his second descent. The Bombay was a slow monoplane but under-powered and lacking in range but it did have a side door. To convert it into a 'troop carrier' the side door was lifted off its hinges and the top one was used as the strong point to which the static lines were attached.   During July 1940 more descents were made, and a recommendation by the CLS was made to discontinue the pull-off method. This initially was overruled by some staff wallah at the Air Ministry, however after a test in which dummies were used to simulate a rapid exit it was dropped completely. This test had ended up with the steel bar at the back of the Whitley breaking and a mass of dummies falling to the ground.

Then after 135 descents from a variety of aircraft had been undertaken the first fatal casualty of the British airborne forces occurred. T/175282 Driver Ralph Evans originally from the Royal Army Service Corps died on 25th July 1940. He had become entangled in the rigging lines of his parachute, which prevented it from deploying fully and hence fell to his death. He is now buried at Walton-on-Thames in St Mary's Churchyard. This first fatality caused a temporary stoppage in training while the accident was investigated.

16. Two of the pioneers of the airborne forces – Lieutenant Colonel
Jackson and Major Rock discussing tactics with RAF officers at
Ringway, while the stick emplane. (IWM CH2617)

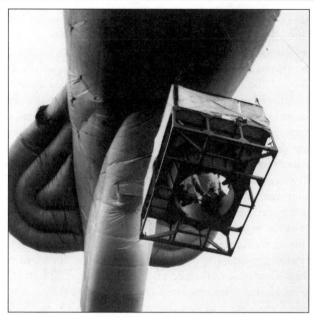

17. An unusual view of the cage suspended beneath the balloon. For many of the trainees their first jump was from a similar cage. The circular hole represented the exit from a Whitley. (IWM H9393)

It became clear that the cause was the way the parachute deployed from its pack. So perhaps it may be best to give a brief explanation of some history and how a parachute deploys, or did in the Second World War. It is also worth adding that for the British, a reserve parachute was an unknown addition.

The Russian Army was probably the first major Army to take on board the concept of using 'airborne troops', indeed it is recorded in their 1930 summer manoeuvres that the Red Army had successfully dropped a small force by parachute and successfully captured an 'enemy' HQ. The aircraft used for this was the Tupolev ANT-6, a large four-engined, fixed-undercarriage plane. There was an exit hatch on top of the fuselage and braving the aircraft's slipstream, men had to clamber down to the wing before dropping off and pulling their own ripcord to deploy their parachute as soon as they were clear of the aircraft. The Russian manoeuvres of 1935 and 1936 were attended by military observers from most of the major powers including Britain and Germany. The effect in these two countries is interesting. The British Army observers seem to have been unimpressed and even though they witnessed successful heavy drops of light tanks, field-guns and armoured cars, one said: 'Such novelties would not have a great deal of influence on the future course of war.' The German Military Attaché on his return to Moscow sent an immediate top-secret signal to Berlin saying that he had seen a revolutionary transformation in the technique of war. In October 1935 orders were issued which led to the formation of the first German parachute battalion, with the intention of forming a future parachute corps. It should be noted here that the German airborne forces were part of the Luftwaffe – the air arm rather than the army as was the case with British airborne forces. In January 1936 a parachute training school was set up, aircraft allocated to it and production of a suitable glider was started. This glider had the stipulation that it could carry 10 men but cost no more than 10 parachutes. After 1936 the Russians changed to static-line parachutes.

The Germans also went for a static-line parachute called the RZ. This had a single point anchor point in the middle of the back, which had the disadvantage that the parachute could not be steered and all landings became forward ones, hence the rubber kneepads often worn by German paratroopers. The British used a two-point attachment with webbing risers at the shoulders which at least meant that the parachute could be steered by pulling down on the appropriate riser. All parachute harnesses also had a couple of straps that went between the legs and could be painful if these straps were not fastened correctly when the parachute deployed.

The parachutes used by the Germans and Russians were similar to those used at Ringway in that the static line first pulled the canopy from the pack followed by the rigging lines. However, if the jumper made a bad exit, which could lead to his body turning or twisting in the slipstream, he risked becoming entangled in the rigging lines. Or as one RAF Parachute Jumping Instructor said at Brize Norton in the 1980s whilst on ground training: 'Come out of the aircraft like that and you'll be turning somersaults down the side of the aircraft counting every rivet as you go past.'

As stated before training was suspended after the death of Driver Evans whilst trials using dummies were carried out which again led to several more failures. The two parachute manufacturers, Irvin's and GQ, were asked to advise and between themselves and the CLS a hybrid design was decided upon. This consisted of a Irvin parachute in a GQ bag, this had the subtle difference of letting the parachute pack itself break away from the wearer's back as he left the aircraft. It was of course still attached to the static line and then the aircraft, as the jumper continued to fall away from the aircraft, his momentum first pulled his webbing risers and then his rigging lines out of the pack. Finally, when these were fully deployed, the canopy itself came out of the bag, attached to the static line by a length of string. This piece of string being a weak link broke under the weight of the jumper and in theory the canopy was then deployed with negligible chance of a jumper becoming entangled in his own rigging lines. This became known as the X series of parachute and was the standard parachute for the rest of the war and indeed up until the 1960's.

However, this is not to say that this worked 100%, as during trials of the new system a canopy became entangled in the tail wheel of a Whitley. Perhaps Rock and the staff of CLS briefly made the decision to stop jumping from Whitleys. Perhaps they had been looking enviously at other parachuting aircraft such as the German Junkers Ju 52 which had a door in the side of the aircraft. Jumping through a hole in the bottom of the aircraft was obviously running the risk of something catching on the tail wheel. The top RAF officer at the CLS, Squadron Leader L Strange is reported to have commented:

The Whitley fuselage is dark and gloomy with its hole in the middle, and is bad for the nerves. The sight of other men disappearing through the hole is an unpleasant one, and the prospect of scraping one's face on the other side is not encouraging.

Another RAF officer commented:

Most of the men were of a good type and were a loss to the Commando. The majority got to the edge of the hole in the aircraft before refusing. Four men fainted in the aircraft, while a number jumped in a state of collapse having forced themselves to do so by sheer will-power.

In spite of these comments Strange together with a number of RAF PJI's jumped using the new parachute from a Whitley to try and improve morale and confidence. Major Rock was initially insistent that the Bombay be used instead of the Whitley. The debate went all the way to London and Whitehall, the War Office backing Rock's suggestion. The Air Ministry though would have none of it, commenting that all Bombay aircraft were required to ferry aircrew round the country as the Battle of Britain was at its height. They also got a bit of 'retaliation in first' by suggesting that in future airborne forces should be modelled on the German lines, with the RAF providing men who would train as paratroopers then receive infantry training. These comments together with those mentioned before in their paper of 12th August 1940 put a bit of a rocket up the War Office and they agreed that training using the Whitley could again be restarted, which indeed happened on 14th August.

18. Looking back down the fuselage of a Whitley at Ringway, also showing the different types of aircraft based there. A lucky bunch of trainee paratroopers are getting to know their way around. (IWM H22881)

It does appear that some lucky people managed to get a jump out of a Bombay as this account recalls:

After a few days of instruction at Ringway in the packing of parachutes and how to drop through the hole of a Whitley, we were told that the next morning we would be making our first descent. We were all keen to get the first one over. We arrived all raring to go; we noticed, however, that all the RAF personnel seemed very subdued and we were told that we would not be jumping that morning. We then paraded in the gym and amid a deathly silence we were told that a fatal accident had occurred in the first batch of jumps, but were earnestly assured that it was a one in a million accident. After a week of expecting to jump, we arrived one morning and were told to draw our parachutes, after which we were marched to a Bristol Bombay, into which eight of us were loaded. The door had been taken off and a handle had been fixed to the fuselage structure on the left of the door, to which the end of our static line was tied. I noticed after the first three had jumped the handle became very loose, but no one would say anything about it as we were all too scared at what would be said if we did.

During this somewhat uncertain time the second fatal casualty at Ringway occurred. This was Trooper Watts, originally from the Household Cavalry, who died as a result of a parachute malfunction on 27th August 1940. By the end of September 1940 21 officers and 321 other ranks had been selected for commando/airborne service and sent to Ringway. Of these two had been killed, twenty badly injured or otherwise unsuitable and thirty had refused to jump. These two deaths were followed by another accident involving Corporal Carter in which his hook which connected his static line to the aircraft twisted open and he exited the aircraft before the PJI noticed. This led to a different design of hook which prevented this happening again. But all of these incidents did in the early days make some people question the whole idea of airborne forces. After all an average of two descents per man and a fifteen per cent attrition rate were not exactly helping the case, given that all the men were volunteers. However, the decision was taken to soldier on, perhaps due to the enthusiasm of the RAF and by the end of the year over 2,000 jumps had been made with a lowering in the attrition rate. Finally, one of the best innovations adopted by the British was the use of balloons. Someone probably as a result of an economy measure suggested that spare barrage balloons with a suitable cage beneath it be used for the first jumps. This was a brilliant idea, a cage with a hole in the floor to simulate the Whitley exit was knocked up. It allowed trainees to make relatively straightforward exits free of twists, somersaults or slipstream. It also was a quick and cheap method of getting large numbers jumping in a short space of time. Finally it was possible for a PJI on the ground to give each trainee personal instructions and advice on the descent via a loud-hailer. The use of balloons for the first couple of jumps continued up into the 1980s.

Meanwhile, although the original volunteers were welcome, not enough had either come forward or been released by reluctant commanding officers to form the large numbers envisaged by Churchill. Efforts, therefore continued into the autumn of 1940 to attract new men. It seems further appeals were sent round. One of these appeals ended up at the 3rd Battalion The Grenadier Guards, in October 1940 stationed at Louth in

Lincolnshire. At one parade the Regimental Sergeant Major read out a letter, present on parade was L/Cpl R Curtis. He had originally joined up in 1937 with the intention of serving for four years before joining the City of London Police. Like many others he had been in France and suffered the ignominy of the Dunkirk evacuation and also seeing his family home in London destroyed earlier in 1940 by German bombs.

Anyway he recalls this particular parade:

A letter was read out by the RSM shouting that "Volunteers for a new type of fighting soldiers are required." He glanced over the top of the paper, beady eyes registering some amusement. "SOLDIERS," he carried on, "to be trained as commandos or parachutists. NOW I know that you would not wish to desert the Regiment, but..... Anyone wishing to volunteer, one pace forward, march!" Glaring as he did so, he took three very stealthy steps towards us. "WELL? You all chicken then?" There was not a titter; not even a hesitant shuffle. I thought back to the days in France. I thought of the carnage, of Calais, of the British prisoners of war belonging to the Warwick Regiment who were herded into a field just outside Dunkirk and machine-gunned to death by the Waffen SS. I thought of my home being blown

19. A regular sight to any trainee paratrooper – the infamous early morning run, supervised by PTS staff. (IWM H22852)

to smithereens, and how Jerry had prevented me from carrying on my ambition of becoming a London Policeman. On which – not wishing to jeopardise my chances of not going – I abruptly took a pace forward before it was too late.

Then in early November the decision was taken to change the name of No 2 Commando to the 11th Special Air Service Battalion, possibly to fool the Germans into thinking we had more airborne troops than we actually had. Also in late 1940 a Wing Commander M Newnham was posted to Ringway to run the administrative side of parachute training. Major Rock was also promoted to Lieutenant Colonel. Numbers in the 11th SAS Battalion started to rise, even if some people didn't hear any news for some time. Reg Curtis recalls:

> Weeks went by without any notification of my move on this new venture. Christmas came and the Battalion sat down to an excellent dinner with all the trimmings. A few days after Christmas I was called to the CO's office and informed that I would shortly be on my way, and that the destination was to be given on the day of departure. I received a pep talk of never to forget that I was a Guardsman and to uphold the traditions at all times. The CO seemed to challenge us to dare thinking of leaving the Regiment. It was sacrilege after being together for so long, but then, why not? I could read his thoughts as he glanced in my direction. Why not go out and carrying on spreading the deeds of the Regiment to others in this new-found adventure. His expression and tone changed from one of discouraging undertones to anticipated acceptance of this wonderful opportunity.

So it turned out that in early January 1942 Reg was posted to Congleton, a small town close to Ringway. Here he met up with other volunteers from the Guards and they were formed into L Troop under the command of a Grenadier Guards officer- Captain P Bromley-Martin. Reg recently stated that his troop was first sent to Achnacarry in Scotland for some special commando training before doing the Ringway course.

To end this chapter it might be good to sum up the assets and progress made so far.

On 31st August 1940 Churchill was informed that with the current resources the figure of 5,000 parachute troops would not be reached for another 12 months.

The RAF pointed out owing to the need to expand the bombing force, there could be no question of having resources solely dedicated to dropping parachute troops. They saw it as an alternative role for the heavy bomber squadrons.

They also pointed out the need to train parachutists in the same aircraft that would be used on operations. The only aircraft with the necessary range to reach Europe at this stage was the Whitley.

11th Special Air Service Battalion was to form a glider wing and a parachute wing.

In September 1940 a report was sent to Churchill which outlined the RAF's view of the deployment of airborne forces. The main points of this report were as follows:

(a) There appeared to be three types of raid for which airborne troops might be used:-

    (i) A raid on a selected position, to be followed by the evacuation of the raiding force by air.

    (ii) A raid to be followed by evacuation by sea.

(iii) The dropping of parachutists as saboteurs, pure and simple.

(b) For the first two roles the best method would be to use a small force of parachutists, who would be followed by a larger body landing from gliders.

(c) For any particular operation about 1,000 men would be required, of whom 100 would be parachutists, and 900 glider-borne. To enable more than one raid to be carried out, plans are being made to train three such forces by the spring of 1941, plus 200 parachute saboteurs.

(d) The total airborne force envisaged, therefore, was:-

500 parachute troops.

2,700 glider-borne troops.

360 glider pilots to fly the glider-borne troops.

To secure the RAF's continued involvement in airborne forces a concession was made at the time which probably was dismissed as insignificant at the time, but had far-reaching effects in 1944. The RAF requested and got approval for the landing and dropping zones for any future operations to be selected by them. Although there was of course in the coming years the usual horse-trading, the RAF had the final word on the zones. If the Army didn't like those selected it was a case of 'tough luck, old boy, you'll just have to get on with those selected'. As a student of the Arnhem battle in September 1944 it is easy to lay the blame for the failure of the plan on the distance from the ultimate objective of the dropping and landing zones. However many people are not aware of the decision agreed to by the Army earlier in the war and so it is wrong to blame solely the RAF.

It was expected that the 500 parachute troops would probably be trained by the spring of 1941, however, the plans for an increase in this number were vague. The only equipment they could carry was small arms and no trials had been undertaken as to how to provide support weapons.

Apart from the notional 'glider wing' of 11th Special Air Service Battalion no other units had been nominated to provide the glider-borne forces. It was felt better to provide them when the gliders themselves were ready. To back this up plans had been drawn up for the design and manufacture of four types of gliders as follows:

(a) An eight-seater, later named the Hotspur. Originally intended to go on operations, but later became the standard training aircraft for aspiring glider pilots. It had the advantage that it could be towed by a relatively small aircraft.

(b) A medium glider, the Horsa, able to carry cargo or up to 25 passengers.

(c) A slightly smaller medium glider able to carry 15 passengers, called the Hengist. This was planned purely as an insurance policy should the Horsa prove unsuitable.

(d) A heavy glider able to carry heavy cargos including a light tank or 40 passengers. This subsequently became known as the Hamilcar.

In the light of the somewhat hazardous nature of parachuting, officers were allowed an extra four shillings (£0.20) a day and other ranks two shillings (£0.10) a day parachute pay. This was allowed after the completion of three jumps, when they would also qualify for parachute wings. This allowance was later changed to two shillings a day (£0.10) for everyone. The number of qualifying jumps also increased to seven.

Chapter 3

11th SAS Battalion go into Action

It was not easy in these early months to maintain morale and motivation, many people had volunteered to join the new units to get to grips with the enemy and nothing seemed to be happening. The number of troops asking to go back to their parent units was on the increase and minor cases of ill-discipline were occurring. However as was often during the struggle Churchill was unhappy with the lack of progress and wanted action. Perhaps more importantly Britain was virtually fighting alone and wanted to show to the outside world that she was still capable of fighting back. In early 1941 the only real theatre that any fighting was taking place was in North Africa, where British and Commonwealth troops were fighting the Italians, although the Italians were also involved in Albania fighting the Greeks. It was felt that the Italian forces were being supported logistically through the ports of Taranto, Brindisi and Bari. As well as supporting the troops in North Africa an operation against the Italians would be good for propaganda purposes but had to be cost-effective in terms of the effort expended.

As early as June 1940 it had been suggested to the Air Ministry by a British engineering firm (in fact one of their board members Mr. W G Ardley of George Kent and Sons) that destroying a vital aqueduct in southern Italy might wreak havoc with the water supply to a large part of that area. This does to some extent mirror the idea of Barnes Wallis and his plans to disrupt the German steel industry by hindering their supply of water. This suggestion contained the information that the aqueduct was part of a extensive pipeline system supplying around two million people in the areas around the towns of Bari, Brindisi, Taranto and Foggia. The aqueduct in question was near a small hilltop town called Calitri, and as it crossed a small river called the Tragino, it was known as the Tragino Aqueduct. This area was part of the Apennine Mountains region.

Perhaps a few words about the water system in this area of Italy would be appropriate. It is probably fair to say that the idea of a system of aqueducts dated back to about 1868 when a junior Italian Government engineer suggested a canal taking water from the head of the river Sele (about 1300 feet above sea level) and transfer it south of Taranto. Initial surveying of the route took place in 1901 and construction started a few years later on 150 miles of the main canal/route from the Sele to a place called Villa Castelli approximately halfway between the towns of Taranto and Brindisi. The design of the system called for many tunnels to go through mountains as well as soft ground and aqueducts to cross valleys where the depths of the valleys were not too excessive. Where there were deep valleys a system of siphons was employed. This was vital to the entire network. The siphon design provided the technical breakthrough that allowed the system to work in conjunction with the use of reinforced concrete pipes (which allowed for the more technically minded to reduce the operating pressure to 5.3 atmospheres). In total there were 68 miles of tunnel and 77 bridges, some up to 690 feet long. The bridges were either constructed using a masonry arch design (for use on wide valleys) or in reinforced concrete (narrow valleys). The flow rate of the water through the aqueducts was between

3 to 4 feet per second. The control of the flow of water was critical to the management of the system and this is where a British firm played a part. Towards the end of the 1920s and in the early 1930s the entire system was completed. George Kent and Sons had begun business in 1838 as mechanical engineers and specialised in flume and metering systems. They had supplied the flow metering and measuring system to the Italians and as such would have known the actual operating volumes of water. As stated before one of the board members of George Kent and Sons had suggested the Tragino Aqueduct as a suitable target but it took a few months for the military to get their heads round the idea.

A planning meeting was held at the Air Ministry in December 1940, which, although stating they deemed it to be a suitable target, it was not feasible to attack it with bombers. An important reason would probably have been the distance to the target. It was therefore decided to hand this one over to Keyes and his Combined Operations HQ.

A further meeting was held at Combined Operations HQ on 12th December 1940, at which amongst others a Colonel J Davidson (late Chief Engineer to the Metropolitan Water Board) and Mr. W Ardley were present. The meeting considered the likely effects of blowing up the aqueduct and the effect on the Italian war effort. It concluded that if all

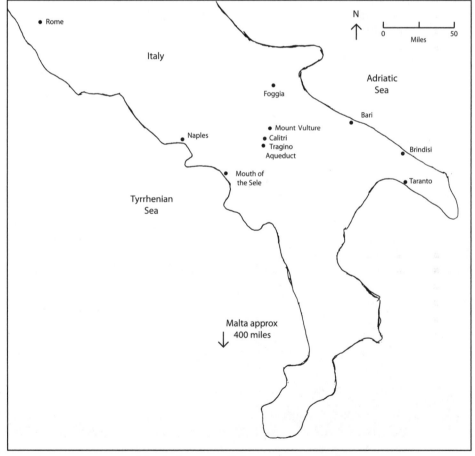

Map 3: Operation Colossus, Southern Italy

the necessary pipes, concrete mixers and labour were available, then 10% of the original flow might be got across the valley by D+14, 20% by D+21 and 40% to 50% after 30 days. These numbers were based on day and night working. The meeting minuted that if the RAF could follow up with a bombing raid then it would obviously delay the work even more. However, it was considered that there was no reason to abandon the plan even if the RAF did not want to carry out a later attack. Subsequent discussions also suggested that if the water supply to the towns of Bari, Brindisi and Taranto could be interrupted this would reduce their fire-fighting capacity. This might lead to greater bombing damage should raids be launched. Also it might possibly affect the morale and motivation of the civilians in these towns which were all important in the logistical tail in support of Italian operations in North Africa and Greece.

As a double banker the idea of attacking the Tragino Aqueduct was handed over to Major Gubbins of SO2 (otherwise known as the people responsible for Irregular Warfare in Europe – later known as the Special Operations Executive). They reported back on 2nd

20. An aerial photograph of the Tragino Aqueduct area used in the planning for the raid on Malta. (National Archives)

January 1941 that they did not have the resources in terms of equipment or explosives to carry out this attack let alone have the time to prepare, train and transport people for such a job. According to some records they were asked to supply two interpreters. So the ball went back to Combined Operations.

After assessing their options it was decided to accept the target and in January 1941 Operation Colossus came into being. The decision was taken to give the 11th SAS Battalion the chance to take part, probably because they had done nothing so far and it would be an ideal opportunity to test this new arm.

The plan called for a party from 11th SAS to first go to Malta by air and then mount the operation from there. It was proposed to spare eight Whitley bombers for the operation, six to carry the men and two to carry out a bombing raid on the railway yards at Foggia. It was hoped that the Italians would believe that all eight aircraft were going to bomb Foggia. After destroying the aqueduct the raiding party was to make its way on foot to the west coast of Italy where they would be picked up by a Royal Naval submarine. So again we have all three services involved so it certainly appeared there was reasonable co-operation in the early days.

With the benefit of hindsight this does seem a risky venture as up to the end of 1940 the maximum number of men dropped simultaneously from Whitleys was 20 on Salisbury Plain and this was of course in the UK. Now it was envisaged to drop nearly 40 in enemy territory after a long approach flight.

After several months training both in soldiering, parachuting and commando skills, the morale of the unit was starting to fall. Then in the middle of January 1941 a rumour started going round that 'something was going to happen soon'. So on a parade of the

21. The Tragino Aqueduct in the middle distance, this photograph also gives an idea of the tough terrain in the area. (H Pexton)

whole unit at Cliffe House in Knutsford, the CO Lieutenant Colonel Jackson informed them that a top-secret operation involving a long-range penetration into enemy territory was being planned. He also said that it was unlikely that any arrangements for the evacuation of the assault party could be guaranteed and capture by the enemy was highly likely. It was also revealed that although the party would be dressed in normal army uniforms, it was possible they might be regarded as secret agents and treated as such. He ended his address by calling for volunteers for a dangerous mission, it is reported that every single man on the parade of around 500 stepped forward. L/Corporal Harry Pexton was present on this parade and recalls:

> The Colonel had the whole unit paraded on Shaw Heath in Knutsford and said something like the following: "Now this is serious, I'm being told there is something coming up, and I'll need some volunteers." By that time everyone was feeling pretty browned off, fully trained with nothing much exciting to do. So when he asked for volunteers everyone stepped forward. It was as it turned out up to Colonel Jackson to decide who should go.

Obviously Lieutenant Colonel Jackson now had a tough decision who to pick. Jackson decided that the unit's second-in-command Major T A G Pritchard, originally from the Royal Welch Fusiliers would lead the operation. Obviously as the ultimate aim of the operation was blowing something up a number of Royal Engineers would have to be included and Captain G Daly was selected as the chief engineer. From this first decision the other officers were chosen as follows:

To command the three infantry sections:
- Captain C Lea originally from the Lancashire Fusiliers
- Lieutenant A Deane-Drummond originally from the Royal Signals
- Second Lieutenant A Jowett originally from the Highland Light Infantry

To act as the assistant demolition officer:
- Second Lieutenant G Paterson from the Royal Engineers

These six officers were all told to select 'five good men' to take part in Operation Colossus, but with the provision that half of the party had to be Royal Engineers. One officer and two men were selected as reserves (Second Lieutenant Davies, Corporal Rowe and Private Humphries). An additional man from 11th SAS Battalion, a Private Nicol Nastri, was added to the party as he could speak Italian which obviously someone thought might come in handy. He was issued with identity papers and tags calling him John Tristan to try and protect him in case of capture and any possible charges of treason! This collection of volunteers from all over the 11th SAS Battalion was to be called X Troop. Harry Pexton again:

> The Colonel had picked five officers and then left it up to them to pick who they wanted. I think I was selected by Captain Lea- I don't think he ever liked me. We then went onto a separate training programme including a dietician to make sure we were all in tip-top shape. We concentrated on infantry training but I don't recall any special demolition training.

Here is the programme for some of the last days before the move to the airfield:

Programme of Work
Wed. 29th January to Sat. 1st February 1941
Nos. 1 and 2 Parties

DATE	TIME	DETAIL	DRESS	PLACE OF PARADE
Wed 29th January	0730 hrs	Run	PT Kit	Main Gate
	0930 hrs	Anti-tetanus injection	Clean Fatigue	Hut
	1000 hrs	Demonstration- Equipment	" "	Armoury
	1200 hrs	Model (No 1 Party) Min. Range (No 2 Party)	Clean Fatigue " "	Armoury "
	1415 hrs	Min. Range (No 1 Party) Model (No 2 Party)	" " " "	"
	1845-2300 hrs	Rehearsal Tatton Park	" "	"
				"
Thurs 30th January	0900 hrs	Pack parachutes (No 2 Party) Discussion, Rehearsal (No 1 Party)	Clean Fatigue " "	Armoury Decontamination Room
	1100 hrs	Lecture on escaping by S/L Keeling	" "	"
	1200 hrs	Lecture by MO	" "	"
	1400 hrs	Pack parachutes and containers (No 1 Party) Discussion, Rehearsal (No 2 Party)	" " " "	Armoury Decontamination Room
	1630-2000 hrs	Dress Rehearsal	Clean Fatigue and Gabardine Jackets Rifles (No 1 Party)	Armoury
Fri 31st January	0900 hrs	Run	PT Kit	Main Gate
	1030 hrs	Kit inspection	Clean Fatigue	Hut
	1130 hrs	Container Drill (No 1 Party) Aircraft Drill (No 2 Party)	" " " "	Armoury "
	1400 hrs	Container Drill (No 2 Party) Aircraft Drill (No 1 Party)	" " " "	" "
	1500-1630 hrs	All, Pay and Range (.32)	" "	Hut

DATE	TIME	DETAIL	DRESS	PLACE OF PARADE
Sat 1st February	0900 hrs	Run	PT Kit	Main Gate
	1030 hrs	Lecture, withdrawal	Clean Fatigue	Decontamination Room
	1200 hrs	Range (No 2 Party)	" "	Armoury
		Container Drill (No 1 Party)	" "	"
	1400 hrs	Range (No 1 Party) (.32 & TSMG)	" "	"
	1500 hrs	Range .32 (No 2 Party)	" "	"
	1830 hrs	Range (No 1 Party) (.32 & TSMG)	" "	"
	2000 hrs	Range .32 (No 2 Party)	" "	"

You will recall that Whitley bombers had been earmarked to carry the raiding party with the rider that none of the aircraft based at Ringway for parachute training be used. A composite group of eight Whitleys from Numbers 51 and 78 Squadrons were selected to take part, under the command of Wing Commander J Tait. He later went on to command 617 Squadron, of the famous Dambusters raid later on in the war. These pilots had to quickly adjust to dropping men from 500 feet rather than bombs from around 10,000 feet. The men of X Troop were moved from their billets around Knutsford into a segregated block at Ringway and started an intensive period of training. PT, runs, route marches, lectures on escape and evasion and so on, then in the evenings they did parachute jumps. A model of the area around the Tragino Aqueduct was made by an RAF officer and used as a training aid by the RAF aircrews.

Here is what Lieutenant Anthony Deane-Drummond had to say about this period:

We all trained hard in that cold month of January 1941. We left our very comfortable billets in Knutsford, and moved to Ringway for the final rehearsals. In the months to come, we were to look back nostalgically on how well we'd been fed and looked after in Knutsford.

Ringway was hard. 3 mile runs followed by 30 minutes PT before breakfast and usually a 12 to 15 mile after it. With full marching order we were expected to do 5 to 6 miles per hour.

A full-size wooden mock-up of the part of the aqueduct that the explosives were to be lodged in was built in Tatton Park and used to practice against. Plans called for about half a ton of explosives to be placed against the aqueduct piers. It is reported that after practice the time taken to place the explosives in position was just over 30 minutes.

Other preparations were finalised including long-range tanks and container release apparatus for the Whitleys. The men could not jump with the necessary half-ton of explosives and so the German method of using containers was copied. It was quite a bad winter and a fatality occurred in training when Bombardier Dennis on a training descent was blown by a strong gust of wind into an ice covered pond, sank and unable to free himself, drowned. The practice of wearing a lifejacket in the airborne forces did not

22. Second Lieutenant A G Jowett at the time of Operation Colossus. (H Pexton)

come till much later and it is now standard practice to wear one. This happened on the 22nd January 1941 and he is now commemorated at the Manchester Southern Cemetery.

As is usual in military circles an advance party was sent out to prepare things for the raid, and Lieutenant Deane-Drummond was selected to be in charge of this and left Ringway on 24th January for Plymouth. It was intended for the party, which also included some RAF fitters to service the Whitleys, to move to Malta by Sunderland flying boat. Due to bad weather they didn't manage to leave the UK till the 31st January, and after a stop at Gibraltar arrived at Malta in the evening of 1st February. He did say that he was told the objective of the operation before leaving for Malta.

That same day a full dress rehearsal for the operation took place around Tatton Park. This can best be described as somewhat unsatisfactory. Large amounts of cloud and strong winds prevented the RAF from dropping around half the men of X Troop in the correct location. Several men were blown into tall trees and had to be later rescued by the Knutsford Fire Brigade. Those that were dropped close to the mock-up of the aqueduct had the ignominy of being dragged across the ground by their parachutes, also it was difficult to locate the containers. In spite of this the following day the eight Whitleys flew to RAF Mildenhall in Suffolk which was to be the departure airfield for the operation. There were a few last minute rehearsals for X Troop before they too travelled to RAF Mildenhall on 4th February although by low flying Army buses. There were a few last minute additions to the party, two more Italian speakers were added to the group. One was an RAF officer – Flight Lieutenant R Lucky and the other was virtually a civilian – Fortunato Picchi. To the officers and men of X Troop both of these men were treated with suspicion. It was thought that the RAF officer was more than an interpreter, and it is reported that some of the officers from X Troop thought the operation was just a front to get a secret agent from the Special Operations Executive (SOE) into Italy. The other interpreter Fortunato Picchi was 42 years old and had been in the recent past head-waiter at the famous London hotel, The Savoy. In 1941 he was though, a naturalised Briton and extremely anti-fascist. On the outbreak of hostilities with Italy he had given up his job at The Savoy and had volunteered for service with the British armed forces.

In the early 1990s Karel Margry, now editor of *After the Battle* magazine, asked the SOE Adviser at the Foreign Office to confirm or deny Flight Lieutenant Lucky's involvement with SOE. He advised that Lucky had never had any connection with SOE. However it did become clear that Picchi was indeed a SOE man. He apparently had been recruited at the end of 1940, and he was the first Italian person to volunteer to return to Italy with SOE. His SOE report stated: "non-politically minded, but anti-fascist. An idealist, an excellent worker and organiser who cannot allow failure. Wants above all things for everyone to be treated fairly. Is prepared to shine in all England's trials and has no desire to be treated in any way differently from an English soldier." However, he was going to be treated somewhat differently to the average British soldier, and I believe he had not done a lot of the physical training the men from X Troop had undertaken. A question was asked about his fitness to take part in this somewhat strenuous operation and the apparent answer was he was 'quite fit and moderate in his habits'. He underwent a crash course in parachuting at Ringway and to try and protect his identity he was given the alias of a Free Frenchman as 3846154 Private Pierre Dupont.

So the final number of men selected for Operation Colossus (including interpreters) was 8 officers and 31 men; 7 officers and 29 men were scheduled to take part in the actual operation and the others were as stated before the reserves. By 7th February all the preparations had been completed and the group was ready to leave on their 1,400 mile flight to Malta. The Chief of Combined Operations Admiral Sir Roger Keyes arrived at RAF Mildenhall to see them off. The concern about Flight Lieutenant Lucky's involvement in the operation was not eased by it being noticed that he appeared to be on very friendly terms with Keyes. At a final parade in one of the hangars Keyes made a short speech ending with the comment: "I know you will tackle this job with determination and enthusiasm, and with a bit of luck I am sure you will pull it off. We shall be waiting to hear how you have got on, waiting to learn what British paratroopers can do. I decided that I just couldn't let you go without coming here to say goodbye to you." He then saluted them, perhaps acknowledging their slim chances of getting back. Captain Christopher Lea recently recalled the following about this episode, "When he saluted us, one realised he must be thinking that the chance of this little collection of men coming back was tiny. And someone – not me – heard him mutter to himself, What a pity."

Harry Pexton commented that Admiral Keyes shook all of their hands at this final parade, and he certainly was not told he was going to Malta.

Anyway the eight Whitleys left RAF Mildenhall around 10.00 p.m. on 7th February and their route took them over occupied France. The Whitleys carried five men each – nearly all from X Troop but also including several extra RAF bods. These included two officers from the CLS, one Wing Commander Norman acting as an observer and another Flight Lieutenant Williams nominally in charge of the parachutes. The long flight was uneventful and all Whitleys arrived at RAF Luqa on Malta around dawn on the 8th. I feel it fair to say that the arrival of all eight was somewhat unexpected, the journey took 11 hours and apparently was a record for a Malta flight, and all aircraft had made it. This had not always been the case on 'ferry flights' out to the Mediterranean. Harry Pexton recently told me:

23. The first casualty of Operation Colossus – Bombardier W Dennis. who is commemorated at the Manchester Southern Cemetery. (G Teece)

24. X Troop on the Tatton Park DZ taken during the training period. (ABF Museum)

25. Fortunato Picchi, the Italian who volunteered to go on the raid (Silvio Tasselli)

I don't have any special recollections of the flight, except it was like travelling in a coffin for many hours, it was a bloody long cold flight. The feel of solid ground under my feet again was a real pleasure and I do recall the bright sunshine after leaving England in snowy conditions. We were carried onto the aircraft from the truck at Mildenhall so as not to bring too much snow onto the aircraft with us.

Meanwhile on Malta over the previous few days Deane-Drummond had managed to get the explosives and other items out of the supply people. After a rest in the billets organised by Deane-Drummond, the equipment was checked on the 9th, with the intention of launching Operation Colossus on the night of the 10th February. The Governor of Malta, General Dobbie, visited on the morning of the 9th, wishing the party good luck. A final preparation was undertaken on this morning and that was sending an RAF photographic reconnaissance aircraft to take pictures of the area. This was undertaken by one of the pioneer PR pilots who later gained the reputation of being one of the best – Flying Officer A Warburton. He flew at 24,000 feet in a Martin Maryland aircraft and took not only shots of the aqueduct but a rolling strip from there to the coast. This was a vital mission as the only previous intelligence source was a photograph of the aqueduct being built which dated from 1928. After Warburton had returned and his films developed it was discovered there were two aqueducts about 250 yards apart in the Tragino valley. After careful consideration it was decided to attack the larger or the more easterly one. There was some good news in that the planned drop zone appeared to be entirely suitable with no signs of defensive measures or indeed troops in the area.

That evening some of the more enterprising members of the troop, like all good soldiers, went out looking for some liquid refreshment which was duly found. Jock

Davidson shall we say overindulged himself and thought it would be good idea to go for a drive in General Dobbie's car. Regretfully it broke down and soon two Redcaps came sniffing round. One of them asked where the Governor was, soon Jock was under arrest and spent the night in the cells. The next morning he was rescued on the condition that when he returned to Malta he'd be charged and have to answer for his actions. Harry Pexton is still under the impression that this was one of the major reasons for not coming back.

The final piece of the jigsaw for the officers of X Troop now fell into place and they were briefed about their exit route. They were told that on the night of 15th/16th February a Royal Naval submarine HMS *Triumph* would be in position off the mouth of the River Sele (south of Salerno). This in theory gave the men from X Troop about five days to cover the 60 miles or so from the Tragino Aqueduct to the pick up point. To the men of X Troop this did not seem too arduous as they had undergone many sessions of physical training both at Ringway and in Scotland. As a fall back position HMS *Triumph* would return on the night of 17th/18th February if no-one showed up at the first rendezvous. This was the last chance saloon and the commander of the operation Major Pritchard had talks with the submarine commander Lieutenant Commander W Woods to make sure there were no misunderstandings about the plan.

The men were briefed on the forthcoming raid on the afternoon of the 10th, and there was much relief when it was found out they were heading for Italy to blow up an aqueduct. The rumour machine had come up with the guess that the target was in Abyssinia, which was way off the mark. Harry Pexton recalled, "We were told that the target was actually in Italy. It had been a well-kept secret as we had often discussed and suggested where the target was, several blokes saying Abyssinia, Albania or North Africa. I can't recall anyone ever suggesting Italy."

However, only the officers were let into the evacuation plan. It was explained that X Troop would split up into smaller parties and rendezvous near the coastal pick-up point on the agreed date. The actual route to that spot would be left to the groups themselves. It was also explained that six of the Whitleys would carry six men and (depending on their weight) between four and six containers with the arms, ammunition, explosives and other necessary equipment. A boffin had also come up with detailed instructions as to where the parachutists were to sit during take off, the flight itself and action stations. The other two Whitleys were as previously stated to drop their loads (two 500 lb bombs and six 250 lb bombs) on Foggia as a diversion to the parachute landing. It was intended for the first aircraft to arrive over the drop zone at 9.30 p.m., with the others arriving at six minute intervals after this. At 5.00 p.m. after a brief meal, the men of X Troop fitted their parachutes and then were bussed out to the waiting aircraft. Before getting on board the commander, Major Pritchard addressed the assembled company and stated: "You are pioneers or guinea pigs – and you can chose which word you prefer." In spite of this the men entered their allocated aircraft in high spirits. The first group to leave were the three groups of men who were to act as the covering parties under Lea, Jowett and Deane-Drummond. These all left around 5.30 p.m. and Deane-Drummond commented that it was a gin-clear night. Next to leave were the two Whitleys heading for Foggia, and the last group of three Whitleys with the commander, his small 'HQ' group and the engineers around 6.00 p.m. However, there was a last minute hitch in that one of the engineers (a Corporal) reported that he suddenly felt quite sick. Not wanting to go with this man, Captain Daly ordered him off the aircraft. This led to a small delay of around 15 minutes so this aircraft was lagging behind the others. The decision was also taken not to call up the reserve engineer so Daly's party took off one man short. One final note was that all the parachuting aircraft were meant to continue to Foggia and also drop a few bombs so hopefully fooling the Italians into thinking it was just a bombing raid.

This is what Lieutenant Deane-Drummond had to say about his last couple of hours on Malta and the flight to Italy:

> The weather report was satisfactory and at about 5.00 p.m. we gulped down some hot tea and some hard-boiled eggs. I did not feel at all hungry and as one of the men said, "These Maltese eggs seem coated with glue." We were dressed in all our paraphernalia – over the webbing pouches we wore a loose jacket called a jumping jacket and on top of that went the parachute. Feeling very over-dressed and clumsy, we took a truck to the waiting aeroplane and squeezed laboriously down the narrow tunnel fuselage of the Whitley. While the men settled down in unaccustomed silence, all the lights and bomb-release switches were tested. Then we heard crackling through the intercom, "N for Nuts now ready to take-off. Over."
>
> Back came the reply, "Hello N for Nuts, OK, Good luck. Out."
>
> Our eardrums tightened as the aeroplane climbed through the sky and soon the pilot told us that we were flying at ten thousand feet over Sicily. Just over the northern coast the aeroplane started to rock and bump and we could hear the engines speed up and then slow down. This was the flak about which we had been warned, but it did not seem very alarming from the inside of a Whitley.

As Deane-Drummond had said it was a clear night and visibility was good, also in most of the aircraft the navigation was spot on and when the target area was reached it was apparently pretty easy to spot the aqueduct amongst the snow covered countryside. In N-Nuts, piloted by Sergeant Lashbrook, the warning order of 15 minutes to target was

TRAGINO: THE PHOTOGRAPH FROM WHICH THE ATTACK WAS PLANNED

26. The only ground photograph available to the planners for Colossus was this one, taken in 1928 when the aqueduct was being built. The huts were used by the construction workers and were not there in 1941. (ABF Museum)

given and this meant that the men from X Troop did a final check on their equipment and probably more importantly their static lines. Also the parachute exit doors were loosened. In this aircraft it was a nervous time as Deane-Drummond recalls:

After what seemed a very long fifteen minutes, we were astonished to see the rear gunner come back from his turret and shout to us; "You are due to drop in under a minute. Get cracking." It turned out the intercom had failed virtually at the last minute and the 'rear gunner' was Flight Lieutenant B Williams from Ringway, who had come along as an observer. Perhaps he had been allowed to study the model and had recognised several features and acted to prevent a disaster.

The next few seconds inside the Whitley were a scene of frantic activity as the parachuting doors were removed and the men took up their jumping positions. The exit of the first parachutists over the drop zone was planned to be at 9.30 p.m. and it is believed N-Nuts was first there at 9.42 p.m. As the covers to the exit were hastily removed Deane-Drummond looked out and later said:

Suddenly I saw the light of a village flash by underneath, not a hundred feet below. I now knew we might expect our red light in a few seconds, as the run-in to the drop zone went straight over the middle of the village of Calitri. Sure enough, on came the red light and we all braced ourselves for the jump. I glanced at the rest of my section, wondering what was going through their minds. They looked cheerful but pale, and they too, were looking round at their companions. Through the hole

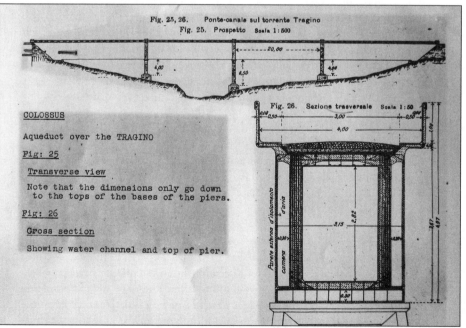

27. A pre-war Italian technical drawing of the Tragino Aqueduct used for planning purposes. (National Archives)

at my feet some houses and then a river, flashed by in the moonlight. It could not be long now.

Then the green light came on and the six parachutists all exited the aircraft. There was a brief pause between numbers three and four to allow the containers to be released. One of these contained a Bren gun, another had three Thompson sub machine-guns and two were packed with explosive charges. For the uninitiated the idea of putting the containers towards the middle of the stick was to make sure that hopefully the weapons landed somewhere near the men. It is believed that Flight Lieutenant Williams reported to Sergeant Lashbrook that the last two parachutists would be in trouble as it appeared the Whitley had not climbed quickly enough to clear the rising ground towards the end of the drop zone. Fortunately he was wrong and the six men jumped high enough to allow their parachutes to fully deploy before landing.

The following is Lieutenant Deane-Drummond's recollections of the time after leaving the Whitley:

We had been dropped rather low, from not more than 500 feet, which gave us about 15 seconds before we touched down. I could only be about 200 feet up at the most, and I started to take a more intelligent interest in the few square yards of Italy that I was going to land on. It seemed that I was going to drop on to a small bridge with a few cottages about a 150 yards away from it. This was our bridge. It stood out clearly, looking just as it did in the air photograph. The cottages were those that my section had to clear of all inhabitants to prevent them giving the alarm. The aqueduct was exactly as it had been described to us except that the surrounding country was far wilder and tilted at far sharper angles than we had expected. I was drifting towards the hillside just above the bridge. The ground was rushing upwards at me now and I braced myself for the landing. Just as my toes touched, I pulled on my rigging lines with all my might. Over I went on one side and the canopy of the parachute slowly lost its shape and flopped its yards of silk and rigging lines all over me. It was the best landing I had ever made.

Also in this stick was Sergeant Arthur Lawley and he commented:

I was acting as stick commander so it was my job to dispatch us all. The green light came on and I shouted "One, Two, Three, Containers, Four, Five then Six." It was a bit silly really me shouting "Six", as that was me and I walked through the hole. When my chute opened I found myself floating steadily down in beautiful moonlight and everything was deathly silent – suddenly I can see the mountains on each side of me and that the one I am going to land on is very steep – I know however, by the rate of my descent that I will have a perfect landing. The next instant I have touched down and for a second I listen intently, but can only hear the distant drone of the aircraft. I whip off my chute and draw my .32 pistol and advance stealthily towards the aqueduct which I can see a short distance down the valley. Suddenly I see what appears to be a form lying on the ground with chute attached. I think it is one of our blokes and rush forward and to my relief find it is a container. I soon have it open and get a Tommy gun. I then wait and listen, and before long I could see a figure coming towards me. Under my breath I give the password 'Heil Hitler', to receive back 'Viva Duce'. It was Lieutenant Deane-Drummond.

Credit must be given to Sergeant Lashbrook and his crew as they managed to drop their stick of parachutists and containers after a flight of over 400 miles with minimal navigational aids within 250 yards of the Tragino Aqueduct and probably bang in the middle of the intended drop zone. This first group all landed pretty close to each other and soon five of them had assembled together. The sixth member of Deane-Drummond's stick was missing, Lance Corporal H Boulter had had a bad landing amongst some rocks on the banks of the Tragino and broken his ankle.

The container containing the Thompson sub machine-guns was quickly found, and then Deane-Drummond divided his gang of five into three. Two of them, including Picchi, were to clear some farm buildings just up from where they had landed. Two others, including Sergeant A Lawley, were to go to some cottages on the other side of the Tragino around 150 yards from the aqueduct. Deane-Drummond himself went to the aqueduct and his instructions were that all the occupants of the buildings were to be brought to the aqueduct. Perhaps the only problem nagging at the minds of this small group was that no other aircraft had been heard, anyway they got on with the task at hand. Over twenty locals were rounded up including an Italian soldier by Sergeant Lawley. He was approaching the cottages, when a door opened and a man came out with a dog. Freezing they saw him go into a small outbuilding, and then after a few minutes return to his home. They followed him, kicked open the door and surprised a peasant family. Lawley lowered his gun and held out his hand, hoping to show that he meant

28. A close-up of the western-most pier of the Tragino Aqueduct. It was around this that the explosives were hung. (R Voskuil)

no harm to them. They allowed themselves to be shepherded outside, whilst the second house was searched. Inside this one they again found a family and an Italian soldier in uniform. Lawley again stepped forward to offer a hand in friendship but the soldier made a move for a shotgun nearby. Lawley beat him to it and with a raised weapon and although he spoke no Italian, the tone of his voice left him in no doubt that this soldier meant business if he tried anything again.

29. A general view of the area around the Tragino Aqueduct showing the somewhat inhospitable terrain. (R Voskuil)

According to the plan Deane-Drummond's party should have been the third to jump at 9.42 p.m., and it is believed they were virtually on time. However no other signs of any men from X Troop could be seen or indeed heard. The party of Italians were marched over to the aqueduct. Then at around 10.15 p.m. the noise of approaching aircraft could be heard. It seems that the other aircraft had been targeted by flak over Sicily and had taken evasive action which led to them temporarily losing their way. On the ground the reinforcements could be clearly seen gently floating down. The Whitley (K-King) carrying Major Pritchard, Captain Lea, Flight Lieutenant Lucky and three men, piloted by Wing Commander Tait, arrived in the area of the aqueduct and the party jumped in good order. The only problem was that they landed around a mile away from the aqueduct close to the Ofanto river. Pritchard jumped first and virtually landed on the bank of the river, another from this stick L/Corporal H Pexton, landed in a tree and was only able to free himself after a considerable struggle. At least he didn't have to wait for the Knutsford Fire Brigade. After the group was reunited, they again set about finding their containers, one of them containing three Thompson sub machine guns had failed to release from the Whitley. They successfully found their supplies and set off for the aqueduct. They were armed with three weapons from the other arms container, the majority of the food for the whole party and a ladder. The decision was taken to leave the explosives behind in the hope they could be collected later.

Two other Whitleys then arrived and it is reported that Wing Commander Tait assisted the pilots of these aircraft in dropping their loads, perhaps he realised his mistake and was hoping to make amends. W-Willie, piloted by Flight Lieutenant Williams was believed to be the next to drop. He had flown Second Lieutenant Jowett's stick of six. The first man in the queue to jump was Sergeant P Clements. His experiences of 'sitting in the door' are worth recounting. He was sitting on the edge of the hole ready to go, briefly saw the green light flick on for a second and then go out to be replaced by the normal red warning light. The pilot had put the aircraft into a sudden climb to avoid flying into a ridge, and then it seemed to be flashing on and off, it stayed green for a few seconds and so Sergeant Clements launched himself into the exit, only to be grabbed by numbers 2 and 3 in the stick, as the green had gone out to be replaced by the red. The pilot had decided to abort and was circling round to make a fresh approach. The unfortunate Percy Clements was held by his comrades for around five minutes half in and half out the aircraft. Then at last the instructions came through that the drop zone was approaching and they could go on the next green light. The stick followed Clements out and all made it safely to ground, although one of the weapon containers was again held up on the Whitley.

Whitley E-Edward piloted by Pilot Officer Robinson with Wing Commander Norman from Ringway along as an observer, carried Second Lieutenant Paterson and his party of sappers. Again this group had a small mishap; the first three men jumped in good order and then Paterson pressed the container release switch. Nothing seemed to happen, so he pressed it again, still nothing seemed to happen. Time was running out so he exited the aircraft followed by the last two members of the stick. The aircraft post-mission report claims that that all six containers were released on the fifth run over the drop zone. These six containers contained (in five of them) explosives and in the last a further ladder. The men all made it to the ground safely, although the last man in the stick L/Corporal Jones just managed to avoid a clump of trees but landed instead in the Tragino and emerged soaking wet.

The fourth aircraft of the 'late arrivals' (making five in all so far), D-Don piloted by Sergeant Holden and again carrying six sappers, identified the drop zone and all six made a safe landing. This Whitley didn't have any gremlins in the release mechanism and all six containers (again five explosives and one ladder) were released and were collected. So by 10.45 p.m., about an hour behind schedule, five of the six Whitleys had deposited their loads of containers and parachutists roughly in the right area.

You will recall there were six Whitleys despatched to the Tragino Aqueduct area which leaves one Whitley unaccounted for. This was J-Johnnie piloted by Lieutenant Hoad (a Fleet Air Arm pilot) carrying the chief engineer Captain Daly and his party. This aircraft made some navigational errors and followed a river which they thought was the right one, but of course wasn't. They eventually realised their mistake when they crossed the Italian Adriatic coast. They turned round and eventually found the right area around 90 minutes behind schedule around 11.15 p.m. The misfortunes continued when Daly's group was dropped in the wrong valley around two miles to the north-east. To compound this none of the six containers (with explosives and a ladder) were released. The loss of this party and their stores was a serious blow to the others at the objective. Here the various parties were all heading towards the aqueduct, and one of them found Corporal Boulter, dragging himself towards it. He was helped to a grassy area and then left on his own. An entirely proper decision as the objective took precedence over casualties.

Major Pritchard arrived at the bridge as Lieutenant Deane-Drummond recalled:

There was a loud crashing through the bushes and thorn ash in the valley bottom. My men took the cue and prepared to fire, only waiting my signal in case it should be one of our own sections. But when the trees parted out came old Tag by himself, a little out of breath, as his plane load had been landed about a mile away. I reported that I had found the aqueduct unguarded and that we had rounded up all the Italians in the vicinity and that so far Captain Daly had not arrived.

As more men arrived the covering sections were sent to their allocated positions. Captain Lea's section was sent to guard the two ends of the aqueduct, Deane-Drummond's group was positioned astride the track leading from the cottages to the aqueduct. Second Lieutenant Jowett's section was in a covering position on the other side of the Tragino, securing the sloping ground on which Deane-Drummond and his men had landed. This left the rest of X Troop, mainly the few sappers who had arrived, to collect the containers containing the explosives. They had been widely scattered but to help find them small battery powered lights had been fitted to them, but the power in these was starting to run out. Major Pritchard quickly realised that the sappers would soon get tired collecting and carrying the explosives to the objective over the rough ground. The decision was therefore taken to 'ask' the male Italian prisoners to help. They had all been collected together and locked in one of the cottages, when one of the interpreters put this suggestion to them, they all readily agreed. One of them apparently said nothing ever happened in their remote valley and this would give them something to talk about in future times. They then trudged off to comb the surrounding countryside under the watchful eyes of men from X Troop, the containers they did find were heavy and it was hard work. It is reported that during the movement of one of these containers an elderly Italian peasant asked, 'Are you guys English?', the question was posed in a broad American accent. It seems that he had spent several years in New York working in a hotel. One of the men in the vicinity without a hint of sarcasm answered, 'No chum, we are Abyssinians on our way to Sunday School.' Soon the Italians were grumbling about the physical effort. However, it is reported that later most of these Italians were awarded medals for their 'gallant behaviour in the face of the enemy'.

The night remained silent apart from the sounds of the container movement and the occasional barking of a dog in the distance. Things were looking good, no opposition had materialised and it seemed no Italians were on their way to investigate. Then from the direction of Calitri a man on a bicycle could be seen pedalling towards the farm buildings. He was intercepted by Deane-Drummond who later recounted:

> Our orders were to give warning of anyone coming up the valley and, if necessary, to prevent interference with the parties carrying the explosives. There was to be no firing unless it was unavoidable. As it happened the only man in uniform who appeared was the local station-master from Calitri. He was duly pressed into the labour gang and made quite a good porter. His biggest worry was that he would be late taking over from his relief and might get the sack. If he was sacked he would be put in the Army and sent to the front, which he pointed out was far too terrible a punishment for kind people like us to inflict on him. We told him his skilled labour was required, but that if he liked we would give him a certificate to say that he had been detained against his will. This cheered him up tremendously and from then on nobody could stop him talking.

While all of this was going on, Major Pritchard went with Second Lieutenant Paterson to survey the aqueduct, to him it was very much the same as the model they had trained on back in England. However, it was not exactly the same – they had been led to believe from the information supplied by the engineering firm who assisted in its construction that it was made of brick. Paterson after seeing the aerial reconnaissance photographs had suspected it might not be brick and after attacking one of the piers with a hammer and chisel he found it was of reinforced concrete. Additionally the centre pier was not low and squat as the models had suggested, but was 30 feet high and with its feet resting in the centre of the water flow. Perhaps here is a good point to detail the explosive resources loaded into the containers on Malta:

Tools:
Mash Hammers 5
Cold Chisels 10
Entrenching tools 5
Saws hand 26" 5
Tensioners 5
Windlassing sticks 10

Detonating Agents:
Cordtex drums 5
Primers 111
Detonators 36
Safety Fuze 162 feet

Gun cotton:
2240 lbs wet slabs (this was packed into 160 boxes each weighing 14 lbs)

Rope:
Spunyarn 10 lbs
Whipping twine 5 balls
Alpine cord 1000 feet
Steel wire rope 300 feet

General:
Insulating tape 18 rolls
Angle plates 20
A quantity of sandbags (empty)

Demolition Equipment:

ITEM	THREE PIERS	SPARE FOR OPERATION	SPARE	TOTAL
Charge boards, complete with end plates, cordage, sheepshank, top hook and short hook	30	12	2	44
Angle plates	12	8	1	21
Balloon cable strops, soldered to ratchet tensioners	3	2	1	6
Pairs of ladders, strengthened and fixed together to extend	6	4	-	10
Alpine rope strops	6	4	-	10
Windlass sticks	6	4	-	10

These were all packed in 25 containers except for the detonators which were carried by the men themselves. In all 33 containers were carried.

Back on the ground at the aqueduct, the guinea pigs of X Troop were the first parachutists to experience the Airborne Murphy Law; in that anything that can go wrong will go wrong. Only around a third of the explosives (800 lbs) expected to arrive could be found, this meant a quick change in the plan. In the original plan it had been intended to blow up two of the three piers plus the supporting abutments. But Second Lieutenant Paterson worked out he had only enough explosive to blow up just one pier. Of the 800 lbs of explosives collected Paterson decided to place around 600 lbs against the western most pier (this was the one easiest to reach from the farm track), with the balance going against its supporting abutment. The sappers started to pack the gun cotton against this concrete pier, using the collapsible ladders that had been found. It is reported that L/Corporal D Jones was one of the sappers foremost in this work.

Sapper D Struthers recounted the actual method fixing the explosives to the aqueduct:

By using the portable ladders we were able to run a steel cable round the column, about ten to twelve feet from the ground. Four boxes of guncotton were attached to a plank of wood with a hook at either end and we suspended the charges from the cable until we encircled the column.

Additionally, as Lieutenant Deane-Drummond had discovered a bridge over a small stream about 150 yards from the aqueduct, Paterson got permission to blow this as well. It was hoped the destruction of this would delay the repair effort. He got two 40 lbs boxes of gun cotton carried by L/Corporal R Watson and Sapper A Ross, and ordered them to get the bridge ready for demolition. He sent a message to Major Pritchard that he would blow his bridge up when he heard the warning sound for the main aqueduct explosion. One of the few interruptions to these actions was the sound of a low-flying aircraft, which was probably the Whitley piloted by Hoad who ended up dropping his load in the wrong valley.

Soon after midnight, the charges had been placed and the Italians were escorted back into one of the farm buildings close to the bridge found by Lieutenant Deane-Drummond. They were told that a sentry had been posted outside with orders to shoot anyone who came outside. It is reported that at 12.30 a.m., Major Pritchard let off the

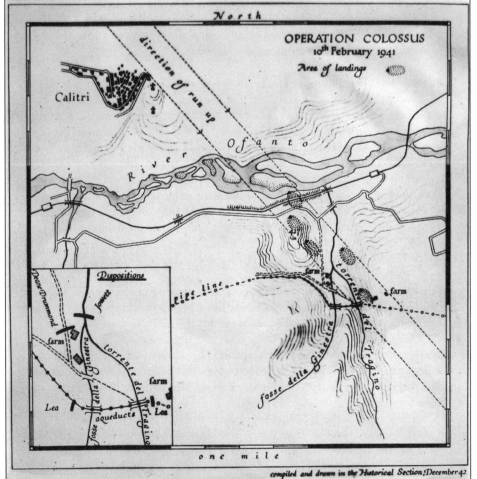

OPERATION COLOSSUS
10th February 1941
Area of landings

Calitri

North

direction of run up

Ofanto

River

Dispositions

pipe line

farm

farm

torrente del Tragino

fosse della Ginestra

farm

Deane Drummond

lowest

farm

torrente del Tragino

farm

Lea

Lea

fosse della Ginestra

aqueducts

one   mile

compiled and drawn in the Historical Section, December 42

The point of aim for the parachutists was hill 427. They came down in a good "pattern". The spot in each landing area marks the point of landing of the first man down from each aircraft.

Map 4. The December 1942 map giving details of the landing places of most of the participants in Operation Colossus. (National Archives)

warning sign (of a single slab of gun cotton), to advise everyone except for the demolition party to withdraw to safe positions about 200 yards from the aqueduct. Shortly after this Second Lieutenant Paterson lit a 60 second fuse to set off the main explosion and he and Major Pritchard quickly took cover behind a rocky outcrop. At the smaller bridge L/Corporal Watson also lit his fuse and took cover.

The air was silent as the men of X Troop waited expectantly for the explosions, the seconds slowly ticking by. After what seemed a minute nothing happened, so Pritchard and Paterson decided to return to inspect what they thought was a defective faulty fuse. They had only taken a few steps towards the aqueduct when it went up before their eyes; the air was full of smoke, concrete and masonry. Almost simultaneously Deane-Drummond's bridge went up with debris showering him and L/Corporal Watson, some also landing on the farm buildings. However, the job here had been done and the small bridge lay in the stream bed. They then went towards the spot where the rest of X Troop had gathered and as Deane-Drummond commented:

> We then slowly clambered up to where the rest were standing and eagerly asked for news of the aqueduct. Tag and Pat had gone back to look at the damage and had left the rest of the men at the assembly position. Impatiently we awaited their return, all wondering what on earth we should do if there was no damage. We had been keyed up for this moment for the past six weeks and failure would have been unbearable. Tag and Pat came back without a smile on their faces. Was it a fiasco? Tag put up his hand and everybody stopped talking. All he said was "Listen." We all strained our ears and sure enough we heard the sound of a great waterfall. It was a success. How we cheered and cheered! We could hardly imagine that we were in enemy country. Those British cheers must have been heard a good mile or two away.

Arthur Lawley only had a few words to say:

> We inspected our handiwork and found that we had made a good job of it! To hear the water rushing down the mountainside like a raging torrent was music to our ears; we had achieved what we had set out to do.

The explosion was clearly heard by Captain Daly and his party of five sappers in the next valley and must have cheered their somewhat downhearted spirits. Hoping that the aqueduct had now been destroyed this party now decided to head straight for the coastal rendezvous.

Meanwhile back at the aqueduct everyone then went down to inspect the damage that had been caused, one pier had gone completely and another leaned at a drunken angle and half the aqueduct was down. Water was pouring from both ends, this was due to water coming out at the western end from the pumped supply. It was also coming out at the higher eastern end due to the lack of pressure. However, it was not the time nor the place to spend long admiring their work as distance was needed to be put between the aqueduct and the pick-up point. Major Pritchard revealed for many the plan that a submarine would be coming to pick them up in a few nights' time.

For some men a degree of fatigue now set in, Lieutenant Deane-Drummond commented:

All our inward hopes and fears about the success of the venture were now soothed and the reaction made us all feel very tired. What was more tiring still was the thought of having to walk some sixty or seventy miles across the mountains to the coast. Tag had decided before we started that we would have the best chance of getting to our coastal rendezvous if we split up into small parties and made our own way to the sea, and accordingly he divided us into three, each with about ten men and two officers. The barks of a dog pierced the night. It seemed impossible that we would not have all Italy on our heels by the morning.

Chapter 4

On the Run

The three parties, all of whom were to travel independently and on separate routes, were led by Major Pritchard with Lieutenant Deane-Drummond, Captain Lea and Second Lieutenant Paterson in charge of the second whilst Second Lieutenant Jowett with Flight Lieutenant Lucky looked after the third. The plan was to travel lightly and move by night, hiding up in the day. A large amount of equipment was left behind, including all the 'spare' demolition kit, and most of the heavier weapons – the Bren guns and all of the sub machine guns (except one per group) were stripped down to pieces and scattered in the immediate area of the aqueduct. However this still meant everyone had a pack to carry weighing at least 30 lbs. Everyone had five days rations and personal equipment such as mess tins. Everyone carried a revolver or pistol and two grenades together with the soon-to-become-famous commando knife. Shared out amongst everyone were water bottles, cooking stoves and petrol. All the officers had been given ten gold sovereigns to act as 'escape money' which was left to them to decide where to secrete on their body. It was hoped these may of enable some people to buy their way out of trouble.

There was a small problem to consider and that was what to do with the injured and virtually immobile L/Corporal Boulter. To try and carry him would be impossible and so Major Pritchard broke the news to him that he would have to be left behind. Boulter was left with a Thompson gun and a quantity of painkillers. It was clear that sooner or later the Italians would be visiting the aqueduct and find L/Corporal Boulter and so Major Pritchard gave him a quick course in anti-interrogation techniques. This involved giving him the news that he should only divulge his name, rank and number, and then shook hands with him. It seems that nearly everyone else came over to say goodbye some giving him extra cigarettes and chocolate. Just before setting off one of the Italian speakers returned to the farmhouse and repeated the warning about staying inside. The time was now around 1.15 a.m., and it was time to get going. Major Pritchard's plan (with his group of ten men) was to first climb the mountain behind the aqueduct and then follow a ridge till it joined the start of the river Sele and when compared to the other two parties can be looked on as the central route. To the south of this route was the party led by Second Lieutenant Jowett with Flight Lieutenant Lucky and for unknown reasons five other men.

Finally to the north of the Pritchard group were Captain Lea and Second Lieutenant Paterson with eleven others. Perhaps it would be best to look at the actions of these three groups separately, but first a word or two about the two Whitleys on the diversionary raid on Foggia. It is believed one of the Whitleys made it to the area of Foggia and dropped some bombs, however, the other Whitley then put a severe spanner in the works of Operation Colossus. This aircraft, S-Sugar, piloted by Pilot Officer Watherspoon, developed engine trouble on the flight and it was severe enough to force him to crash land. The area he chose to crash land near was the mouth of the Sele, south of Salerno.

This was of course, the same rivermouth where in five nights' time HMS *Triumph* was due to pick the men of X Troop up. It is reported that a coded radio message was sent to Malta, advising them of their location and requesting a rescue. The Navy on Malta were of the opinion that the code used had probably been broken and the chances of the crew staying undiscovered not very high. They concluded that the pick up point had been compromised and not wishing to risk a valuable submarine on such a dangerous mission, recalled it. The submarine was already at sea but a message was sent recalling on them at 8.30 p.m. on the evening of 13th February. Obviously no such niceties were accorded to the men of X Troop as they had no means of communication with anybody except by torch, which was of little use in this situation.

So back in the early hours of 11th February the groups started to struggle up the steep hillsides on their way to the coast. This left poor old L/Corporal Boulter on his own, as his ankle was starting to swell up, he cut away his boot to try and ease the pain. Later he limped into a small farm building and soon fell asleep. Waking up later after dawn, he saw the Italian soldier cautiously come out of his overnight prison and getting on a bicycle pedalled off in the direction of Calitri. Harry Boulter, perhaps foolishly, fired a burst from his Thompson at him but missed. Realising this had revealed his position, he did his best to find alternative cover, and dragged himself up the hillside a short distance and positioned himself behind a large boulder. Shortly afterwards several vehicles arrived carrying *Carabinieri* and soldiers who proceeded to sweep the ground for

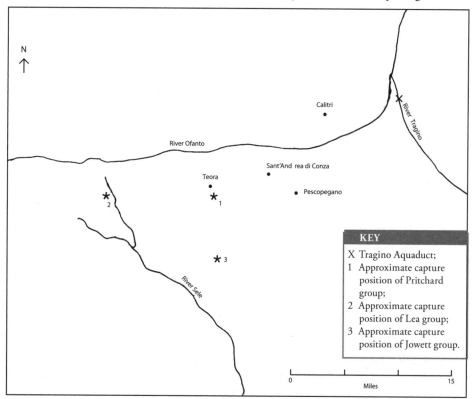

Map 5. Tragino Aquaduct Area

him. It is reported that Harry kept them at bay until his ammunition ran out. He was handcuffed and beaten up and then made to hobble to Calitri and then taken to Naples, where he finally received some medical treatment.

It is perhaps worth giving a brief description of the terrain in the area of the aqueduct which was virtually similar to that they faced over their trek of 60 or so miles. Most of the ground was around 2,000 feet above sea level (at least) and snow was on the ground, there was plenty of mud and numerous small streams had to be crossed. The terrain was seriously undulating and even though the trip was in theory only 60 miles it became a very trying experience, you must also remember that it was also a manhunt and the men were behind enemy lines.

The largest group was that led by Major Pritchard with Lieutenant Deane-Drummond and eleven others including Picchi. One of the group, L/Corporal D Henderson, in spite of orders, had kept his Bren gun with him and I suspect this 22 lbs load soon became a burden. The plan was for them to follow a ridge line until they reached the course of the Sele, and then travel down the north side till this emptied into the Mediterranean and hopefully meet HMS *Triumph*. This basic outline can also be applied to the other two groups. Major Pritchard's group first climbed the steep hill behind the aqueduct and then at the top headed in an almost south-westerly direction. The going was pretty arduous and at least one halt an hour had to be made for a brief rest. It soon became clear that certain gorges were impassable, which led to many detours, all of which were extremely frustrating and time-consuming. After walking for most of the time since leaving the Tragino valley the decision was taken just before dawn to hide up in a wooded ravine. This is Lieutenant Deane-Drummond's recollections of that first night's march:

> Right from the start we met difficulties. Fields knee-deep in mud, impassable little ravines, innumerable farm houses all with noisy dogs, were only a few of our obstacles. We soon learnt to disregard the dogs, as does everybody else in Italy. Every three quarters of an hour Tag stopped and we sat down, munching chocolate or sipping a little water till we were sufficiently recovered to continue. On and on we tramped, pulling ourselves up the sides of steep little gorges by hands and then slithering down the other side on our backsides. All the jagged prominences and rocks were exaggerated by the moonlight and appeared twice their real distance away. Occasionally we had a glimpse from the tops of some of the ridges and the countryside seemed endless in its variety of obstacles, all supremely difficult for marching troops. How we cursed all Italy, the Italians and everything Italian that night!
>
> We had left the bridge at 1.30 a.m. and we halted about 7.00 a.m. By that time we must have covered at least fifteen miles over the ground, but had only done six out of the sixty we had to do before reaching the coast.

According to the plan they hid up in this wooded area and when it was deemed to be safe tea was brewed on the primus stoves they were carrying. According to several of the veterans the main type of food issued to them was pemmican. This was one of the staple foods taken on many of the polar expeditions both before and after the Great War. It was made of meat extract with added fat and tastes like concentrated greasy

Bovril, but as I've never eaten pemmican I shall bow to their superior knowledge. In the daylight Pritchard and Deane-Drummond studied the surrounding countryside against their maps and thought they were near the village of San Lorenzo. It was a difficult day as Italians could be seen working the fields and on several occasions a light aircraft flew back and forth over the valley, clearly searching for signs of the men from X Troop. Also on one occasion some children playing with some dogs came close to this group's hiding place, but fortunately they remained undiscovered. Lieutenant Deane-Drummond commented on the area around their hiding place as follows:

> I shall always remember the boulders. The little ravine in which we were sheltering was filled completely with enormous boulders of all shapes and sizes. Some seemed strung together like a necklace whilst others were perched on top of one another in defiance of all the laws of gravity. Straight in front of us, not more than a quarter of a mile away, rose a sheer cliff which we would have to scale that evening. More hell to come!

Anyway with the darkness they set off once again, first having to scale the cliff previously mentioned by Deane-Drummond. This climb was eventually accomplished and at the top they could ascertain a mountain road and so Major Pritchard decided they would travel parallel to this about 400 yards to one side of it. Shadowing the route of this road they skirted the villages of Pescopagano and Sant Andrea di Conza. However so far they had been moving for several hours and seemed on the map at least to be making little headway on the distance they had to travel. After a brief discussion it was decided to march on the road and take the risk of being discovered. Initially they made good progress, marching uphill for the best part of two hours it is believed they reached the high point of their journey, an isolated crossroads from which it was now in theory downhill all the way into the Sele valley and the coast.

The following is Lieutenant Deane-Drummond's recollections of that second night:

> Night came at last and on went our packs, with our pistols at our belts. Tag had noticed a shepherd with a flock of goats come down a path in the cliff during the day, and he said he thought he could find it. Before climbing we had to cross a small stream, not more than thirty feet wide, but most unpleasant to fall into as it had deep pools and a swift current flowing between round, slippery boulders. Eventually we found a crossing place which provided stepping stones most of the way over except a gap in the middle. Nearly all jumped it successfully, but I saw one man slip and tumble in. He had to travel the rest of that night in soaked clothes.
>
> Tag led the way and we started to approach our cliff. When we reached its foot, we discovered that it was not so steep as it had appeared from our hiding place and with a bit of difficulty we could pull ourselves up. Every bit of scrub and long grass came in handy now, and we sweated and heaved our way up the three hundred feet of mud and shingle which formed most of the surface. As we arrived at the top each man threw himself down panting on the ground. It had taken every ounce of our energy to climb that hill and we felt it later on.
>
> I was leading now and slowly we crept on in single file with ears strained for the slightest sound. We could see a few cottages against the skyline and we assumed

it must be the outskirts of Pescopagano. Dogs could be heard barking all over the village and further up the valley. Perhaps it was one of the other parties that was causing the disturbance. I kept wondering how they were getting on.

The country became wilder and more impossible than ever. The moonlight distorted every natural hummock and glade into grotesque and weird shapes. Before us stretched mile upon mile of the roughest country we had ever seen. Few landmarks could be picked out so we decided to march by compass to a large crossroad near the source of the Sele river. During this night's march we had to cover some twenty miles and then find hideouts for the following day somewhere along the north side of the Sele valley. We crossed countless small streams and stumbled through wild junipers and stunted oak thickets. We were always walking either up or down or along the side of a hill. Compass marching, in this sort of country is not easy, but we managed to strike a small road which we were expecting to find.

At this stage we decided it was too risky to walk along the road, but preferred to use it as a guide, keeping it about a quarter of a mile below us. Gradually we worked our way forward, trying to avoid the scattered little farmhouses, which were becoming more numerous. At each brook we came to we first threw ourselves flat on our faces and sucked up some clear ice-cold water. Our mouths were dry with exhaustion and some of the men were completely worn out.

We skirted several villages and eventually Tag decided to stop and make some sweet tea to keep us going. Soon the primus was spurting and hissing, and a welcome steam was coming off the mess tin. It was the best dixie of tea I've ever had. New energy seemed to pour into our veins as we sipped the hot sugary liquid, and when we got up a new briskness was obvious in all our party.

It was about one o'clock in the morning and as we had not seen anything on the road for some time, Tag very wisely decided to march straight along it and damn the risk. The change of walking along that road after trudging through the mud revived us both mentally and physically. For five or six miles we tramped along the road and eventually we reached the big crossroad which was the highest point on our route to the coast. From now on the way ran downhill and our only task before dawn was to find a hiding place for the following day. As we scurried over the crossroad, we looked down the valley. We could see it stretching for miles in the moonlight with rugged cultivated sides. The country looked forbidding and we could hardly believe that things would continue to go as well.

Then up ahead the distinctive sounds of a horse and cart could be heard approaching the crossroads, Major Pritchard quickly formed the men up into a marching formation. He then got Private Nastri to go to the front of the column as if in command and call out the orders and time in Italian. As it neared it could be seen that it was driven by a woman with a load of vegetables. As they passed the cart Nastri called out 'Buon giorno' and they passed without incident. This process was repeated on their way through other signs of inhabitation until at one point a farm worker engaged Nastri in conversation. Nastri explained that they were a group of Austrian soldiers on an exercise and politely declined the offer of a meal in his farmhouse. Soon after this they stopped walking on the road.

These are Sergeant Arthur Lawley's recollections of this period:

We spent the day hidden in a wood, from where I watched an Italian bring his flock of goats down the opposite mountainside and up which we would have to climb the next night, so I tried to memorize the route. We started off at dusk and went to the bottom of the valley and had to cross a fast flowing stream, some of the party fell into it getting across, and we all got our feet wet. On reaching the opposite bank I told Major Pritchard what I had seen during the day and so we started off up the goat track; but we were very soon on our hands and knees clinging for dear life to anything within reach, one slip and that would have been the end. However, everyone got up somehow. Still moving westwards we kept in the fields by a road, rounded a small town, and for the next few miles made good going along a road. It was along this road that we ran into a farmer going to market, but it was approaching dawn and so we began to look for somewhere to lay up for the day.

During the previous day when at their lying-up point Major Pritchard and Lieutenant Deane-Drummond had hoped that their group would spend the following day in a wood marked on their maps. However when they got to it, it was discovered there was a farm in the middle. Dawn was now approaching and the nearest suitable place appeared to be another wood at the top of a feature called the Cresta di Gallo overlooking a small village called Teora. After the dislocation of expectation at their intended hiding place it was a difficult move to this new location as spirits were low as the group trudged on through deep snow. They managed to get to the top of the Cresta di Gallo and found that the trees had been felled. There was no option but to stay here. This is what Lieutenant Deane-Drummond said:

My feet ached as they had never ached before, and my whole body was limp with exhaustion. Immediately we left the road we had to pay attention to avoid stumbling. This added to our general weariness. Some of us were near the end of our tether and a hiding place had to be found soon or we would have men falling out, which was unthinkable. The hill with trees on it was close by so we decided to head for it. We were still among ploughed fields with occasional farm houses nestling in a fold of the valley side. We climbed gradually now, hoping to strike the trees but none could be found. Eventually we came up to cloud level which was here below the tops of the hills. At last some trees loomed up through the mist, but when we approached we discovered that they sheltered a farmhouse. To have our hopes raised so high and then dashed mercilessly to the ground a moment later was no medicine for men in our condition, and we collapsed on the ground as one man. Our sweat-soaked clothes quickly became ice-cold and in the raw mist we were soon shivering from cold and exhaustion. Tag and I decided to climb up a little higher, to try to find a hiding place. We knew we could not go much further and the men were in the same state, so it seemed the only course to take. Less than fifty yards higher up cultivation ceased, and we came upon boulders and small juniper bushes which we thought might serve as temporary hiding places. Tag went back and brought up the men and soon we all found cover of some sort to hide in. Two or three men found a tiny cave which just concealed them. It was not good, but we were unable to move another step from sheer exhaustion. We had passed the caring stage and I suppose were a little overconfident of our powers of avoiding detection.

The time was about 5.30 a.m. and we had been on the move about ten hours and had covered twenty miles as the crow flies, across enemy country which had truly lived up to its name. Our feet must have travelled a good forty miles through the mud and so it was hardly surprising that we had not much energy left.

It was a miserable time for this group, it was not possible to light fires as this would certainly attract interest from the locals. In any case within about an hour, a local with a donkey started walking up the hillside and the men from X Troop thought he had spotted them. He acted as if he had seen nothing, perhaps he hadn't, but the footprints in the snow were a dead giveaway. Major Pritchard took the decision to send Picchi after him and tell him that everything was ok and the men up on the hillside were German and Italian mountain troops out on an exercise. Picchi did as he was told and spoke to the local but he seemed unconvinced and did not want to continue the conversation and started walking down the hillside towards the village of Teora. The uneasy atmosphere in the men of X Troop was not helped by the brief glimpse of two locals armed with shotguns who appeared on a ridge line a short distance away. However, these two men shortly disappeared. Meanwhile back in Teora the donkey man (for want of better words), reported what he had seen to the local *Carabinieri*. It is difficult after over sixty years to judge the scale of the effort expended by the Italians to find X Troop, but there had certainly been many radio broadcasts to the locals and the *Carabinieri* had been told to look out for 'enemy parachutist saboteurs'. It seemed they had their first breakthrough in the manhunt and an appeal went out for reinforcements. Whilst waiting for them to arrive, the armed locals looked on from a discrete distance, appeared briefly then disappeared. If the men of X Troop were going to avoid capture it was vital they did so quickly. Before they could act however, lorry loads of *Carabinieri* and troops from a mountain battalion began to arrive. In defence of X Troop it is difficult to see what they would have gained by breaking out as their mobility was limited and they were very tired from the previous night's exertions.

The following is Deane-Drummond's recollections of this time:

> I woke up around dawn and every bone in my body ached and shivered, my clothes were still soured with sweat and my teeth would not stop chattering. At first I could not believe my eyes but it was unfortunately too true. A peasant was standing not a hundred yards away looking intently in our direction. He had obviously spotted us and started to walk away. Tag made a quick decision and sent Picchi after him to try and convince him of our honest intentions. I knew in my heart that the game was up, but I could not believe that this was the end. We were fools to think so, but failure when we had travelled so far was unbelievable after the success that our venture had had up till then.

It was decided to try and bluff it out and 'draw the wagons into a circle', all the maps and any other useful items were either buried or destroyed. Corporal Henderson still had a Bren gun and it was hoped this would be the main defensive weapon, everyone else had a pistol and grenade.

However, to the men of X Troop the first people they saw were not armed police or soldiers but a large number of locals coming up the hill towards them. This was probably the most exciting event that had occurred in this village for many years and they had not waited for the Army or the *Carabinieri* to act. The children arrived first, followed by the local men and women some armed with shotguns, bringing up the rear were the soldiers and the *Carabinieri*.

This now put Major Pritchard's group in a very difficult position, for a few minutes a 'Mexican Stand Off' occurred, some of the men glancing at Pritchard waiting for an order to open fire. It has been said that this group was prepared to fight it out with the limited ammunition they did have, but what would this have achieved? All the time the locals were getting closer and closer and completely surrounding them until they were within about 20 yards. Major Pritchard said to Deane-Drummond, "I think we've had it". Deane-Drummond started to protest, suggesting that they could fire in the air or throw a grenade or two to scare them off a bit. Major Pritchard replied, "All right, Tony, you throw a grenade at those people on the right and I will throw mine over there". Deane-Drummond could sense the impossible situation they were in and agreed with Pritchard, who then told his group that they had to surrender. This is what Deane-Drummond remembers:

> After Picchi came back and said he thought he had satisfied the farmer, Tag said he had decided that it was useless to try to move off as it would only attract even more attention and so we sat where we were, feeling apprehensive about what was going to happen next.
>
> Some half-naked and filthy Italian children with a few mongrel dogs were our first spectators. They sat down about a hundred yards away from us, sucking their dirty thumbs and gazing at us as if we were men from the moon. A minute or two later a peasant appeared with pointers and a shotgun from over the hill just above our position. He seemed very frightened as he pointed his shotgun straight at Tag and kept up a running commentary, which of course was unintelligible to most of us. By this time quite a ring of spectators had collected, including a few peasant women who seemed to be the children's mothers. Picchi was now asking the man with the shotgun what it was all about. The man then gabbled something and ended by waving his gun around to emphasise his sentences. Eventually we discovered that he wanted us to lay down our arms. As these mainly consisted of pistols it seemed a lot of fuss to make about singularly ineffective weapons.
>
> The crowd surrounding our position had now become quite large and we were rather uncertain what to do. One easy way out would have been to chuck two or three hand grenades about and then make a bolt for it. On the other hand the whole countryside seemed to be on the move towards where we were and we would not have lasted long. In addition the grenades would have killed some of the women and children, who had in the meantime been joined by more men.
>
> I remember telling Tag that I did not agree with him when he gave the order to lay down our weapons, however I soon saw that we could not fight on. Women, children and unarmed peasants were everywhere and we would not be able to avoid casualties amongst them. All we could achieve were a few extra hours of freedom at the price of a particularly odious and inglorious action. Disconsolately I agreed with Tag and he told the men. There was dead silence for a moment and then one man asked in an incredulous voice: "Aren't we going to make a fight for it, Sir?"

I had never seen such a look of anguish on anybody's face as on Tag's at that moment. He just looked at the women and then at the man who had asked the question, and said that he was sorry but they would have to give in. Our hearts ached as we put down our pistols and Picchi was told to tell the Italian we were giving in because of the women and children. As soon as the peasants saw that we had dropped our weapons they came surging up to us and took all our equipment from us, much to our chagrin and disgust. I have never felt so ashamed before or since, that we should have surrendered to a lot of practically unarmed Italian peasants. This was the morning of 13th February 1941.

One man Corporal Henderson tried to make a break for it but he did not get very far and was soon captured. There was one small drama still to act out, as Major Pritchard held a grenade with the safety pin removed. If he dropped it as ordered by an Italian sergeant it would of course explode. Private Nastri managed to explain the situation and the crowd was ordered to one side so the grenade could be thrown to a safe area.

These are Sergeant Lawley's recollections of this time:

I remember telling Major Pritchard that we had been spotted by a local and he sent Picchi to go and tell him that we were Italian and German troops on manoeuvres, but it was of no avail. Soon we were surrounded by dogs, men, women and children then armed troops and police. Major Pritchard had no choice but to surrender, but before doing so all maps and other material was collected and burnt.

Now that everyone had been disarmed, the men from X Troop were now subjected to a humiliating experience. The Italians taking no chances, they were then handcuffed and chained together in three and fours, every second man also getting an iron ball. Major Pritchard was spared this treatment and complained but to no avail. They then had to run the gauntlet of taunting and spitting by the locals as they trudged down to the village of Teora. In the village they were lined up in the main square where two local officials not only spoke to the gathering crowd but to the men of X Troop, one calling them 'English desperadoes' and the other inciting the crowd to lynch them. Fortunately the Italian soldiers realised their prize was more valuable alive than dead, managed to maintain order, although shots had to be fired over the crowd to keep it. Then they were taken to the local *Carabinieri* station and locked in the cells. Later an elderly Italian General arrived, who had some knowledge of English, spoke with Major Pritchard and advised that if they all gave their word of honour not to escape, they could drive themselves in a lorry to their next prison, escorted only by armed troops in front and behind. Pritchard declined, fearing this way be an ideal opportunity for the Italians to claim that these 'English desperadoes' had all been shot and killed whilst trying to escape. So later that evening all still under heavy guard and back on the chain gang they travelled to the railway station at Calitri, where they were placed in the waiting room, again under heavy guard.

Lieutenant Deane-Drummond had this to say:

A narrow winding track led us down into the nearby village of Teora where a small crowd was out to meet us. A few shouts went up, "Viva *Carabinieri*!" "Viva Duce!", as if the *Carabinieri* had had any part at all in our inglorious capture. We were led into the local *Carabinieri* police station which struck us as damp and cold after the warm sunshine outside. The room in which they locked us up had bare whitewashed walls, and a cold red-tiled floor. Its windows looked out through heavy one-inch bars on to the green hillside which we had just come down.

After being thoroughly searched again we began to feel the reaction to all our adventures. Food and water were asked for and eventually they appeared with hunks of bread and a few tins of Italian bully beef. These we greedily devoured and immediately felt a new energy and hope surge through our veins. A tiny little man with a very big hat came into the room and started shouting and bellowing for all he was worth. Of course we went on munching our hunks of bread and eventually it transpired that he was a General and expected us to stand up when he entered. After a bit of hesitation Tag told us to get up, and said with a laugh it might get us some more food if we tickled the little chap's vanity. The only thing he wanted to know was how many more of us there were and he received the usual answer "I can't say."

Nastri and Picchi were called outside soon after the General's departure and were questioned by a Black Shirt officer. When they came back they said that he

30. Most of the men of X Troop in Sulmona Prisoner of War camp. Back row left to right L/Corporal J Maher, Sergeant J Walker, Sergeant H Meddings (RAF aircrew on raid), L/Corporal D Jones, Corporal P Julian, L/Corporal H Tomlin, Sapper G Pryor, L/Corporal H Pexton, Sapper D Struthers, Corporal J Grice, Sergeant A Lawley, Sergeant Southern (RAF not on raid) and L/Corporal D Henderson. Middle row left to right Sapper R Davidson, Private J Parker, L/Corporal R Watson, Sapper A Ross, unknown RAF man (not on raid), Sergeant E Durie, Sergeant P Clements, Private A Samuels, Sapper O Phillips and Private E Humphrey. Front row left to right Sergeant J Shutt, Corporal P O'Brien, Sergeant E Hodges (RAF aircrew on raid), Sergeant B Albon (RAF aircrew on raid), Private J Tristan, Corporal D Fletcher and Sapper A Parker. (H Pexton)

had told them that we were all going to be shot at dawn the next day, so that we might as well tell everything.

Anyway that evening we were all pushed into a lorry and driven to a railway station a few miles away. Guards sat on all sides of us and the men were kept chained together. We felt like a travelling circus moving its animals from one town to the next. But we were the animals. Hungrily we gazed at the free world outside the lorries, with a deep, hopeless feeling inside which increased with every minute as we sped along. The Italians were obviously taking no chances with us, and we never had a hope of making a dash for it. After about 30 minutes we arrived at a railway station and were immediately hustled into an evil-smelling waiting room which we were told would house us for the night. Not that we smelt too rosy ourselves.

It will be best to leave this group here and now look at the exploits of the group led by Captain Lea. This group consisted of 11, as well as Lea he had with him amongst others, Second Lieutenant Paterson, Sergeant Walker, Corporals Fletcher and O'Brien, L/Corporals Maher, Pexton and Watson and Private Parker. Perhaps it is worth pointing out that for unknown reasons this party had no Italian speaker with them. Their route was planned to be to the north of that taken by Major Pritchard and his group. They had to endure the same testing conditions as the others; Lea called a halt every two hours or so of marching. L/Corporal H Pexton commented:

> The ground we had to walk across was some of the worst, if not the worst I've ever walked over. It had snowed several days beforehand, and it was now starting to melt turning the ground into a mixture of mud and slush, which was like walking through treacle.

Towards the end of the first night's marching they chose a hiding up place in a tree-covered ravine. They originally settled in what appeared to be the bed of a dried-up river, but had to move when later after dawn water started streaming around them, so they found an alternative spot. They did hear and see during the day light aircraft flying around and the sounds of trucks but they remained unmolested during this day.

The next day probably through sheer bloody guts and drive they slogged on seeing no one and near dawn found a very good laying-up point. This was a large cleft in the rocks on a pretty bare mountain slope. During the day they heard and saw a small Italian boy tending a flock of sheep, but they remained undetected. However the effort and lack of food started to take their toll and on the third night's march the pace was a lot slower and spirits were sagging. Captain Lea was not helping by wearing on the operation a pair of mountain boots he had bought in Malta, and these caused him problems with his feet. However, in spite of this Captain Lea also took the decision on this night (12th/13th February) to walk on the road and again good progress was made, six or seven miles being covered in relative ease. One of the members of Lea's group remembers him saying that he couldn't walk any more on that – referring to the treacle like slush and they would have to walk on the roads.

Then the group came across a small bridge over the river Sele with a sharp bend in the road just beyond the end of the bridge. Captain Lea went forward to scout the likely position ahead. All seemed quiet and so he waved the rest of the group forward, just as they were getting onto the bridge, half of Italy seemed to appear at both ends of the bridge- they were well and truly surrounded. It again was a motley crew of locals both men and women, some armed with shotguns and a few *Carabinieri* thrown in for good measure. Captain Lea tried to tell them that they were German soldiers by saying 'Deutsch...Deutsch.' However, his bluff was called by a *Carabinieri* who pointed his bayoneted rifle at Lea's stomach and shouted: 'You speak big lie.....Youse all Inglesi!' There seemed little point in trying to resist and Captain Lea ordered his men to surrender. They had managed to walk about 30 miles to the coast, around half way. Treated in a similar way to the Pritchard group (handcuffed and chained) they were transported on mule carts to Calitri railway station. Here on the following morning they were reunited with that group.

The following are Captain Christopher Lea's recollections of the whole operation:

We took off from Malta, lying on the floor of eight Whitley bombers. Our mission was to blow up an aqueduct, one of Mussolini's achievements, over the river Tragino in southern Italy. We were guinea pigs; they wanted to know if the Royal Air Force could drop bodies on a pinpoint target. The jump went all right – we were dropped within a few hundred yards. I was in command of a party covering the sappers, but they didn't need us, so we had nothing to do. We were minus a load of explosives, as one aircraft made its drop in the wrong valley, so we blew up one pier instead of two.

We were about sixty miles from the coast, where a submarine was supposed to collect us. The exciting bit was over, now we had a hell of a slog ahead. The snow was melting and it was very hard going – we had four days to reach our rendezvous. We could only move at night and had to hide during the day. By the third night, hopelessly tired, we were making such slow progress that we took to the road instead of open country. We had to cross a bridge, it was completely quiet and I had a feeling it was too quiet. We were beautifully ambushed. Out of the hedges came this motley crew of Italians: civilians, men and women, soldiers and *Carabinieri*, variously armed with pitchforks, ancient muskets and rifles. We couldn't attack them without killing civilians and maybe women. One man said, "Shall I shoot, Sir?", and I replied in the negative. If we'd had a battle there would have been needless deaths and we'd never have got very far without being picked up by the military. They walked us to a barn.

They thought we were spies and were all for shooting us. Fortunately, an Italian General turned up and said; "Certainly, you can't shoot them." We were later taken to join up with Major Pritchard's group. I'm not being dramatic, but one had recruited these men, trained them, loyal and good and obedient, and here we were having to give up our weapons, captured by a mixed bag of angry, shouting people. It was a rational decision, but a painful one. I was sitting alone in the barn, exhausted, feeling about as miserable as any young officer could feel, when a couple of my chaps came and sat alongside me. One of them said, "We think you made the right decision, Sir." I'll always remember that.

Harry Pexton was convinced they were the only group that had been captured but he was soon to find out he was wrong.

This means we can now look at the actions of the smallest party, that led by Second Lieutenant Jowett assisted by Flight Lieutenant Lucky. As well as these two officers also present were Sergeant Clements, Corporal Grice, Driver Crawford and Sappers Ross and Struthers – making seven in total. It was planned for them to take the most southerly route to the coast. Needless to say they faced the same problems with the terrain as the other groups, although the leader Second Lieutenant Jowett did try and set a tough pace. It is worth adding here that at least two of this group carried their Thompson sub-machine guns with them. At the end of the first night's march, this group descended off a ridge line into a ravine hoping to find a decent hiding place. However they found most of the area distinctly boggy and had no option but to spend the rest of the day in a decidedly uncomfortable position. It gave them no opportunity to dry out their wet clothes. Moving off again as darkness fell, spirits were a bit low, they soon came across a road which Second Lieutenant Jowett felt led to the Sele valley. Jowett wanted to walk on the road, and although Flight Lieutenant Lucky initially disagreed with him, they eventually agreed to walk on the road. After making good progress for a while and meeting no-one, they approached a blind bend, when round the corner they found themselves very close to an isolated village. As you might have guessed by now, their approach was greeted with a chorus of barking from various dogs. There was no way round the village and so they passed through it as quickly and as quietly as possible. Fortunately no one came out to see what all the barking was about, but this incident persuaded Jowett and Lucky that walking on this road was not a good idea. They came across a small stream which it was felt fed into the Sele and so the gang of seven followed this, and it did as expected lead them to the Sele river. Just before dawn on this second night, they came across a small area full of fruit trees and this seemed as good a place to hide up as they might possibly find. Then just as they were entering the wooded area an Italian farm worker appeared. Second Lieutenant Jowett went after him drawing his commando knife as he went, but the Italian disappeared and they did not have the time to hunt him down. They were certain he would report this sighting to the authorities and so had no option but to move off. Moving close to the river bank, they quickly came across a point where the river widened a bit and there were some small islands in the middle of the river with what appeared to be in the darkness small clumps of bushes. Thinking this might be their best option the group waded out to one of these islets and found some cover and settled down to rest. However, with the growing daylight it became apparent that the bushes were not as densely foliated as first thought and worst still barely concealed them at all. It meant that movement had to be kept to a minimum if they were to remain undetected and lighting their primus stoves was certainly out of the question.

After several uncomfortable hours their luck ran out as before noon a local appeared on the river bank with a barking dog. It seemed clear that the dog had picked up the scent and was leading his owner to them. The dog even swam over to the islet they were on and for several moments ran up and down between the bushes the seven parachutists were hidden in. The dog eventually returned to his owner and they both disappeared, it did not take a genius to work out they had again been discovered. L/Corporal D Struthers did recall that they had been issued with black pepper and been told to put it down at changes in directions to try and fool any dogs trying to follow a scent. Obviously it failed to work on the Italian dogs!

It was time to leave and when trying to cross the river one man fell into a pothole, disappearing under the water and in the process losing one of the Thompsons. He was dragged into shallower water by two of his comrades. Quickly climbing a hill by the riverbank, they decided to take cover in a small patch of shrub. Each man was now left alone with his thoughts but company was not long in arriving and vehicles could be seen heading along the river road towards their position from both east and west. They halted almost immediately below their position but to each side and around 100 armed civilians and *Carabinieri* started to assemble from each convoy on the road. They were virtually surrounded and the only way relatively free would have been up the hillside and over the top. However, the hillside was virtually devoid of cover and anyone moving would have stood out like a beacon on a dark night. Then even more lorries arrived this time with soldiers and once deployed they started to fire in the general direction of the gang of seven. Meanwhile the locals started converging on the men from X Troop's position. It was not looking good and as the locals neared their position Second Lieutenant Jowett fired some warning shots over their heads. This failed to stop their movement forward and so he loosed off three bursts from his Thompson, several men fell either injured or killed. This did cause the rest to lose heart a bit and they rushed back down the hill. While this was going on Second Lieutenant Jowett ordered a quick lift and shift to a smaller copse further down the hillside. He shouted he would give covering fire.

The others made it to this new position and only one of them, Driver Crawford, was hit in the arm by a bullet. From this new position they fired back as best as they could with their pistols, but it was clear it was a lost cause. Ammunition was starting to run out and there was nowhere else to go. Jowett shouted down that it was time to surrender but he would go on fighting. Sergeant Clements using his experience as a SNCO suggested that they would not surrender without him, and Jowett reluctantly agreed. Sergeants Clements then stood up and waved a somewhat grubby white handkerchief.

However, the local Italians were not in a very happy mood as several of them had been killed and wounded by Jowett's first burst of fire. One heavily-armed local appeared to take charge and at the position they had surrendered first gave instructions for the group of seven to strip to the waist. Once this had been done they were moved downhill a little and lined up against a large outcrop of rock and a group of men with rifles stood opposite them. It appeared they were about to be summarily executed. The group's Italian speaker Flight Lieutenant Lucky tried explaining that they were British soldiers and once taken prisoner they were protected by the Geneva Convention. This request was answered by one of the Italians putting a pistol to Lucky's temple and shouting they were ex-convicts and murderers- it was not looking good. Fortunately the 'appointed' leader then started to give a little speech apparently justifying his actions and inciting the crowd to take revenge for the death of their friends and to have no mercy on the English 'banditos'. He raised his arm and the firing squad settled into an aiming position – then in the nick of time an Italian Army officer on a horse appeared and rode his horse between the prisoners and the locals. He got off his horse and it is reported he then slapped the local appointed leader round the face, then turning to the men from X Troop explained in English, that they were now prisoners of the Italian Army and would be treated as prisoners of war. Other Italian soldiers appeared and took charge, allowing the men from X Troop to retrieve their clothes and they were then marched off to a local village. Here Driver Crawford's wound was dressed by a doctor and they were locked up for the night under heavy guard. Next morning they were also taken on lorries to Calitri, to join the other two groups at the railway station there. They were the last to arrive but not long after Captain Lea's group. So by the morning of the 13th February all the main participants in the blowing of the Tragino Aqueduct had been caught, this just leaves the small group led by Captain Daly to look at. One small comment to end with here is that you may remember that the officers had been given gold coins for any unforeseen emergencies and as Lieutenant Deane-Drummond commented:

> My stash of coins didn't escape detection very long and led to everyone else being thoroughly searched, even though most people didn't have any. Perhaps in their haste to find the gold other items were overlooked, which came in handy later.

Captain Daly and his four sappers (L/Corporal Tomlin, Sappers Davidson, Parker and Pryor) had been dropped somewhat later than the others and in the wrong valley. They had heard the explosions going off and so had decided to head independently for the coast. L/Corporal H Tomlin recalled that Captain Daly remarked after they heard the explosions. "Well, that's it, it's gone off, there's no point heading for the aqueduct now, we'll go towards the coast."

The first night was spent in a deserted hut they found just before dawn and remained undetected here for the rest of that day. The route they chose was mainly confined to cross country travel and they did not venture onto the roads at any time. During the third day leaving the rest of his group in a hiding place, Captain Daly and one other man boldly approached an isolated farmhouse and asked for food, but they did not get any, the owners locking all the doors and windows. In spite of this they seemed to bear a charmed life and by the morning of 15th February had managed to get to within about twenty miles of the rendezvous point. By now they were pretty hungry and extremely tired. The submarine was due to pick them up that night and so a decision was taken to risk it and travel in daylight. Initially making good progress, their luck ran out around noon, when they ran into a group of Italian soldiers. They tried to bluff their way out of this situation with Captain Daly stating they were aircrew from a crashed German aircraft and needed to be in Naples by 2.00 p.m. and could they please have some transport. However the officer in charge of the Italians was not convinced and pulled Daly's jump jacket open to reveal his British battledress with his captain's insignia. The game was now up and they were marched to the nearest village, from here they were handcuffed and chained and taken initially to a civilian prison in Naples.

One of this group, Sapper Alfred Parker escaped later in the war and the following is taken from his post-escape debrief by an officer of MI9:

> We were unfortunately tipped out into the wrong gorge. While we were making our way to the correct gorge, we heard explosions and guessed that the aqueduct had been blown. We altered our course for the coast and the pre-arranged rendezvous at the mouth of the river. On 11th February 1941 we first heard sounds of pursuit and of dogs. We therefore lay up in ravines by day and marched by night.

On the night of 13th February we ran into a snow storm and lost our direction, travelling in a circle. In consequence we were then well behind time. We had to be at the rendezvous at 2200 on 16th February. At dawn on the 16th February we were 18 miles from the rendezvous and short of food. Therefore Captain Daly decided that we must walk by day, and at 1000 we were captured by a mixture of soldiers, *Carabinieri* and civilians. We told them we were German airmen on special duty carrying despatches and had to be in Naples by 1400 that day. We asked for a car. All went well until the local mayor arrived. He asked for our papers. None were forthcoming, we were handcuffed and chained and taken by car to an HQ in Naples. We were searched, interrogated and even threatened with being shot. Apparently in consequence of a skirmish with our main party two civilians had been shot and died. To all questions I replied, "I can't say". This eventually stopped the questioning, although all sorts of tricks were employed, food, cigarettes and drinks being offered. That night we were moved to a civilian jail. Our officer was taken away separately. Three of us were in one cell, the fourth in another cell.

In an interview Harold Tomlin gave a completely different account of how the Daly group came to be caught, and it is included to let the reader make up his own mind! He recalled,

On what was our last day of freedom we were getting a bit desperate, we knew we wouldn't make the coast in time on foot. So a plan was hatched that we'd walk on the road and if we came across a small cafe or bar we'd make out we were crashed German aircrew and see if we could get a taxi. We did find a small cafe and sat inside and then one of the blokes went up to the counter not realising he was holding a box of Swan Vesta matches and this was noticed by the man behind it. Soon afterwards he disappeared into a side room and probably phoned the authorities. All of a sudden there was a screech of brakes outside and soldiers everywhere and that was it. Operation Colossus was over for us.

However, at this prison Captain Daly, after being locked up on his own in a cell, managed to escape from the jail. He did not have much freedom as he was recaptured the next day after trying to jump on a moving train but managed to knock himself out in the process.

The following is apparently the story of how Captain Daly managed to escape and his subsequent escapades. He noticed that the wood surrounding the lock to his cell door was rotten, and when at around 11.00 p.m. on his first night in captivity he pushed at it with his feet it broke. Walking almost silently due to his rubber-soled boots he slipped past three sentries and spent the rest of that night wandering around Naples. Eventually he found a railway line with the intention of hitching a lift on a goods train still aiming for the coast and the submarine pick-up. It was not until about 11.00 a.m. that a train moving slow enough to jump on came along. He made a jump for it but somehow missed his grip and went sprawling. He was knocked out cold and awoke to find an Italian soldier standing over him jabbering in Italian and was eventually hauled off back to prison.

Meanwhile we need to go back a couple of days to the three groups led by Pritchard, Lea and Jowett who we left at Calitri station on the morning of 13th February. During the morning they were visited by a General from the Italian Army who praised them for their bravery and said they would be treated as prisoners of war according to the Geneva Convention. This is what Lieutenant Deane-Drummond recalls:

> Morning came at last and brought with it the other two parties which had been captured not very far from where we had been taken. One of Geoff Jowett's party had fired a tommy gun he had kept and killed an Italian officer and two peasants. When they were captured soon after, due to lack of ammunition, their clothes were ripped from them and they were rather roughly handled until they arrived at the station.

Anyway it was not until the morning of the 15th February that a train arrived to take them to an undisclosed destination, although we now know it was Naples. After a journey lasting most of the day they arrived at Naples, where once again they were chained together. To the local civilians present on the station it must have been a strange sight. It is reported that the men from X Troop marched erect and with pride in spite of their shackles. Very soon word was going round the locals that these men were 'Ingleshi paracadusti'.

This is what Lieutenant Deane-Drummond remembers about the journey from Calitri:

> About 10 a.m. our train came in. The men were all put together in a carriage like a dining saloon with a *Carabinieri* in every seat near a window. The officers were split into pairs and put into ordinary six-seater compartments with four *Carabinieri* who sat in each corner. They certainly did not mean to lose us, and we had so many guards that it was laughable. It rather flattered us that the Italians thought us such desperate characters. We sat in the same seats all that day and eventually arrived at Naples about an hour after sunset. Lorries were waiting to take us to the local military detention barracks, but before the men were allowed to leave the train they were all chained together once again and taken across the station to the waiting trucks. They were outwardly very cheerful and many jokes were dropped about the Italians and people said things like: "They say you get to like a ball and chain after the first ten years." Eventually they had us all in the trucks and within about ten minutes we were in a prison of some sort.

Soon after arrival much to their delight and surprise they were reunited with L/ Corporal Harry Boulter who they had not seen since leaving him at the aqueduct some five days before. Then soon afterwards the whole party was reunited when Captain Daly's party was moved from their prison to the Naples Central Prison.

The men from X Troop took no communication equipment on Operation Colossus and with the submarine pick-up being cancelled, the high command in both London and Malta had no idea if the operation had been successful. All they knew was that six groups of parachutists had been dropped in the vicinity of the aqueduct (or so it was hoped). A second photographic reconnaissance flight was undertaken on the 12th

February and when the results were studied it appeared no damage had been done to either aqueduct.

No doubt to much relief the Italians made an announcement on the 14th February which confirmed that the raid had achieved some success. The official Italian press agency, Stefani, issued the following communiqué:

> During the night of February 10th/11th (Monday night) the enemy dropped detachments of parachutists in Calabria and Lucania. They were armed with machine guns, hand grenades and explosives. Their objectives were to destroy our lines of communication and to damage the local hydro-electric power stations. Owing to the vigilance and prompt intervention of our defence units all the parachutists were captured before they were able to cause serious damage. In an engagement which took place one gendarme and one civilian were killed.

A further statement from this agency also said:

> The parachutists, who carried automatic arms and explosives, certainly intended to damage the regional water supply system, a magnificent achievement of the Fascist regime which made possible an agricultural revival throughout the district, together with railway lines, bridges and roads. Having landed in a clearing surrounded by forests, the parachutists occupied some farms and immobilised the peasants. One parachutist who had broken a leg was left in one of these farms, where he was later arrested by guards. The British parachutists deceived the peasant farmers by shouting 'Duce', and so inducing them to open their doors to them. After abandoning their injured companion the British made their way to the springs which feed the irrigation system, guiding themselves by means of maps which they were provided with. But the alarm had been given, and guards, co-operating with the military police and the military organisations of the Fascist Party, drew a cordon round the area. A search was instituted making the position of the parachutists very precarious. Speedily surrounded they were unable to execute their plans and had to hide in woods to avoid capture.
>
> To make capture more difficult they divided up into several groups hoping that some at least would be able to break through the cordon and carry out a part of their plans. Their plan failed for while eleven parachutists were seized in one place, seven others were arrested at the same time a mile or two away. The latter attempted to put up a resistance turning a tommy gun on the patrol consisting of one guard, one police constable and a shepherd who was guiding them over the mountain paths. Shots from the British officer's gun put the policeman and the shepherd out of action. The guard left alone defended himself with his rifle, forcing the parachutists to remain behind a rock until other guards, hearing the shots came up. Seeing that all resistance was hopeless the parachutists surrendered. Another group which had taken to the scrubland remained to be found. The search went on and the rest of the parachutists, including a Captain, were seized without trouble. The men claimed they were British parachutists, were dressed in khaki clothing, Air Force caps, spoke fluent Italian and had plenty of Italian *lira*.

These statements found their way into the headlines of nearly every newspaper in Britain on the 15th February. It led to much press speculation as the War Office in London basically declined to comment, one newspaper commented, "If these parachutists are British this would be the first hint that has been given to the public that such parachutists exist, and there is immense curiosity on the subject, but last night the War Office was entirely non-committal and would not even admit the existence of parachutists. If, however such a body does exist it will be an additional worry for both Mussolini and Hitler, for their very bases and invasion ports will be exposed to a fresh peril." These words were of course no comfort to the men from X Troop in Naples Central Prison.

Over the days following their arrival at Naples Central Prison every one was interrogated several times, it is believed that the Italians learned very little from their questions. Some men resorted to the usual name, rank and number. Whilst others gave humourous answers such as when asked what aircraft had brought them over to Italy, one 'new' aircraft type was the Heinz 57. Most of these question and answer sessions ended with the threat that the prisoner would be shot at dawn the next day. However, for two men the questioning was a little bit more serious. Firstly, Fortunato Picchi, even though he maintained he was French, was very afraid that he would be identified as an Italian and even worse a civilian. This would lead him open to charges of treason, even though he was a naturalised Briton. His downfall was that he looked very 'Mediterranean' and his English was not as good as the others. The others did their best to keep his morale high but after one lengthy interview without coffee, he was brought back to his cell very disconsolate. All through the night his cell mate (L/Corporal Jones) tried to keep his spirits up. Alas, it was all in vain as on the following morning he was taken away from the group and no-one ever saw him again. He was tried as a traitor and was executed on Palm Sunday, 6th April 1941. The next news the rest heard was when they were in PoW camps from the Italian newspapers. The death of Fortunato Picchi was also reported in several British newspapers, an 'in memory' entry reading as follows: "Picchi – On Palm Sunday, 1941. Fortunato Picchi sacrificed his life for the cause of freedom. A brave man of high ideals. Until the day breaks, dear – F. R.I.P.', appeared in the London *Times*.

Harry Pexton recently commented, "I have always felt sorry for Picchi, he was a very nice guy but he stuck out like a sore thumb amongst the rest of us. He just looked like an Italian."

After Picchi had been recognised as an Italian, the spotlight then fell on the other Italian-looking interpreter, the so-called 'Private Tristan'. It is worth adding here that even though Flight Lieutenant Lucky spoke Italian, he was so obviously British in his appearance and bearing that he was never accused of treason. Private Nastri (which is almost an anagram of Tristan), stuck to his story that he was a British soldier and citizen. He had the advantage of speaking like a Londoner as he had spent most of his life there. Somehow or other the Italians thought his real name was indeed Nastri and confronted him with one of his aunts who lived near Naples. Fortunately she had the presence of mind to say she didn't know him and so the intense interrogation of him abated. Harry Pexton backed him up frequently and said, "Johnny Tristan was lucky because even though he did look Italian, his English was so good it put a doubt in their minds and he was able to get away with it."

These are Lieutenant Deane-Drummond's recollections of the Naples prison:

My cell was about ten feet long and five feet broad. Along one side there was a large concrete block about two feet off the ground and about six feet long. On this was scattered a little straw, which had obviously been used before and had become damp from condensation in the cell. A very small square pane of glass high up in the end of the cell gave the only light. The door was heavily barred and bolted with a small peephole for the sentry stationed in the corridor.

Our depression was at its lowest when we were pushed into those cells. All that night we slept by fits and starts, turning over from one hip to the other and back again. Morning came at last and with it a sentry who banged open the door and plonked down a bowl of ersatz coffee with a small piece of dried fig. We heard that we were soon going to be interrogated and I think we rather looked forward to it. We were all quite confident that nothing would be got out of us, but we had heard so much about the questioning of prisoners of war that we were all curious to see what it was really like.

When the interrogator arrived he was given a room and we were all herded together in the passage outside our cells. I saw Picchi looking very depressed and tried to cheer him up. All he would say was that he was going to make a clean breast of it. "I know nobody likes the Fascists, they will soon see that I am a true lover of Italy, but at the same time a hater of the Fascist regime." It alarmed me when I heard him talking like that and I told him to keep quiet and stick to his story that he was a Free Frenchman. I am sure he did not take my advice when he went in to be questioned and I can well imagine him telling the Fascists what he thought of them till he was led off. We never saw him again.

Two months were to go by before we read in the Italian papers that he had been shot as a traitor on Palm Sunday. We were all to feel sad at his passing. The job he had been given had been so small compared with the risks he had taken. He was a great little man.

Eventually it came to my turn, and wondering what was going to come next I went into the room. A well-dressed man in civilian clothes was seated at a desk in one corner and immediately behind him were two obvious Fascists. They did not ask any questions themselves, but just stood and listened. At each of the interrogations that I had in the next fifteen months in Italy there were always two black crows standing behind the questioner. "I am the Commandant of the camp you are going to," he said, "and all I want are a few details for the Red Cross." This was a lie of course, but it was designed to put me at ease. Then I butted in and said, "My number is 71076, my rank is Lieutenant and my name is Deane-Drummond and you can expect nothing else." He then followed up with a few innocent questions like the address of next-of-kin, mothers name and so on. To all of these I told him "I can't say." Eventually he gave it up and I was sent out. Heaving a sigh of relief at having finished something unpleasant, I went out and rejoined Tag and Christopher who had already been through. They told much the same story, but the questioner had used the line that all he wanted to do was establish who was guilty of shooting the three men. This was absurd as they already knew the answer, and anyhow we were quite within our rights to shoot anybody who attempted to interfere with us, while we were getting to the coast.

It became clear to us that the Italians believed we must be semi-lunatics or at least criminals who had been reprieved on the scaffold provided we jumped out of an aeroplane. This seemed the attitude of the average Italian. They could never understand that we enjoyed our job. The word *paracadusti* always raised awe in the Italians when mentioned and we found it a disadvantage later when it came to trying to escape from prison camps.

After spending a short time in the Naples Central Prison the six officers were separated from the men and were transferred to an Italian Air Force detention centre in the military part of Naples aerodrome. Here they were relatively well-treated and the food appeared to be better than what they had previously received. Apparently they were also allowed the luxury of baths and visits from a local barber who shaved them. It is also said that the base commander even complained about the treatment of the whole group after learning they had been photographed and fingerprinted.

For reasons that are difficult to work out after such a time, Flight Lieutenant Lucky seemed to get special treatment and was allowed out on many occasions to 'go shopping' in Naples. Deane-Drummond remembers this time:

On arrival at the aerodrome we were immediately hustled up the stairs of a four-storey building, and discovered that we had been allocated bedrooms on the top floor. Here were clean sheets and comfortable beds, with a washroom not far off down the corridor. I was put in a room with Geoff Jowett and we were soon fast asleep.

Lunch and dinner we had together in Tag's room. The food was sent up from the officers' mess and was plentiful and good. We were still hungry and polished off enormous plates of minestrone soup, followed by equally large dishes of macaroni, meat and vegetables. Fruit and wine were put on the table as a matter of course. During the fortnight that we were in Naples, we ate solidly and took practically no exercise with the result that we all put on weight.

Eventually we persuaded the authorities that some exercise was necessary for our health and we would be escorted round the aerodrome at a slow stroll by an equal number of guards. The average Italian appeared to have an aversion to walking and we were told that unless we walked even slower we would have no more walks. We did get permission to walk around the flat roof our block, this suited both sides as the guards could just sit and watch, while we tried to go as fast as we could, trying to regain fitness.

We asked for baths, hardly expecting them, but the CO of the aerodrome was a humane man and we were allowed one every other day in the officers' mess. We were marched over by guards and then had a bath. It was apparently not used much by the Italians as the water had to be specially heated up for us each time. On one occasion some German pilots, who had arrived in a Junkers Ju 52, in transit to Libya, were queueing up for one bath, while we were queueing up for the other. A remarkable funny situation, but we were the only people who laughed. I rather think the Germans thought it was an Italian idea of a practical joke and were distinctly not amused.

Lucky was allowed to go down into Naples, under escort, to buy clothes for us, which at that stage of the war were very plentiful. I don't think Lucky realised that he was getting more freedom then than at any time afterwards when he was a prisoner. By the time we were moved on to our proper camp we had accumulated quite a reasonable wardrobe of washing kit and shirts, underclothes and so on. These we found invaluable later.

The so-called easy existence (especially at the aerodrome) ended at the end of February when the remaining 34 men from X Troop were moved again. Before moving however, they were subjected to a vigourous search which revealed that many of them had up till then managed to retain maps, button compasses and Italian money. Needless to say this did not remain with them for much longer. After a long train journey they ended up at a small town in the Abruzzi mountains at a small town called Sulmona about seventy miles east of Rome. They then had a five mile march to what the Italians called 'Campo di Concentramento 78 PoW Camp.'

The search before leaving was in the case of the officers at the aerodrome not as thorough as at the Central Prison as Lieutenant Deane-Drummond commented:

The search was quite good, but very stupidly they left a little on everybody, and when we arrived at the camp we were able to muster just about one complete set of escaping equipment, which was a great help to us later on. We moved on the last day of February. We were told that we were going the night before and to have everything ready to move at 4 o'clock in the morning. We packed our few clothes into some suitcases that Lucky had bought and at that early hour in the morning we were ushered into a convoy of ambulances. The *Carabinieri* were all dressed in their best blue and the guard consisted of one Colonel, one Captain, one subaltern and 35 *Carabinieri*, all for the 34 of us. We were always considered desperadoes by the average Italian. We were taken to the railway station and eventually the train slowly puffed its way out of Naples, after a lot of talking and gesticulating by every railway official in the station. We thought we were being given a special send-off, but Lucky told us that the same sort of thing preceded every train departure in Italy. We did not believe him at the time but later on I was to discover how right he was.

The track wound its way through the mountains to Sulmona all that day. At times we were perched on the side of precipices and at others we clattered through evil-smelling tunnels. The scenery grew wilder and more desolate as we neared Sulmona. Wide open stretches of virgin snow, followed by nearly vertical pine-covered hillsides, did not serve to raise our spirits. We were all the time wondering how long we would be in the country. As each barren and deserted scene moved past the train's windows, our depression increased, as it seemed humanly impossible to escape from a country like this with so many natural obstacles.

About four o'clock in the afternoon we burst out of a tunnel and found ourselves rattling along a hillside high above a green and beautiful valley, sparkling in the sunshine with little streams and red-roofed whitewashed farmhouses. After the desolate country we had come through it was like looking into a real promised land. Before many months were out though, we had all come to hate that little valley, surrounded as it was on all sides by 5,000 feet high mountains.

The final five miles to the isolated camp was on foot, which for the men of X Troop was a welcome chance to get a reasonable piece of exercise, but the Italians hated it, especially as it was raining heavily. One man commented that the road was little more than a farm track and very muddy, and the *Carabinieri* Colonel spent most of his time trying to keep his coat tails out of the thick mud. Eventually they arrived at the camp and to their surprise they were not allocated quarters with the rest of the prisoners, but in two separate areas within the camp, one for the men and another for the officers. These areas had been specially built for the *paracadusti*, and as usual they were treated as though they were still desperate and dangerous characters. After about one month the American Military Attaché from the Embassy in Rome, Colonel Fiske, was allowed to visit them. America of course at this stage was still regarded as a neutral power. He put pressure on the Italian authorities to treat them as ordinary prisoners of war.

Deane-Drummond later said:

In a way we had rather looked forward to getting to the camp. We had visions of Red Cross parcels and plenty of company from the others. We were soon to realise what a mistaken idea we all had of prison camps. On arrival we were led in through tall barbed wire gates, and then through a door in a brick wall about ten foot high, and up a narrow passage between more high walls to a long low hut devoid of any furniture whatsoever. One end was partitioned off and one by one we were searched. Nothing was found on us and soon we were led off through a maze of walls and passages and shown our new homes. The Italians had gone to the trouble of making a small walled-off compound in the middle of the camp especially for our benefit. The officers were put in this, and the men led off by themselves and locked up in another one which again had been specially constructed in their honour. All the view we could see from outside the hut was the sky and a sheer mountainside. Halfway up, an old hermit's house had been built into the side of the rock, and it was the only sign of habitation that was visible from our prison. Our depression was not eased when we heard that we were not to be allowed out of our compound for any reason whatsoever. We had to eat, sleep and exercise all in an area thirty yards long by three yards wide. It was not long before I went down with a mild attack of jaundice.

The next two months were hell. It hurt us more than most because we were used to an active life with plenty of exercise. The only saving grace was the food. At this stage of the war Italy had not yet introduced rationing, and we were able to gorge ourselves on as many eggs and as much meat as we wanted. Later on we were to know the meaning of starvation rations, but at this time we had far more than was good for us. Tag became larger every day and was reaching a colossal size when he suddenly realised it and started cutting down on his food. We soon saw that with a guard on a tower just above our yard, and also one inside all night, escape was hopeless for the time being.

The American Military Attaché from Rome, a Colonel Fiske, visited us towards the end of our first month, and we were vociferous in our complaints of

31. Second Lieutenant G Paterson who stepped in as the main demolition
officer after the non-arrival of Captain Daly. (Silvio Tasselli)

unfair and prejudicial treatment, just because we were parachutists. "You sure got the Wops scared," he said, "but I will plug the Geneva Convention at them, and I reckon I will get you out of here pretty soon." He cheered us tremendously, but the Italians could never quite rid themselves of the idea that no one could possibly want to parachute and would only do so to avoid service in Russia or a long term of imprisonment.

Finally after about two months in these specially-constructed cages the men from X Troop were finally allowed out into the normal PoW compound, joining the other 800 or so officers and men already there. Most of the previous arrivals had been captured by the Germans in the Western Desert and handed over to the Italians for safe-keeping. Soon they integrated themselves into prison camp life and for the majority they spent the rest of the war in captivity. Once inside the normal PoW system they started to receive Red Cross parcels and mail. Indeed they had been taught a code at Mildenhall to be used in communications home in the event of them being captured. This was duly put into practice and over the coming months maps, money and messages were received from the UK hidden in food parcels. However, it was not long before the thoughts of many men turned to trying to escape – even if their comrades in the camp didn't want to try. Major Pritchard headed an escape committee and many attempts to escape were made, mainly by the officers. At the beginning of December 1941 Captain Lea and Lieutenant Deane-Drummond posing as two civilian electricians repairing the lights on the camp wall and carrying a ladder made it over the wall of the camp. Unfortunately Captain Lea was shot at by a sentry and hit in the leg but Deane-Drummond managed to get away in the confusion. The sentry apparently fired a special type of exploding bullet, one fragment grazed Deane-Drummond in the cheek but he did not stop. In any case they had decided to split up over the wire as they both favoured different escape routes and Lea had shouted out for him not to stay. The Italians left Captain Lea bleeding profusely from several wounds to his leg and initially refused to treat him. It was only the actions of the camp Medical Officer who insisted he was brought in and treated that saved his leg. Deane-Drummond nearly made it all the way to Switzerland before being recaptured. Whilst he was on the run Flight Lieutenant Lucky also made it over the wall using a ladder but was quickly recaptured. The Italians lost patience with the parachutists and shipped Pritchard, Lucky, Paterson and Deane-Drummond off to another camp. This was Campo 27, a special camp for dangerous prisoners in a monastery near Pisa. Deane-Drummond, after temporarily getting himself hospitalised away from the camp, successfully escaped in June 1942 and made it back to Britain – he was the first member of X Troop to make it home. He later in the war took part in the Battle of Arnhem as a Major and second-in-command of the 1st Airborne Division's Signal Regiment. He was also captured at this battle but again managed to escape, on one occasion staying in a locked cupboard with the Germans the other side of the door for nine days. But that's another story....

The rest of X Troop left back at Sulmona did not just roll over and stop escaping, Second Lieutenant Jowett also managed to get over the wall assisted by Sergeants Clements and Lawley. He managed to get on a train heading towards Switzerland but was caught when changing trains. The other ranks also dug a tunnel over 170 feet long before it was discovered. But no-one succeeded in getting very far until the Italian surrender in September 1943 after the Allied invasion. The guards just seemed to vanish into thin air and several people took the opportunity to disappear before the Germans arrived to take over. Sergeants Clements and Lawley were prominent in this as they went over the wire and had a testing four week trek towards the Allied lines which they reached in mid-October. Another was L/Corporal Boulter, now fully recovered from his broken ankle. He joined a group of Italian partisans and stayed with them for nearly nine months. He was eventually recaptured by German troops and probably was very lucky to be spared his life and was sent to a PoW camp in Germany. When the Germans did arrive at the two camps that the men from X troop were at, they were all quickly shipped off to camps in Germany. During this move, Second Lieutenant Paterson succeeded in jumping from the train he was on, and joined up with a group of partisans, and stayed with them for some time before crossing over into Switzerland. He later returned to Italy as a member of the Special Operations Executive assisting the Italian partisans. The rest of the group did not get their freedom until their camps were liberated by the advancing Allies in 1945.

Operation Colossus: A Balance Sheet

So what can be said about the first British parachute raid of the Second World War?

In purely strategic terms the raid achieved little as the aqueduct was repaired within about 3 days, well before any local reservoirs ran dry. It also failed in the aim of affecting the Italian war effort in North Africa or Albania. However the tactical effects of the raid were far-reaching. Much effort in the days after the 10th February 1941 were spent in looking for the parachutists, and the Italians were unsure for many days if everyone had been rounded up. In the spin of the time the Italian propaganda machine told the public that the raid had been a total failure. However, the Italian Government considered it

32. Anthony Deane-Drummond on a return visit to the aqueduct in 1989. (Silvio Tasselli)

to be a serious threat and with there being the possibility of more raids, new security measures were introduced. Additionally soldiers were posted to dams, bridges, power stations and other likely targets the length and breadth of Italy. Lieutenant Deane-Drummond commented that in his view, "The raid had a profound psychological effect upon the Italians. It was a slap in the face for Italian pride. It meant that troops were brought from the front to be on guard duty all over Italy protecting bridges and other vital installations". So it can be said that the small force of 35 was able to punch well above their weight and certainly caused problems with a lasting effect.

Additionally once details of the raid had been released in Britain it gave a fillip to morale and encouraged more men to volunteer for the airborne forces. There was initial caution about the raid from the War Office due to the lack of news and the photographic evidence. Indeed in his report of 13th February, Wing Commander Norman, who had gone along as an observer, commented that either the raid had been expected and X Troop had been captured immediately on landing, or that the aqueduct had been of a different construction to that thought and could not be destroyed with the explosives taken.

Fortunately he was wrong on both counts, as on 24th February 1941, information was received via the American Embassy that the raid had achieved some success. Also as stated earlier Colonel Fiske was able to report back via the Rome correspondent of the *Chicago Daily News* who was expelled from Rome in early March. Definite confirmation came from a coded message in one of Major Pritchard's letters home. Then finally in August 1942 a first-hand account came from Lieutenant Deane-Drummond when he arrived back in the UK after his successful escape.

Like the somewhat ineffective commando raid on Guernsey in 1940, Operation Colossus provided valuable information on what to do and what not to do. Perhaps the most important element to come out was the need for proper reconnaissance especially using aerial photographs. Also the methods of dropping the containers came under scrutiny. It is perhaps no surprise that within months paratroopers were jumping with their own weapons and equipment rather than relying on containers.

In February 1941 the Russian-German non-aggression pact was still intact and America was still not involved in the war – Britain was virtually on her own. Perhaps it is worth ending by saying that it showed in the dark days of 1941 that Britain was willing to strike back at the Axis powers.

Chapter 5

Striking from the Sea

After the somewhat disappointing raids on the French coast and Guernsey in 1940, it was realised that whilst relatively small-scale commando raids could be undertaken, it would need a lot more resources to sustain effective raids. Perhaps the most important lesson was the need for suitable landing craft, and a second was the need for more men and close co-operation with the Navy. Soldiers are in most cases all at sea when dealing with the Navy. On 11th November the so-called 'Special Service Brigade' was formed consisting of five Special Service battalions each consisting of two Special Service companies. With the benefit of hindsight it is difficult to work out why the powers that be wanted to label British troops as belonging to the SS. The name was unpopular and one commanding officer said to his Adjutant 'Never let me see the words Special Service Battalion appear on our Orders.'

Another officer compiled a list of rules in which the words 'special service' managed to appear. These rules are listed here:

1. The object of special service is to have available a fully trained body of first class soldiers, ready for active offensive operations against an enemy in any part of the world.
2. Irregular warfare demands the highest standards of initiative, mental alertness and physical fitness, together with the maximum skill at arms. No Commando can feel confident of success, unless all ranks are capable for thinking for themselves; of thinking quickly and of acting independently, and with sound tactical sense, when faced by circumstances, which may be entirely different to those which were anticipated.
3. The offensive spirit must be the outlook of all ranks of a Commando at all times.
4. The highest state of physical fitness must at all times be maintained. All ranks are trained to cover at great speed any type of ground for distances of five to seven miles in fighting order.
5. Cliff and mountain climbing and really difficult slopes climbed quickly form a part of Commando training.
6. A high degree of skill in all branches of unarmed combat will be attained.
7. Seamanship and Boatmanship. All ranks must be skilled in all forms of boatwork and landing craft whether by day or night, as a result of which training the sea comes to be regarded as a natural working ground for a Commando.
8. Night sense and night confidence are essential. All ranks will be highly trained in the use of the compass.
9. Map reading and route memorising form an important part of Commando training.
10. All ranks of a Commando will be trained in semaphore, morse and the use of W/T.

11. All ranks will have elementary knowledge of demolition and sabotage. All ranks will be confident in the handling of all types of high explosive, Bangalore torpedoes, and be able to set up all types of booby traps.

12. A high standard of training will be maintained in all forms of street fighting, occupation of towns, putting towns into a state of defence and the overcoming of all types of obstacles- wire, rivers, high walls etc.

13. All ranks in a Commando should be able to drive motorcycles, cars, lorries, tracked vehicles, trains and motorboats.

14. A high degree of efficiency in all forms of fieldcraft will be attained. Any man in a Commando must be able to forage for himself, cook and live under a bivouac for a considerable period.

15. All ranks are trained in first aid and will be capable of dealing with the dressing of gunshot wounds and the carrying of the wounded.

16. These are a few among the many standards of training that must be attained during service in a Commando. At all times a high standard of discipline is essential, and the constant desire by all ranks to be fitter and better trained than anyone else.

17. The normal mode of living is that the Special Service soldier will live in a billet found by himself and fed by the billet for which he will receive 6s 8d per day to pay all his expenses.

18. Any falling short of the standards of training and behaviour on the part of a Special Service soldier will render him liable to be returned to his unit.

The naval designers had been hard at work and came up with the concept of the 'Assault Landing Craft' or ALC. This was 35 feet long, 9 feet wide with a draught of 3 feet – a definite improvement as it would allow the troops to get a lot closer to the shore than previously. With a crew of one officer and three sailors it was capable of carrying at the most 35 troops. It may be a good place to have a look at the structure of the Special Service Brigade as it was in late 1940; its first commander was Brigadier J Haydon.

It consisted of five Special Service Battalions:

(a) 1st Special Service Battalion was based in Devon and consisted of:
   (i)   Special Service Company formed from Nos.1, 2, 3 and 4 Independent Companies.
   (ii) Special Service Company formed from Nos. 5, 8 and 9 Independent Companies.

(b) 2nd Special Service Battalion was based in Scotland and consisted of:
   (i)   A Special Service Company formed from Nos. 6 and 7 Independent Companies and No 9 Commando.
   (ii) B Special Service Company formed from No 11 Commando.

(c) 3rd Special Service Battalion was based in Scotland and consisted of:
   (i)   A Special Service Company formed from No 4 Commando.
   (ii) B Special Service Company formed from No 7 Commando.

(d) 4th Special Service Battalion was based in Scotland and consisted of:
   (i)   A Special Service Company formed from No 3 Commando.
   (ii) B Special Service Company formed from No 8 Commando.

(e) 5th Special Service Battalion was based in Scotland and consisted of:
   (i)   A Special Service Company formed from No 5 Commando.

(ii)   B Special Service Company formed from No 6 Commando.

The decision was also taken to base each Commando on the lines of six troops rather than the original ten, with each troop consisting of three officers and 62 men. This was in part based on the number of men that could be carried in an ALC, so now each troop could move in two of them. At the end of 1940 it was felt there were now enough ALCs to contemplate another raid and so many of the commando units were centred around Inveraray in Scotland. The first raid planned was one on the Azores but this was soon cancelled as it was probably beyond the range of practical resources. Perhaps the planners thought that it was also time to look at hitting some strategic targets rather than the two rather ineffectual previous raids on France and Guernsey. Consideration was also given to targets in the Mediterranean – Pantellaria being one such option. As it turned out none were actually undertaken and in late 1940/early 1941 three units were despatched to the Middle East where they were supplemented by two locally-recruited Commandos from troops already stationed there. These later became known as Layforce after their commander Colonel R Laycock. The Chief of Combined Operations Admiral Keyes turned his eyes northwards as a likely area for commando raids, however it is worth adding that for many months Keyes had found dealing with the War Office very difficult. To the Top Brass, the Commandos were an unacceptable use of capable men and scarce resources. To them they would be better employed defending the UK or fighting in the North African campaign. But the fledgling commando units had a supporter at the top, Winston Churchill, and he continued to press for raids against German-occupied territory and wanted action. In particular he felt the need for raids and commented: "There comes out from the sea from time to time a hand of steel which plucks the German sentries with growing efficiency".

However the men of the Special Service Brigade were becoming frustrated, similar to those at Ringway and morale and discipline was on the decline. All they seemed to do was carry out exercises or train for a raid which was then cancelled. Then shortly after news had broken in the UK of the Tragino Aqueduct raid, it was announced to the 3rd and 4th Special Service Battalions that they had been selected for a raid on Norway. The target was a place that probably many of them had never heard of – the Lofoten Islands. Norway had fallen into German hands in the early summer of 1940 together with the bulk of her industrial capacity. The Lofoten Islands were a sparsely populated group of islands just to the north of the Arctic Circle and situated about 900 miles from Scotland. Their main activity was fishing in the rich waters of the Northern Cape. As well as the actual fish themselves, there were associated industries using fish by-products, namely cod and herring liver oil for medicinal purposes. Another important asset for the Germans were several factories involved in the manufacture of glycerine, this was deemed to be an important raw material used in the manufacture of high explosives. The factories were located in four ports on different islands in the group – Brettesnes, Henningsvaer, Stamsund and Svolvaer. The whole operation was given the codename of Operation Claymore. The assets allocated to the operation were two converted cross-channel ferries now known as infantry landing ships- the *Princess Beatrix* and the *Queen Emma*, loaded with newly-constructed ALCs. These were commanded by Commanders T Brunton and C Kershaw.

Naval support under the command of Captain C Caslon came in the shape of five destroyers – HMS *Bedouin*, HMS *Eskimo*, HMS *Legion*, HMS *Somali* and HMS *Tartar*. The commando forces under the overall command of Brigadier Haydon came from Nos. 3 and 4 Special Service Battalions numbering around 500 men. Also present were 52 Royal Engineers to provide additional demolition support and 52 volunteers from the Free Norwegian Forces to act as guides and interpreters.

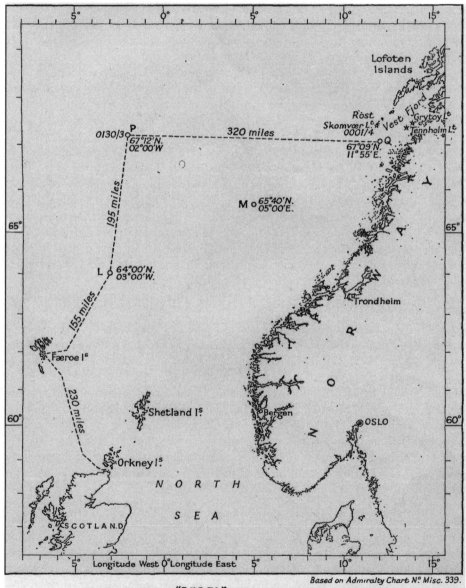

Map 6. Route to the Lofoten Islands

The aim of the operation was to destroy the fish-oil factories, sink any shipping they could, enlist volunteers for the Free Norwegian Forces and to round up any Quislings. This was the name given to any supporters of Vidkun Quisling who was helping the Germans to run Norway as a puppet state.

The two commanding officers (Durnford-Slater and Lister) were both told to report to one of Admiral Keyes Staff Officers at Troon in Scotland in the early part of February to be given details of the raid. Basically they were told that the operation was primarily for the benefit of the Ministry of Economic Warfare. Around 50% of Norway's herring and cod oils were produced on the Lofoten Islands. Additionally large amounts of fish, salted, chilled and fresh, were exported mainly to Germany. So it would be a good chance to hit the German economy.

Intelligence (such as there was) told the commandos that the Lofoten Islands were 850 miles from Scapa Flow, the temperature was expected to be below freezing, snow would fall every other day with gales expected every ten days. In January 1941 three U-boats had been reported in the vicinity of the islands. There was a small bit of good news in that German air intervention was expected to be minimal or non-existent. No airfield north of Trondheim was in theory fit for flying in this midwinter period. It was expected, however, that there could be the appearance of an unarmed Ju 52 on its thrice-weekly reconnaissance patrol. There would be no air support from the RAF. It was thought there were around 20 German military personnel in the area, the local population were in the main said to be friendly, but the port officials were German and the local mayor was a Quisling. The four ports were connected by telegraph and a telephone cable connected them to the Norwegian mainland.

The force concentrated at the Scottish port of Gourock on the 21st February 1941 and that evening sailed for Scapa Flow in the Orkneys, which was reached the next day. A week was then spent on the Orkneys fine-tuning the planning and training., Around this time the news was received that the name Special Service Battalions was no longer to be used. With typical Army logic No 3 Special Service Battalion became No 4 Commando and No 4 Special Service Battalion No 3 Commando.

At the time the operation appeared to be fraught with difficulties, again as at Tragino no real reconnaissance had been possible. The approaches to the ports were hazardous for large ships which would make it almost impossible for the destroyers to get close inshore. This would make naval gunfire support difficult. It was decided to ask the leading landing craft to act as scouts and so draw any fire from the defenders. They could then hopefully be neutralised before the main body of Commandos landed. The troops were also given rations for 48 hours, should it be necessary for the destroyers to temporarily leave the area to deal with any German naval intervention.

The plan called for No 3 Commando commanded by Lieutenant Colonel J Durnford-Slater, to land in the western area of attack and assault the ports of Stamsund and Henningsvaer. Durnford-Slater looked after Stamsund while one of his senior Troop Commanders, Captain Ronald, was in charge at Henningsvaer. The other part, the eastern group from No 4 Commando led by Lieutenant Colonel Lister, were to look after the ports of Brettesnes and Svolvaer.

Lister set down seven tasks for his Commando whilst it was ashore and these were as follows:

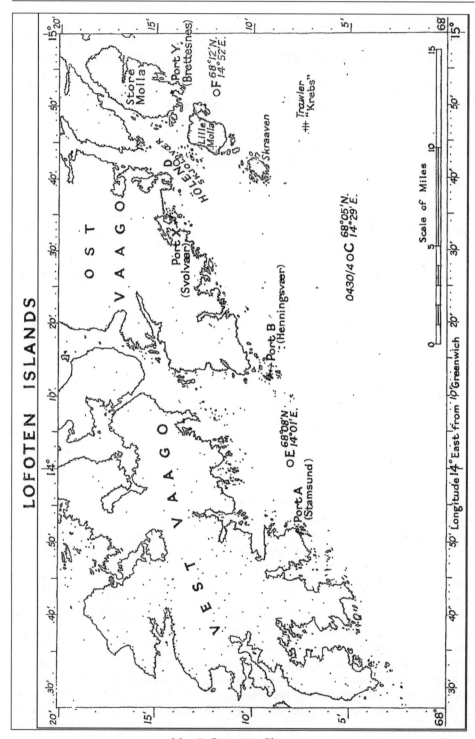

Map 7: Operation Claymore

Task 1

(a) Lister with his HQ and supported by Captain Hunter's G Troop to secure a small bridgehead on the main quay on Svolvaer and to seal off the area with road blocks etc.

(b) Lieutenant Webb and his section with guides to take over the post office and main hotel, then also to try and find and destroy a Luftwaffe wireless station known to be in the area.

Task 2

Lieutenant Lewis and his section, assisted by Captain Linge and 19 Norwegians, to gather information and papers from the mayor's, harbourmaster's and other port offices, then arrest known Quislings. Captain Lord Lovat, as Admiral Keyes's observer, to be attached to this party.

Task 3

Captain Emmett and C Troop to land near the major 'Cuba' fish factory and destroy all its production facilities, then to destroy any other facilities in the area.

Task 4

Lieutenant Style and his section, plus the specialist sappers, to destroy the main storage tanks, together with any other small cod presses located in private properties in this area. Lieutenant Style to be responsible for giving the order for any demolitions once having assured himself that all civilians in the danger area are clear.

Task 5

Captain Cook and E Troop, together with Captain Montgomerie and A Troop, to form the local and general reserve force, provide local AA defence with Brens mounted on tripods. This force to be embarked in the two MLCs (Mechanised Vehicles Landing Craft).

Task 6

Major Kerr (2 i/c) with one section of F Troop, to land on Brettesnes and establish a bridgehead with local AA defence and also to be prepared to assist with Task 7 if required.

Task 7

Captain Duveen and the rest of F Troop and specialist sappers to destroy the oil-producing facilities in three factories on Brettesnes plus any other smaller presses in the area; capture any enemy and quislings in the area.

After a few days at Scapa a signal was received on the 1st March ordering Brigadier Haydon to execute Operation Claymore. So at midnight the force of the two infantry assault ships plus the five escorting destroyers set off initially sailing to the Faroe Islands, arriving there on the evening of the 2nd March. The arrival at the port of Skaalefjord was probably greeted with much relief by the soldiers. Their infantry landing ships, more suited to the short trip across the English Channel, did not handle the waters of the North Atlantic Ocean very well and it is reported that nearly every soldier suffered from seasickness. However, their relief was short-lived as within five hours the force was again on their way. It had only been a short stop for the destroyers to top up their fuel tanks. The area of the Lofoten Islands was reached in the early hours of the 3rd March 1941, and so far so good, no sign of any Germans. Indeed, the navigation lights in the vicinity could be seen burning brightly. Any Germans in the area fell into the malaise of any soldier in a quiet, rear area thousands of miles from the front line, in that 'it'll never happen to me'. Indeed there were very few Germans in the area, the Lofotens probably not even registering on their radar as a potential target. It is worth adding here that the Royal Navy had deployed a covering screen of capital ships including HMS *Nelson*, HMS *King George V*, HMS *Dido* and HMS *Nigeria*, together with five destroyers, should the German Navy decide to try and attack what appeared to be a relatively lightly defended group on their journey to and from the target. Additionally, a submarine HMS *Sunfish* was going ahead to act as a navigational aid for the force.

The lights in the various fishing ports were visible from several miles away as the Commandos started to climb into the ALCs for the final part of their journey. In the intense cold they tried to keep as warm as they could, many huddling under their gas capes. One officer later commented on the efforts he had taken to try and keep warm: "I was wearing two vests, two pullovers, a shirt, a Gieves waistcoat, a wool-lined mackintosh and a pair of fur-lined boots and I was still cold". The initial intelligence had suggested that the islands were lightly defended by small parties of Germans at various locations but none had been reported at Stamsund or Svolvaer. The nearest big base of Germans was believed to be at Bodo, some sixty miles away and after that Narvik, around one hundred miles away. There was a seaplane base in the Lofoten islands but the aircraft here were felt not to be much of a threat, and the closest main fighter base was at Trondheim, 300 miles away. This meant that there would only be a limited German aerial intervention in the raid.

Soon after 6.00 a.m. the leading ALCs began their run in, with Durnford-Slater leading from the front heading for Stamsund and met a few fishing vessels heading out to sea. One of the Free Norwegian interpreters shouted out asking "Where are the Germans?" The answer came back that there were none – confirming the view of intelligence, however the answer probably left Durnford-Slater and the others feeling a bit flat, as I'm sure they were itching to get to grips (finally) with some Germans. However, the Norwegians were immensely happy to see the British troops and hoisted their national colours to the top of their masts, rather than at half-mast as the Germans had ordered.

Also around 6.00 a.m. an armed German trawler, the *Krebbs*, appeared and opened fire on HMS *Somali*. It was very much a one-sided engagement, and soon the *Krebbs* had been set on fire and several of her crew killed by gunfire, including the captain. She ran aground on a small island and remained there for about three hours before the incoming tide set her free, she was then sunk by gunfire and the survivors taken on board the *Somali*.

Meanwhile, as it was clear there was going to be little or no opposition, the bulk of the ALCs approached the harbour at Stamsund. Here intelligence had got it slightly wrong, what had been described as a 'gently shelving beach' turned out to be a quay. Initially it was difficult to get on the quayside but enthusiastic locals pulled many a commando up from their launches once they realised the troops were not German. Soon afterwards the men of No 3 Commando moved off to search the town and start the demolition process and their other allocated tasks. A similar experience was repeated with the eastern group in that no resistance was met and the local German garrison quickly surrendered.

33. A small group of commandos watching a burning oil tank during Operation Claymore. The man on the extreme right appears to be wearing some decidedly un-military gloves. (IWM N396)

34. Ashore on the Lofoten Islands, commandos and locals exchanging gifts. (IWM N444)

35. A Commando wearing the unpopular rope-soled boots. (IWM H17536)

Meanwhile, some time in the morning a message was passed to Lieutenant Colonel Lister's HQ that there was a Luftwaffe wireless station on an island some miles from Svolvaer. This seemed too good an opportunity to miss. So a coach was commandeered and some of the reserve, together with Captain Lord Lovat set off there. On the way they ran into a group of Germans who had withdrawn after an encounter with the commandos led by Major Kerr, who had landed on Brettesnes. A burst of machine gun fire over their heads led to a quick surrender and they together with a small escort went back to Svolvaer. The remainder were quickly back on their way and found the wireless station, a converted police station flying a swastika flag. From speaking to locals it was learned that there were only a few technicians inside and several bursts of Bren gun fire through the windows led to a rapid exit out of the rear of the building into the arms of other waiting commandos. Now that the station was clear some of the party set about destroying the equipment. Most of the damage was done with iron bars, much to the chagrin of their attached signaller who looked on with envy at the apparently far superior German radio equipment. He was carrying a Number 18 set and was unable to contact HQ even though they were less than 5 miles away. Taking the swastika flag as a souvenir, they returned to Svolvaer with a small number of prisoners.

One of the officers (Lieutenant R Wills) from No 3 Commando went to the post office at Stamsund and asked for a telegram to be sent to a Mr A Hitler, Berlin. It read, "You said in your last speech German troops would meet the English wherever they landed STOP where are your troops? Wills 2-Lieut". Regretfully it is not recorded whether the telegram was ever delivered.

After around six hours ashore the forces withdrew, taking with them around 215 Germans, these mainly being merchant seamen but there were a few Luftwaffe men and soldiers. Additionally ten locals believed to be quislings were taken back to the UK. Perhaps the most significant event on the personnel front were the 314 local men and women who volunteered to come back to serve with the Free Norwegian Forces.

On a material front the aims of the raid were probably exceeded – it was estimated that 800,000 gallons of fish oil and petrol were burnt, eleven cod oil and herring oil or fish meal factories were either demolished or severely damaged. It was said that the largest factory in Stamsund was the Johannes one. When two of the officers from No 3 Commando arrived here the sound of other demolitions could be heard and they were greeted by the sight of the owner arguing with one of the demolition officers, Lieutenant Williams. The conversation went along the lines of:

Local: "But I've never sold oil to the Germans. I'm pro-British".

Commando: "Then where does the oil go?"

This was met by a stony silence so the order was given to carry on and demolish the factory.

An electricity-generating plant was also destroyed. Five ships in addition to the *Krebbs* with a total tonnage of more than 20,000 tons were sunk, four by demolition parties and the last, the *Hamburg*, a large factory and refrigeration ship, by naval gunfire. In addition the crew of one trawler agreed to sail it back to Britain. As the commandos left Stamsund it seemed the whole population of the town was on the quayside cheering them off. Gifts were distributed by the commandos which had been brought from Britain such as tea, coffee and toys. In return gifts of gloves, sweaters and scarves were pressed on the commandos. As the last of the men moved out to the waiting ships the sound of singing could be heard which gradually stopped. Many men felt they had a big lump in their throats at this time and were sad to go.

Sergeant J Dunning was a member of F Troop from No 4 Commando who went to Brettesnes with Captain Duveen. He commented:

My specific role in the operation was to make sure my section took two bamboo ladders on our landing craft and secure the quay while the rest landed. Once everybody was ashore I was to go to a certain house, get the occupier out of bed and take him to one of the cod factories and make him give us certain papers. This bit of the operation went exactly to plan. I went to the house got the chap and together with my Norwegian guide took him to the factory and got him to open up. After we had finished our little job the demolition team moved in.

Sapper K Kennett, a member of E Troop of No 4 Commando said the following about Operation Claymore:

I did very little at Lofoten. I went into the village but saw very few Germans. We did get a very warm welcome from the locals. However, my overriding memory of the Lofoten raid was the absolutely useless rope-soled boots we had been issued with. Whoever came up with the idea of them deserved shooting as it was very difficult to keep your feet. Afterwards they were taken away and I never saw a pair again.

Lieutenant Webb from No 4 Commando heading for Svolvaer had been given detailed instructions as to his main tasks here by Lieutenant Colonel Lister. He later recounted:

Colonel Lister told me in no uncertain terms that I was to take the hotel and arrange for his breakfast to be got ready! I believe he had been once the Army

36. Lieutenant Colonel Durnford-Slater returning from Operation Claymore. On his left is Lieutenant-Commander Kimmins and the civilian is Mr Hawes, the bank manager from Svolvaer. (IWM N406)

37. A group of happy commandos returning with the spoils of war after the Lofoten Islands raid in March 1941. (IWM N416)

middleweight boxing champion so I wasn't going to argue with him. With six men I went to the hotel which was only a small one, six rooms only I think. I did the necessary with the hotel staff and indeed later the Colonel came for his breakfast. I also managed to pinch some silver arctic fox furs which a high-ranking German officer had left in the hotel pending collection. After making sure the Colonel was having his breakfast I then had to go to the bank to see what I could find there. Imagine my astonishment to find an English bank manager there. The bank was called Allen and Hanbury and the manager's name was Mr Hawes. He had been caught at Svolvaer during the German invasion in 1940 and unable to get away. I said I was going to burn all his Kroner currency but he persuaded me from doing so as he said the Germans would only print more. He did however, come back to England with us.

Perhaps even more importantly it had been decided to send a film unit to accompany the Commandos and much footage was shot. This was an important propaganda coup when little was going right for Britain. The footage showing captured German prisoners and Quislings being arrested was of much value and was shown in cinemas across Britain.

The casualty figure for the Commandos is thought to have been only one – an officer who managed to achieve a negligent discharge from a pistol he had put in his pocket. How much his CO fined him is regretfully not recorded. Another commando who was the subject of much ridicule was a Sergeant. Before the raid everyone had been issued with 100 Kroner for use as escape money if they should be left behind. On the journey back the money was collected back but this NCO could only hand back 70 as he had spent the rest comforting an apparently attractive Norwegian blonde, no doubt many of his comrades were somewhat jealous. Not recorded at the time was the liberation of an incomplete set of rotor wheels for the German Enigma encoding machine, these were passed to the codebreakers at Bletchley Park and subsequently proved to be of much value. It took a while for the men to thaw out but overall there must have been a warm glow inside every man after having taken part in a successful operation.

The force arrived back at Scapa Flow on the 6th March to a rapturous welcome, and Lieutenant Colonel Durnford-Slater later wrote: "Altogether it had been a highly successful operation with no casualties and a good start to large-scale raids." It certainly took away the bad taste from the fiasco at Guernsey. However things did not really develop as Durnford-Slater had hoped for several months. The main reason for this was the transfer of many of the ALCs to the Middle East and it would be towards the end of the year before the UK based Commandos got their next taste of action.

Chapter 6

The Latter Part of 1941

For the next few months after the success of the Lofoten Islands raid, the spotlight for commando activity fell on the Middle East. Three Commandos (Nos. 7, 8 and 11), had been sent to the Middle East to supplement the three Commandos already raised in that theatre. These were Nos. 50, 51 and 52 (Middle East) Commandos. The first commando operation in that region was planned to occur at the end of October 1940, with an attack on an Italian seaplane base at Bomba. However, like so many other operations it was cancelled at the last minute because of the Italian invasion of Greece. As a result of an invasion scare No 50 Commando was hurriedly despatched to Crete to act in an ordinary infantry role. Then over the months of December 1940 and January 1941 Nos. 51 and 52 Commandos were sent to the Sudan to take part in fighting against the Italians there. Both were destined to play a significant role in the defeat of the Italians in Ethiopia and Eritrea over the latter months of 1941.

The three Commandos sent from the UK arrived in the area in early 1941 aboard three infantry assault ships – HMS *Glenearn*, HMS *Glengyle* and HMS *Glenroy*. This was a major step forward as these three ships had been converted to take ALCs and other motor launches from specially installed davits. United with the Commandos from Crete and the Sudan there were now around 2,000 trained troops with suitable transport to carry them available for offensive operations. To try and fool the Germans and Italians the unit's designations were changed as follows:

No 7 Commando becoming A Battalion
No 8 Commando becoming B Battalion
No 11 Commando becoming C Battalion
No 50 Commando amalgamating with No 52 Commando and becoming
D Battalion

Various operations were again planned and then cancelled, although on the night of 19th/20th April A Battalion undertook a raid against the Cyrenaican port of Bardia. This port had been captured during General O'Connor's January offensive but had been recently retaken by the Axis forces. The intention of this raid was to harass the enemy's lines of communication and to inflict damage on his supplies and shipping. It was appreciated that for most of the voyage there and back that the ships would be out of the range of fighter cover, but it was decided to accept this risk. HMS *Glengyle* with A Battalion aboard set sail on the night of 19th/20th April, escorted by an anti-aircraft cruiser HMS *Coventry* together with three Australian destroyers HMAS *Stuart*, HMAS *Voyager* and HMAS *Waterhen*. It was planned for the submarine HMS *Triumph* (the same one involved in the abortive Operation Colossus rescue mission), to take up a position two miles or so off Bardia and show a white light as a navigational aid. Regretfully she was attacked by friendly aircraft on the voyage and was delayed. Additionally a green light was meant to be lit from a small island outside Bardia, courtesy of an officer from the Special Boat Section but he again was delayed. In spite of these difficulties the

Glengyle reached the right position and launched her landing craft around 1.30p.m., the troops were intended to land on four different beaches. A Beach was the most northerly and the men got ashore without difficulty wading ashore in pretty shallow water, soon afterwards they were joined by the men from B Beach. The Navy had managed to land them in the wrong place. Both parties destined for C and D Beaches arrived at the correct place albeit somewhat delayed. All the landings had been unopposed and except for a few motorcycle patrols and the sound of a couple of lorries there were few enemy about. One officer attempting to move from one group to another failed to give the reply when challenged with the password and was shot and fatally wounded. A dump of tyres was discovered which was set alight with four incendiary bombs. Some of this group went back to B Beach but the landing craft did not come and many were taken prisoner. The group from C Beach whose main objective was a pumping station, took a lot of time to find it and were running out of time so failed to accomplish this. However, as a secondary target they did manage to damage a bridge. The party from D Beach probably had the major success in that a battery of four guns was found and these were blown up.

It must be said that this raid was not much of a success – only minimal damage being caused and there being over 70 casualties, the majority being 'missing presumed taken prisoner' mainly due to problems picking up the troops from the beaches. However, the raid did force the Germans to pull back an armoured brigade from Sollum to guard rear areas.

Around this time the small number of British troops in Greece were coming under increasing pressure and it looked inevitable that another 'Dunkirk' would have to be put into operation. There was a lack of suitable transports so the three Glen class ships were taken away from the commando forces. It is reported that when A Battalion left HMS *Glengyle* for the last time at the beginning of May one wag left a sign saying 'Never in the whole history of human endeavour have so few been buggered about by so many.' Over the next few weeks the units were again broken up and sent all over the place. C Battalion was sent to Cyprus and the others to Crete where they arrived on 27th May. The aim here was to try and stop the German takeover of the island. But it was all a case of too little too late, as the Germans had already been on Crete for over a week. Harried from pillar to post, the Commandos fought a number of desperate rearguard actions across the island. They ended up at a small port called Sphakia on the southern coast where the Navy managed to evacuate the survivors. However it was not without grievous losses – the Commandos had gone ashore around 800 in number, yet only 200 escaped from Crete, not a very good use of highly trained men.

Two more operations followed with B Battalion conducting a successful raid (but with many casualties) on Tobruk and C Battalion fighting in Syria. However the casualty rate was too high for the Top Brass in the Middle East and in August 1941 decided that Layforce (as the commando troops were called after their commander Colonel Laycock) would be disbanded.

Admiral Keyes was said to be very unhappy with this situation and someone else was even more unhappy. The irregular forces had always been a pet project for Winston Churchill and he was said to be furious when he heard of the decision from GHQ Middle East Command. He immediately demanded that a new commando force be created but this time under the command of the Senior Service because in his view, "Middle East Command had indeed maltreated and thrown away this valuable force."

The now Brigadier Laycock was appointed as the Director of Combined Operations in the theatre and he tried to pull together the various elements of the special forces in the area. One of the survivors from all this blood letting was the original No 11 Commando who had been sent out from the UK earlier in the year. Although they had had many names, such as C Battalion and then No 3 Troop, they still regarded themselves as No 11 Commando. Under the command of Lieutenant Colonel G Keyes (Admiral Keyes's son), around 60 members of the unit were selected to take part in one of the most ambitious commando raids of the war. This was codenamed Operation Flipper and was to coincide with the launching of a major offensive by the 8th Army to relieve the encircled garrison at Tobruk under the code name of Operation Crusader. Whilst the aim of the main operation was to relieve Tobruk a side operation was to try and assassinate General Erwin Rommel, the commander of the German Afrika Korps. An additional aim of the plan was to also disrupt the German High Command just before the offensive which was to take place in mid-November 1941.

Early in October 1941 six officers and 53 men from the Scottish Commando (as No 11 Commando liked to be known), were selected for special training for Operation Flipper. The party was split into four groups; the first was to raid Rommel's quarters at Beda Littoria, the second going for the Italian Army HQ at Cyrene, the third an Italian Army intelligence base at Appollonia. The last was more of a sabotage party designed to create as much mayhem as they could do by destroying telephone, wireless and telegraph communications. Brigadier Laycock intended going along as overall commander. The plan was to move the commandos to the area of their attacks in two submarines – HMS *Talisman* and HMS *Torbay*. On reaching their destination the commandos would paddle themselves ashore in rubber boats, with the reverse happening on completion of the operation (in theory). On the evening of the 10th November the two submarines left Alexandria, heading westwards. It is recorded that the men were in high spirits, "All ranks were greatly interested in what was to us a novel method of approaching our objective, and the soldiers were high in their praise of the way in which they were fed and accommodated." Landfall at what was thought to be the correct location was made by HMS *Torbay* around nightfall on the 14th November, her commandos were to land first. Things were helped by Captain Haselden, who had been living as a native behind enemy lines for several weeks and signalled from the beach that all was well. However the weather now took a hand and in deteriorating conditions the commandos from the *Torbay* started to try and get ashore. A task that was meant to take about an hour grew into a five-hour marathon. The men from *Talisman* were to land when all the party from *Torbay* were ashore. The weather continued to get worse and Brigadier Laycock had just about made up his mind to delay departure for his group to the following night when the expected signal was received. The party left in their rubber boats but most of them were capsized, and only Brigadier Laycock and seven men made it ashore, the rest fortunately being able to swim back to the *Talisman*. Once ashore Laycock joined up with the party from *Torbay* and took cover for the rest of the night and the following day in a nearby wadi. It was hoped that on the following night the others would be able to make it ashore. But during the laying-up period the weather was not good, high winds followed and accompanied by torrential rain. Given these conditions it was debatable whether the men from *Talisman* would be able to make it safely so Laycock decided on a quick change of plan. He split the available men into three parties – Lieutenant Colonel

Keyes together with Captain Campbell and 17 men would go for the ultimate prize, that of Rommel and his HQ. A second group consisting of Lieutenant Cook and six men were to go to a crossroads south of Cyrene and demolish the telephone and telegraph wires here. Laycock himself together with three men would remain at the beach and guard the spare rations and ammunition. It was also hoped they would be able to guide in any men from the *Talisman* who could make it subject to sea conditions.

Anyway around 8.00 p.m. on the evening of the 14th November the Keyes group left the coast heading inland towards Beda Littoria. In common with the men from X Troop the going was difficult, mainly rock-strewn undulating tracks. At dawn the following morning they took cover on a small hill. They did not remain undiscovered for long as some locals armed with Italian weapons soon found them. However, as on Operation Colossus, a soldier who spoke the local language had been included and with his help the Arabs were won over to the British side, Keyes even managing to buy some cigarettes from the Arabs with some Italian currency that had been issued to him. The Arabs were also kind enough to bring the group a hot meal of some goat stew. When it got dark again the group set off guided by some of the friendly natives who took them after a march of about three hours to a large cave, which although dry and offered very good protection from the elements smelt strongly of goat. They rested till dawn when the guide said it would be safe to move in daylight and then took them to a small wood not too far from Rommel's perceived HQ. From here Keyes and a couple of the guides set off on a close target reconnaissance which proved very useful and enabled a sketch map to be produced which was used to brief the men on the coming raid. Each group was briefed as to its role in the assault. At around 6.00 p.m. on the 17th the group set off for their objective in pouring rain, which although was uncomfortable did provide some sort of cover. After a somewhat tortuous journey their guides said they were now on the track which led to the rear of Rommel's HQ.

At this point Lieutenant Cook and his party broke away to go and do their task of disrupting the enemy communications. The others edged closer to the HQ. Keyes was in front with Sergeant J Terry with the rest under Captain Campbell about fifty yards behind. The guides were also left behind while the commandos went on alone. When the two lead scouts were within about 100 yards from the HQ building a dog started to bark and an Italian soldier came out of the darkness close to the main group. Captain Campbell told him in German that they were a German patrol and Corporal Drori spoke to him also with the same message in Italian.

The Italian seemed happy with these comments, probably happy in the belief that no British soldiers were within many miles of here. As the sentry turned away to continue his patrol Keyes and Terry returned to the main group. The final go-ahead for the attack was given and Keyes, supported by Captain Campbell and Sergeant Terry, got through the hedge surrounding the garden compound of the HQ and neared the house. They went up a flight of steps to a set of double doors when a German officer appeared. Captain Campbell later commented:

> Geoffrey (Keyes) at once closed with him, covering him with his Tommy gun. The German seized the muzzle of Geoffrey's gun and tried to wrest it from him. Before Terry or I could get round behind him he retreated, still holding on to Geoffrey, to a position with his back to the wall and both of his sides protected by the first

38. The house at Beda Littoria, the main objective of Operation Flipper. (IWM E30463)

39. HMS *Talisman*, one of the submarines involved in Operation Flipper. The caption on this photograph states that it was taken after her return from the operation. (IWM A7822)

and second pair of doors at the entrance. Geoffrey could not draw a knife and neither could Terry nor I could get round Geoffrey as the doors were in the way, so I shot the man with my .38 revolver which I knew would make less noise than Geoffrey's Tommy gun. Geoffrey then gave orders that we could use Tommy guns and grenades, since we had to assume that my revolver shot had been heard. We found ourselves in a large hall with a stone floor and stone stairway leading to the upper floors, with a number of doors opening out of the hall which was very dimly lit. We heard a man in heavy boots clattering down the stairs. As he came to the turn and his feet came in sight, Sergeant Terry fired a burst with his Tommy gun. The man turned and fled away upstairs.

They then started to search the rooms, in itself a risky business as anyone who has ever done fighting inside an occupied building will know. Some of the rooms were empty, but one door had light shining out from under the door. Keyes quickly opened the door to see around ten Germans inside. Captain Campbell again:

Geoffrey fired two or three rounds with his Colt .45 automatic pistol, while I said I'd throw a grenade in. Geoffrey shut the door and held it shut while I pulled the safety pin from the grenade. I said to Geoffrey that I was ready and he opened the door and I threw the grenade into the room. Geoffrey said "Well done". Then almost at the same moment one of the Germans fired and caught Geoffrey just above the heart.

Keyes slumped to the floor, while Captain Campbell quickly shut the door, just before the grenade went off. The light went out in the room and for a few seconds there was silence. Campbell and Terry quickly carried Keyes outside and laid him on a patch of grass by the front steps. Captain Campbell commented, "He must have died as we were carrying him outside, for when I felt his heart it had ceased to beat." It now felt like it was time to go, there was no sign of Rommel and Captain Campbell went back into the house to give new orders. Unfortunately one of the Commandos mistook him for a German and shot and badly wounded him in the leg. His men offered to carry him back the thirty miles or so to the coast but Captain Campbell ordered them to leave him behind. It fell to Sergeant Terry to lead the survivors back to the coast. Shortly afterwards the Germans found Captain Campbell and took him to hospital where his leg could not be saved and it was amputated. Lieutenant Colonel Keyes was graciously awarded full military honours at his funeral.

Sergeant Terry and his party made it successfully back to the coast and met up with Laycock. Regretfully Lieutenant Cook and his group never made it back, after successfully carrying out some demolition work, they had been captured on their way back to the wadi. HMS *Torbay* returned on the night of the 20th November and sent a message by lamp, which said that the sea was too rough and she would come back the following night. The submarine's crew did launch a dinghy filled with food and water which floated ashore. There was no option but to try and hide up during the coming day and Laycock placed men in various caves and ordered a watch to be kept all day. The Italians and Germans however, were out searching for the Commandos and around noon on the 21st a small party of Arabs working for the Italians engaged the western flank of his perimeter. Two parties were sent to try and outflank the attackers, but some German reinforcements arrived and foiled this manoeuvre. Further reinforcements arrived and by around 2.00 p.m., the enemy had closed to within 200 yards and it was not looking good. Laycock now decided to divide the group up into smaller parties and make a break for it. It was a hopeless exercise as most men were quickly captured. Only two, Laycock and Terry, managed to get away from the perimeter area and set out to join up with the hopefully advancing 8th Army. On Christmas Day 1941, forty-one days after setting out on the raid, they reached friendly troops at Cyrene. Brigadier Laycock later commented:

> Our greatest problem was the lack of food, and though never desperate we were forced to subsist for periods, which never exceeded two-and-a-half days, on berries only, and we became appreciably weak from want of nourishment. At other times we fed well on goat and Arab bread, but developed a marked craving for sugar. Water never presented a serious problem as it rained practically continuously.

Later it was found out that the house they had attacked was used as the HQ for the German and Italian Logistic Services and had never been used by Rommel. On the night in question he had been up in the forward areas visiting his troops. For his determination, gallant and skillful leadership Lieutenant Colonel Keyes was awarded a posthumous Victoria Cross, the first awarded to one of the Commando Forces. His citation read:

> Lieutenant Colonel Keyes commanded a detachment of a force which landed some 250 miles behind the enemy lines, in North Africa, to attack Headquarters base installations and communications. Lieutenant Colonel Keyes deliberately selected the command of the party detailed to attack the residence and Headquarters of the General Officer Commanding the German Forces in North Africa. This attack meant almost certain death for those who took part in it. The disposition of his detachment left with only one officer and a NCO with whom to break into General Rommel's residence. On the night 17th/18th November 1941, he boldly led his party to the front door and demanded entrance. It was unfortunately necessary to shoot the sentry; the noise aroused the house, so that speed became of the first importance. Lieutenant Colonel Keyes instinctively took the lead and emptied his revolver with great success into the first room. He then entered the second room but was mortally wounded almost immediately. By his fearless disregard of the dangers which he ran and of which he was fully aware, and by his magnificent leadership and outstanding gallantry Lieutenant Colonel Keyes set an example of supreme self-sacrifice and devotion to duty.

He is now buried in Benghazi CWGC Cemetery.

Sergeant F Birch was a demolition's expert who was attached to No 11 Commando for Operation Flipper but only at the last minute. Here is his account of the immediate time before the operation and then what happened to him ashore in Libya.

> The day before the men were due to leave, one man in a tent of six caught scabies, so all of them were quarantined, so the group was six men short. I had been training

the men of 11 Commando in demolition techniques and was therefore press-ganged into service at the last minute. The time on the submarine was great – really good food and the navy boys did their best to look after us. However, when we came to get ashore it was in small two man dinghies. It was a really tough and slow job getting ashore. I was in the second dinghy and after struggling ashore, Colonel Keyes who had been in the first dinghy told me and my mate to go inland a bit and keep watch for any enemy soldiers. This we did but perhaps due to the problems of others getting ashore we were there the whole night until I sent the other bloke back to find out what was happening. They had indeed forgotten about us and we joined the rest and spent the day hiding.

On the raid itself I was with Lieutenant Cook and we were going to try and blow up a communications pylon at about the same time the attack was going to take place at Rommel's HQ. But due to a number of reasons we got to the pylon about an hour late. It was a four-legged pylon and we laid the charges and fuse but I had problems with the matches supplied to light the fuse. Everything was so wet due to the torrential rain that had been falling. One of the blokes suggested using an incendiary bomb to get them going. I thought it was better than nothing and so telling everyone else to put some distance between themselves and the pylon, I set an incendiary off, lit the fuses and ran for dear life.

The charges went off and the pylon fell to one side. Regretfully a lot of the telephone lines hadn't been cut so we cut them by hand. It was now time to try and get back to the coast and the pick-up point.

We hid by day and walked at night and on the second morning we found ourselves pretty much in an open spot but a local shepherd took us to a cave. Sometime later that morning we heard Italians out searching for us and inevitably an Italian appeared at the cave entrance. Someone opened fire and hit an Italian in the leg. They withdrew and threw in some hand grenades. Lieutenant Cook said he would go out first and if we heard shooting, we must assume he'd been shot and we were to come out fighting. As it turned out he was not shot and he called for us to come out. We were then obviously taken prisoner.

While all of this activity involving his son was going on in the Middle East, Admiral Keyes was becoming increasingly frustrated at his role as Director Combined Operations and the use of these so-called Special Forces. He felt that many in the military saw the Commandos as Churchill's Private Army and few in the Top Brass had ever seen the need for them. In fact, their arguments were strengthened when in August 1942 a very successful raid by Canadian regular troops against the coal mines on the German occupied island of Spitzbergen was carried out. This, to the Top Brass, proved to them that there was no need for elite troops to carry out such raids. This encouraged them to deny to the Commandos resources they desperately needed such as training areas, supplies and intelligence reports and photographic reconnaissance. Keyes's morale was probably not helped when he heard that the airborne troops had been allowed to wear a distinctive coloured beret when his request for one for the Commandos had been turned down, although one was later approved.

Perhaps it may be worth adding a word or two about the Spitzbergen raid as it is a little-known event of the Second World War. On the 22nd June 1941 Germany invaded Russia and so Britain was no longer fighting alone. Things initially went well for the Germans and the Russians requested whatever help they could from Britain. Three hundred and seventy miles from the most northerly point of Norway lies a group of islands (belonging to Norway) – the Spitzbergen Islands. These islands in the pre-war years although being in a very inhospitable location, were being extensively mined for coal mainly by around 2,000 guest Russian coal-miners. The total population was around 3,000. An agreement was reached between Britain, Norway and Russia in July 1941 that immediate steps should be taken to deny the Spitzbergen coal to the Germans. It was decided that it would not be possible to maintain a permanent garrison in the exposed position well north of the Arctic Circle. Therefore the decision was taken to disable the mines to ensure the Germans could gain no benefit from them, to destroy any stocks of coal and evacuate the inhabitants.

The question was who would go, perhaps it was not a job for the Commandos as it was pretty certain there would be no Germans on the islands, but still it could be argued that some sort of amphibious warfare experience would be necessary. Perhaps one of the resentful Top Brass in the War Office heard that some of the Canadian Army troops had spent time training in landing craft techniques at a Combined Operations base in Scotland and suggested their use. In any case the job was given to the Canadians and a Brigadier A Potts was selected to lead the Canadian troops. The bulk of the men came from the Edmonton Regiment and the Saskatoon Light Infantry, supported by (as usual) explosive experts from the Royal Canadian Engineers. Also coming along were some Royal Canadian Corps of Signals men, a few Royal Engineers with mines experience and as interpreters and local liaison some members of the Free Norwegian Forces. The group arrived in the main port Long Year City on the 25th August 1941.

As predicted no opposition was met on the islands, the inhabitants showed great warmth to the Canadians, even when they were told to get ready for immediate evacuation. It had been decided to send the Russians back to their homeland, while the Norwegians would be brought back to the UK. The mines were all disabled, with vital components either being destroyed or removed. Additionally the aerial conveyor belt bringing coal from one of the biggest coal mines to the dock side was destroyed. It is estimated that 450,000 tons of coal and 275,000 gallons of petrol, fuel oil and grease were set on fire. This must have been some blaze and taken several days to burn itself out. An additional bonus was the return of the ships from Russia with around 200 French Army troops who had volunteered to join the Free French Forces. They had escaped to Russia from German prisoner of war camps and were eager to carry on the fight.

The final part of the operation was the destruction of the two radio stations on Spitzbergen, who continued right up to the last minute to transmit weather reports which were of use to the Germans. As it turned out the Germans neither interfered with the Canadians nor indeed had any idea that the raid had occurred until the night of 3rd/4th September when a radio station at Tromso could be heard calling up Spitzbergen and, demanding in vain for them to answer.

Perhaps for all these reasons, Admiral Keyes had had enough and on 27th October 1941 he resigned as the Chief of Combined Operations. He later announced in a speech,

After fifteen months as Chief of Combined Operations and having been frustrated at every turn in every worthwhile offensive action I have tried to undertake, I must fully endorse the Prime Minister's comments on the negative power of those who control the war machine in Whitehall. Great leaders of the past have always emphasized the value of time in war, time is passing and so long as procrastination, the thief of time, is the key-word of the war machine in Whitehall, we shall continue to lose one opportunity after another during the lifetime of opportunities.

The War Office's response was to send him a copy of the Official Secrets Act and to remind him of his responsibilities under the Act to try and keep him quiet. It is worth adding here that about three weeks later he would learn that his son Geoffrey Keyes had been killed on Operation Flipper.

The question was now who would replace Admiral Keyes as the top man? Given what had happened in the past with one of his pet projects, it is certain that Winston Churchill had thought long and hard about who he wanted to replace Keyes. His attention was drawn towards a 41 year old sailor who had already seen a lot of fighting in the war and had made a name for himself when in command of a destroyer HMS *Kelly*. This ship had been sunk off Crete during the evacuation earlier in the year. The person in question was Captain The Lord Louis Mountbatten, who had spent most of his active life as an officer in the Royal Navy, he was also a cousin of the King. Someone commented on his appointment as follows, "The discerning eye of the Prime Minister had long had him in view. He had energy, brains and determination of the highest order, all qualities in which a Chief of Combined Operations must excel. To these, as well as to his youth, his vigour, and his frank personality, he owed his appointment." He was appointed to the role on 27th October 1941 and promoted Commodore and to give him some clout with the other services given honourary commissions in the Army of Lieutenant-General and in the Royal Air Force as an Air Marshal. As previously mentioned Germany had invaded Russia in June 1941 and in October 1941 the Russian Army was in virtual total disarray, retreating at a rapid rate towards Moscow. The call went out to Britain to do something, anything, to try and take some pressure off the Russians. At this stage of the war Britain realistically had only two ways of striking at Germany, by sending bombers over by night to try and disrupt the German war machine and by Commando raids. On the first of these two subjects I will briefly look at the bombing war in a later chapter, which means we can concentrate on the first real major Commando raid of the war so far. One of the first tasks given to Mountbatten was to identify a suitable target and raid it as soon as possible.

During the latter months of 1941 a few minor raids had been carried out by the men of Nos. 2, 5, 9 and 12 Commandos on the French coast, but it cannot be said that any of them did any damage worthy of much German attention. So Mountbatten decided it would be an opportune time to return to Norway. Now with Mountbatten at the helm of the ship a new sense of urgency began to sweep through the whole of the Commando organisation. Mountbatten was expert at oiling the wheels of inter-service co-operation and also helping to unblock administrative foul-ups. Within two months of taking charge a raid was proposed at a location on a part of the occupied coast of Europe, where it was hoped, the enemy would least expect it. The country chosen was again Norway and the location a place called Vaagso, several hundred miles south of the Lofoten Islands which had been visited in March 1941.

Chapter 7

Operation Archery

The raid on Vaasgo was given the codename of Operation Archery, its main aim was to attack and destroy military and economic targets in the town of South Vaagso and on the nearby island of Maaloy. Additional aims were the capture or sinking of any shipping found in the strip of water known as the Ulvesund. Ulvesund is the name of the channel that separates the island of Vaasgo from the mainland of Norway. Situated in the channel is Maaloy Island which again had some military and economic targets situated on it. It was known that there was a German garrison in South Vaagso and so would provide an opportunity to either kill or capture some Germans. The area was again heavily involved in the fishing industry so destroying factories would have a material effect on the Germans. Additionally as a more strategic effect it was hoped that it might force the Germans into diverting troops away from the front line areas (Russia and North Africa) to guard rear areas. That is not to say that the area was totally devoid of defences, in fact it was a difficult approach for shipping and there were several defensive positions dotted around. The Germans had fortified the southern end of the Ulvesund, as well as a battery of guns on Maaloy together with positions in the town of South Vaagso. The intelligence available also stated there was one tank in the town.

Almost at right angles to the southern end of Ulvesund was Husevaago Island but it was thought there were no German positions here. It was decided to approach the target up Vaagsfjord, the entrance of which was marked by two lighthouses at Hovdeneset and Bergsholmane. On reaching a small bay behind Halnoesvik Point, about half a mile south-east of the village of Hollevik, the ALCs would be lowered from the assault ships and then go to their objectives. The landings were planned to be made under cover of a naval bombardment from the accompanying ships and then a smoke screen laid by aircraft of the RAF. So it can be seen that the three services were, at last, starting to pull together after a number of months of mistrust.

From the Army came the men of No 3 Commando still commanded by Lieutenant Colonel Durnford-Slater, probably the country's most experienced commando leader, supported by two troops from No 2 Commando (not to be confused with the earlier version which became 11th Special Air Service Battalion). Also helping to swell the numbers were some men from No 6 Commando (mainly sappers and medics) and again a party of around 20 Free Norwegian Forces to act as local liaison and interpreters. It was again hoped to round up some Quislings and recruit any locals to join the Norwegian Forces in Britain. The total number of army personnel involved came to 576 and all were under the overall command of Brigadier J Haydon. The Naval involvement consisted of a cruiser HMS *Kenya*, four destroyers, HMS *Chiddingfold*, HMS *Offa*, HMS *Onslow* and HMS *Oribi*. To transport the commandos were two infantry assault ships, HMS *Prince Charles* and HMS *Prince Leopold*. These two ships were purpose-built assault ships, no longer did the landing troops have to rely on converted cross-channel steamers. HMS *Tuna*, a submarine, was also present acting as a navigational aid off the island.

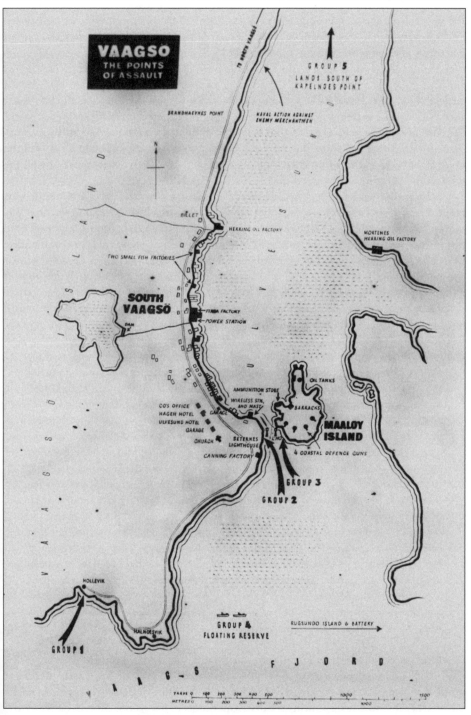

Map 8. Vaagso Area. A planning map for Operation
Archery December 1941. (National Archives)

The navy element was commanded by Rear-Admiral H Burrough who was on board HMS *Kenya*. The RAF element of Operation Archery were ten Hampdens from No 50 Squadron and some Blenheims from 110 and 114 Squadrons to provide close support over Vaasgo. To try and prevent the Luftwaffe from interfering with the raid, Blenheims and Beaufighters from Nos. 235, 236, 246, 254 and 404 Squadrons were tasked with airfield raids, these being tasked to support operations from Sumburgh in the Shetlands and Wick at the extreme northern part of Scotland. These two airfields were around 250 and 400 miles respectively from the Vaagso area. One final point to mention is that around 300 men from No 12 Commando were to mount another raid on the Lofoten Islands at the same time called Operation Anklet. This then was the three services involvement in the operation.

A couple of weeks were spent training for the operation before the Commandos met up with the Navy element at Scapa Flow on Christmas Eve 1941 and left that day sailing for Sullom Voe in the Shetland Islands which was reached on Christmas Day. Mountbatten visited the troops at Scapa Flow and is reputed to have told the commandos: "One last thing. When my ship, the destroyer *Kelly* went down off Crete earlier this year the Germans machine-gunned the survivors in the water. There's absolutely no need to treat them gently on my account. Good luck to you all!"

Two rehearsals were carried out on the Orkneys together with extensive briefings and here is Private C Stacey's recollections of these events:

> On both rehearsals at Scapa Flow, where the black-faced sheep were the only onlookers each time we hit the beach from our assault craft, No 3 Troop was on the left flank, hitting the beach and going like the very hammers of hell all the way to the make-believe objective. Non-stop, breathless, sometimes with a red mist and black dots before our eyes from our all-out endeavours, we'd hit the objective in really good time. On the voyage from Scapa Flow, we were allowed to see the model that had been made of the area around Vaagso and Maaloy together with air photographs. Each troop had a turn in studying them. The briefings were very thorough and the chaps were extremely interested in their individual parts in the raid. Questions and answers were certainly a part of the briefing given to my troop (3 Troop) by Captain Giles, the other officers and the senior NCOs. I remember several of the questions as it was going to be my first operational experience as a commando and wanted to make sure I did nothing wrong. They came thick and fast certainly from Captain Giles such as "You, Stacey, what objective has been assigned to your section? How are you going to attain this objective? What happens if your section leader is wounded, killed, lost etc. etc." Over and over again these questions were put to us and we had to memorise the air maps, the coast line, other troop's objectives, the overall plan of the raid, buildings, factories, wharfs etc.

It had been intended to raid Vaasgo on Boxing Day hoping to catch the Germans even more unaware, but due to very bad weather in the area of the Shetlands it was decided to postpone the departure by 24 hours in the hope of better weather. To gauge the weather it is worth recounting a story from the secretary to the captain of one of the infantry landing ships who invited his commanding officer to his cabin, and showed him the table moving up and down the wall a distance of about six inches. Rather than some 20th Century poltergeist it was later discovered that the levitation was due to the heavy seas literally squeezing the ship in several inches. Again many of the Commandos found the journey uncomfortable and were badly seasick. The ships did also suffer some damage from the heavy seas so a pause of 24 hours was welcome to everyone, the men were able to eat their Christmas dinner in relative ease and running repairs were carried out on the ships where necessary. It was said that the *Prince Charles* had shipped in around 120 tons of water which was pumped out at Sullom Voe with the assistance of HMS *Chiddingfold*. The weather did indeed abate and with the promise of settled conditions in the coming days the force sailed at 4.00 p.m. on Boxing Day. The voyage was uneventful and by the time the area of the southern Norwegian coast was reached weather conditions were said to be perfect. Landfall was apparently right on track helped by the navigation beacon shown by the submarine *Tuna*. The flotilla made for the entrance of the fjord, passing Klovning Island and the Skarningerne rocks. Around this time the sound of aircraft could be heard coming from the west. The Brigade Major of the Special Service Brigade- Major R Henriques was on the bridge of HMS *Kenya* and later commented:

We approached from the west into the promise of dawn. It was a very eerie sensation entering the fjord in absolute silence and very slowly. I wondered what was going to happen, for it seemed that the ship had lost her proper element, that she was no longer a free ship at sea. Occasionally I saw a little hut with a light burning in it and I wondered whether the light would be suddenly switched off, which would mean that the enemy had spotted us, or whether it would continue to burn as some Norwegian fisherman got out of bed, stretched himself and went off to his nets.

As we entered the fjord the naval commander gave the order to hoist the Battle Ensign. This is apparently a tradition that the normal flag is lowered and replaced with a thing the size of a double sheet to give the enemy something to shoot at.

Another man present said the following:

We lay down to sleep at the end of a rough evening with the ship moving uncomfortably and the wind noisy. When we woke up it was very still, and we went on deck with the usual holiday expectation of finding that overnight the scene had changed, that we had come to a new land to enjoy a promised excitement. The wind had gone; the sea was quiet – everything was completely quiet – there was a fine moon in a clear sky and, ahead, the first suggestion of morning twilight. The other ships were neatly in line astern, and the whole force appeared to be shut in by high steep, snow-covered mountains. A long way above us, a window shone out brilliantly, the lovely sight of a lit window hung in the darkness; this was peace again.

It was most disturbing that there was so little left to do because everything had been done beforehand. We noted the time, exactly one minute late, that the landing craft were lowered, and could just be seen through glasses, black beetles crawling in the shadow of the mountains up the black waters of the fjord. We heard our aircraft overhead and saw their welcome of heavy, familiar tracer fire rising quite slowly from the surrounding slopes. Our ship was moving very quietly towards the headland where we should come into sight of the battery, which ought by now to be expecting our arrival. As we nosed round the point, everyone was waiting for the order to open fire and get in first with a salvo. It should have been a thrilling moment; but all the same, it was difficult to look at anything except that nostalgic window, now astern of us, still lit and still shining brightly in the dark morning.

The raid had been planned for a winter's morning, and due to the northern latitude it would be dark for most of the time, relieved only for a few hours of murky daylight.

Meanwhile what was the initial German reaction? To the Germans on Vaagso Island 27th December 1941 was just another normal working day. The diversionary raid by No 6 Commando had in fact gone ahead on Boxing Day when they landed many miles to the north at Reine in the Lofoten Islands. This probably served to some extent to divert German eyes here and it is believed there was no inkling by the Germans about the blow to come further south. According to contemporary documents the programme was for the infantry platoon in South Vaagso to work on their defensive position at the south end of the town, so by a quirk of fate were already at their action station. Not that this mattered much as we shall soon see. In a hut on Maaloy Island an NCO was giving a lecture to the men from the artillery battery on the subject of 'How to behave in the presence of an officer.' The time was now between 8.30 and 8.45 in the morning, the OC of the battery, Captain Butziger had yet to appear, he was still in his quarters with his batman getting ready for the day to come. The batman was apparently cleaning his officer's boots when the telephone rang, being a methodical man he decided to let it ring and carry on with his polishing. The caller at the other end of the line, a lookout on Husevaago Island, unable to get an answer from the battery, then rang the harbourmaster's office in South Vaagso. He was more lucky here and someone answered and reported that he had seen what appeared to be to him seven blacked-out destroyers entering Vaagso Fjord. The clerk at the harbourmaster's office assured him all was well as a small convoy had been expected that morning, it just seemed they were a little ahead of schedule. The lookout was not convinced and replied along the lines of they didn't look like merchant ships to him. A reply came from South Vaagso implying that he was still hungover from the Christmas festivities and he'd better not be found drunk on duty.

Things now seem to take an almost comical turn. The lookout was apparently a conscientious German and wrote a message saying 'unidentified warships entering fjord'. He passed this to a signaller and asked him to send a message by lamp to the naval signal station on Maaloy Island. This message was duly received and handed to someone called Van Soest, who instead of informing the army officer who was only a couple of hundred yards away, rowed across to South Vaagso to tell the harbourmaster there, a *Leutnant zur See* Sebelin. He found him in his HQ at the Hagen Hotel and Sebelin listened to Van Soest's story. "Did you notify the army battery on Maaloy?", came the question from Sebelin. Van Soest replied "No, Sir. After all, they are army and this is a naval signal!"

Perhaps here would be a good place to pause and cover the roles and make-up of the assaulting commandos. The top-level forces have already been detailed and for Operation Archery it was decided to divide them up into five different groups all with different objectives. The following details their roles:

Group 1 was to land at Hollevik. This consisted of No 2 Troop from No 3 Commando and four Free Norwegians. Their initial objective was to take out a German artillery piece which was suspected to be on the hill directly behind the village of Hollevik. After this to clear the village of Hollevik and then move along the coast road and act as a reserve for Group 2.

Group 2 was tasked with landing at the village of South Vaagso. This was the main assault force and comprised Nos. 1, 3 and 4 Troops from No 3 Commando. It was intended that 3 Troop would move along the left hand side of the main street as their line of advance and 4 Troop the right hand side, at least initially. 1 Troop to follow along as reserve.

Group 3 was to head for the island of Maaloy. Their role was to neutralise the four 75mm guns from the coastal battery situated on the island, the troops going here were Nos. 5 and 6 Troops again from No 3 Commando.

Group 4 mainly consisting of a troop from No 2 Commando was acting as the floating reserve, to be deployed wherever needed. They were initially based on HMS *Kenya*.

Group 5's task was to land somewhere between South Vaagso and North Vaagso and to disrupt any reinforcing moves from the north and disrupt communications. This group was carried on HMS *Oribi* and consisted of a section of No 6 Troop from No 2 Commando.

So this then was the brief outline of the raid and the troops had got into their ALCs in good order and were slowly heading for their objectives. The island of Maaloy could be seen in the murky greyness from the bridge of HMS *Kenya* and at 8.48 a.m., Admiral Burrough gave the order to start the preliminary bombardment. The first shots were a salvo of starshells which not only illuminated the island of Maaloy for the naval gunners, but also aided the dropping of the smoke bombs by the Hampdens. It is then recorded that *Kenya* fired around 500 6 inch shells into a space of 250 square yards, more than enough to keep the German heads on Maaloy close to the ground. Later HMS *Offa* and HMS *Onslow* added the weight of their 4 inch guns to the party. This was probably of great benefit to the men of Group 3, many of them wondering how long it would be before the guns opened up on them as to some of them felt they were like the Light Brigade charging into the Valley of Death. At 8.57 a.m. as the ALC Lieutenant Colonel Durnford-Slater was in neared its landing point, he gave the order for ten red flares to be shot up into the sky. This was the signal for the Hampdens of 50 Squadron to come in and drop their smoke bombs around the landing spots. This was also the signal for HMS *Kenya* to stop firing. As one man commented, "There was now a sudden calm disturbed only by the odd burst of machine gun fire, but the main noise was the skirl of Major Churchill's bagpipes piping *The March of the Cameron Men* from his landing craft."

Perhaps it might be best to deal with some of the groups separately in the early stages of Operation Archery. Group 1 as you will recall was to land at a small village called Hollevik about a mile south of South Vaagso. The force numbered around 70 men all under the command of Lieutenant R Clement. They got ashore unmolested and quickly got to the gun position and found it deserted. One of the men in this party was Private A Ashby, who had been called up in January 1940 and served for around 5 months with the Royal Berkshire Regiment before volunteering for special service. He had been trained in what today's terms might be called a Mountain Leader and so was the first man up the steep slope to the supposed location of the gun. As he recalled:

> As I had been trained in rock climbing I was specially selected to go first. I was a bit nervous about this but had to get on with it. The slope appeared to be about sixty degrees and covered in ice and snow. However, when I reached the supposed large German gun position there was absolutely nothing there.

The commandos then went to the village and searched it and found two German marines who had both been wounded by the naval shelling. One of them said that the other eight men from the position had gone to South Vaagso for their breakfast and had not yet returned. Lieutenant Clement attempted to report the situation to Commando HQ, but failed to make contact with them. However, it was possible to use *Kenya* as a relay post and Durnford-Slater gave instructions for Group 1 to move up the coast road and act as a reserve in South Vaagso.

Whilst this group were making their way towards South Vaagso they could clearly see one of the RAF Blenheims circling overhead. As they neared the town a Me 109 suddenly appeared, flying at about 50 feet over the fjord parallel to the coast road. They opened fire with everything they had but it was just flying too quickly. They watched with growing horror as it suddenly pulled up into a power climb straight under the Blenheim's tail, which was a well known blind spot to German fighter pilots. It manoeuvred itself slowly into a position directly under the Blenheim's tail and then opened fire with predictable results.

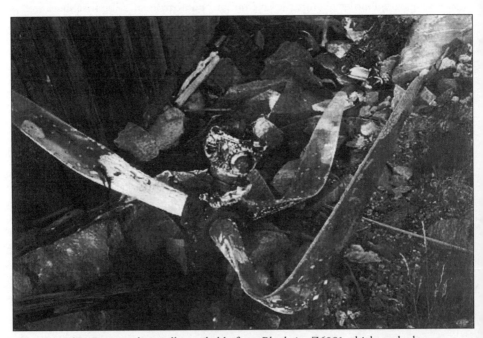

40. Recovered propeller probably from Blenheim Z6081 which crashed in Maaloy Sound during Operation Archery. (K Sørensen)

It would probably be best to look at the actions of Group 3 next for reasons that will become clear shortly. As their objectives were relatively close together the ALCs were formed up in two columns, the left column going to Vaagso and the right-hand file going to Maaloy. This group, consisting of Nos. 5 and 6 Troops of No 3 Commando, was led by the colourful figure of Major J Churchill. Originally a member of the Manchester Regiment, he had won a Military Cross during the fighting in France in 1940 and led his group ashore at Maaloy brandishing his Claymore sword. That was of course after handing his bagpipes over for safekeeping after piping the group ashore. The actual landing spot was well chosen as it was a gently shelving cove and the majority got ashore with dry feet. Just behind the beach was a low rocky cliff, and the Commandos formed up on the top of it and advanced inland. The preliminary bombardment and smoke screen had done their job well and the landing was unopposed. Their initial aim was to destroy the four guns on the island. These were later found to be four 75mm Belgian artillery pieces captured during the fighting in 1940 and moved to Norway. They had been mounted on platforms which gave them a useful 360 degree field of fire. The gun crews were quickly captured and it was found that only one of the four guns was still serviceable and with the help of some ex-gunners in the commando ranks it was used to fire at the German armed trawler *Föhn*. Regretfully the two gunners, Troopers Hannan and Mapplebeck, did not know much about fuse setting and whilst they managed to hit the trawler none of the shells exploded. However, it must have been a shock for the crew of the *Föhn*.

These are Sergeant G Herbert's recollections of the time just before and after landing:

> The Verey lights went up for the bombardment to cease; the RAF then came in and laid a smoke screen for us. The Major in our boat started playing the bagpipes, and I must say it seemed to put new life into everyone. About five minutes later we were landed on the edge of the Island, and for once it was a dry landing. I got off and under cover of the rocks and smoke, collected my section together. We then advanced in extended order until we came to the barbed wire which we had already been told about; my section got down in a firing position while I cut the wire. While I was struggling to cut it one of men pointed out that most of it had been destroyed by the bombardment and it was in fact easy to walk over it. The smoke screen was so good it had obscured my view. We carried on and took our first objective which was unmanned.

The second objective for this group was the barracks situated behind the gun pits. Whilst the fighting at the gun pits can be described as easy, it was a different matter at the barracks. The Germans, probably recovering from the shock of realising they were under attack, rallied and it took a stiff firefight to overwhelm the defenders. 11 of them were killed and 31 taken prisoner. It was reported that these 31 comprised the following:

- 1 officer and 24 German Army artillerymen
- 2 naval signallers
- 1 groom
- 1 pay clerk
- 2 female German auxiliary helpers (1 Norwegian and 1 Italian)

Sergeant Herbert again:

We then carried on towards the barracks, this is where we first came into contact with the enemy. I was watching the barrack door when I saw a Jerry run towards us; I fired at him and I got a misfire. By the time I loaded again he seemed to have disappeared beneath me. I told my section to give me covering fire while I went down after him. I crawled down the slope and on reaching the bottom I saw a huge hole in the side of the hill. I had one grenade ready and I shouted for anyone inside there to come out, but received no reply. My Bren gunner then came down the other side, so that he covered the opening. I went in. Here I had another shock; I was only expecting one Jerry inside and, when I got in, there were at least 15 Jerries and the Officer commanding the island. I was quite surprised, as they were fully armed, and I don't know why they didn't make a fight for it – perhaps it was better for me they didn't. After disarming them, they were marched back to the beach under escort.

A useful hour was spent searching the barracks for intelligence material and indeed it is said that most of the files from the offices were removed for shipment back to Britain. After a brief reorganisation, the men of 5 Troop led by Captain S Ronald were sent to a place called Deknepol, situated on the eastern side of the Ulvesund to blow up the Mortenes herring oil factory there – this was successfully achieved. The landing craft had remained on the beach awaiting the return journey. Additionally, around 10.30 a.m., it was clear that things were not going too well in South Vaagso and so most of 6 Troop led by Captain P Young were ordered to get into a ALC and go to help Group 2. There were several pieces of high ground on Maaloy and the men from Group 3 could see and hear heavy fighting going on across the brief stretch of water that separated Vaagso from Maaloy.

A final comment about Maaloy from Sergeant Herbert:

About an hour later orders came from Vaagso for reinforcements. My section was one of those selected to go. We embarked and within five minutes of receiving the order we were landing at Vaagso. Here it was much different than on the island, as we had to go through the streets and warehouses. Our orders were to push through the town and make contact with the troops the other side of Vaagso.

There was particular resistance from a small warehouse which I distinctly remember. When the Captain put his head around the door the Jerry fired and so did the Captain, but both missed. I threw about ten grenades in, and then Jerry just came to the door and dropped two stick grenades near us. We were very lucky here, as both failed to go off. One of our officers who had already been wounded through the shoulder, took a Tommy gun and went in after him, but again Jerry came into action and shot him through the face, here Jerry could have killed him but just let him walk out. One of my own section then dashed in and sprayed one magazine of Tommy, but again Jerry shot him through the thigh and let him get away to fight again. There was only one thing we could do here and that was to burn him out. We got petrol from one of the little sheds and threw it in and set light to it. We left one man here to take care of him, which I can now say he did. From here we fought northwards until eventually we made contact with those who had landed at the other end of the town.

So perhaps it is a good place to turn attention to the main assault group – that of Group 2 led by the CO of No 3 Commando Lieutenant Colonel Durnford-Slater and mainly consisting of Nos. 1, 3 and 4 Troops from that Commando. Most of the run into the beach (which was just south of the southern houses of Vaagso) was uneventful, the barrage helping to keep the Germans heads down. As stated before just as the craft were nearing South Vaagso, Durnford-Slater ordered the firing of the red flares. This unfortunately led to a small disaster. One of the Hampdens dropping 60 lb phosphorous smoke bombs was hit by anti-aircraft fire from the armed trawler *Föhn* in Ulvesund. Whether by design or accident the bomb aimer from this aircraft released his bombs as the aircraft was falling out of the sky. The Hampden crashed in the bay and only one crew member survived. However, some bombs fell into an ALC.

A young commando by the name of George Peel was present and recently commented:

It wasn't a very good start, because we were supposed to arrive in Norway on Boxing Day, hoping we'd catch the Germans with hangovers. But the sea was so rough we arrived on 27th December, escorted by the cruiser HMS *Kenya* and four destroyers. It was dawn, the lights were coming on along the fjord, it was all very picturesque. Suddenly all hell broke loose as *Kenya* opened up with her big guns. We were all on deck, ready to board the landing craft. You're too young at 21 to think you might not come back.

Unfortunately, the Germans were already on parade, ready for a long march. As soon as they heard our guns, they took up positions in the trees, firing down at us. As we approached our beach, our own bombers were dropping a smoke screen, but one was hit by machine gun fire I think; it shuddered, dropped its bombs too soon and hit our first four landing craft. You could hear the lads crying, being burned to death – all chaps we knew. We tried to drag them out of the water, but they were too badly injured.

It is possible George is mistaken on four landing craft being hit as reports state that only one craft was hit. This contained No 4 Troop under the command of Lieutenant A Komrower and around half of them were either killed or badly burned. Komrower was able to leap 'out of the frying pan into the fire' as when he leapt ashore he got trapped under the front of the ALC crushing his leg and he had to be rescued from the icy waters. It is very possible it would have been drummed into the commandos that the operation took priority over casualties and they would be gathered up by the accompanying medics and not to waste time on them. The damaged ALC (still ablaze) was later pushed out into the fjord where it sank a short distance from the shore.

Another member of this group, Private Charles Stacey commented on the approach to Vaagso:

It was a fairly steady run-in to shore. The Royal Navy personnel were, as they usually were, utterly superb, calm and steady, dead on time and dead on the landing spot. As far as I was concerned I was wet up to my waist (I'm a small chap) in the icy waters of the fjord on landing although the craft was very close to the shore. I then floundered in some deep snow drifts as soon as we hit the shore but we soon got going. It was just like an exercise landing as far as I was concerned with the difference that the 6 inch shells of the cruiser *Kenya* went hurtling overhead like coal being tipped down a chute. The Hampdens were on time and roaring around overhead dropping their phosphorous bombs and making the smoke screen and causing a diversion.

Two small machine gun posts close to the landing place were quickly dealt with and the way was clear to advance into the town itself, but towards the town centre considerable opposition was met and casualties inflicted on the commandos. The Germans had woken up from their slumber and were starting to defend almost house by house. Additionally riflemen were on the hillsides to the west of the town where they had excellent views and excellent cover. By around 10.00 a.m. most of the southern part of the town had been cleared, but the northern part was proving a tough nut to crack. The two forward troops were finding it difficult to move forward and both of them (Nos. 3 and 4 Troops) had had their troop commanders killed and other officers wounded. George Peel was in No 3 Troop and here are his recollections of the first couple of hours:

We got ashore, over the brow of a hill, and our OC, Captain J Giles, stood up and said: "Come on, 3 Troop!" Bang! He dropped dead in front of us. His younger brother, a Lieutenant was also in the same Troop. How he did it, I don't know, but he stood up and said: "Come on, No 3!" So we charged, tearing down the road, looking for cover to rethink the situation, and suddenly we saw this wooden house by the church. We jumped over the fence, through the back door. It was wonderful- suddenly we realised it was Christmas. There was a Christmas cake on the sideboard, a tree and decorations.

Five of us dived under the table. Being a wooden house, bullets were coming through and out the other side, so we had to keep low. But then I saw this little pewter box on the sideboard. It had a cross on it and when I flicked it open, inside were little papers. It was all in Norwegian, but I could see it was extracts from the New Testament because the first one said Matt.14, 27. It's hard to explain but it didn't feel like stealing. Somehow, I felt it was telling me something. I thought it's getting rough around here and I need God to be with me. So I put it in my pocket and I was never without it for the rest of the war.

Then there was the rattle of machine gun fire and a scream from outside. We opened a French window and it was poor Corporal Pike. We heaved him in, but his leg was shattered and he was screaming: "Please don't leave me." We broke a door off its hinges, with our bayonets and tossed up. I was the one who had to go outside and pull the stretcher through the window. My spine was going hot and cold, but nothing happened. Whether those young German soldiers took pity on me, I don't know, but we got it out and pushed it down the road like a toboggan. Norwegian men were carrying our wounded back to the ships so we left Pikey with some of them. We moved forward, using house-to-house techniques, diving into porches, our Lee-Enfield rifles at the ready. I was in a doorway and I had a feeling, the door behind me opened slowly. When it was half open, I gave it a kick and standing there was a German officer. Without even having to think, I whipped my knife out and stabbed him. But then I couldn't bring myself to pull it out of him. It suddenly appalled me what I'd done. For all the training we'd had – and it was the reaction I'd been trained for – that was one of the worst episodes of my career.

The body of Captain Giles was initially taken back to one of the landing ships but he was buried at sea together with two wounded Commandos who died on the way home. He is commemorated on the Brookwood Memorial to the Missing.

I have received several accounts from veterans about the qualities of Captain J Giles, originally from the Royal Tank Regiment. They were unanimous in saying that in their opinion he was one of the best, if not the best officer in No 3 Commando. One said

Shortly after the raid I noticed how empty our troop headquarters was without the tall, commanding figure of our former Troop Commander. With his death a gap was made in the Troop which was never filled. He asked us to do absolutely nothing that he was not prepared to do ten times better himself. I have seen him at the head of our Troop on a really tough forced march with blood seeping through the welts of his boots from broken blisters. He was always standing at the end of a long march and inspected our feet or listened to our moans and groans before he ever looked after himself. I remember once when training on the rough moorland at the back of Largs that the Troop, at the end of a field firing exercise, we had to put in a bayonet attack on the objective. We were running like mad downhill at the time and my momentum was such that I drew level (almost) with Captain Giles at the front. Breathless, almost, he panted out, "Who is leading this bloody troop, you or me? Get back!"

He once led us fully clothed and armed off the end of the wooded pier at Largs into the sea at the end of a forced march. We almost swam out of the sea in formation, formed up and marched back to our headquarters before the astonished gaze of several holiday-makers. With Captain Johnny Giles in front of us we always went straight to our objectives in the final assaults when on exercise- and he went to his death in the same way.

Another, Paddy Habron, commented that Captain Giles and his brother were two of the best officers he ever served under and remembers one day when they got their greatcoats mixed up. Now this may not have meant much but Johnny Giles was a lot taller than his brother and the greatcoat Bruce was wearing nearly came to the ground while his brothers scarcely fitted him.

Things were now falling behind the planned timetable and it was time to try and sort the situation out. Around 9.30 a.m. Brigadier Haydon ordered the floating reserve (a Troop from No 2 Commando under the command of Captain R Hooper) to go to South Vaagso. Also a message was sent to Major Churchill with Group 3 from Durnford-Slater asking if any men could be spared to go to South Vaagso. All he could spare was 18 men from Captain Young's No 6 Troop and these were quickly on their way together with two men from the accompanying film and photographic unit. To save time Captain Young ordered the commander of the ALC to ignore the original landing place for Group 2 and to land nearer to the church as soldiers in British uniforms could be seen on the waterfront near it, and this was successfully accomplished. Just to go back a little in time, the main advance was along the town's single main road with

41. Men from the Captain Young party approaching Vaagso after
being released from their task on Maaloy. (National Archives)

42. Commandos from Group 2 stand guard on anti-aircraft watch with a Bren gun
on its special tripod at the southern end of South Vaagso. (National Archives)

No 4 Troop on the right hand side. This troop was a little depleted by the loss of most of Lieutenant Komrower's section as previously mentioned. Then casualties among the senior commanders started to mount up; Lieutenant W Lloyd, an Australian, was shot through the neck and seriously wounded. However the men under command of senior NCOs pushed on and eventually got to the area of the Ulvesund Hotel.

Here *Leutnant* Sebelin and a few soldiers he had collected together improvised a relatively strong defensive position and progress was basically stopped here. It seemed the only way forward was to first storm the position in a frontal assault. The OC of the Troop Captain A Forrester pulled the safety pin from a grenade and made a dash for the front door of the hotel. Apparently taking the Germans by surprise he managed to get inside when a German opened fire and hit Forrester, he then fell forward and his grenade detonated beneath him. His body was left behind and it is now believed he is one of the three unknown British soldiers in the graveyard at Vaagso. In any case as he in theory has no known grave he is commemorated on the Brookwood Memorial to the Missing in Surrey.

The only fit officer left with No 4 Troop was an attached Norwegian one, Captain M Linge. His main role on the raid was to collect as much documentation and books from the German HQ as possible. However, without hesitation he now assumed command of No 4 Troop and called for them to follow him in a second assault. The men did so although they did not get very far, as soon as Captain Linge broke cover he was hit in the chest by small arms fire and fell dead virtually in the doorway of the hotel. The rest of the assault petered out. The problem now was what to do next? It fell upon the initiative of Corporal White to shout out a few orders and finding they were responded to (even by other senior ranks), covering fire was put down on the hotel. Then fortunately, a message was got back to the HQ element of No 3 Commando further south. At the HQ at the time was the presence of the OC of No 1 Troop (Captain W Bradley) who volunteered his 'special services'. This Troop had not been destined to take part in clearing the town but to follow up Nos. 3 and 4 Troops to demolish or damage any vital installations or equipment discovered by the other two Troops. Somehow he had managed to scrounge a 3-inch mortar and take it on the raid, it was really the Commandos only internal support weapon. Lieutenant Colonel Durnford-Slater readily accepted Bradley's offer. The hotel was probably a little difficult to hit from the warships in the bay. The crew was not that experienced but under the leadership of Sergeant Ramsey they were ordered to set up the mortar about 100 yards from the hotel, this short range was pretty dangerous as the mortar tube was almost in a vertical position and the bombs were being fired on their lowest charge. It is said that around ten bombs hit the hotel including one that went down a chimney. If so the round that went down the chimney would have detonated inside the hotel with disastrous consequences. These bombs gave the men led by Corporal White renewed impetus and with the use of grenade, Tommy gun, rifle and bayonet they were able to overcome the resistance. They pushed on only to be stopped at another improvised German strong point, this time the German harbourmaster's office. Again this proved difficult to neutralise so the mortar was again called forward and after a barrage of rounds into the building it too was overrun.

Meanwhile the reserves were starting to arrive, Group 1 had arrived from Hollevik and the men from Group 3 on Maaloy were nearing the shore after the short voyage across the narrows. Also the rest of the floating reserve had been sent in as a result of a

43. The memorial to Martin Linge close to the spot in
South Vaagso where he fell. (O-A Langstøyl)

message from Durnford-Slater, this said: "Fairly strong opposition being encountered in centre and north end of Vaagso. Please send remainder of Group 4 to Group 2's landing place." Fortunately these groups decided to act on their own initiative as command and control from Durnford-Slater was proving difficult except to those close around him. It seems the radios did not work too well, at least forward to Nos. 3 and 4 Troops. Durnford-Slater could hear fighting going on all over the place but was not getting any accurate reports. He decided to go forward with a small Tactical HQ to find out for himself. We shall return to this small group shortly.

The 18 or so men from No 6 Troop approached Vaagso and as previously mentioned landed near the church, and it looked to Captain Young that most of the opposition was coming from two warehouses. The first was searched and found to be empty, so attention was turned to the second, which became known as the red warehouse. It was being defended by a small group of determined Germans. Captain Young placed two men at a window on the third floor of the first warehouse to give covering fire to the rest of the Troop as they rushed the red warehouse. Between the two warehouses was a small building with a pile of timber beside it, which looked like it would provide a useful forming up point for the attack on the red warehouse about 50 yards away. The small group reached here for the loss of one man killed and another wounded, Sergeant Hughes and Trooper Clarke. There were four Germans here and all quickly surrendered, although one of them appeared to be a civilian. Around this time some members of Group 1 under Lieutenant O'Flaherty also appeared to add weight to the small group led by Captain Young.

It is worth continuing with the words of Captain Young:

I decided to advance immediately to our front and seize the red warehouse on the steamship wharf. It was about 50 yards away and, I thought, unoccupied. When, however, I was some ten yards from the door I saw a German soldier standing there, wearing a steel helmet and a long overcoat. I fired at him from the hip, swerved to my left and got down behind a crate standing against the warehouse wall. My men were coming up at the double in the most determined manner; Lance-Sergeant George Herbert came first. The Germans threw three stick bombs at us without doing any damage, though one fell within ten yards but did not explode. Our retaliation was to put a dozen Mills bombs into the building, mostly through the door. I then ran into the building shouting "Hände Hoch!", thinking that they had been done for; I was immediately shot at from an inner door, I returned the fire and came out of the warehouse. Lieutenant Denis O'Flaherty and I posted men to cover every window and the door of the warehouse while we reconnoitered it in order to find a way in. The Colonel, however, then came up and told us we must push on. I decided to burn the place down. We removed three draught horses from the stables where they had been slightly wounded when Lance-Sergeant Connolly flung a grenade into the place on hearing movement in it. There was not an entrance into the warehouse from the stables.

It was while I was organising the job of burning down the warehouse, as opposed to rushing it, that I suddenly saw Lieutenant O'Flaherty and Trooper Sherrington dash into the building by the front door. They were both armed with Tommy guns. I felt I had to go too. I was at the bottom of the stairs leading to the second floor, when I heard two shots and both O'Flaherty and Sherrington fell. I then fired at the inner door and again withdrew. It was difficult to see how we could rescue them, as they were both lying in the middle of the room covered by the enemy, who could not be seen, for they were standing in the darkness of the inner room not five yards away. Sherrington gasped out that he had been shot from the next room. It seemed to us that the best thing to do would be to go up the stairs and try to shoot the enemy through the ceiling, though this was obviously going to be difficult. At that moment, however, O'Flaherty and Sherrington walked out of the room, Sherrington had been hit in the leg and O'Flaherty looked as if he had had a plate of strawberry jam flung in his face. Trooper Hannan caught O'Flaherty as he fell and Lance-Corporal Darts got hold of Sherrington. I sent them back to the rear, and dispatched Corporal Chapman of No 2 Troop to get fire bombs while Trooper Dick Hughes fetched a bucket of petrol. Lance-Sergeant Herbert flung this into the room.

The results of this were obvious – the warehouse was set on fire, Captain Young decided to push on, but left two men with a Bren gun watching the situation. When things became too hot for the Germans, they came out firing and were all mown down by fire from the Bren gun. It is perhaps worth here saying a few words about Lieutenant

Denis O'Flaherty. A section commander in No 2 Troop he had gone ashore with Group 1 at Hollevik. As stated before there was no sign of the gun meant to be covering the area there and so he and his men had marched to South Vaagso. Moving along the area to the right of the main street, they bumped into two Germans in an alley close to the fish factory. O'Flaherty shot the first, but the second threw a grenade at him, which hit him on the nose breaking it. One of the others then shot and killed the grenade thrower. Soon afterwards, as they advanced further, O'Flaherty was nicked in the shoulder by a small arms round, but he carried on. Eventually they joined up with Captain Young's party, and his forward movement was stopped at the red warehouse. He took a bullet in the face, which broke his jaw, carried on through his palate and took out one eye. He was briefly knocked unconscious, when he came to he was able to stagger out of the warehouse and tried to explain the situation inside, but suffering from shock and facial injuries, he was virtually incoherent.

He later commented:

I heard a shot and as my companion fell I was thrown to my knees against the outside wall by a blow on my head. When I had stopped seeing stars and got up and picked up my gun I saw a figure in the door and he fired, how long then elapsed I have no idea. I came to on my face. The flashing lights had passed and I remember looking at my hands which were moving themselves with pins and needles. I sat up against the wall and saw the two Germans near me, ignoring me but peering through a window. My Tommy gun had gone. I heaved myself up and together with Trooper Sherrington walked or staggered out.

44. The 3 inch mortar crew in action in South Vaagso. The range is very short as the barrel is nearly vertical. (IWM N533)

As stated before he was then sent back for evacuation, Denis O'Flaherty spent most of the next two years in hospital, undergoing eight major operations, he rejoined the commandos minus one eye after all this but still wanting to take the fight to the enemy.

The time was now approaching midday as the leading elements pushed northwards, this was not without difficulty, as there were still a few pockets of German resistance often just one or two in a house or industrial building. Prominent in the advance was again Captain Young who was later awarded a Military Cross for his actions on this day. One of his men commented:

Our Captain always seemed to be up the front, and although it was slow as we had to go from house to house, we were able to spot and shoot the Germans who were doing the damage. One of our sergeants received three shots in the back from a German who had let us pass. We opened fire on the window and settled him. We dashed to the next house, often we threw in petrol, set fire to it and carried on.

Intelligence had stated there was one tank in Vaagso, admittedly it was an obsolescent one, but still could have caused a lot of damage to the commandos. It was eventually found in a garage around 100 yards from the Ulvesund Hotel. Two men from No 1 Troop started with the demolition work to blow it up, this was successfully achieved, although they overestimated the amount of explosive and Sergeant A Cork was killed in the subsequent explosion whilst making his escape. The other man Private Dowling escaped uninjured. In spite of several people saying that Sergeant Alfred Cork was killed on the 27th December, his date of death according to the Commonwealth War Graves Commission is the 28th December 1941. In any case, Alfred was brought home and a man of Dorset who was born in Poole, is now buried in Poole Cemetery, section 18, grave 13018. He died aged 34 and had originally served in the Devonshire Regiment before volunteering for special service.

Up at the front end of the attack No 3 Troop had managed to reach the northern edge of the town, although they had encountered several problems on the way. Their Troop Commander, Captain Giles, had been killed shortly after landing. His brother, Lieutenant B Giles, had taken over command. One of the troop members explains what happened next:

The situation of being led by a very young and untried (like most of us) officer and the brother of our Troop Commander was, to say the least, unexpected. I personally feel that young Bruce Giles must have been affected by the suddenness of his brothers death and it was asking a lot from this young officer to overcome his personal grief and loss in a moment and put into effect alternative plans for the progress to the objective. I remember going to the head of the section with Sergeant Thomas on our dash round the flank and we had to use wire cutters to cut a gap for the section through a wire fence at least 10 feet high. This wire fence ran laterally across our path of attack and I do not remember seeing it on the photos. It may have had something to do with the dam or its works. Sergeant Thomas and I were under fire from the high ground at the back of the town at the time and I believe that one of our slower moving troopers, a chap called Pike, got shot in the stomach shortly after we had got through this wire fence. Shortly after this we got to a

45. Lieutenant O'Flaherty being helped back after being seriously wounded
in the assault on the Red Warehouse. (National Archives)

46. Stores being prepared for demolition at South Vaagso. (National Archives)

double storied building (near the youth hostel I think) where I took up position at an open window on the top floor with my sniper's rifle and fired at flashes whenever I saw them. Downstairs, the rest of the section were spread out round the base of the walls of the front room with a huge Christmas tree in the centre of the floor. I remember getting some tinsel caught in the camouflage of my helmet when I was told, in a very outraged voice by someone, to crawl and not walk upright. Apparently a burst of machine gun fire had been fired into the room just before I came down the stairs. We took a door off its hinges in this house and laid poor old Pike, whose face was grey and who was losing a lot of blood, on it. We bandaged his stomach with his shell dressing and later four of the section carried Pike on the door back through the town to the beach.

It was obvious to me even though I was only a Trooper that we had undertaken some very bitter street fighting and without our leaders we had stalled a little. I still felt, though that our progress was steady, from house to house, but lacked the dash which we usually had on exercises but the Germans helped to lower the pace. I believe that our section went as far north as it possibly could in the circumstances. Our numbers had been whittled down as we crossed the open ground at the back of the town and we were sited in the solidly constructed house out on the left flank by the early afternoon, I think the time was around 12.40. There were no other troops from the Commando directly in front of us but there were some to our right flank. The withdrawal was ordered by Sergeant Thomas and I think Sergeant Allen was also in the same house at the time. I believe it was obvious that we would not be able to reach our objective in time and we were to filter out in twos and threes to cover each other. I went with another man from my section and we went down hard-packed snow-covered side streets before coming out on the main street, a little north of the Firda factory. On the left-hand side of the road I saw some of our men from I think 6 Troop in a house. They were facing up the street away from the beach and I got a nod of recognition from one of them who was standing in the doorway guarding the entrance to the house and keeping watch to his front. Eventually we pulled back to the embarkation point and then back to the landing ships.

Captain Young later recalled:

We went on until we got quite near the Firda Factory and then we were put into a good solid house on the right of the road by the Colonel who told us to act as a stop in case the Germans counter-attacked down the road. We could see the youth hostel to our left front where there seemed to be firing going on. The Colonel, Captain Head, Second Lieutenant Giles and I held a conference in the garden behind a wooden fence. The Colonel handed over to me and told me to fall back not later than 1310. Captain Bradley who was also turned up, was ordered to destroy the Firda Factory which he obviously could not do because he had only one man, Trooper Habron, with him and no demolition material. My own party consisted of five Troopers and Sergeant Herbert. He and Trooper Mapplebeck were armed with Tommy guns. We saw no more Germans and as time was marching on we eventually withdrew back to the landing craft.

Meanwhile further south back in the town the job of destroying the installations that the Commandos had come for was well underway. The fish oil factories were of particular importance because as well as producing glycerine, used in the manufacture of explosives, it is also a rich source of vitamins A and B. These would have been of benefit to the submarine arm of the German Navy, to compensate for their lack of exposure to sunshine. The stocks of oil at the canning factory at the southern end of Vaagso was set on fire and produced a huge blaze. Additionally Major Churchill had sent a party to Deknepol to destroy the herring oil factory there. The last German opposition in the northern part of South Vaagso had been eliminated by around 12.30 p.m., and enabled the search and demolition operations to be carried out unhindered.

This has now told the story of most of the Commando assault forces except Group 5, this was to go further north up the Ulvesund and disrupt communications and prevent any German movement south. This group consisting of around half a troop from No 2 Commando led by Captain D Birney and were carried on two of the accompanying destroyers HMS *Onslow* and HMS *Oribi*. Their voyage up the Ulvesund started at about 9.45 a.m. and there are two parts of the story to tell here. Firstly the actions of the commandos on shore and then what happened to the two naval ships.

First steaming up the narrow channel between Maaloy and South Vaagso the two ships, with HMS *Oribi* leading and her sister ship *Onslow* following, were heading for a place called Rodberg about three miles north of South Vaagso. They were to land their cargoes of commandos using boats from the ships themselves. Once ashore this small group was to crater the road between North and South Vaagso and generally cause as much nuisance as they could. The landing was completely unopposed and the required

47. HMS *Oribi* steaming up the narrow passage between Vaagso and
Maaloy during Operation Archery December 1941. (IWM N548)

craters were duly blown in the road, additionally one Norwegian Quisling (Johan Setland) was captured and perhaps more importantly a group went into North Vaagso and destroyed the telephone exchange there. This severely hampered German efforts to find out what was happening in South Vaagso. While the commandos were busy on land, the two destroyers were not missing out on the action. In fact ships were seen in the Ulvesund even before the commandos had been landed. The first ships were seen steaming northwards and it was believed they were two German merchant ships and an armed trawler. Soon after this sighting, the two destroyers went past a ship anchored close to the shore, it was a ship of about 2,000 tons called the *Eismeer* and as they passed the crew waved the Dutch flag to try and show they were friendly. Additionally many Norwegians recognised the ships for what they were and cheered them. The three ships up ahead ignored all requests to heave to and rounding a place called Brandhaevnes Point, all beached themselves. Nearing them the destroyers opened fire on them and they were identified as follows:

- The *Norma* (merchant steamer) 2,200 tons
- The *Regmar Edzard Fritzen* (merchant steamer) 3,000 tons
- The *Föhn* (armed trawler) 250 tons

The reader will probably recall that we have met the *Föhn* before, armed with twin Oerlikon cannons, she had probably damaged a Hampden earlier in the day causing an own goal on an ALC. Now she had shepherded the other two merchant ships northwards up the Ulvesund. It was decided at about 10.00 a.m. to send a party from HMS *Onslow* to board both of them, first the *Föhn* and then the *R.E. Fritzen*. Both of the ships had in theory been abandoned by their crews, but from the shore line they sniped at the boarding party, which was led by Lieutenant-Commander A de Costabadie, a member of Mountbatten's planning staff who had been allowed to come on the raid as an observer and liaison officer. When he got to the bridge he found that the ship's captain, *Leutnant zur See* Lohr, had been killed in the process of trying to throw the ship's confidential code books over the side. He had most likely been killed by fire from HMS *Onslow*. This was the major intelligence coup of Operation Archery, as they revealed the call signs of every German vessel in Norway and France, together with challenges, countersigns and emergency signals. It was a most useful find as there was every reason to hope the Germans would believe that the books had in fact been dropped into the water in the lead-weighted bag supplied for such an emergency situation. After this seizure, de Costabadie took up an abandoned rifle and started to take pot-shots at the crew of the *Föhn* on the shore line. They were soon driven off as a result of fire from the boarding party assisted by a few well-placed shells from the destroyers.

However, Sub-Lieutenant M Vaux went ashore with four men and did take 17 other German merchant seamen prisoner, who somewhat foolishly had remained in the area. The rest under Lieutenant-Commander de Costabadie then boarded the *Fritzen*. It is said that upon finding a locked cupboard in the captain's cabin, de Costabadie fired a shot from his pistol at the lock, which broke the lock but the repercussion also broke three bottles of brandy inside. The next ship to be boarded was the supposedly Dutch vessel the *Eismeer*, but was found to be crewed by Germans. As de Costabadie and his party approached the ship in a whaler, they were fired at from the shore, and one of the oarsmen was killed. They managed to get aboard and tried to raise the anchor but were prevented by small arms fire from the shore. The commander of HMS *Onslow*, Captain

Armstrong, realising that it was all becoming a bit of a stalemate, called the boarding party back and then the *Eismeer* was sunk by gunfire. Then one of the few German aircraft to appear over the Ulvesund that day was shot down by the *Onslow*. Captain Armstrong writing shortly afterwards in his report: "Yesterday was excellent for a new ship. At one moment we were sinking a merchant vessel with the after 4.7, covering the military with the foremost 4.7, engaging aircraft with the 4 inch. The close range weapons were covering the landing party against German snipers. Unfortunately there was no torpedo target."

Then up ahead two other merchantmen could be seen steaming southwards down the Ulvesund towards the two destroyers. One was an armed tug, the *Rechtenfleth* (200 tons) and the other the *Anita L. M. Russ* (2,800 tons). The *Anita L. M. Russ* flashed a signal at the *Oribi*, who replied in kind, thus momentarily deceiving the crew of the Russ. Suddenly the two German ships realised the other ships were British and both turned away, one to port and the other to starboard. Both ships ran aground and were destroyed by gunfire. Some of the crews were picked up and admitted that they had first thought the destroyers were Germans, they soon found out their mistake. Soon after this the commandos re-embarked on the ships after doing their mischief ashore. This group suffered no casualties. Another armed trawler, the *Donner*, was boarded by a party from HMS *Offa* in open waters near the entrance to Ulvesund and later sunk after everything of intelligence value had been removed.

We will now return to the HQ Group of No 3 Commando and Lieutenant Colonel Durnford-Slater somewhere close to the middle of the town of South Vaagso. Durnford-Slater was now on this third commando raid and was still waiting to really get to grips with the Germans. By around 11.00 a.m. with all the reinforcements that were available ashore in South Vaagso there was not much else Durnford-Slater could do except perhaps go and have a look himself at what was happening at the sharp end. Accompanied by his signal officer Captain Head and two orderlies, Corporal Barrington and Sapper Allen, he set off towards the sounds of battle. It was the first time Durnford-Slater had been under fire but with his pistol in hand, he walked briskly up the main street, not looking to either the left or right. It is reported that Captain Head suggested that "You keep a lookout for snipers on the left, Sir, and I'll take the right". Durnford-Slater is reported to have snapped back, "Lookout nothing. I'm in a hurry." He and Captain Head reached the Ulvesund Hotel, which was one of the first sticking points. The after-raid report stated, "His two orderlies were both wounded, but with great coolness and complete disregard for personal safety, he reorganised his forces and directed a northward drive through the town until, when he judged the situation to be well in hand, he left Captain Young in charge and returned to report progress to the flagship."

A slightly different version of some of the exploits of Durnford-Slater can be seen from the following comment:

> The Colonel had collected together some members of 2 and 6 Troops and was leading them forward. A German sailor emerged from a side lane and threw a stick grenade at us. He dived into a doorway and only got minor shrapnel wounds but his two orderlies were both more seriously wounded. Sergeant Mills then went towards the German with his rifle at the advance position. This sailor shouted "Nein, nein". Mills replied "Ja, ja", and shot him. The Colonel went up to Mills and

said "Well, Mills, you shouldn't really have done that," but that was all that was said about the incident.

The attacks on the Ulvesund Hotel and the red warehouse were successful and it is probably fair to say that soon after noon all opposition in South Vaagso had been neutralised. However, for some time before this ALCs had been ferrying wounded, prisoners (including Quislings) and Norwegians who wished to serve in the Free Norwegian Forces out to the *Prince Charles* and *Prince Leopold*. The list of military material destroyed included all the German offices in the town, the radio station and transmitting/receiving mast, numerous German vehicles, four commandeered Belgian artillery pieces, one anti-aircraft gun, one tank, an ammunition dump, one searchlight and finally all the barrack huts used by the German military. In addition the following civilian targets – but these of course had virtually became 100% geared to German military use – the main fish canning factory in South Vaagso and the herring oil factory at Mortenes, had both been completely demolished. Other industrial targets such as the Firda factory in South Vaagso and two other fish by-product factories were left blazing from end to end. In addition the Sternes lighthouse at the southern end of South Vaagso and two telephone exchanges were put out of action. It was estimated after the raid that damage to the extent of 5,000,000 Kroner had been caused.

There is still one element of this tri-service combined operation yet to be looked at – the air-support side of things. Almost for the first time a commando raid was within range of a number of different aircraft to provide in theory both bomber and fighter support. The RAF certainly supported this operation by allocating a number of aircraft flying at almost the extreme limit of their range. The first sight of the RAF that day was on their way to bomb the artillery battery located on Maaloy. There were ten Hampdens from No 50 Squadron and these were led by Wing Commander A Willetts. Their first task was to bomb a German coastal battery at Rugsundo (about 5 miles to the south-east of the Ulvesund), which they did although not well enough to completely put it out of action. They later went to Maaloy to drop a smoke screen to cover the commandos landing there and at South Vaagso. Remember the problems encountered by one of the Hampdens while dropping its smoke bombs? Willetts circled around and watched the naval bombardment of Maaloy. The battery at Rugsundo continued to fire at the naval fleet in the Ulvesund and Willetts later commented on this shelling, "While I was looking at the bombardment of Maaloy, I saw what looked like red-hot meteors streaking out from the Rugsundo battery, I could watch the whole length of their flight from the mouth of the gun to the moment when they burst in the sea, when they gave off a cloud of purple smoke."

After a couple of minutes HMS *Kenya* opened fire on this battery to the south-east and this battery remained a thorn in the side of the naval ships for most of the morning. Opening fire at sporadic intervals, she managed to keep firing until finally silenced around 1.30 p.m. by then she had managed to hit HMS *Kenya* twice, one of these hitting her just above the waterline below the bridge.

As well as the Hampden bombing support, three other elements made up the RAF contribution. One was the bombing of the closest German fighter airfield at a place called Herdla. Secondly was general fighter support over the Ulvesund, and finally a general diversionary raid off Stavanger. The attack on Herdla airfield (about 80 miles south of Vaagso) was apparently very successful. Thirteen Blenheims were detailed to bomb this base at noon, the runway at this base was made of wooden decking and it was felt if bombs could be dropped on it, it would render it unsuitable for take-off or landing. For once the bombing was spot on and several large craters were blown in the runway, indeed it was seen that one Me 109 fell into one crater on its take-off run. It must be presumed that this aircraft was either taking off for Vaagso or to attack the 13 Blenheims. It is reported that the runway was out of action for several days. Given the experience of Hampdens and Blenheims in the war to date when in combat with Messerschmitts it is fortunate that none took off otherwise RAF losses would have been greater than they actually were. The losses on this particular element of the raid were two Blenheims, after they collided into each other after one or both of them were hit by flak from guns around the airfield.

It should be remembered that whilst the dark winter days were ideal cover for the ships and the commandos, this had the reverse effect for the RAF. Northern Scotland, where most of the air support was flying from, is a far from hospitable place at the best of times and in December 1941 it lived up to all expectations. Most of the aircraft were lucky to even get off the ground. Readers may recall the severe storms which affected the ships on their voyage to the Shetland Islands. This also affected the airfields and on the day before the operation a blizzard hit most of northern Scotland and on the morning of 27th December most aircraft had several inches of hard-frozen snow on their wings. This had to be cleared off as best as it could be. The RAF did their best to fly a standing air patrol over the Ulvesund from around 9.00 a.m. till 4.00 p.m., they managed to achieve nearly 100% air cover, no mean feat when some aircraft had to fly 300 miles just to get to the area. This was provided by Blenheims and Beaufighters from RAF Wick and RAF Sumburgh. The first casualty was a Blenheim shot down soon after 10.00 a.m. after an aerial combat with at least two Me 109s. In all on this day 7 Blenheims were lost, four from 110 Squadron, two from 114 and one from 254 Squadron.

Here is a comment from Flight Lieutenant B Rose a pilot from 254 Squadron:

> When we were still about 100 miles off the Norwegian coast, we could see smoke. It was a dirty browny-black colour and went up to about 4000 feet in a thick cloud. So we had no trouble in making a landfall. When we arrived the landing zone was in the process of being evacuated. Maaloy seemed to be a heap of ruins with smoke coming up from every part of it. The town of Vaagso was burning fiercely and we could see flames shooting from what appeared to be factories and oil dumps, the commandos had certainly done a nice job of work.

Some Junkers 88's were also sent to the area but these were beaten off by some Beaufighters, a more suitable aircraft for a combat air patrol than a Blenheim. There were no more losses until the afternoon when two Beaufighters were shot down. However, in spite of the inadequacies of the aircraft the main objective of stopping the Luftwaffe from bombing either the ships or the commandos ashore was achieved. The most serious and largest attack came in the early afternoon when a number of German medium bombers, Heinkel He 111s, tried to attack the British forces. They were driven off by a combination of anti-aircraft fire from the ships and the fighters. Four Heinkels were claimed as destroyed and all the bombs were dropped wide of the ships, which must be assumed were the main target. The final RAF action was to launch a diversionary raid against the port of Stavanger with the additional aim of attacking any shipping found near the port. This raid was launched and even if it did not cause a great deal of damage, it certainly had the effect of diverting German eyes away from Vaagso and Maaloy.

It appears that the Luftwaffe reaction was probably a bit slow, RAF aircraft flying into Norwegian airspace over the previous two years was probably a rare occurrence. The Germans were probably therefore taken completely by surprise and slow to react. All in all the air cover option had been a big gamble for the RAF, sending some unsuitable aircraft (Blenheims in particular) to do the job of fighter, and these had ended up suffering fairly heavy losses. It was another example of how difficult it was to get modern aircraft to cover combined operations. No 2 Group RAF, which had supplied the majority of the Blenheims, suffered the heaviest number of casualties since mid-October 1941 when seven aircraft were lost whilst attacking enemy shipping. Two of these Squadrons, 110 and 114, had suffered a total of 27 aircraft losses in 1941. Another sobering statistic is that from the crews of these 27 aircraft only one man had survived.

The attrition rate of these obsolete aircraft did give cause for concern, another example following on from the Battle of France in 1940, when the Fairey Battle fleet had been reduced from 135 to 72 in two days. In four actions trying to bomb pontoon bridges around Sedan in May 1940 60 out of 108 aircraft were lost, a monstrous 55% loss rate.

Back at South Vaagso, the raid was coming to an end, and around 3.00 p.m. when it was felt everything that could be done had been achieved, the commandos started to withdraw back to their transports. For the first hour or so the armada was escorted by Beaufighters; it did of course get dark quite early in Norway at that time of year. One German aircraft did try to attack the ships but this was again beaten off.

Contemplating his first taste of action on the way back was the 20 year old Private Charles Stacey, who also felt a bit guilty. As a member of 3 Troop No 3 Commando he had moved through the outskirts of the town and in the early minutes had cause to enter one of the houses and realised he had left his gloves behind. As he commented:

> I saw a pair of black and white woolen gloves next to the family Christmas tree and slipped them into my pocket knowing they might be vital in keeping the chill from my trigger finger. None of the people in the house spoke English and I've always remembered the concerned face of a little girl. I think I must have knocked the gloves off the tree as I passed it and picked them up and popped them in my pocket. I do recall it being freezing cold outside with heaps of snow on the ground and as a sniper it was always a problem trying to keep your trigger finger warm. It was just instinct.

For the next 64 years between the day Charles left Vaagso and his first return visit in 2005, he carried the nagging feeling of unfinished business, an unopened Christmas present to be replaced. In May 2005 Charles and seven other veterans were invited back to commemorate the raid and also the 60th anniversary of (for the Norwegians) liberation. On the journey back to Vaagso Charles took with him a pair of woolen gloves in a symbolic attempt to return the gift reluctantly borrowed in his hour of need all those years ago. Taking a short break from the official celebrations, he tracked down the house where he and his fellow commandos had been. The first time he knocked on the door he spoke to a young girl who appeared not to understand his English. Undeterred he returned the next day when the door was opened by the same person who had stared at him on that chaotic morning 64 years ago. Charles commented,

> It was an incredible moment. I didn't even have to explain myself. The little girl who had answered the door the day before must have understood what I was saying and passed it on to her grandmother, the girl I had seen during the raid in 1941. When she answered the door she said; "I've been expecting you, I knew you were going to come." We had a big hug and it was so nice, so warm and natural despite all those years. I've always had at the back of my mind to make up for that little misdemeanour; to put it right. Now that I have, it feels like I have completed the circle.

That 'little girl' was Anne Osmunsvaag who at the time of the raid was three years old, and along with her brother Andreas still vividly remember the events of December 1941.

As on the raid to the Lofoten Islands in March 1941 a number of cameramen were taken to gain propaganda material for consumption at home. One of this group was a civilian, John Ramsden of Movietone News, who had managed to talk his way onto the raid as an old colleague from Fleet Street was now in the Army Film Unit. Soon after the raid he recorded,

> It was the most exciting job I've ever been on and I've been around quite a lot. I had no special orders, I just shot from cover like the commandos, except they shot to kill and I shot to give the operation life. However, my best moment was on the way across which was pretty rough. On one of my many trips to the ships rail, I was next to one of the toughest commandos and I don't know what I looked like but he looked pretty green.

The returning ships from Operation Archery arrived back in Scapa Flow in the Orkneys on 28th December after a pretty uneventful journey. Some of the commandos who had been killed on the raid and some of the seriously wounded who died on the way back were buried at sea. There was also time for reflection for those who had been in action as Private Charles Stacey recalled:

> I was inordinately tired at the end of the action. Lots of us, including me, had never seen a German soldier before or been in action. The prospect of immediate bodily contact during the desperate close-quarter fighting was over and I relaxed once we got on board the *Prince Charles*. It was reaction, I suppose, and I remember, when the bombers were overhead and one of the boilers was put out of commission on the ship when a bomb fell really close, that I was quite happy to leave the rest of the fighting with the anti-aircraft guns to the very efficient Navy personnel. On the voyage home, I was sobered quite a bit when we were on deck at evening time and the body of Captain Giles, sewn and weighted in heavy canvas, slid slowly off a plank erected on the depth charges at the aft end of the ship. It slid down into

the depths through the churning wake of the vessel on his very last journey and I remember the scene so very well. The cold air, the Union Jack which covered the bodies before they were consigned to the deep, the short prayers of committal, and the intensity of those present. I do recall that we listened to Lord Haw-Haw on the German radio on the way back and he announced that nearly all of the attacking force had been bombed out of existence and I remember how this was greeted with roars of laughter. We were looking forward to our return to Largs, leave (perhaps) and our first Scottish Hogmanay, and girls and wives for those who possessed them.

So before drawing up a balance sheet for the operation, I will briefly give some details about Operation Anklet, the diversionary raid for Vaagso again aimed at the Lofoten Islands. 223 men from No 12 (Irish and Welsh) Commando and a number of attached men from the Free Norwegian Forces all under the command of Lieutenant Colonel S Harrison landed at 6.00 a.m. on Boxing Day 1941. As had been planned at Vaagso this time was chosen in the expectation that the German garrison would be caught off guard after the Christmas festivities of the day before. The naval element consisted of a cruiser HMS *Arethusa*, a landing ship HMS *Prins Albert*, 8 destroyers (2 Polish Navy) and a number of minesweepers and corvettes all under the command of Admiral L Hamilton. The landings were in a different place than the previous March, aimed at two ports on the westerly island of Moskenesoy. The commandos went ashore clad for the first time in white hooded snow suits, and the two towns of Reine and Moskenes were soon

48. A wounded commando being evacuated to a waiting
ALC at South Vaagso. (National Archives)

secured and a small number of Germans and Quislings taken prisoner. The German radio station at Glaapen was raided and demolished, with the detachment of Germans there taken prisoner. There was very little resistance to the commandos. An additional bonus particularly for the locals was the discovery of the German garrison's hoard of French chocolates and cigarettes, together with pork and wine and many of these were distributed to grateful locals. However there was concern about German reprisals and many locals wanted the British to stay, which of course was totally out of the question. Admiral Hamilton in overall charge was considering an extended stay, the main threat it was felt coming from the air, although this was mitigated by the fact that this far north there was no daylight between 10th December and 3rd January. However a German seaplane did appear over the islands on 27th December and dropped a bomb (which did no damage) close to the *Arethusa*, so the decision was taken to withdraw back to Britain. On this raid two radio transmitters were destroyed, a German armed trawler was sunk and 29 Germans and some Quislings taken prisoner. Two Norwegian coastal steamers were commandeered with the intention of sailing them back to Britain but had to be abandoned due to lack of coal to fuel them. 266 locals volunteered to come back with the commandos to join the Free Norwegian Forces.

49. A commando surveys burning buildings at Maaloy, while across the sound another building burns. (National Archives)

50. The memorial to the 52 dead of Operation Archery on Maaloy Island. (O-A Langstøyl)

Not all the men destined to go on Operation Anklet made it to the Lofotens. The ship that Lieutenant C Purdon and his men were travelling on suffered a series of engine failures and struggled to make progress. This group clad in their new shiny snow suits were looking forward to going into action but found it a very frustrating time. To make matters worse about halfway between the Shetlands and Norway their ship met the main force sailing back. Corran Purdon commented that as a result of him complaining long and hard to his CO he was told he would definitely go on the next operation.

Whether it diverted any German eyes away from Vaagso is doubtful, but it certainly made the Germans think that a raid could be undertaken virtually anywhere in Norway. The force suffered no casualties and returned unscathed back to Britain.

Both sides issued communiqués about the raid on 28th December 1941. The one from London stated:

On Saturday, 27th December, a small-scale raid, mainly against enemy shipping, was carried out on the Norwegian coast by the combined force of the Royal Navy, Army and RAF. The operation was entirely successful in all respects and all of our ships returned fit for immediate service.

A further communiqué will be issued as soon as details are available.

The Berlin version said,

British naval forces on 27th December attempted a surprise attack at two remote points of the Norwegian coast. After brief violent engagements the British landing detachments were ejected by local patrols of the Army and Navy. The British landing detachments retired to their ships.

German bombers sank a destroyer of the fleeing warship formation. A cruiser and another destroyer were damaged. Ten enemy bombers were shot down in air fights and by our anti-aircraft artillery.

During the approach of the enemy, the German patrol boat *Föhn* was attacked by numerous bombers. The patrol boat shot down one enemy bomber and then was lost in heroic struggle against the superior fire of a British cruiser and several destroyers. Some Norwegian merchant ships which were engaged in peaceful coast traffic were attacked and sunk by the British.

So what can be said about Operation Archery? It is fair to say it was both a successful and instructive raid. Successful because most of the tactical targets had been achieved, there had been much material damage done as previously outlined. As well as this 98 Germans were brought back to Britain and 70 locals volunteered to return to Britain. A number of Germans had been killed in the raid, but it is difficult to be precise about German casualties. One report says that of the army garrison at South Vaagso, who were there over the Christmas period, 11 were killed, 7 wounded and 16 stated as missing. The marine detachment lost 6. Every man on Maaloy was either killed or captured and the Germans had great difficulty in later working out what had happened due to the almost total absence of any reliable witnesses. The figure including seamen from the ships that were sunk probably points to a German killed figure of 140 to 150. Nine ships had been sunk with a total tonnage of around 15,000 tons.

The casualties amongst the commandos were two officers and eleven men killed with six officers and forty six men wounded with five later dying of wounds sustained on the operation. Additionally the Free Norwegian Forces suffered one officer killed and two men wounded. This gives a total casualty figure for the commandos of 68. The Royal Navy had two men killed. The total figure for all services who died on Operation Archery are today recorded on a memorial on Maaloy – it has 52 names on it. The RAF

51. German prisoners being escorted back to the beaches. The commando on the left looking towards the camera is Sergeant Chitty, the Provost Sergeant of No 3 Commando. (National Archives)

casualties include men from Australia, Canada and New Zealand. This points to the first time in the war so far that in an operation of this kind all three services had worked together in one harmonious pattern and sung off the same hymn-sheet. It showed that given close co-operation a relatively well-defended enemy garrison could be assaulted and overcome. However, this is not to say that everyone on the Allied side was happy; the Norwegian Prime Minister in exile, Mr. John Nygaardsvold expressed his concerns and commented,

> Who could be so blind as to delude himself that this effort could have done anything to shorten the ordeal of Norway? Undoubtedly the enemy had been annoyed by the very impudence of the operation lancing deep into the shoreline he sought to secure, but it could only have one result: the Germans would now strengthen their defences making the ultimate victory even harder to achieve than it would have been if the raid had never taken place.

In one respect the comments were quite right, in that it did convince the Germans to beef up their troop levels in Norway. However, since the Allies at that stage had no intention of invading Norway it certainly achieved the strategic aim of moving troops from other areas to a quiet backwater. If Nygaardsvold was upset, the Germans and in particular Hitler were infuriated. Even before Operation Archery he was of the opinion that Norway was a likely candidate for an Allied invasion especially after the American entry to the war earlier in December 1941. As a result of his interest the High Command in Berlin had ordered a fresh appreciation of the troop levels in Norway. The commander in Norway, General von Falkenhorst, had already requested an additional 12,000 troops to bring the divisions he had up to their full fighting strength and an extra three complete divisions to increase his reserves and give more depth to his defensive plans. Following on close behind this request from General von Falkenhorst was the news that his very command had been raided not once but twice and that a ship carrying troops home on leave to Germany had been sunk by a mine, apparently British, off the Norwegian coast. Hitler lost no time in demanding a full report from his military chiefs. Foremost in his mind was that this was all a precursor to a larger British landing to disrupt the German war machine even more. It is worth remembering that Norway was supplying quite a lot of vital raw materials to Germany at this time. Hitler commented before the end of 1941,

> If the British go about things properly, they will attack northern Norway at several points. By means of an all-out attack by their fleet and ground troops, they will try to displace us there, take Narvik if possible, and thus exert pressure on Sweden and Finland. This might be of decisive importance for the outcome of the war. The German fleet must therefore use all its forces for the defence of Norway. It would be expedient to transfer all battleships and pocket-battleships there for this purpose.

There were such ships, the *Scharnhorst* and *Gneisenau*, many hundreds of miles away in the French Atlantic port of Brest, and if the High Command hoped that Hitler would forget what he said, they were wrong. In mid-January 1942 Hitler sent for Admiral Raeder (head of the German Navy) and told him, "Norway is the zone of destiny in this war. I demand unconditional obedience to my commands and directives concerning the defence of this area". This meant that the ships would have to go. The battleship *Tirpitz* sailed from its then base in the Baltic to Norway soon after this and then on 11th February 1942, *Scharnhorst*, *Gneisenau* and *Prinz Eugen* left Brest. Taking advantage of some horrible weather they made a dash up the English Channel. In the Straits of Dover *Gneisenau* was badly damaged and had to stop off in Kiel for repairs. She was later attacked by Bomber Command but again repaired and eventually joined the *Scharnhorst* in Norway. The *Prinz Eugen* reached Trondheim, but on the way she had also suffered damage from a torpedo attack, which took off one of her rudders and was compelled to return to Germany for repairs. Even though there was some flak directed towards the services in the papers about the so-called 'Channel Dash', the Admiralty was probably happier with these ships in Norway, as they were easier to monitor and keep out of the North Atlantic. Later on in March and April 1942 two other capital ships, the *Admiral Hipper* and *Lützow* joined them.

The German Army was not forgotten either and General von Falkenhorst got almost all he asked for. First, his 12,000 reinforcements arrived, closely followed by 18,000 men organised into fortress battalions. An armoured division was also formed to act as a mobile reserve. Additionally new equipment was sent to replace the captured weaponry mainly used, an example being the Belgian 75mm guns on Maaloy and Russian guns used at Rugsundo to fire at HMS *Kenya*. In February 1942 *Generalfeldmarschall* List, made an inspection tour of Norway as Hitler's personal representative. As a result of his report three more divisional commands were established, more coastal artillery was deployed and more static defensive positions built. By the time of the Normandy invasion in June 1944 nearly 400,000 German troops were stationed in Norway, a response out of all proportion to the less than 1,000 commandos who raided the Lofotens and South Vaagso. Indeed Hitler still feared an invasion of Norway right up to the end and those 400,000 troops were still there in May 1945. Men from the 1st Airborne Division plus a few other troops were sent there to disarm them after the German surrender, but that's another story. The raid on South Vaagso was the last big raid on Norwegian territory, perhaps as a result of Nygaardsvold's comments. However two more small raids were undertaken against Norway and these will be looked at in a later chapter.

Attention now turned towards France as a more suitable target as it was within reasonable range for air cover. This is perhaps one of the great lessons of the 1941 raids as was the need for close co-operation between the three services, especially in the planning stages of operations.

Chapter 8

Bomber Command and the Radar War 1939–1942

After war broke out in 1939, in common with most of the other British armed forces, the RAF was somewhat unprepared for what was to happen over the next few years. Whilst it was realised during the height of the appeasement period in the mid 1930s that the RAF would have to be expanded and more modern aircraft put into service, this was a lot easier to say than put into practice. It was normal in those days for it to take an aircraft around 5 years to get from the drawing board to front-line service. For example, in 1935 the majority of Bomber Command's front-line strength was based on aircraft designs from the Great War. Examples would be the Heyford, the Hart and the Hind. Several new bombers had been planned in 1932 and these were the Whitley, Hampden and Wellington, but in 1935 they were not yet ready for mass production. These were planned to be 'heavy' bombers and there were also plans for two light bombers – the Battle and the Blenheim. However, by 1939 these aircraft basically formed the main offensive capability of Bomber Command. In 1936 specifications were drawn up and sent out to the aircraft industry for designs for a four-engined heavy bomber and a two-engined medium bomber. From these came the Short Stirling, the Handley Page Halifax and the Avro Lancaster and the twin-engined Manchester. Indeed there was some hostility to the idea of four-engined bombers not only for the strain on the engine manufacturers but also a larger maintenance force. However these reservations were overcome and eventually all these four aircraft came into service, although the plan stated that it would take until 1943 for the Whitley, Hampden and Wellington to be phased out.

When war broke out in 1939 Bomber Command had thirty-three operational squadrons, sixteen were light or medium (ten Battle and six Blenheim) and seventeen heavy squadrons (six each with Wellingtons and Hampdens and five with Whitleys). It was not long before Bomber Command was tasked with operating over enemy airspace, although in a limited capacity. There were a number of reasons for this limited offensive. It had been predicted in the inter-war years that the manned, self-defending bomber would always get through to its target and rain a hail of high explosive from the sky on the belligerent's cities, ports and industry. Indeed the majority of the high command in Britain felt that the German Luftwaffe was vastly superior in number and could therefore wreak more havoc than the RAF. So if an onslaught from the air could be delayed for a time, then time would be gained to build up the fighter and air defence resources of the RAF. Time would also be gained to build up Bomber Command. In fact the option of expanding Bomber Command would in the early days lead to a contraction of front-line strength. Instructors and aircraft would have to be found to train new recruits and work up the reserves. Most of these could only be found from the operational squadrons. A high rate of casualties in the remaining squadrons before the new recruits were trained would not only virtually turn Bomber Command into a toothless weapon but might endanger the entire future for it. It must be remembered that the RAF still had lots of enemies in the Joint Chiefs of Staff, with both the Army and the Navy feeling the RAF would be better off under their command, either in the shape of Army Co-operation Regiments or amalgamated into the Fleet Air Arm. The need to conserve and expand Bomber Command was, at the outset, second only to the need to avert defeat.

The RAF were certainly helped in the early days by the fact that in spite of many attempts to try and agree on a 'Geneva Convention' for the air, nothing was ever settled. So whilst there were elaborate rules and regulations for the conduct of war on land and sea under the Geneva Convention, the Second World War opened with in theory no limitations at all on the use of bomber aircraft. This led to an appeal in the early part of September 1939 by the US President, Roosevelt, for all the belligerents to refrain from unrestricted air warfare.

The policy of the Bomber Barons in the high command of the RAF was based on the idea that the proper (and to some the only use) of an aircraft in war was to strike at the enemy's means of production and deprive his armed forces of the raw materials with which to wage war. Civilian targets were to be avoided at all costs. In theory if this was carried out successfully the defeat of the enemy forces in a land battle would automatically follow. With the benefit of hindsight it seems that nothing had been learned from the previous unpleasantness in 1915. For example, during research for a previous book on the Gallipoli campaign, I found a statement that suggested if the Royal Navy sent a couple of battleships up the Dardanelles to Istanbul and bombarded the only munitions factory it was believed the Turks possessed, their surrender would shortly follow. It is not the place here to look in detail at that campaign but the Royal Navy battleships got nowhere near Istanbul thanks to stiff Turkish resistance at the mouth of the Dardanelles and the Gallipoli campaign was little short of a total disaster.

Soon after the Roosevelt initiative the French Government asked Britain not to bomb any German land targets because they were more likely to suffer the retaliation. Britain agreed to both the American and French requests, probably pleased to have more time to build up her bomber assets. However, this is not to say the RAF did not do anything. Soon after noon on 3rd September a reconnaissance flight by a Blenheim from 139 Squadron over the German Naval bases around Wilhemshaven was undertaken. Although this aircraft found several ships at anchor, this information didn't immediately get back to England. When the wireless operator attempted to send a message back he found that his radio had frozen and he was unable to transmit. By the time the Blenheim got back it was too late to launch an attack that day so a raid was planned for the next day to 'knock the German Fleet out of the war'. Also that night ten Whitleys flew to the Ruhr area in Germany to drop propaganda leaflets on what became known as Nickel operations.

So on the afternoon of the 4th September between 3.00 and 4.00 p.m. fourteen Wellingtons and fifteen Blenheims took off from airfields in East Anglia heading for the north German coast. It should be remembered that in those days each squadron flew independently of any other squadrons tasked. On the outward flight rain and cloud caused most of the bombers to lose their positions in their respective formations. Added to this problem were navigational difficulties and five Blenheims and five Wellingtons returned back to their bases having been unable to find any targets. Three more nearly bombed British warships but turned away when these ships showed the correct recognition colours. These three also returned without having bombed anything. One more aircraft, to put it kindly, suffered severe navigational difficulties and bombed the Danish port of Esbjerg and killed several civilians. The British Government had to apologise to the-then neutral Danes and paid compensation for the deaths and damage. This aircraft was 110 miles out in its navigation. It is similar to an aircraft being told to fly from Edinburgh to bomb Cardiff and ending up dropping its bombs on London. It is reported that due to the problems those aircraft that did find the correct area attacked individually, thus offering the German gunners good targets. Forced by the low cloud to bomb from around 500 feet it is believed fifteen aircraft actually attacked. The attacks were gallantly pressed home with the battleship *Scheer* being hit by at least three bombs, but these all failed to explode, while other hits on the cruiser *Emden* caused only slight damage. Five Blenheims and two Wellingtons were shot down. The Operational Record Book of Bomber Command HQ includes for this raid the following comment: "An eyewitness account obtained from secret sources shows that the action by the Blenheims was a most gallant affair and according with the best traditions of the Royal Air Force." This rhetoric may have been fine, but the facts were that almost 50% of the force that set out had failed to find in daylight a target 270 miles from England and of those which did find the target almost 50% again had been lost. It was perhaps a disappointing start but it did nothing to defeat the theory that the self-defending bomber formation was still valid as a few fighter attacks had been beaten off. It was thought by the bomber theorists that the principal reasons for the failure of the raid had been the formation keeping and target finding in poor weather. However, in the cold light of day if it was considered that out of thirty aircraft despatched seven had failed to return – this was a loss rate of 23%, thus it was possible that the entire strength of Bomber Command could be lost in five operations. Over the next few weeks and months care was taken to follow the pre-war doctrine of attacking only military targets which limited attacks to naval targets actually at sea, as ships in ports were deemed to be too close to civilians to risk attack.

Some aircraft were sent over Germany in the winter of 1939-1940 but the majority of them carried nothing more dangerous than bundles of leaflets on Nickel operations. Even if these did not achieve anything and did lead to losses they were allowed to continue because they gave the aircrews some valuable operational experience.

The mode of actual operating was at the time pretty crude as this comment from a member of 61 Squadron recalls:

We flew on operations independently, not in formation, and there would probably be only six crews from the squadron out at any one time. There was no such thing as mass bombing, as we simply did not have the number of aircraft. As far as briefings, before the raids were concerned, the crews were called together in the early evening and simply given details of the target, the weather forecast and the wind directions. Normally it was not difficult to find the target area but almost impossible to be anywhere near a specific target, so we just dropped at an estimated position and hoped for the best.

Even though this comment points out some of the difficulties encountered by the aircrews there was activity going on in the background by a wonderfully named body –

the Air Targets Sub-Committee, who were working out which targets could be attacked in the future. Mainly these consisted of the infrastructure of Germany's power supplies particularly oil refineries, power stations and coal depots. Transport links were also not overlooked and targets included canal locks, railway stations and sidings. However bombing these latter targets ran the risk of causing civilian casualties so the attacks got no further than the planning stage.

Daylight raids continued but at a heavy cost, for example on 29th September 1939 11 Hampdens from 144 Squadron were sent to bomb enemy shipping near Heligoland Two ships were actually found and bombed but without causing them damage. The real damage came when German Me 109s appeared and shot down five Hampdens including that of the squadron commander. From these five aircraft 18 men were killed a staggering 45% loss rate. For a while daylight operations were suspended but the Nickel operations continued with a probably 'satisfactory' 2% loss rate. However, in December some more daylight operations were attempted which again helped and probably finally convinced the RAF that the cost of mixing with the German Luftwaffe in daylight was too high. On 12th December twelve Wellingtons from 99 Squadron were sent out to attack two German cruisers, the *Leipzig* and the *Nürnberg*. Even though the weather was not good, they managed to find the ships and bombed them at low level amid a storm of flak. Then several Me 109s fell upon the Wellingtons, within minutes five had been shot down and another damage, which crashed on landing back in England. This was a 50% loss rate and although it appears one Me 109 had been shot down it was a very small crumb of comfort. Following this, on 18th December 24 Wellingtons from 9, 37 and 149 Squadrons were sent again to Wilhemshaven to attack targets of opportunity, i.e. any shipping they found. Strict instructions were given to fly above 10,000 feet so as avoid the worst of the German flak. Even before they found anything to attack, the Luftwaffe again appeared and within minutes shot down 12 Wellingtons – half the aircraft sent This time two Me 109s were shot down. Obviously this could not continue and the commander of Bomber Commander, Air Chief Marshal Ludlow-Hewitt, was ordered to consider a switch to night bombing, which eventually happened. This of course had its own difficulties which will be briefly mentioned shortly, but daylight operations did continue although on a much-reduced scale. For the next few months whilst the moratorium on bombing targets which might cause civilian casualties was still in force the main focus was on anti-shipping patrols in the North Sea. Also important were the mine-laying flights called 'Gardening', aimed again at disrupting German naval and merchant shipping.

So for the main part of the bomber force it was now necessary to fly by night with all the inherent problems caused by this. We have seen that it had been difficult in daylight for the RAF to find targets in Germany and it was now going to be even more difficult by night. The best method for the RAF navigators at the time was the use of a method called dead reckoning or DR, supplemented by (at night) astro-navigation. This was a method pioneered by sailors many years before and used fixes on stars to plot the position of the aircraft. Both had been taught to the navigators in peacetime but were totally inadequate for war time. In fact it is probably fair to say they had not worked well in peacetime either. It is recorded that in early 1939 a special ten week course was run to try and improve the standards in navigation, and whilst this must have helped, during an exercise in August 1938 more than 40% of the aircraft sent out were unable to find their way to various cities the length and breadth of the UK even in daylight.

Dead Reckoning in theory is simple, using a wind speed of a certain direction and strength, it is possible to plot a course between the airfield and the target. Allowing for the speed of the aircraft and factoring in any deviation due to the wind it is possible to work out the time over the target. Many leaflets were probably dropped at this calculated time over Germany when in practice the aircraft was nowhere near their target. The pilot flies on the plotted course and the flight crew members check progress by using the Mark 1 eyeball to spot places on the ground they should be flying over. This is of course assuming that the effect of wind has been accurately calculated and the wind had not changed direction or strength; also factored into this, has the pilot kept to the correct compass heading? Obviously this is easier in daylight but even then the European weather often stops an aircraft seeing the ground from even relatively low heights. Given these constraints I feel even the most experienced navigator would find flying over Germany at night using DR difficult. This is not to say that astro-navigation was any easier. This relies on fixing the position of the aircraft in relation to the position of certain stars. This requires someone to be skilled in the use of a sextant and also clear skies above the aircraft. Using this method was probably acceptable for sailors in a relatively slowly moving ship, but in an aircraft moving at around 200 mph it was a different matter. By the time the navigator had taken his shots, returned to his position and calculated his position the aircraft would have moved a considerable distance and there would be always a margin of error in the calculations.

A good example of this would be on the night of 19th/20th March 1940 when 50 aircraft, a mixture of Hampdens and Whitleys, were sent to raid a seaplane base on the German island of Sylt (off the western coast of Schleswig-Holstein on the northern peninsula leading to Denmark). During the routine debrief back in England 41 crews claimed to have bombed the base during a bright moonlit night. However, when the photographic reconnaissance aircraft had returned and the pictures studied, the base appeared to have suffered no damage whatsoever. A few days later when the navigation logs were again studied it was found several aircraft had bombed Esbjerg in Denmark. Again the British Government had to issue an apology and pay compensation. Scenes such as this were commonplace until the advent of the real war in May 1940 when the Germans invaded France, Holland and Belgium. One of the turning points in the bombing war was the bombing by the Luftwaffe of Rotterdam in Holland on 14th May 1940. This raid was carried out after a warning calling on the Dutch to surrender otherwise they would suffer complete destruction. It later transpired that the Dutch garrison had surrendered before the raid, and a recall signal did not get through to all the bombers. Much of Rotterdam was laid waste and finally the gloves came off. On the night of 15th/16th May 1940 99 bombers were despatched from Bomber Command with the targets of oil installations and railways in the Ruhr area. In spite of many crews coming back stating they had not only found the right area but actually dropped their bombs right on target, the efficiency of the German war machine was hardly affected. After the withdrawal from France much of the attention of the RAF and the British people was directed towards Fighter Command and the Battle of Britain. Bomber Command was still active in this period, bombing invasion barges in various ports and attacking German troop concentrations and airfields in France.

It is probably fair to say that the Battle of Britain would not have been won without the advantage of radio direction finding (RDF, or in today's language, radar), that enabled ground controllers to know exactly where the enemy were and in roughly what strength. It is difficult to say who discovered the power of radio beams first, as it seems most of the major players were in the pre-war years experimenting amid conditions of great secrecy. The Germans certainly took the steps of developing RDF for both defensive and offensive purposes while the British preferred to use it for home defence only. So as well as the men in the front line waging war, there was an army of scientists battling away on the so-called 'Battle of the Beams'.

During the Great War on many occasions Germany had bombed England, either using Zeppelin airships or Gotha bombers. One attack on London causing 600 casualties. Initially some fighter squadrons were recalled from France to defend London, but once the Germans started flying by night it was virtually impossible for the fighters to find them. The attacks continued for over a year and killed or injured nearly two thousand people, mainly civilians.

Once the war was over in 1918 the lack of success at shooting down any Gothas was virtually forgotten until the mid-1930's when, with a new war being almost inevitable, ways were looked at to defend the mainland of Britain. One of the ideas suggested by the Air Staff was a 'death-ray' to be produced by radio waves. The intention of this was to kill or incapacitate the crews with a secondary objective of disabling the engines of aircraft. This was pretty fanciful stuff and the notion was quickly dispelled by the boffins as it was quickly realised that radio beams of sufficient power to damage humans could not be guaranteed. The man initially charged with looking into death-rays was the Director of Scientific Research at the Air Ministry, Mr H Wimperis. One of the boffins he consulted was the chief of the National Physical Laboratory's Radio Research Station at Slough, Robert Watson-Watt. However it was suggested that whilst a death-ray was totally impracticable, it was possible to use radio beams to search for objects in particular flying aircraft. Watson-Watt was alluding to a system that would work essentially in the same way that a bat uses sound to 'see' in total darkness. The radio transmitter produces strong and extremely short (about a millionth of a second) pulses of radio energy. The pulses are transmitted through the air in a known direction by a directional antenna. When the pulses hit an object, such as an aircraft, ship or the ground, they are reflected back from it. The reflections are received back and can be converted by a receiver to an electrical signal that can be displayed to an operator. Since the speed of the signal is the speed of light, the time between the transmission and the reception of a pulse indicates the distance of the target, and together with knowing the direction at which the antenna transmits, the position of the detected target can be worked out.

After some initial theory meetings, a demonstration was planned and on 26th February 1935, Watson-Watt with three others, set up his equipment in a caravan at Weedon in Northamptonshire, close to the BBC transmitting station at Daventry, which many people drive past on the M1. Using a 10 kilowatt (kw) signal produced from the BBC's short-wave overseas transmitter, the group watched a green spot being deflected on a cathode ray tube as a Heyford bomber flew back and forth on a pre-determined course in the centre of the beam being transmitted from Daventry. It at last proved that the theory of radio location was practicable. An additional research grant of £10,000 was allocated to Watson-Watt and the team moved to Orfordness in Suffolk as it was on a commercial aircraft flying route. By July 1935, an aircraft had been detected and tracked for nearly 40 miles. Refinements to the system followed and by September an aircraft had been detected at a range of 15 miles and its height accurately assessed. More staff and money arrived and by March 1936 the distance at which an aircraft had been detected had been extended to 75 miles. The RAF were most impressed and intended setting up a chain of RDF stations around the coast. The first station in what became known as the Chain Home (CH) stations was opened at RAF Bawdsey, also on the Suffolk coast, south of Orfordness.

Meanwhile on the other side of the North Sea the Germans were also experimenting with radio waves. At the beginning of 1936 an experimental set had managed to detect an aircraft at a range of 28 kilometres (nearly 18 miles). This experimental set developed into a radar known as 'Freya', and at a demonstration to Government and Military officials in July 1938 it detected an aircraft at a range of 90 kms (55 miles). The Germans as well as looking at radio waves for defensive purposes also looked at them for offensive purposes to help their bombers and in this it is fair to say they were years ahead of the British. They developed them in tandem and the majority of their bombers were equipped with a number of bombing aids by 1939. Some early indications to the British scientific community of these aids came in the anonymous Oslo report of 1939. This was a package pushed through the letter box of the British Embassy in Oslo which amongst other things mentioned that the Germans were developing a method of measuring the distance of an aircraft from a ground station by transmitting a modulated radio carrier wave which was picked up by the aircraft, amplified, and re-sent back to the ground station. This ground station could then determine the distance of the aircraft by measuring the delay in the return signal. Whilst this by itself would not pinpoint the aircraft's position, if used in tandem with another ground station or another aid it would pinpoint the position.

The system referred to in the Oslo report and by captured German airmen in February 1940 was known as X-Gerät or X-apparatus. To add to the complexity, another aid then came to light. In April 1940 a scrap of paper was found in a shot-down German bomber with the words 'Radio Beacon Knickebein, from 0600 hours on 315°'. The boffins decided this 'Knickebein' must be a radio device and the bearing must have some significance. The bearing of 315° points directly north-west and made it unlikely to be a bearing from an aircraft. The alternative, it was felt, was that it was a radio beacon pointed in the direction of 315° like a searchlight along which an aircraft could fly to a known location. Indeed a prisoner revealed under interrogation that he thought that Knickebein was something like X-Gerät and involved a beam not more than a kilometre wide directed over London. As it turned out they were both similar systems and Knickebein consisted of two radio beams laid over Britain. If one beam basically ran north-south and the other east-west, they could be made to cross over at a known point. If a bomber pilot flew along the north-south beam, kept on course by two different sounds, dots and dashes, if he flew off track, eventually he came across the point where the beams intersected and another note was sounded, telling the crew that the plane was over the target and the bombs could be dropped.

Other German blind bombing aids were discovered later such as Y-Gerät and attempts made to jam them. There were limitations in the range of these aids due to the curvature of the earth but they were far better than the dead reckoning used by Bomber

Command. Indeed the Luftwaffe carried out several very successful raids using these aids, particularly at Coventry on the night of 14th November 1940. 500 tons of bombs fell that night on Coventry and around 60,000 buildings were destroyed, including more than half of the private homes in the city centre and the cathedral. Over 500 people were killed and 1,200 injured. This raid made people sit up and take note and work started on some blind bombing aids for the RAF similar to those used by the Germans. Three of these were Gee, Oboe and H2S. One of the British scientists who worked on the German aids felt they could give an accuracy of around half a mile. To jump the story forward to mid-1941 there was disquiet amongst several advisers close to Winston Churchill that in spite of the spin put out by the Air Ministry that the bombing war was effective and destroying the targets, this was not quite the case. Around July 1941 Churchill's scientific adviser Lord Cherwell asked a civil servant D Butt to carry out a careful study of photographs taken on recent bombing operations. Starting work in August 1941, Butt examined over 4,000 photographs taken during the course of 100 raids to 28 different locations and came up with some uncomfortable statistics. Not every aircraft had a flash photography camera fitted to their aircraft, in theory only the best crews, and for all targets Butt concluded that of all the aircraft recorded as having attacked their targets, only one-third had got within five miles of it. The percentage of successes, however, varied greatly with the geographical position of the target, the weather conditions and the intensity of the anti-aircraft defences. Over the French ports, he calculated that two-thirds of the aircraft reported to have attacked the target had actually been within five miles. Over the Ruhr the proportion was reduced to one-tenth. His report also contained the opinion that a French port was more than twice as easy to find as a target inside Germany outside the Ruhr, but one there was four times more difficult to locate as one elsewhere in Germany. In full moon conditions, the so-called 'Bomber's Moon', two-fifths of aircraft reported to have attacked the correct target had actually got within five miles of it. Without the benefit of the moonlight the proportion fell to one-fifteenth. This would on its own have been an uncomfortable read for the high command and it would be even worse when they realised that the figures only applied to those aircraft which claimed to have attacked their targets. An additional factor was the five mile rule, which actually became an area of seventy five square miles when correctly applied. Lord Cherwell told Winston Churchill after reading it, "However inaccurate the figures may be, they are sufficiently striking to emphasise the supreme importance of improving our navigational methods."

Churchill laid down quite a lot of importance on the bombing war and as early as July 1940 he had written:

> But when I look round to see how we can win the war I see that there is only one sure path. We have no continental Army which can defeat the German military power. The blockade is broken and Hitler has Asia and probably Africa to draw from. Should he be repulsed here or not try invasion, he will recoil eastward, and we have nothing to stop him. But there is one thing that will bring him back and bring him down, and that is an absolutely devastating, exterminating attack by very heavy bombers from this country upon the Nazi homeland. We must be able to overwhelm them by this means, without which I do not see a way through.

The Butt report forced a change in Bomber Command tactics, which in Europe was the only one of the armed forces to be regularly striking back at Hitler's European empire. They dropped the notion of precision night bombing and went for a new tactic which remained in force for many months, that of the so-called area bombing. In spite of this change in warfare nothing stands still for very long and in late 1941 the German defenders were becoming more experienced and starting to take an increasing toll of the numbers of bombers sent out from England. On the night of 7th November 1941 around 400 aircraft took off to attack Berlin, Mannheim, the Ruhr, Cologne, Boulogne and to carry out mining and intruder operations. Thirty-seven failed to return. The major part of the force, some 169, went to Berlin and twenty one (12%) failed to return. Fifty-five bombers went to Mannheim and seven (13%) were lost. The other major part of the force sent out went to the Ruhr and to carry out 'Gardening', and here nine aircraft out of forty-three sent failed to return. Somewhat surprisingly there were no losses among the other 133 aircraft sent to the other locations – Cologne, Ostend and Boulogne. So if we add up the losses on the three main raids, 267 went to Germany and her coastal areas and 37 failed to return. A loss rate of nearly 14%, when everyone had previously agreed that for a sustained bombing campaign to be undertaken losses needed to be 4% or less on every raid.

On the following night the head of Bomber Command at that time, Air Marshal Sir Richard Peirse, had the misfortune to be a guest of the Prime Minister at his country retreat at Chequers. It was a difficult meeting and Churchill explained that in his opinion losses such as those sustained on the previous night could not be allowed to continue, especially as in Winston's words "He did not think we had done any damage to the enemy lately." Sir Richard tried to reassure Churchill but Winston would have none of it, as he held a very strong opinion that Bomber Command's strength should be conserved and indeed built up for the future. Churchill was probably under a lot of pressure from the Russians and the only effective way of tying down large numbers of Germans in Western Europe was by bombing them. Every anti-aircraft gun positioned in Germany was one that probably had been diverted from the Eastern Front.

Instructions were soon issued that for the time being Bomber Command was to send out much smaller forces and the more distant targets were to be avoided. In due course a new commander, Arthur Harris, would be appointed and the new four-engined bombers started entering front line squadrons. Meanwhile there was work going on in the background to manufacture the new navigation aids which it was hoped would greatly increase the effectiveness of Bomber Command.

However, there was also disquiet about the increasing losses which it was felt were due to the growing German experience of radar and fighter control. When the Germans had overrun much of Europe in 1940, they began to develop a system of defence similar to Britain with an early warning radar system installed along the coasts of Denmark, Holland, Belgium and France. Information for a time was scarce about how the radar worked and it was some time before clues were found by a brilliant scientist, photographic reconnaissance and enigma transcripts. Obviously if the British knew how the German systems worked it would help the boffins beavering away at such places as the Telecommunications Research Establishment (TRE) at Swanage in Dorset. Eventually nearly all the pieces of the jigsaw fell into place and HQ Combined Operations was invited to fit the last piece.

Chapter 9

The Road to Northern France

In the summer of 1940 Churchill suggested that he wanted to see a corps of around 5,000 parachute troops. By the summer of 1941 this idea was still in its infancy with only the 11th Special Air Service Battalion on the order of battle. Whilst the Tragino Aqueduct raid had gone a little way to keeping this somewhat rebellious gang in check by June 1941 things were starting to go wrong again. Churchill, for one, was unhappy with the lack of progress towards his goal of 5,000 and it is fair to say there were less than 500 parachute troops trained by then. There were many reasons for this, some of which have been touched on before but a study of the records of the Army and the RAF do not paint a good picture. There were certainly difficulties between the two services which probably have a great deal to do with the slow growth in numbers. In May 1941 the Germans once again used airborne troops to spearhead an invasion, this time in the Mediterranean at Crete. Churchill wrote another memo towards the end of May asking for a progress report and this seemed to galvanise things into action. Another question was what to do with the 11th Special Air Service Battalion? One school of thought was that it should be disbanded and its members spread across the units of the planned 1st Parachute Brigade. It was however spared this fate after a new CO, Lieutenant Colonel E Down, was posted in and he oversaw a radical shake up of the unit, thus saving it from disbandment. However, they were assigned another new name, this time the 1st Parachute Battalion in September 1941. This occurred on the same day (15th September) that the 1st Parachute Brigade officially came into existence. The other two units for this new Brigade, the 2nd and 3rd Parachute Battalions, began forming at Hardwick Hall near Chesterfield in Derbyshire. An advance party of office wallahs had been sent here to oversee these two units' formation. They were meant to be formed up by 1st October and then have a month's training before the parachute training for the thousand or so volunteers was to start on 1st November 1941.

So where were all these new recruits to come from? The ball was set rolling by a further communication from the AAG (Assistant Adjutant General) branch at the War Office on 28th August 1941 entitled 'Urgent Memo Re:Formation of Two Additional Airborne Battalions', this was addressed to all units then serving in the UK. The two new CO's had already been selected and it was up to them to choose their officers, similar to the way the officers for the Commandos had been done in 1940. So with a core of officers the men who had answered the appeal started to arrive at Hardwick Hall. One of those officers who saw the notice in September 1941 was Martin Willcock. He recalled:

> On the 8th September 1941 I saw that volunteers were required for the Airborne Forces (parachute duties) and so I put my name down, having looked through the minimum health requirements. [Author's note: these health requirements from the memo were that a good standard of physical fitness was required, soldiers with glasses were ineligible, had to be aged between 20 and 32, but with exemptions for

officers and NCOs who otherwise met all the physical fitness requirements, in the A1 class with good hearing and eyesight, weigh no more than 196 lb and with a minimum of eight good teeth including two molars in the upper set.] On the 26th September 1941 I received a telegram instructing me to report to Hobart House in London at 10.00 hrs for an interview on the 27th. On that afternoon I was interviewed by a Lieutenant Colonel Flavell, who I later found out was selecting subalterns for his 2nd Parachute Battalion which was being formed and he was commanding. I had no idea how I fared. In the adjacent room another Lieutenant Colonel was selecting his subalterns for the 3rd Battalion. I like to think that I picked the right room to be interviewed in.

I returned to my unit and on the 29th I heard that I had been accepted, and then events moved at a bewildering speed. I was instructed to report the next day to the 2nd Parachute Battalion at Hardwick Hall Camp near Chesterfield. I got on the train at St Pancras and met up with two other subalterns and whilst rather naturally our conversation was a little guarded, when we all got out at Chesterfield it was obvious where we were all heading.

On the morning of the 1st October the CO spoke to all of us, six subalterns and about 20 NCOs were detailed to go on a parachute course at Ringway starting that afternoon! It didn't give us much time to think about things. We arrived at Ringway about 4.00 and started to settle in. The next morning there was a delay for our first training session in the gym as Mass was being said for a Pole who had been killed three days before! I rang my mother to tell her what I was doing, and for the first and only time in my life she hung up on me!

52. Syrencote House in Wiltshire. In 1942 this was the HQ of the 1st Airborne Division where much of the Bruneval planning was carried out. (S Elsey)

The next seven days were taken up with PT, talks, films and synthetic training. We expected to make our first balloon jump the next day but this was cancelled due to the weather. The following day was full of hopes and disappointments. After breakfast we were told during PT that we would be jumping by balloon. So a quick change and out to Tatton by bus, only to be told it was cancelled and that we might make our first jump from a Whitley, and so back to Ringway where we waited and hoped. There was no decision till after lunch when we put our parachutes on and were all set. Again it was cancelled on account of the wind. We waited until about 4.30 when we changed into PT clothes and got on parade, only to be told we would be jumping after all. So we changed once again, put on our harnesses and waited. One stick went and when the plane returned we marched out full of hope. On arrival at the plane all was cancelled, the plane was U/S.

Next day, Saturday the 11th, after morning PT we were told once again we would be jumping. We hurriedly changed, collected our chutes, formed up and got into the plane. We took off and circled over Tatton. I was Number 4. It must be the real thing this time! Numbers 1 and 2 jumped and we waited expectantly, and then we got the wash-out signal! It did not seem possible to be so near to jumping and then not to do it! And so we returned and carried on with normal training. I forget now why, on this occasion, jumping was stopped but I expect it was on account of the wind. Sunday was a day of rest and so Peter Naoumoff and I walked to Wilmslow Church for the Harvest Festival Service.

On Monday the 13th of October we went to Tatton Park and did two balloon jumps. We had been warned that we would drop about 180 feet before the canopy fully develops and this takes about two seconds. On my first jump I distinctly remembering thinking to myself "It's about time this bloody thing opened!"- which of course it did – and in due course I landed quite safely. The second jump was even easier and I landed on my feet. I thought this is a piece of cake, that afternoon taught me otherwise. The man I most admired was an NCO whose name I do not remember, he refused the first time but went up a second time and had to be pushed out. He also had to be pushed out on his third attempt and after that he was all right and I believe he got his wings. After lunch we returned to Ringway to make our first Whitley jump. I was Number 1 in the third plane and in my enthusiasm went too early causing some consternation in the aircraft. I landed with a bit of an oscillation and the shock of hitting the ground so hard taught me not to take jumping too lightly.

On the 14th and 15th we did two further drops without any problems that I can remember. On the 20th the news media descended on Ringway. Cameras and newsreel cameras took pictures of us doing synthetic training from every angle. In the afternoon we did a drop for them at Tatton Park either in pairs or sticks. Later we all watched the 1st Battalion do a massed drop of about 60 men – I think every available aircraft was used. Anyway the weather was good and they took lots of photos. Some of us found ourselves in the national press a few days later.

On the 21st we made two more attempts to make a further jump but the weather stopped it. On the 23rd we were issued with our wings although we had only done 6 jumps. This was because the next day we would return to Hardwick and be dropped in the Park before the assembled ranks of the 2nd and 3rd Battalions and it was felt that as we would be making our 7th and qualifying jump it would be appropriate for us to land qualified. We thought this was a nice gesture.

On the 24th we fitted chutes etc. in the morning, but we were unable to go before lunch. We emplaned at 1.45 and taxied out to the take off point, but then returned as one engine was U/S. We got into another aircraft and took off about 2.25 – about 25 minutes after the others. I was Number 8 and thus I was the last to land. Thus we completed our course, at least most of us. Looking back on it, it seems incredible that none of us had had any medical examination and we made our first three jumps 14 days after joining the Battalion! Guinea pigs, I suspect.

Martin Willcock certainly took an unusual route to joining and this was repeated for a lot of the early volunteer officers. Another officer who volunteered was a pre-war regular by the name of John Frost. In 1940 and 1941 he had been with his unit, the Cameronian Rifles, on beach defence duties in Suffolk. According to an account from him it was a most boring period and as part of the 15th Scottish Division felt he was earmarked for a most inactive war. He recalls:

One evening after returning from a solitary walk the company office clerk handed me a letter marked 'Secret'. The War Office were looking for volunteers for special units, I had little idea what they were about, but wanted something better than I had at the moment. I went up to London and did really badly in the interview. I couldn't remember the name of my divisional commander or any other important detail. So I thought I'd failed and was quite glad to be back in Suffolk again. However, about ten days later I was posted to Hardwick Hall near Chesterfield. I recall it was a terrible place, hideous countryside, horrible camp, only half-built and bitterly cold, with mud everywhere. The whole atmosphere was very strange. I wasn't at all sure I'd done the right thing or could possibly compete on the physical side. Then I got caught for the Adjutant's job.

Amongst all the normal duties of an Adjutant in these two newly forming parachute units, it was his job to allocate the newly-arrived volunteers to the companies and duties which in theory they would be best suited to. However, even a relatively experienced officer like John Frost was concerned at the quality of the men arriving in his office, saying they were ready to parachute and wanted to do so with the 2nd Battalion. He later recalled:

In my humble opinion I thought around half of those I saw in my office were unsuitable for one reason or another. Some of the old commanding officers had played the Army at their own game and when the call had come for volunteers in September 1941 had shunted off their naughty boys and misfits. Some of them had conduct sheets about six pages long. [Author's note: in spite of what it sounds like to have even one entry on your conduct sheet is not good.] There were few good NCOs because the units were reluctant to let them go. To me it seemed that I would never be able to get the Battalion up to strength, which did not seem to be happening with the 3rd Battalion, who were also at Hardwick. Then I found out my counterpart in the 3rd Battalion had stationed a man at the entrance and told all new arrivals to report to the 3rd Battalion Guardroom. Here their RSM inspected them all and kept the best ones for himself and sent the chaff down to me! I decided to send a few men with a truck to just outside the camp and for them to pick up all the new arrivals. This worked out well for a while, till the 3rd's Adjutant sent a truck even further down the road, we then called a truce and both units started to build up fairly equally.

Other people had a less formal introduction as Hugh Levien recalled:

My personal record shows that on 4th September 1941 I travelled from Beverley in Yorkshire to Chesterfield, leaving the 10th Battalion The Queen's Own Royal West Kents. At Chesterfield railway station we were ferried to the camp at Hardwick where there were many newly-built red brick huts along partially constructed roads. As a Sergeant I was one of the first in the queue to report and was welcomed, if that is the right expression, by a Major full of jocularity who enquired what Regiment I was from, in spite of the fact that we all had our own cap-badges. He made a most offensive remark, mispronouncing the county, accompanied by an inane cackle. On being told that I had been the Intelligence Sergeant of the unit I came from, he said something like, "Oh, I think we still have a vacancy for one of those chaps in the 2nd Battalion. You had better trot down there and see how you fit in." So I followed his directions and was duly taken on in that capacity with Dicky Ashford as the Intelligence Officer.

I didn't really have any duties, and made out my own programme, which mainly consisted of joining a squad undergoing intensive PT and synthetic training under qualified parachutists. I moseyed around Battalion HQ a bit each day to make sure I kept up to date with what was going on, and after parades if I still had the price of a few pints I fairly often took the free transport provided into Chesterfield. As soon as I discovered that C Company was to be the first to go to Ringway I got myself a temporary posting to that Company.

So by fits and starts during the month of October 1941 the two new Battalions grew in number and in physical fitness, following the plan that the first 'large parachute course' would start on 2nd November. This first contingent travelled by a special train and arrived at Heald Green station on Saturday 1st November 1941. As one account put it:

Seventeen officers, two warrant officers, twenty-two sergeants and two hundred and twenty-eight other ranks tumbled out on to the platform laughing and joking and wondering in their hearts what it was going to be like. Every man was a free volunteer, character and courage were innate in them, for not only had they shown the desire to meet and fight their King's enemies but they were willing to challenge the unknown perils of parachuting in order to hasten the day of combat. Short days and the notorious November weather would add to the difficulties. In fourteen days, if all went well, those men would be leaving Ringway after having completed their training.

As it turned out these 250 or so trainees mainly from C Company of the 2nd Battalion and A Company of the 3rd Battalion, started their training on 2nd November. On 15th November a message was sent to the War Office from Ringway that Number 1 Parachute Training Course had been successfully completed at 1330. Descents were around 500 from balloons and over 1,200 aircraft descents, some of them in front of the newly appointed 'Major-General Airborne Forces' – Major-General Browning. It can be said that it was a most successful course with only one man not completing the course. It is also probably fair to say that the extra PT and high altitude training at Hardwick was doing its job. The ethos of this time is carried on today in the rigorous pre-parachuting course known as 'P Company' which a soldier must pass before being allowed anywhere near an aircraft to throw himself out of!

Over the next few weeks large courses for the men from Hardwick ran almost continuously, as the following details show:

- Number 2 Parachute Training Course 18th to 30th November 1941 – 270 successful trainees encompassing 924 balloon and 1633 aircraft descents.
- Number 3 Parachute Training Course 5th to 15th December 1941 – 270 successful trainees including 24 Poles.
- Number 4 Parachute Training Course 17th to 25th December 1941 – 209 successful trainees.

There were some trainees unable to complete their course due to various injuries and records show that in the six weeks after 1st November 39 students could be included in this category. The overall number of descents in this six weeks was 5,239 or a 0.75% failure rate, which was entirely acceptable. Within a period of about eight weeks virtually two Battalions completed their training and were ready to take part in any operations that may come their way. Around this time the glider element of the Airborne Forces was not being ignored and on 10th October 1941 the War Office selected 31st Independent Brigade Group to become airlanding troops. This unit was mainly a collection of Regular units, some of whom had recently returned from India. It was probably a good choice as they had just completed mountain warfare training in Wales, and were already trained to operate in a light role. It was left up to the units involved to solve the problems of converting from a light mountain role to a light airborne role, but it is not the place here to go into any more detail. However, I will add that the gliderborne men did not receive any extra money for being airborne troops unlike their parachuting counterparts. It was also felt that there was no need for the men to be volunteers just as long as they were physically fit and deemed suitable for airborne service.

So from somewhat tortuous circumstances in 1940 by the start of 1942 there were a relatively large number of airborne troops ready to take the fight to Hitler and it would not be long before an opportunity came their way. The reader may recall the mention in the previous chapter of the work of the scientists in the so-called 'Battle of the Beams'. One of the scientists who had a prominent role in this was a Dr R V Jones, who had helped with the identification of the X-Gerät and Knickebein systems. In 1940 he had started to work closely with the fledgling RAF Photographic Reconnaissance Units (PRU) and had asked them to reconnoitre a place on the northern coast of France where a beam transmitter was suspected to be located. Based on this continuing work together with some Enigma transcripts, Jones and other members of the Intelligence Staff at the Air Ministry felt they were getting an understanding of a long range, somewhat coarse German radar system which was known as Freya. Eventually through listening to the airwaves, they could locate it, work out the frequencies and so on. It was starting to be used to detect Bomber Command aircraft on their trips over German-occupied Europe. Additional information was gleaned from Enigma transcripts around 5th July when a broken message revealed that German fighters had intercepted some British aircraft due to the excellent 'Freya Meldung' (Freya Reporting). Then a few days later another decoded message revealed the existence of the 'Freya Gerät' or Freya Apparatus. It must be said that the Germans sometimes lacked imagination in the choice of code words for their 'secret equipment'. The name Freya originally came from Norse mythology and was a god who could see for about 100 miles. It was also discovered that at least two coastal stations had been set up in the coastal belt of France. From decoded Enigma messages it was discovered that the station located near Cherbourg had been able to detect a Royal Navy destroyer, HMS *Delight*, at a range of about 60 miles and direct Luftwaffe bombers towards her with the result that she was sunk on 29th July 1940. As Dr R V Jones commented:

> Since HMS *Delight* had neither balloons nor air escort, the Freya apparatus must have been able to detect her directly. It appeared to be sited near the village of Auderville on the Hague peninsula north-west of Cherbourg, but it had to be very different from our own coastal chain stations, since it was completely undetectable on the best air photographs that we possessed of the area. This confirmed the idea that Freya was a fairly small apparatus, which had already been suggested by the fact that it had been set up so quickly after the Germans had occupied the Channel coast.

The Freya continued to avoid the boffins efforts to find a glimpse of it on a photograph until early 1941. One of Dr Jones's contacts in the RAF Photographic Reconnaissance Unit by the name of Claude Wavell spotted something he thought was of interest on a shot of a German radar installation on the Hague peninsula. In the photo he could see amongst the Knickebein, X and Y Gerät turntables, two small circles about 20 feet in diameter that had not been present on a previous photograph. Wavell suggested they might be nothing more than feeding enclosures for local cattle, but when Dr Jones asked where they were located and was told near Auderville, Jones remembered the *Delight* incident and wondered if they could be the elusive Freya radars. The photos were examined in detail and it could just about be ascertained that there were the shadows of a fairly tall structure at the centre of the two circles. Then one of Jones's staff, Charles Frank, spotted that the two shadows were of different widths on two shots taken at slightly different times. Frank suggested that it could be caused by the fact that whatever the object was, it had rotated during the series of exposures. On the original prints the difference in width was around one-tenth of a millimetre! It was indeed the rotating apparatus of the Freya and the difference had been caused by the different positions relative to the sun. The RAF PRU at Benson was requested to take a low-level oblique photograph of the mysterious circular pens. This duly happened some days later and the pilot commented on his return that he had been sent to take a photo of an anti-aircraft position, which did not impress him much especially as he had virtually risked his life in getting the picture. When the pictures were examined there was indeed an anti-aircraft gun in the picture and the pilot had slightly misjudged the area he was meant to photograph. However, to Dr Jones's relief just on the edge of the shot was the area he had requested and he thought he could make out some form of aerial. He therefore told the RAF they would have to return and this time Flying Officer W Manifould got the area spot-on and brought back one of the classic PR pictures of the war. The date of the sortie was 22nd February 1941 and when the pictures were examined it confirmed that the Germans had a new type of radar. This was an entirely opportune moment as Dr Jones was to attend a meeting on 24th February with, amongst others, Air Marshal Joubert (in charge of radar and signals in the RAF), there was only one item on the agenda: 'To discuss the existence of German radar.'

Perhaps the fact that such a meeting needed to be held was a sign of the naivety of the service community to the benefits of science. Dr Jones attended this meeting armed not only with the photographs but also the news that at last the Freya's radar transmissions had been located. The discovery of these was also a bit of a 'lash-up' as will now be shown. Dr Jones had been saying for quite a few months that Britain needed to set up a proper listening service to help find out what the Germans were up to. Although minor steps had been taken by November 1940 the service was still inadequate. Around this time Air Marshal Joubert noticed that Dr Jones was working virtually single-handed and instructed the TRE to send someone to help him. The nominated person was Derrick Garrard and during the time it took for him to get 'security cleared' for the Broadway office building (it was also the Headquarters of MI6), he had to work as best he could at the Air Ministry in Dr Jones's office there. This he found relatively boring and with little to do, decided to get out on the road. He begged, borrowed or stole a suitable radio receiver and drove in his own car to the south coast to see if he could find the elusive Freya transmissions. Bear in mind here that so far the 'official' listening services had failed to locate them. In the space of a few days, he succeeded in hearing the Freya transmissions on frequencies of about 120 Megacycles a second or a wavelength of 2.5 metres and also managed to achieve rough bearings on their origins. He also managed to get himself arrested as a 'Fifth Columnist' for unauthorised activity in a prohibited area. Some of the bearings when plotted showed their origins as being near Cherbourg. When the meeting started Jones let it run on for a while letting the doubters state they did not believe the Germans had any radar. Jones then produced his trump card and Joubert looked long and hard at Jones, perhaps thinking he had kept this information up his sleeve for several weeks. His attitude softened when the date on the photographs (two days before) was pointed out to him. This was perhaps the first brick in building up a picture of the German radar capability. As time went on and as the Resistance groups became more professional other coastal Freya stations were located. The Oslo Report is mentioned in Chapter 8 and this alluded to the naval radar system working on a wavelength of 80 centimetres, as well as another system working on about 50 centimetres with a paraboloidal aerial. Dr Jones had found no trace of this until soon after the discovery of the Freya system when a decoded Enigma message stated that a Freya set together with a Würzburg was being sent to Romania for coastal defence and later two Würzburgs were being sent to Bulgaria for similar purposes. From these seeming innocuous messages Dr Jones assumed that these were the minimum requirements to cover the Black Sea coasts of the two countries. He worked out that the two countries had coastal belts of 260 kilometres for Romania and 150 for Bulgaria. As no other sets were going to Bulgaria he assumed that each Würzburg would have to cover 75 kilometres of coast, which it could just about do if it had an all-round range of 37.5 kilometres. Applying this theory to Romania, the Freya would have to cover (260-75) kilometres, which meant it could have an all-round range of 92.5 kilometres.

Having had many discussions with the radar users in Britain, Jones had discovered that to carry out an effective night time interception of any aircraft the ground controller needed to know its height as well as the direction of flight. He felt the Germans were encountering the same difficulties and be tempted to use a second type of radar to determine the height of aircraft. It was felt the Freya system was unlikely to be able to measure height, so was the missing link the Würzburg? A paraboloidal system was capable of measuring height as it could be tipped up and down and rotated in contrast to the flat vertical aerials of the Freya. The Oslo Report had suggested this. So perhaps it was necessary to find a paraboloidal aerial looking like, in the words of the time, 'a large electric fire bowl.' If the Oslo Report was correct, its transmissions should be around the 50 centimeter wavelength range; and if the maximum range was 40 kilometres, its pulse repetition should not exceed 3750 per second. It was detected that most of these transmissions, if not all, were coming from German-occupied areas of the Channel coast and the next obvious step was to find a site on the pictures taken on the regular photographic reconnaissance missions. This was easier said than done, it had taken quite a time to find a Freya site and it was expected that the Würzburg was smaller than the Freya. All the British could hope was that for ease of guarding in often occupied countries the Germans would place a Würzburg close to a Freya and eventually one would be spotted. Things went quiet for a few months until in the autumn of 1941 pictures were taken of a Freya station located about 15 miles north of Le Havre on some cliffs known as the Cap d'Antifer. From the original photographs two Freyas could be seen with a path leading from them for a couple of hundred yards or so to a large villa closer to the small village of Bruneval. The villa had been owned by a Paris doctor-Professor J Gosset but had been requisitioned by the Germans in 1940.

These photos had been looked at by Claude Wavell at Medmenham and then been sent to one of the people working for Dr Jones, Charles Frank. The initial assumption had been that the villa was the headquarters of the radar site and the path had been worn by people moving between this and the Freyas. Upon close examination Charles Frank noticed that the path did not go right up to the villa but ended up at a loop a short distance from it. At this loop in the path was a small speck which might, under different circumstances, have been taken as a spot of dust on the negative. Upon this hunch or speck of dust a request was made for a further photographic sortie at low level, and Claude Wavell warned to look for anything that looked like a large electric fire bowl. A few days after this request two pilots from RAF Benson were visiting Wavell and he told them of this request. One of them, Flight Lieutenant A Hill, said he would give it a go. At that time in the war it was difficult for the pilots to get decent low level oblique photos. The only camera position in the PR Spitfire for this type of photography was a camera pointing sideways and slightly downwards located behind the pilot's seat. The technique needed was for the pilot to put his aircraft in a dive and fly past (at high speed) the object or area to be photographed. The target would eventually disappear under his wing, the trick was guessing when it would reappear behind his wing and then press the camera gun fire button. This may sound simple really except when you consider the aircraft might be at 50 feet, travelling at around 300 mph and probably under fire from light anti-aircraft and small arms fire. On the following day (4th December 1941) Tony Hill went over to Bruneval and although he successfully flew past the target and later confirmed he had seen what had been expected, i.e. a large fire bowl about ten feet across, his cameras had failed and no photographs had been taken. He stated he would go back the following day and repeat the exercise. He duly flew over again the next day in spite of there being rules about repeating flights too soon after the initial mission. It probably does not need to be pointed out that the risks were high of being shot down on the first flight and if an aircraft returned the next day there was a high probability of the defences being strengthened. However, in spite of the risks Tony Hill brought back a selection of photographs with the 'mystery object' virtually in the middle of the shot. They were exactly what Jones wanted and confirmed the existence of a new German system. It was probably no coincidence that as well as the coastal belt of radar, one was in place along the western border of Germany and it was felt that most of the increasing

53. The classic photograph of the clifftop villa and Würzburg radar dish taken on 5th December 1941 by Flight Lieutenant Tony Hill. (ABF Museum)

bomber losses were as a result of radar-controlled searchlights and fighter interception. It would obviously be good to get to examine the workings of a Würzburg at close quarters.

After examining the magnificent photographs brought back by Tony Hill, Dr Jones commented to his assistant Charles Frank that although the Würzburg was on a cliff about 400 feet high, there was a slope down to a small beach a few hundred yards away. This meant it was entirely feasible that a 'commando' type raid could be undertaken. Initially though Dr Jones did not want to be the prime instigator of such a suggestion but after a discussion with the Deputy Superintendent of the TRE, W Lewis, who had also seen the prints, agreed it was a likely location and suggested that the TRE would strongly support any suggestions for a raid. The suggestion went all the way up the chain of command in the Air Ministry to the top when it was passed across to Combined Operations. Admiral Mountbatten accepted that the suggestion was practicable and started to undertake some initial planning. Intelligence also had a hand in this in that they wanted the raiders to positively confirm that the Würzburg was indeed the source of the 570 megacycle transmissions that had been picked up on the south coast of England. Ideally this would be sorted out by bringing back the aerial from the centre of the 'fire bowl'. It was suggested that an RAF radar operator or ideally two be included as part of the raiding party, however this was all for the future.

Chapter 10

Enter Jock Company

So now that a suitable target had been located by intelligence, the question was who would be given the operation? As the location of the radar station was on the coast, it seemed an ideal opportunity for the commandos to carry out a raid. But unlike Norway it became clear from studying aerial photographs that the coastal area was well defended. It was thought that a seaborne assault having potentially to fight their way in, would give the Germans a warning and perhaps destroy the radar equipment before it could be examined. So on 8th January 1942, the Chief of Combined Operations Admiral Mountbatten asked if a unit from the newly formed 1st Parachute Brigade together with support from 38 Wing of the RAF could carry out a raid on the northern coast of France. It is perhaps worth mentioning here that the airborne forces were at last getting their needs addressed and voiced in the right places by a newly-appointed officer, Brigadier F Browning, who was given the rank of acting Major-General and his role in life (at least in the early months) was to be 'Major-General Airborne Forces.' He had won a DSO in the Great War and had been Adjutant at the Royal Military Academy Sandhurst in the 1920s. He may have been lacking in operational experience but he was certainly well connected, a Grenadier Guardsman and a good man to have fighting your corner in Whitehall. Browning perhaps viewed this raid in northern France as an ideal opportunity to get some credit for the airborne forces after their unfortunate baptism of fire in Italy in 1941. So it is said that the same day he was asked if his men could carry out this raid he accepted it. If nothing else Browning was always quick to sense an opportunity to empire build.

One source claims that Browning personally selected the troops to go on this operation, although this is doubtful. It would seem that the choice of who would go was left to the commander of the 1st Parachute Brigade, Brigadier R Gale. The obvious choice would probably have been to use the 1st Parachute Battalion who had previously been our old friends the 11th Special Air Service Battalion, and had been whipped into shape by a forceful commander, Lieutenant Colonel E Down, who had acquired the nickname of Dracula. Instead, it seems that to prove that the entire brigade was ready, he looked away from his 'oldest' unit, to his two newest ones. So the choice was narrowed down to those sub-units of the 2nd and 3rd Battalions who had been through Ringway. The reader may recall that the first large Ringway course comprised C Company from the 2nd Battalion and A Company from the 3rd. An educated guess is that C Company were chosen because the majority of the men had volunteered from infantry units and not from the arms and services as was fairly common in the early days. This meant in theory they would not need extra training in infantry tactics as perhaps a body of men, mainly from such units as the Royal Artillery, Royal Signals and RASC would need.

From a trawl of the surviving records at the National Archive one of my research assistants found a document which was written in early January 1942 addressed to the

HQ 1st Parachute Brigade from the HQ Airborne Division (as it was sometimes known in those early days). Part of this document stated:

> You will therefore detail for this training one complete company of parachutists plus two subaltern officers and twenty ORs as first reinforcements, plus one RE officer and eleven sappers. All personnel must be fully trained in parachute jumping.

Brigadier Gale therefore nominated C Company to be the chosen ones. In early 1942, in spite of the company being all Jocks, its commander was an Englishman from the Royal Fusiliers, Major P Teichman. It is fair to say that the CO of the unit, Lieutenant Colonel E Flavell, wanted a Scottish officer to be in command of a company that had a rough and tough reputation. He felt he had an ideal candidate in his current Adjutant, the previously mentioned Captain J Frost. However John Frost was not really in a position, in early January 1942, to take up command as Frost himself recalled:

> As I said I got caught soon after my arrival for the Adjutant's job. With all the paperwork I had little chance to get fit or train. I thought I could get away without all the training. Came the day and I did my first jump successfully and went up immediately for the next. This time I landed awkwardly and badly damaged my knee. Ten days later, after I'd got out of hospital, I really started to get fit by going for long runs. I returned from a Scottish New Year to relinquish the Adjutantcy and take over C Company, who were all Scots, from Philip Teichman. Two weeks later I was told that C Company were to move to Salisbury for special training. However, as I was not qualified, I would only be given one week at Ringway to pass and get all my jumps in. Philip took the advance party from the company down to Salisbury, and if I failed he would resume command.

It was known that the company would be based on Salisbury Plain for about six weeks undergoing a programme of special training for an undisclosed reason or objective.

So in the middle part of January Frost travelled to Ringway with the threat that he if he didn't complete his course within a week, he would lose the opportunity of commanding C Company. To anyone who has lived near Manchester or in the north of England, they will know that the weather can be somewhat unfavourable in January and also there are not many hours of daylight. However, when Frost started training it appears his card had been specially marked and he seemed to get preferential treatment, indeed he himself said that he heard RAF instructors talking about him and the words 'the last time'. He stated he felt this was a reference to Operation Colossus. He was allowed to do jumps with very little ground training and given priority over other attendees for places on an aircraft. Frost himself commented on the Manchester weather:

> It was notoriously fickle. On the slightest provocation a smoky fog would creep across the airfield from the direction of Manchester, and a wind strong enough to dispel the fog very often made jumping unsafe.

As it turned out Frost overcame the weather and potential shortages of aircraft and managed to get the required jumps in, within the allotted time scale. Newly qualified he hurried back to Hardwick Hall prior to moving south with the rest of C Company. They left Derbyshire on 24th January 1942 for a camp on Salisbury Plain, which turned out to be at Tilshead. Here they were accommodated in a camp with the newly forming Glider Pilot Regiment. Major Teichman was, for perfectly understandable reasons, not best pleased to see Frost and told him so. Teichman did however reveal that C Company was to train for a parachute demonstration to the War Cabinet and that at present there were not any raids on the horizon. The scheme was based upon the lines of landing behind enemy lines at night with a simulated evacuation by the Royal Navy.

So the newly promoted Major Frost took over command much to the annoyance of Major Teichman. Obviously both men were keen to see some action and indeed both would see their fair share over the coming months and years.

Sadly Major Philip Teichman was killed in Tunisia in December 1942 whilst second-in-command of the 2nd Parachute Battalion on the ill-fated Oudna operation behind enemy lines. He now lies at the Massicault War Cemetery in Tunisia.

Soon after Frost took over command, the company was inspected by Major-General Browning. It is perhaps worth pointing out here that the HQ of the 1st Airborne Division was based at Syrencote House near Netheravon in Wiltshire. This was conveniently located relatively close to Tilshead so Browning and his staff officers could interfere as much as they wanted. Frost had not been looking forward to this parade, as he knew Browning was certain to notice any defect in the men's turnout and drill. As he said later:

My men were a wild crew. At that stage of the war clothing and equipment were scarce, and for a few months we had been concentrating on toughness and on weapon and parachute training. We'd had little time for drill, and still less for making ourselves look glamorous, or even clean. After a prolonged and uncomfortable railway journey, the Jocks had found time to work the dreadful Tilshead mud deep into the fabric of their uniforms. They looked horrible.

As Frost had suspected Browning kept his own counsel until the inspection was over when he led Frost aside and said:

Just let Peter Bromley-Martin know exactly what you need in the way of transport, stores and equipment. And see here, Frost! Every man is to get a new uniform, for that is without question the filthiest company I have ever seen in my life.

Peter Bromley-Martin was Captain Bromley-Martin who had interviewed Reg Curtis when he applied for special service in 1940, but he was now a liaison officer at Syrencote House, close to Browning and also a Grenadier Guardsman. Later that day Frost's other officers, Captain Ross, Lieutenant Timothy, Lieutenant Naoumoff and Second Lieutenant Charteris, were all introduced to him and he became a well-known figure over the next few days to Frost and the rest of C Company. At this meeting Bromley-Martin explained that the unit had been moved down to the Salisbury Plain area to stage a demonstration which in Browning's eyes was critical to the future of the airborne forces. It was thought (still) in the top brass that the best way of striking back at Germany was the use of the commandos, and to convince them they were wrong an exercise was being staged on the Isle of Wight. During this exercise C Company was to raid a German HQ and then withdraw, with interested spectators being Winston Churchill and the rest of the War Cabinet together with several military top brass. The added incentive was that if the demonstration went well and the top brass agreed they would carry out the operation for real somewhere near the coast of France later on that year.

An area near Alton Priors close to Devizes in Wiltshire had been selected as the training area for the demonstration. It was chosen as there were some steep hills here which in exercise speak were to represent cliffs by the sea. C Company was to be dropped inland behind some imaginary defences, neutralise the objective and withdraw down a ravine to a mythical beach to be picked up by the Royal Navy.

Here are two comments about the training undertaken at Alton Priors; the first from Sapper Stan Halliwell:

> We did the same thing night after night, up the hill and down again. Us engineers had to do it with about nine bricks in a pack to simulate what I now know to be the weight of the radar equipment. With all this hill work we soon got super-fit, no doubt about it.

Major Frost recalled:

> We built a little replica of the pillboxes and the objectives at the top of a cliff here. There we were able to practice dropping out at night and assaulting the features from the rear and then coming down the cliffs to the imaginary pick-up beach.

Then came the bolt from the blue which greatly annoyed Frost. Bromley-Martin then proceeded to explain exactly how Frost should plan and control the operation, the normal organisation would have to be scrapped and his men divided into four unequal groups each with a specific role. Ever since the Great War the British Army had been, certainly up to company level, working on the rule of threes. To explain this, a platoon (commanded by a Lieutenant or Second Lieutenant) would be formed of three sections (each about 8 men commanded by a Corporal). Three platoons would form a company with three rifle companies in a battalion. Three battalions in a brigade and three brigades in a division. All the Army training was based on this pyramid and Frost was not best pleased and told Bromley-Martin so. It also went against the normal Army logic of giving the commander the task and then let him get on with a plan to solve it. In Frost's view the plan went against the normal command and control by the platoon and section commanders and lacked flexibility to cope with unexpected events, which were almost certain to happen. The meeting ended with each side retreating to lick their wounds and Major Frost spent a few hours reviewing his options.

Frost later commented:

> It was planned in much too much detail by the staff at Divisional HQ which meant splitting my force up into little penny packets, each to do a certain job. Well that's all very well when you're doing it in peace time and nothing can go wrong, but it's the wrong way to go about it when you are actually on operations when something is bound to go wrong.

These deliberations to Frost included his own plan and a visit to Syrencote House to speak directly to Browning, which is precisely what he did. Unfortunately Browning was absent from his HQ when Frost visited and he had to make do with a meeting with one of the senior staff officers. He was basically disinterested in anything that Frost had to say about his own plan and kept telling Frost that it was the four-party plan or nothing. One account relates that Frost was offered the option of either accepting the plan as it was or that another officer would be found to undertake it. To an interested observer it is perhaps feasible to suggest that the plan was Browning's but he distanced himself from it by passing responsibility to a relatively junior 'liaison officer'. Browning had not really in my view (and probably his also) had a decent war up till then. You will recall he was a pre-war officer and had been Adjutant at Sandhurst and did not receive an operational command at the outbreak of the war in September 1939. His war had till 1942 constituted of being in charge of the records at the Small Arms School until mid-1940. After this he spent a few months in command of both the 128th Infantry and 24th Guards Brigade, although neither of these were in an operational mode, before getting the job at Airborne Forces.

The somewhat cold atmosphere thawed very quickly, when on the day after Frost's visit to HQ, Bromley-Martin let Frost into the real story. The tale of training for a demonstration for Winston and the War Cabinet was just a cover story. Major Frost later remarked "I was told that if I didn't like the plan they'd get somebody else who did. So I wasn't going to have that so I said all right I'll be a good boy and I'll do what you say."

The actual intention was to raid a German radar station on the French coast and bring back parts and information about the equipment. Some Royal Engineers and a RAF radar technician would also be included in the party. Frost was also told they would be going over before the end of February and he was not to tell anyone else for the time being, and this news immediately removed Frost's verbal objections. Over the next few days and weeks Browning fulfilled his promise and virtually anything that C Company asked for was provided, often more than was asked for. Weapons came by the crate-load including a relatively new weapon the Sten gun, new Brens, anti-tank mines, mine detectors, radios and new boots and uniforms.

The brand new radios provided were of two types, the Numbers 18 and 38 sets. The Number 18 set was the standard British Army man-pack radio used during the Second World War and had been designed for short-range communications in forward areas. It had been introduced in 1940 and was entirely self-contained in one unit comprising a sender, receiver and batteries. Including the carrying frame it weighed in at about 35 lbs and had an effective maximum range of 5 miles. The Number 38 was first issued in 1941 and was a smaller in size set weighing about 24 lbs and designed for use by assault troops. It was more suitable for inter-company communication and had a shorter range than the Number 18 set. C Company had been issued with four Number 38 sets for communication between the platoons and Company HQ and two Number 18 sets to use to establish communication with the Navy.

Meanwhile, HQ Combined Operations were looking for some volunteers from the RAF to go on the raid. The search eventually settled on two NCOs working in a radar station in Devon, Sergeant C Cox and a Corporal Jones (about whom not much is known). On the 1st February 1942 both were given a railway warrant to London and told to report to an Air Commodore Tait at the Air Ministry. Cox later stated he was somewhat surprised by this and wondered what he had done wrong. At the time, unbeknown to Cox, he had been specially selected due to his proficiency in working on radar sets and had been an amateur radio enthusiast before the war. According to Cox's account his interview at the Air Ministry went along the lines of:

> "Well done, you two for having volunteered for a dangerous job."
> Corporal Jones said "Yes, Sir," while Cox replied "No, Sir."
> "What do you mean no Sir?"
> "I never volunteered for anything, Sir."
> "There must be some sort of mistake, as I thought you had. We asked for volunteers from everyone with the specialist skills we need, including you. But now you are here Cox, will you volunteer?"
> "Exactly what I am getting involved in?"
> "Regretfully, I'm not allowed to let you know at this stage, except, I honestly believe the job offers you a reasonable chance of coming back. The mission is of great importance to the RAF and if you're half the man I think you are, you'll give it a go."
> "I volunteer, Sir."

After this brief interview, Charles Cox was told he was now a Flight Sergeant and given a railway warrant to Manchester and told to report to the Adjutant of Number 1 PTS at Ringway. Cox was at first unsure what PTS stood for and later commented:

> Busloads of soldiers kept entering and leaving. Some had queer pot helmets on, rather like the Boy's Brigade. I eventually asked the Sergeant in the Guard Room what this place was and what PTS stood for. I was somewhat surprised to be told it was the Parachute Training School. The thought of parachuting had never even entered my head before.

F/Sergeant Cox followed in the footsteps of Major Frost and only spent a few days at Ringway training before he was told to report to Tilshead and C Company. When he arrived on the Plain Major Frost decided he should have a week's preparatory training which included PT, route marches, unarmed combat, weapon training and night patrolling. Around this time the Royal Engineer element arrived at Tilshead, this consisted of a section from what was known at the time as the Parachute Field Squadron commanded by Lieutenant D Vernon. Some of the sappers (four) were to be an anti-tank party while the others were to go for the radar apparatus. It was intended to take two RAF radar experts on the raid but the other volunteer Corporal Jones injured himself whilst at Ringway, and as it turned out missed the raid. Soon afterwards a mobile gunlaying radar borrowed from an anti-aircraft battery arrived at the camp and Cox was given the task of explaining what the radar was and how it worked. So this then was the basic framework for the Army side of the operation and Frost's main problem was keeping the actual aim secret for the time being. Training got underway, rehearsing what would be expected of the various groups, which in the spirit of co-operation had all been named after famous sailors. I will give more details on these shortly, but it would be good to look at the various other elements of this proposed combined operation.

In similar circumstances to those which occurred when planning Operation Colossus, it was realised that the meagre resources of the RAF at Ringway could not cope with both training and operational tasks. So the question was again who would fly C Company over to France? Once again Bomber Command was 'invited' to support the operation with a squadron of Whitleys. The unit chosen was Number 51 Squadron commanded by Wing Commander P C Pickard. Wing Commander Pickard was probably one of the best-known RAF pilots in the country at the time as he had been the pilot of F-Freddie who had 'starred' in a propaganda film made in 1941 called 'Target for Tonight.' A visit was arranged between the Army and the RAF aircrew and this is what Major Frost later commented about this meeting:

> We were all concentrated down on Salisbury Plain to practice. Pickard's squadron had been taken off bombing operations and sent to Abingdon in the old-fashioned Whitley bombers, very slow but very safe. I went over there one day with my officers to meet the aircrews and particularly the pilots. When we arrived, the Wing Commander wasn't there. I don't quite know where he was, but, having had a good look round we were having tea in the mess when suddenly he came in, a tremendously bustling, powerful figure, and the first thing he said to his pilots was, "Why the hell aren't you in the air flying?" His pilots replied that they were telling their opposite numbers in the airborne forces about their problems. Anyhow, he soon joined in the party and we knew, having now met him and them, that they were going to do an absolutely first class job for us.

Later 51 Squadron moved to Thruxton, just on the edge of the Plain.

So this covered the way in, now for the way out. The Royal Naval element comprised various assets. The whole group was commanded by Commander F Cook from the Royal Australian Navy. Also included were Motor Gun Boats (MGB) from the 14th Flotilla commanded by Lieutenant Commander W Everitt, the HMS *Prins Albert* (commanded by Lieutenant Commander W Peate) and assorted ALCs and support landing craft.

In 1939, of when war broke out, Commander Cook had been an exchange officer in the battleship HMS *Royal Oak*. He remained with her after the outbreak of hostilities and survived the torpedoing and sinking of her by a German U-boat, the U47 in October 1939. After some sick leave he was posted to HMS *Curlew* and went to Norway in May 1940 but his ship was again sunk, this time by German bombers. In July 1940 he was summoned by the Head of Combined Operations Admiral Keyes to find and then establish a naval commando training base in the Portsmouth/Southampton area and then to command it. After a careful search he decided upon the Household Brigade Yacht Club at Warsash at the mouth of the River Hamble. He later stated that he and some of his men participated in some of the early commando raids. He was also asked shortly after the base had been commissioned to suggest a name for the base. After a discussion in the Mess one night apart from the usual names like 'Impossible' and 'Incredible', one young Sub-Lieutenant suggested HMS *Nobby*. When asked to explain this he came up with 'Night Operations by Bloody Yachts'. Cook commented he was dead right but eventually it was agreed that they should suggest the name 'HMS *Tormentor*', the reasoning being that they could not do much damage but could certainly be a nuisance. This name was eventually approved by the Admiralty. Shortly after taking over command from Keyes, Admiral Mountbatten visited the establishment and saw Cook's armada exercising in the Solent.

Commander Cook was called in the middle of January 1942 to a conference at HQ Combined Operations in London. He later recalled:

> To my amazement there were only three people present at this meeting. Captain J Hughes-Hallett RN (Mountbatten's Chief of Staff), Commander D Luce (Planning Officer) and myself. Hughes-Hallett started to go into the details of a raid when Luce interrupted and said "Sir, shouldn't we tell Cook that he is to be the naval commander of this operation?" From then on I pulled out the thumb and really took notice of what was being said.

Perhaps it worth mentioning here that as well as the initial reconnaissance flights by Tony Hill, it is reported that on 13th February 1942 Wing Commander Pickard flew a high-level photo reconnaissance by Whitley of the area around Bruneval. From the interpretation of these and other photographs a scale model of the area was made by staff from RAF Medmenham. The cliffs at Cap d'Antifer were given their actual height together with all the relevant slopes, fences and buildings. This was studied in great detail by everyone involved and seems to have been a useful aid.

After many rehearsals in the area around Alton Priors the whole group travelled by railway north to Scotland to train with the Royal Navy. I would like to add here that so far in the training no-one had jumped from a Whitley of 51 Squadron as the aircraft hadn't yet had a hole cut in the fuselage to enable a paratrooper to jump through. Also going to Scotland was another volunteer or nominee of HQ Combined Operations. He was put down on the nominal roll of C Company as Private Newman on attachment from the Pioneer Corps. He was in reality Peter Nagel and officially coming along as the interpreter. He spoke excellent German, which was not surprising as he had been born in Germany and his father, who had been an ardent anti-Nazi, had emigrated to England before the war. He did speak good English but Frost decided that he would only tell his second-in-command Captain Ross and the Company Sergeant Major WO Strachan what nationality he really was.

[Author's note: During my research I came across a comment from Jimmy Sharp in 1977 that he felt that Nagel went on the raid as 'Private Walker'. No other documents support this claim except when checking the records from Ringway and intriguingly there is a 'Private Walker' with no Army number nor unit on Parachute Course Number 1 on which many men of C Company also attended.]

Major Frost felt somewhat uneasy about his presence and later commented:

> The Germans then seemed invincible. Their armies knew no halting, and in spite of their recent reverses, or apparent reverses, in the snow in front of Moscow, they were truly formidable. So many things could go wrong with our little party, and we had been taught to fear the enemy's intelligence. With all the talk in England then and previously about the Fifth Column, I could not help thinking that the enemy probably knew all about us, and what we were training for. There was a distinctly eerie feel to have a Hun on the strength.

54. The beach and cliffs at Bruneval (N Cherry)

55. The drop zone at Bruneval. (N Cherry)

So after a long journey by train from southern England C Company, some Royal Engineers, a RAF Flight Sergeant and a German arrived at the small town of Inveraray on the banks of Loch Fyne on the west coast of Scotland. The paratroopers were ordered to remove their wings for this trip north. This town was no stranger to soldiers as many of the commandos had received amphibious training here and it was now the turn of the parachutists to get wet. They were all accommodated in the HMS *Prins Albert*, which as previously mentioned was destined to be the main transport for the force.

Perhaps it is worth mentioning here that often overlooked in the order of battle was a small number of men from the RAMC providing medical support. This group came from at the time the only air-landing field ambulance. By this, is meant a glider-borne unit rather than parachute-trained, and this was 181st (Airborne) Field Ambulance RAMC. There was a parachute field ambulance in existence at the time, 16th Parachute Field Ambulance, but perhaps like the 2nd Battalion, a less senior unit was chosen to show the whole Division was ready to go into action. 181 was then based at Chilton Foliat in Berkshire and the nominated section moved north to Inveraray in Scotland for specialist training. Private W. Scott recalls:

> One morning on parade they called out 21 names, mine included and we were told to pack all our belongings as we were being sent on a course to Scotland. We left Hungerford station on a train for Glasgow with a packed lunch, where we arrived late at night. We were billeted somewhere and I remember being fed porridge for breakfast – the Scottish way with plenty of salt.

Bill recalls it was bitterly cold and had been snowing.

The complete roll call of men from 181 commanded by Lieutenant A. S. Baker, was 20 NCOs and men – these being S/Sgt J. Griggs, Cpl W. Kiddell, L/Cpl D. Pusser, Privates – J. Stanton, G. Rose, W. Scott, E. England, E. Freer, J. Waters, L. Hatcher, B. Tuson, E. McNulty, R. Maltby, J. Newman, J. Devitt, F. Cousins, M. Grinsberg, R. Domone, W. Hoath and W. Elliott.

The mixed group were all billeted on the *Prins Albert*, which after the mud of Tilshead certainly came as a welcome relief. The ship could, in theory, accommodate over 300 men, so space was not a problem. It is also reported that certain foods such as eggs in their shells were enjoyed as part of the fare provided by the Navy. The *Prins Albert* herself was around 370 feet long with a crew of 35 officers and 161 ratings and a maximum speed of 22 knots. Over the next few days time was spent on getting wet in the cold waters of Loch Fyne on joint exercises with the Navy. It was the first time many of the men had come anywhere near an Assault Landing Craft (ALC), which by this stage of the war had been improved from earlier versions. By now they were around 41 feet long, 10 feet wide and with a draft of only 2 feet 6 inches. They were able to carry up to 35 soldiers and their two V8 Ford engines gave a top speed (on flat water) of 10 knots. The many exercises probably did nothing to soothe some of Frost's concerns about the evacuation from the coast of France, as several night exercises did not go well. As Frost himself commented:

> We found that evacuation off the beaches around Loch Fyne was extremely difficult and if the weather was bad, sometimes dangerous. The flat-bottomed ALCs were

prone to being moved by the tide and the navy crews' performance was patchy. Sometimes we couldn't get communication with them on the Number 18 sets and when we could they couldn't find us. It seemed to me that they had difficulty in seeing flashlights or Verey lights. For several nights there was not a single successful evacuation. In the end we finished our time at Inveraray with only one really successful pick-up.

Coupled with this was the strain of trying to maintain the cover story of the exercise for the War Cabinet, although I suspect several of the group had an inkling that something more serious lay ahead. Then to cap it all, in the Navy's eyes was the news that their top man, Admiral Lord Mountbatten, intended to visit the *Prins Albert*. In typical service style the Captain of the *Prins Albert* got rid of his Army 'guests' and probably in his eyes scruffy and smelly ones at that, by asking Frost if 'he wouldn't awfully mind taking his men up into the hills for a few hours.'

This move backfired when Mountbatten asked where was the Army? He was told they were busy ashore but Mountbatten said he wanted to address everyone. So a message was passed and this time the 18 set worked. Frost commented:

There was a misunderstanding about the visit because the Captain of the *Prins Albert* thought that Lord Mountbatten was arriving specially to inspect his ship and the flotilla of landing craft. It was arranged therefore that we should make ourselves scarce, so that morning we moved ashore and into the surrounding hills, where we hid from view until frantic hooting from the *Prins Albert*'s siren told us

56. A group of men from C Company on board the *Prins Albert* prior to boarding an ALC. Most appear to be armed with the newly-issued Sten gun. (IWM H17370)

57. Five ALCs in convoy on Loch Fyne during training for Operation Biting. (IWM H17375)

58. Men of C Company 2nd Parachute Battalion boarding ALC 125 during training for Operation Biting in Scotland February 1942. (ABF Museum)

that all was not well on board. We then scurried down to the landing craft and back to the ship with all possible speed.

The Admiral spoke to all ranks, both naval and military, and this was the first inkling that many of our soldiers and any of the Navy had had as to what we were going to be required to do. Until this moment the sailors had no idea we were parachutists and from then on they took a great interest in us, for we were the first of the breed that they had met. Throughout all subsequent events we had nothing but the most willing co-operation from both sailors and airmen and we were left in no doubt by his Lordship that cooperation had to be the thing.

After Mountbatten had spoken to everybody, he met with Frost. According to Frost there were just the two of them present at the start and Frost was asked if there was anything he wished to ask or raise any concerns. Frost took the opportunity of pointing out his two concerns, firstly the possibility of getting stranded in France given the lack of success so far of the Navy picking them up and secondly Private Newman. Frost stated he would rather do without him so according to Frost:

Private Newman was sent for and subjected to a tremendous barrage of questions in German. He seemed to hold his own and Lord Louis was satisfied. He told me to take him as I should certainly find him invaluable as an interpreter during the raid. In the end this proved to be more than true; as indeed were all the other little bits of advice I received from the same source at that time.

Private Newman later commented about his interrogation:

I recall it being a pleasant and gentlemanly affair. I was asked about my life before the war and my reasons for wanting to go into action. I thought the Admiral was utterly charming.

The day after this meeting the *Prins Albert* sailed down to Gourock where the C Company group left, again travelling down by train to Salisbury Plain. The day after their arrival back at Tilshead, 15th February 1942, there took place what turned out to be their (and 51 Squadron's) one and only practice drop. The modifications to the Whitleys had now been carried out and C Company travelled across to RAF Netheravon for the drop. It should also be remembered that so far in the war 51 Squadron had never dropped paratroopers before, so it was very much a learning exercise. The drop zone chosen was in the grounds of Syrencote House with Major-General Browning being an interested observer. The drop was fortunately to be in daylight and it was got in before the light had gone. According to sources there was a lot of huffing and puffing at Thruxton before things were sorted out. The Whitleys dropped everyone in the correct place, and although the ground was rock-hard there were no serious injuries and just the usual rash of bruises. Browning stated he was satisfied and it was then decided that most of the remaining training time would have to be spent on the naval side of things and the recalcitrant ALCs. As was common with many other operations over the years the weather played an important part in the timings. To assist the men of C Company and the RAF in finding the drop zone a clear moonlit night was called for together with the 'correct' tides. This narrowed the window of opportunity to a few days with one of these looming close on the horizon towards the end of February.

The senior naval officer, Commander Cook, also had concerns and he later commented:

> My biggest worry, by far, was to find the tiny 400 yard rocky beach under the high cliffs after travelling 100 miles across the Channel by dead-reckoning. No fixes after the Isle of Wight and a possible sighting of an EA5 rescue float. I also had to consider the latest time that I could abort the raid because of bad weather, gales, swell, fog, breakdowns or whatever was 2200 i.e. the take-off time of the Whitleys. I would also like to point out that our boats had very little radar and relied to a great extent on the boats' magnetic compasses. Inter-boat communication was difficult – we only had very poor 1942 walkie-talkies. Finally I wanted my little armada to go in on a rising tide, which should help when embarking with tired or excited paratroopers. I also pointed out that any wind or swell above Force 2 or 3 would make for dangerous conditions when lowering craft or embarking from the beach.

59. Practice firing from an ALC for Operation Biting on Loch Fyne in Scotland. Note that two men are using Boyes anti-tank rifles and two men have relatively unusual drum magazines on their Brens. (ABF Museum)

Perhaps here is a good place to detail the roles of C Company and the German forces thought to be in the area for the forthcoming operation. Basically the task of Frost and C Company was to provide protection to Flight Sergeant Cox and the sappers from the Parachute Field Squadron while the Würzburg was photographed and possibly dismantled. A couple of airborne trolleys were going to form part of the Whitley's cargo to enable relative easy movement of any captured booty. Frost had divided his group into various-sized parties all with different roles. The largest was known as Drake and had several sub-groups to it. Major Frost was in command with two sub-groups known as Hardy and Jellicoe. Their objectives were all in the vicinity of the house and the radar pit. Hardy group was tasked with neutralising the house and searching it, collecting any prisoners and intelligence material. In keeping with the inflexible plan imposed on Frost he was to be in command of Hardy and so would be busy dealing with the house rather than being in a position to exercise some form of command and control.

The sapper party, together with Flight Sergeant Cox, were to wait at a safe distance from the radar pit until the sub-group known as Jellicoe had moved up to and secured the area. In the plan the radar pit was known as Henry. The Drake party was to move to an area north-west of Henry as a defensive screen. Another officer, Lieutenant P Young, was temporarily posted in to the company to be in charge of the Jellicoe party. Forty men under the command of Captain Ross assisted by Second Lieutenant Charteris were to form the Nelson party and their main role was to secure the beach prior to the withdrawal, hopefully with everybody who landed, the radar equipment and any prisoners. The last group, the Rodney group, led by Lieutenant Timothy, was to act as a general reserve, dealing with any Germans advancing to threaten either the house area

60. Another training shot for Biting taken in Dorset but now the men are wearing their newly-issued airborne smocks and helmets. (IWM H17407)

or the beach. It was hoped the highly-trained and relatively heavily-armed (compared to the Germans) paratroopers would be able to cope with what intelligence thought were superior numbers of German troops in the area. Whilst outnumbered it must be remembered that a proportion of the 'soldiers' would have been the radar operators and therefore probably not highly skilled in infantry fighting. Also the German Army was heavily involved on the Eastern Front fighting the Russians and it was only to be expected that the troops in this 'quiet backwater' would not have been first line. It was thought there were around 30 radar operators and support staff who would either be on duty in the radar pit or at the house. Another hundred or so were billeted in some farm buildings to the north of the house known as La Presbytère. The final party and probably most dangerous were the troops who manned the defences in and around the beach area these were thought to number around sixty. It was also felt that assistance would soon be forthcoming from other garrisons in nearby villages and might even take the presence of armoured vehicles which is perhaps why the anti-tank sappers had been included in the C Company group. It would have been a one-sided fight as the sappers were only allowed a few mines and anti-tank grenades, the days of an effective lightweight British anti-tank weapon were a long way off. Some veterans might argue that it was post-war before the British Army got one. The spigot-operated Projector Infantry Anti-Tank (PIAT) which was on general issue later in the war to the airborne troops was not a nice weapon to have to fire and had an effective range of about 50 yards.

So after the successful daylight drop in front of Major-General Browning attention turned to training with the Navy, and for reasons that are best known to the high command the decision was taken to mainly leave C Company at Tilshead and make them travel nearly every day to the coast, mostly Dorset. Several training exercises were undertaken at Lulworth Cove, but again the weather played a hand and several amphibious exercises were cancelled. Meanwhile whilst C Company were getting thoroughly wet on the south coast, the boffins back in London had been thinking about and discussing the raid. The main instigator of the raid, Dr R V Jones, thought it would be a good idea to have a word or two with Flight Sergeant Cox and Lieutenant Vernon about the Würzburg radar and what to look for. They were both as a cover story given two days compassionate leave but told on the afternoon of the second day to report to the Air Ministry in London. As Flight Sergeant Cox recalled:

> I went home for one precious night to Wisbech, and when on the following day I got to the Air Ministry, Lieutenant Vernon was there, in the waiting room. I thought it peculiar, him not being an airman. We were taken to an office. Three men sat behind the desk, two Englishmen in civilian clothes and a Frenchman in British Army uniform, battledress. He said little. The Englishmen in the middle, powerfully built, sure of himself, a good bit younger than me, did the talking, while the third man spoke occasionally when what you would call the technical side of matters was under discussion.
>
> There was a lot of talk to begin with about what would happen if we were taken by the Jerries. We were only to tell them, of course, the standard things, name, rank and number. But we must make it clear, if caught on the job, that we were simply a demolition squad out to do mischief to a valuable bit of enemy equipment. We would both come in for special questioning, since I was the only airman in the

parachuting party, and Vernon was the only engineer officer. We discussed alibis. The tall man said the Germans often planted an 'English' fellow-prisoner in the cell of a newly-captured man. He would be an expert at getting information, and there could be hidden microphones. We were warned against the kindness-and-generosity treatment: they might put you in a comfortable room with soft music, a box of Coronas, and a bottle of whisky or brandy....I told the intelligence people I could stand up to any amount of that type of interrogation.

We were given advice on how to escape capture if things went badly wrong with the raid. With the French people in the locality we would be among friends. Granted half a chance, any of the farmers or villagers would hide us and risk their lives, and more than their own lives for us, just as they were doing for all our boys shot down over France. It might well be, the big man said, that even if things went wrong, we would be smuggled, Dennis and me, fairly quickly back to England, either by boat or in a small pick-up aircraft. But in case we were completely on our own over there we were given French money, maps printed on fine silk and collar studs with miniature compasses hidden in the bases. We had to memorise three addresses, two in France and one in Switzerland. If we got to any of the three we had a code word. The people in the houses would do the rest. We would simply be packages in their care. Most of the rest of the interview was technical stuff concerning the German radar set, what was wanted from it and why. Both the Englishmen evidently knew more about radar than we did. Without raising his voice or saying anything dramatic, the main spokesman had made us feel that our job was something really worth doing, and that we were lucky to find ourselves doing it.

Dr Jones also had some concerns about the involvement of Flight Sergeant Cox, in that he would be wearing a blue uniform against a sea of brown should he be captured and come in for special treatment. Jones initial thoughts were to get the War Office to issue Cox with an Army number, uniform and documents. The War Office forcefully refused to do this and Cox ended up going in his RAF uniform, although there were special measures in place to prevent his capture, which will be explained later. Jones did speak about this to Cox and his first idea was to state to the Germans that he had been a despatcher in an aircraft and got carried away and jumped out. Jones suggested that he doubted the Germans would wear that excuse and Cox agreed.

The question of whether any of the civilian radar experts should also go on the raid was discussed and originally a young scientist working with Dr Jones, D Garrard, volunteered to go with the raiding party. Dr Jones stated that once he heard that Derrick Garrard had stepped over the line, he felt duty bound to volunteer as well. However, when news of these two volunteers reached the ears of the-then Chief of the Air Staff Sir Charles Portal, he flatly refused permission for either Jones or any of his team to go because they were in possession of so much sensitive information that it was too much of a security risk. It was agreed, however, that a back room boy with 'less knowledge' was permitted to go at least with the seaborne force. The expert selected was D Preist from the TRE and he was present at the interview with Cox and Vernon at the Air Ministry. He was temporarily commissioned in the RAF as a Flight Lieutenant (no red tape here) and given suitable advice. He was, as stated, to go with the landing craft and a small escort group known as Noah. This part of the plan had a lot of ifs in it, but it was entirely proper to be in the plan. It was suggested that if the fighting ashore was very one-sided in favour of C Company with the beach defences neutralised, with very little German reaction and that the ALCs made the beach in good time, then the Noah group might just have time to scramble up to the radar pit, make a quick assessment of the equipment and supervise the dismantling before returning to the beach. An ambitious plan but it was better to plan for any eventuality than not to plan at all.

So back to C Company – after several days getting wet on the south coast, the window of opportunity for the raid was fast approaching and a dress rehearsal (of sorts) was held on 17th February 1942. On this exercise it was planned to bring all the three services together, albeit not quite exactly as they would on the operation but fairly close to what they would have to do operationally. The Jocks of C Company were dropped from their low-flying troop-carrying vehicles on a flat area of ground close behind the coast, simulating the actual drop zone. Soon after their arrival 12 Whitleys from 51 Squadron would drop the arms and stores containers at the same place, then C Company would attack the objective and then withdraw to a beach and ask the ALCs to come in and pick them up. As it turned out, the paratroopers jumped out of the vehicles at the right place, but the containers were dropped some distance away, although they were eventually collected. The objective was overrun but then the troops mistakenly walked into a minefield and were lucky to get out without any casualties. This was not a good omen as the raid was meant to be carried out in the next few days. With 48 hours to go before the start of the window of opportunity, the Royal Navy, not unreasonably, asked for another rehearsal of the pick-up by night in the Channel. Originally intended to be held on 19th February bad weather caused a delay of 24 hours and even then the wind in the Channel was so bad the pick-up point was moved to Southampton Water, which gave a bit of shelter.

This time things went much better at first, one of the airborne trolleys was loaded with a large boulder to simulate the radar equipment, the timetable was adhered to and radio contact was made on both the Number 18 radios. However, the ALCs could be seen some distance offshore and were unable to get in any closer. C Company were ordered to wade out to the boats. The weapons and trolley were left on the shore under guard. It was a long cold wade out to the landing craft with the water reaching up to the men's thighs. Eventually the ALCs were reached and reverse gear engaged but the craft were all stuck fast on a falling tide. Everybody had to get out to try and push the ALCs off, not an easy job in the cold and dark. The ALCs were all stuck well and truly fast, so C Company had to wade back to the shore and were faced with another cold, wet journey back to Tilshead.

After this somewhat unsatisfactory exercise the coming four days (Monday 23rd to Thursday 26th February 1942) were what had been designated as the window of opportunity when the moon and tides would be right. By this it is meant there would be a full moon (for ease of finding the drop zone) and the landing craft could approach the coast on a rising tide. The time was now right to brief the men and as well as a 'paper order' the topography was depicted by a wonderful briefing model which still exists today as a prize exhibit (in my mind) at the Parachute Regiment and Airborne Forces Museum. This model had been made at RAF Medmenham as someone who worked there recalls:

Really good low obliques are a most compelling form of intelligence; and Tony Hill's magnificent photographs played a big part in bringing about the Bruneval raid. But the detailed planning that was necessary could not be done from photographs alone, however good, and it was at this point that one of Medmenham's most secret departments, the Model Making Section, had to step in. The work of the model makers, which contributed vitally to the planning of innumerable operations all through the war, was far from a merely mechanical task. They interpreted the photographs just as much as all the rest of us; but they translated them into a different language – into solid three-dimensional replicas instead of into written reports.

At the time the Bruneval raid was planned the cellars of Danesfield were the setting for this highly secret activity. There Flight Lieutenant Geoffrey Deeley, a peacetime sculptor, worked with a staff of specialists, many of them sculptors or artists. There they studied all the photographs of the area they could lay their hands on, and with fretsaw and spatula and paintbrush they gradually brought them to life – in precise miniature – the whole setting for the raid. The Model Section was full of the whir of electric fretsaws and the tapping of hammers as the contours that had been traced from greatly enlarged maps were cut out of hardboard one after another, and then mounted and nailed into position. Next, after being smoothed by electric chisel, the land form was given an unbroken surface with a special plastic substance, and after this had set an enormously enlarged photograph, damped to make it supple, was pushed gently into place. Thus the towering cliffs of Cap d'Antifer were given their height, and the little valley near Bruneval its gentle slope. Finally the model was painted in the sombre colours of the winter landscape, and the model makers set in place with tweezers the Lilliputian buildings and trees and fences and of course the fire-bowl itself. Anything over three feet high was shown three-dimensionally, and if you stooped down and looked along the surface of the model, you could see exactly what the troops were going to encounter.

Members of the French Resistance supplied additional information about the radar site and where the Germans in the area were stationed. They were additionally able to confirm that the beach which was intended to be used for the withdrawal was not mined. The model was also studied at great length by the aircrews from 51 Squadron to hopefully enable them to drop their human cargoes in the correct place. The first paratrooper from the Nelson group was due to drop at 0015 and the rest of the groups at five-minute intervals. See Appendix XVII for the operational order for C Company put together by Major Frost.

Major Frost always remembered what some of the questions asked at the end of the briefing were: "What happens when you get to the front door of the villa and you blow your whistle, what do you do if the door's locked?" Frost with a smile answered that he would ring the bell. Another man questioned why they were not 'blacking up', that is using camouflage paint on all exposed areas of skin. Frost relied: "Certainly not. The main aim on this operation is to avoid confusion. I'll have no black faces. I want to be able to recognise you in the moonlight."

So now that in theory everyone had been briefed on what they had to do, there now came the time well known to anyone who has been in the Army, often jokingly referred to as the 'on the bus, off the bus' routine. Monday 23rd February was the first date that had been identified as suitable to go over to France and to all appearances to the rest of the soldiers at Tilshead, it was just another normal training day for C Company. In the morning they checked and cleaned the weapons and stores before packing them in the containers, these were to leave for Thruxton at 2.00 p.m. prior to being loaded on the Whitleys. The Company second-in-command Captain Ross had persuaded the cooks at Tilshead to provide a 'special' midday meal although what this was is unfortunately not recorded, and then everyone was encouraged to undertake some Egyptian PT (i.e. sleep) before yet another meal at tea time around 5.00 p.m. in the early evening. Then in keeping with Army dislocation of expectation a message came through that due to unfavourable weather conditions Operation Biting would have to be postponed for 24 hours. The evening was spent unpacking the containers.

This procedure was also repeated on the following three days, the containers being packed in the mornings, having a return trip from Thruxton, being unpacked in the evenings. Operation Biting was postponed on Tuesday, Wednesday and Thursday, this last day being the last date thought feasible for the raid before the next full moon in March. It must have been a somewhat stressful few days being wound up and then let down. Frost himself commented:

> We are all thoroughly miserable. Each morning we brace ourselves for the venture, and each night, after a further postponement, we have time to think of all the things that can go wrong, and that if we don't go on Thursday we shall have to wait for a whole month to pass before conditions may be suitable. After all, the weather in the English Channel in February and March is not inclined to be 'suitable'.

It was recorded in the orders the comment that 'even if the operation is postponed from 22nd February containers must still be packed during the morning of that day as it is impossible to say until approx. 1500 hours whether the operation will take place on that day. It may be cancelled up to 2215 hours if the weather changes.'

Chapter 11

Off at Last

The men of C Company awoke on the morning of Friday 27th February 1942 to a bright crisp sunny morning, no clouds, indeed it was the best day they had seen for a while. Frost expected to be told to stand down for a short period and give everyone some leave. Instead he heard that the Navy and the RAF were prepared to go that night dependent, as usual, on the weather. In fact the Navy had confidence that it would be on that night as the Commander-in-Chief at Portsmouth, Admiral Sir William James, had sent a signal to the relevant people stating "Carry out Operation Biting tonight 27th February". Commander Cook recorded that on the morning of the 27th February he rang the Flag Lieutenant Portsmouth to ask if he could see the Admiral urgently. Cook stated:

I called on Admiral Sir William James in his new office in HMS *Victory* after he had been bombed out of his old one around 9.00 a.m. I suggested that we try and do the operation that night. There had been a reasonable weather forecast and there was the problem of maintaining security for another month or so. He queried whether the tide would be suitable as at the time of the proposed embarkation it would be a falling one. I showed him a pre-war postcard of Bruneval beach with a lady bather standing close to the water's edge. From this we could deduce that the beach was much steeper than he had previously imagined. The Admiral approved and signalled that the raid should be undertaken that night. I also received a signal just before sailing this read as follows:

To HMS *Tormentor*
From Commodore Combined Operations
Operation Biting -To All Hands-Good Luck. Bite-Em-Hard
Mountbatten 27 Feb. 1942
I had much pleasure in passing it on to all concerned.

It was reported that there was not much enthusiasm amongst the paratroopers on their fifth outward trip on the bus as they packed the containers again. One man however, CSM Strachan, said he felt sure that tonight was the night and he was proved right. Around 5.00 p.m. Major-General Browning arrived at Tilshead to wish everybody good luck as it was definitely on. Even earlier at Portsmouth the *Prins Albert* had quietly slipped her moorings and headed out into the Solent. Whilst she had less distance to go than the Whitleys her speed was a lot slower and she needed a head start. As well as her normal crew she was carrying 32 men from the 11th Battalion Royal Fusiliers and 4th Battalion Monmouthshire Regiment who, armed with Brens and Boyes anti-tank rifles, were going to provide fire support (if needed) from the ALCs to cover the withdrawal.

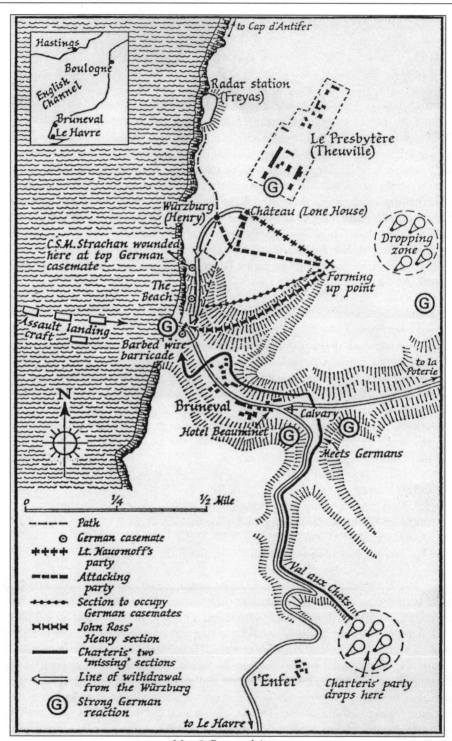

Map 9: Bruneval Area

The following few words are taken from Browning's Operation Biting report written after the raid:

5 OR's per ALC to act solely as escort to the ALS. Each of the parties were armed with four Bren LMGs (with 400 rounds per gun) and four anti-tank rifles (with 40 rounds per gun). To provide the required numbers and reserves, one officer and 25 OR's from each of 4th Monmouth Regiment and 11th Battalion Royal Fusiliers joined HMS *Prins Albert* at Inveraray on 10th February and remained on board her or in the ALCs until 1st March 1942. 20 OR's from each regiment actually accompanied the ALCs but did not land or attack the beach defences.

Also present were the previously mentioned section from 181 Field Ambulance RAMC to look after any wounded on the return trip. The *Prins Albert* had six ALCs and two LSCs slung on her davits and was escorted by five MGBs and two destroyers. Just before 10.00 p.m. off the northern coast of France the *Prins Albert* lowered the eight landing craft with assorted passengers and crew who headed off towards Bruneval. The *Prins Albert* then turned for home.

This is the medical plan for Operation Biting as drawn up by Lieutenant Baker and the Naval surgeons:

The RAMC Section embarked on the HMS *Prins Albert*, a former Belgian ship of 3000 tons, at Gosport for part of the Channel crossing, except for Lieutenant Baker who was on a MGB. Roughly halfway across the channel personnel were transferred to two LSCs and six ALCs and in company with three MGBs continued on their journey to the French coast.

The medical party were divided up as follows among the various ships:-

MGB 317	Lt A S Baker	
LSC1	Pte J Stanton	
LSC2	L/Cpl D Pusser	
ALC3	S/Sgt J Griggs	Pte E Freer
ALC4	Pte J Waters	Pte B Tuson
ALC5	Pte W Elliott	Pte J Devitt
ALC6	Cpl W Kiddell	Pte W Scott
ALC7	Pte W Hoath	Pte L Hatcher
ALC8	Pte J Newman	Pte G Rose

HMS *Prins Albert*		
Sick Bay	Pte M Grinsberg	Pte E England
Forward FAP	Pte R Domone	Pte R Maltby
Aft FAP	Pte F Cousins	Pte E McNulty

Had there been any seriously wounded troops the plan was that these would be operated on aboard the MGBs, Lieutenant Baker being based on one with Naval surgeons on the other two boats. As well as the medics from 181, medical cover was provided for the paratroopers of the 2nd Battalion by training several members of C Company (or they already had training in first aid). These were distributed amongst the various groups as follows: 2 men with first aid packs to both Hardy and Drake and 4 men each to Nelson and Rodney.

After a light meal the men of C Company moved to Thruxton to follow the timetable previously mentioned. There was time for a few last minute conversations; Major Frost remembers the following exchange with Wing Commander Pickard:

> We met again at Thruxton airfield just before we emplaned to be taken over for the operation. Once again we were more than impressed by the way the aircraft were positioned and with the way everything seemed to function absolutely as it should. The only thing that slightly worried me was what old Pick said to me just before take-off: "I feel like a bloody murderer, dropping you poor devils over there in a foreign country when we are all nice and peaceful here!".

The Jocks were piped into the aircraft by Private/Piper Ewing (who was a member of Nelson group), who played the various Regimental marches of the Scottish Regiments represented in C Company. As I have been unable to find any confirmation to the contrary the bagpipes were left behind at Thruxton, probably to the relief of the Germans, had they known. Here are a few more comments from people on the last few hours before take-off; first Flight Sergeant Cox:

> We were put in blacked-out Nissen huts. Inside it was warm and the light was yellow. Parachutes were laid out in rows on the swept floor and we each picked one hoping that the dear girl who'd packed it had had her mind on the job in hand. They were dark parachutes, camouflaged in green and black. They pressed bully beef sandwiches on us, real slabs, and mugs of tea or cocoa laced with rum. We checked each other's straps, and wandered about wide-legged like Michelin men. It seemed brighter outside than in the hut, and bitterly cold. We were formed up in our sticks roughly ten men, as we had done so often in training. One saw then what it had all been about. It was reassuring to know exactly where to go and who with.

Major Frost:

> The Company was dispersed in huts round the perimeter. John Ross and I and Sergeant Major Strachan and Newman visited each little party in turn. Some were fitting their parachutes, some having tea. There was a lot of talk, and one group was singing. It was a glorious night, an utter change in the weather; the kind of thing that only happens in England. Sometimes an aircraft engine would cough into life, and always in the background there was the rattle of a truck coursing round the edge of the aerodrome on some urgent mission. That truck came round again and it was looking for me. I was wanted on the telephone. Were they going to call it off again? But it was Group Captain Sir Nigel Norman who again was dealing with the air side of things: "Just wanted to say good luck, Frost. Latest information is that there's snow on the other side and I'm afraid the flak is lively." I thought to myself, so the RAF has been snooping round there again, annoying what we

wanted to be a sleeping hive of Germans. They had promised diversionary raids by Fighter Command on neighbouring parts of the French coast; it was to be hoped that the weather report came from one of them. As for the snow, in a way it was a relief to me. We had been issued with snow smocks but they were back at Tilshead. No, my feeling was that our main difficulty on such an operation was the fog of war, confusion. I thought the snow would make things clearer.

One man relatively happy to be at Thruxton in one piece was Sergeant Alex Reid who recalls an incident in the latter part of February 1942:

We shared a camp at Tilshead with the newly formed Glider Pilot Regiment, a god-forsaken camp if ever there was one. I shared a bunk with Sergeant Jimmy Sharp (also known as Shorty, short in stature but very great as a soldier). Conditions in the camp were terrible. I had a touch of flu, and one night I was lying in bed trying to keep warm when a Sergeant burst in brandishing one of the newly-issued Sten guns. He departed shouting "Shorty, Shorty". There followed an explosion, and I naturally thought he had shot Shorty. However, midst a lot of laughter and horseplay, Shorty and a bevy of Sergeants arrived a little worse for wear, one of them clutching a massive chunk of cheese he had borrowed from the Mess. I was more than a little apprehensive, for the early Stens were unpredictable to say the least. Discussion arose as to whether the cheese should be shot off the rafters of the hut, but the cheese-bearer invited the Sten-waver to shoot it out of his hand, whereupon the Sten-man told him; "Don't be bloody daft I might hit your hand." Upon which the other suggested they swap roles, such was the ale-inspired logic but being somewhat sober I was afraid that bullets would get sprayed everywhere including my direction. However, it was decided to eat the cheese instead much to my relief.

Back at Thruxton there were no more last-minute hitches and gradually the men of C Company started to get aboard their relevant Whitley, ten to each aircraft, except in the Frost aircraft which carried only nine. This made a total of 119 men intending to drop on the raid, take-off time was virtually to time at 10.15 p.m. Although it was a relatively short flight compared to that experienced on Colossus, it was still a cold trip. Sleeping bags and silk gloves had been provided and this is what Flight Sergeant Cox later recorded:

We put on our silk gloves and crawled into sleeping bags for warmth. The Whitley's ribbed aluminum floor was fiendishly uncomfortable. Ahead we could hear a kite revving prior to take-off and then it was away. Others followed until it was our turn. The whole machine throbbed and bumped and dragged itself off the ground as though it had great big heavy sloppy feet. Nobody slept in that dim-lit metal cigar. There was a green light inside the fuselage and a group of four at the other end were playing cards even though it was very cold and very cramped. We sang a few songs on the way across – *Lulu, Come Sit by My Side If You Love Me* and *Annie Laurie.* Then by popular request, I gave them two solos, *The Rose of Tralle* and *Because*. Somehow the engines made it easier to sing. At least it helped relax my straining nerves.

On an aircraft containing some of the Nelson group three hardened gamblers were playing cards and the big winner was Corporal Stewart who remarked, on putting his winnings in his wallet, that if he got hit on the raid the bloke closest to him should take his wallet and put it to good use. In another aircraft Private Scott (part of Rodney group) remembers Lieutenant Timothy handing round his water bottle around ten minutes before the expected drop time. Expecting it to be water to his surprise he found it was pure Jamaican rum which gave him and the rest of them a warm feeling inside. Soon afterwards the covers in all the Whitleys over the dropping holes were removed which obviously let some really cold air in. To those that were able to see out they could observe the English Channel shimmering in a bright moonlight. Then they crossed the coast to be met by some flak, so perhaps the Würzburg was doing its job. Action Stations was called and the first man in each stick dangled his legs into the exit hole, the dropping height was around 500 feet. Each aircraft was flying independently, relying on the navigators to get them to the right place. The RAF flying that night did a magnificent job. Admittedly it was a short-range mission but when one thinks back to the Butt Report, Frost and his men should have expected to land within about 5 miles of the objective. As it turned out 10 of the 12 Whitleys dropped their loads in the correct place. Perhaps the reasons for this are the bright moonlight, the snow on the ground (which would have outlined the coast), it is also possible they may have obtained a bearing of the Cap d'Antifer lighthouse which would have been a useful reference point and the skill of the crews of 51 Squadron. Flying a south to north course, it would have been possible to see where the white ended and the coast started. It is also worth remembering that much time had been spent studying maps and the model and this probably helped orientation.

The following comment comes from Sergeant M Forsyth, who was a member of Rodney group and recalled this about the last few seconds before the green light came on:

> The red light went on and Corporal Walker, the first man, put his feet into the hole. I was watching him and his face turned a bit of a different colour. Then the green light went on and bang, bang, bang out they went. When everyone was down and organised I said to Corporal Walker what had happened as I had seen his colour change and he said; "So would you have with all that bloody tracer coming up at you." I had no idea as it had been relatively quiet when I left the Whitley.

Major Frost, the first man out of his Whitley, later commented that as he was descending to the ground he was able to recognise exactly the drop zone and other features where he had expected to see them. All the time spent looking at maps, aerial photographs and the model had paid dividends. They landed in the snow and with no German reception committee waiting for them, which was good news. The first action should have been to go and find the weapons and stores containers (which had a small light on them to assist in finding them in the dark), however, after getting out of their parachute harnesses, many of C Company needed to 'ease springs'. The mixture of tea, rum and the cold air that had passed through many of them had caused a pressing need for release. Frost later commented,

> What I hadn't thought of was the effect of the tea and rum and cold. It became very uncomfortable on the flight over and bitterly cold. I'll never forget the relief in being outside the aircraft in the cold still air and dropping exactly on target. I landed in the snow and the first thing I did without any hesitation at all was to have a bloody good pee! I looked down the line of my stick thinking I must be setting a bad example and saw everyone else was doing exactly the same.

Just a word or two here about the identification of the containers:
- The arms containers had a red light.
- The signals containers had a green light.
- The engineer containers had a purple light.
- The trolley containers had an orange light.

These lights were operated by dry-cell batteries which were turned on by the impact of landing.

These were further identified by having wide white bands painted on the containers denoting the groups; Nelson containers had 1 band, Hardy and Jellicoe 2 bands, Drake 3 and Rodney 4 bands. The containers also had a distinctive letter and number painted on the side. It was reported later that these aids helped the troops to find and recognise their containers without any difficulty.

The first group to land, Nelson, was on the drop zone at 00.15 a.m. on what was now Saturday 28th February. In theory, this should have been 40 men under the command of Captain Ross assisted by Lieutenant Charteris, who were to head for the beach defences to secure the withdrawal route. After a quick head count at the rendezvous Captain Ross found he only had 20 men. The rest of Nelson group carried in two aircraft, one piloted by Wing Commander Pickard, had dropped their loads about two miles south of the intended drop zone near a small village called L'Enfer. Fortunately they could see that the other Whitleys were dropping paratroopers to the north, so roughly knew which direction to head. Perhaps it is worth adding that it was a good job that the senior pilot didn't carry the senior paratrooper! About five minutes after half of Nelson group had landed Hardy group landed intact. This is what Flight Sergeant Cox later recalled:

> I remember looking up at the dark belly of the Whitley and how visible the exhausts were. When my parachute had opened, I checked I still had my fighting knife and Colt .45 pistol. The next thing I remember is rolling in the snow. The first thing that struck me was the silence. I suppose it was a reaction to the horrible din inside the aircraft. Then I heard a rustling, and saw something outlined on the snow and a light on it. I was close to a container and also that of one of the containers containing a hand-trolley.

After the men had collected the weapons and stores from the containers, numbers at the forming up point began to increase and within about ten minutes everyone from Hardy group was present. Here Major Frost was given the news about the twenty men from Nelson and so he hastily arranged a new plan with Captain Ross. Basically this

61. The Rectangle/La Presbytère from the forming-up point near Bruneval. (N Cherry)

62. Looking inland from the position of the German beach
bunker towards Bruneval village (N Cherry)

meant telling Ross to go and do his best at the beach with his group. Originally Captain Ross had been in charge of the support group while Lieutenant Charteris's group would do the actual clearance of the beach. So he had to improvise as best he could. Captain Ross was not helped in his new task in that the other Whitley-load of Nelson had been given a task that meant them leaving very soon after reporting in. This was to take and hold a German defensive position codenamed Redoubt on the northern heights of the beach. Quite rightly, after reporting in, they left to undertake their task. In the event, the defensive position was unmanned, and they remained here according to the plan outlined in England. Obviously the villa and radar site took priority and Frost stated that he would send reinforcements in the shape of some of Lieutenant Naoumoff's Drake group as soon as possible. Whilst all of this was going on the last group – the 40 men of Rodney group, could be seen arriving on the drop zone. One of the members of this group, Private R Scott, had an unfortunate incident on exiting his Whitley:

> I was Number 6 in the stick and in the descent just after leaving the Whitley I was clobbered by a container and didn't I curse the RAF despatcher. On landing I found that my fighting knife had gone and my trouser leg was ripped down the seam.

So far so good, with the exception of the 20 missing men, and the various groups started off on their relevant tasks. Captain Ross and his party headed off towards the evacuation beach. Major Frost and the Hardy group went towards the villa, closely followed by the Jellicoe group going to the radar site. The Jellicoe group was followed at what was hopefully a safe distance by the 'dismantling party'. Drake group were to take up a position between the area known in the plan as 'Rectangle' (La Presbytère), where it was thought around 100 Germans were billeted, and the villa. The final group, Rodney, was to move in a south-westerly direction from the rendezvous point to form a defensive line against any German attack from inland. There was no opposition as the groups set off, their main problem being the numerous wire fences surrounding the fields. There were a few stray bursts of machine gun fire somewhere in the distance but nothing was seen or heard from the area of the villa or radar pit. The imposed plan called for Frost himself to lead the attack on the villa, he later commented:

> I didn't like this because there wasn't proper control. I had been told to lead the assault on the villa, when I should have been free to command the situation. Instead I was with a Sten leading a charge on the villa. When I got to the steps leading up to the villa I found the door was open and I nearly forgot to blow my whistle before going in. As soon as I blew it explosions, yells and the sound of automatic fire came from the proximity of the radar set and my party rushed into the house. It was devoid of furniture and we found only one German in a top room who was firing down on the people round the radar pit, however he was quickly dealt with.

Meanwhile at the radar pit, Lieutenant Young and his group had quickly overwhelmed the few Germans there. One German ran away towards the cliffs and ever mindful of the request to get some prisoners he was chased. In his haste to get away he ran over the edge of the cliffs but managed to cling on and climb back. As he reached the plateau he was caught and taken back to the radar pit. Lieutenant Vernon had left Flight Sergeant Cox and the sappers kneeling in the snow some distance from the radar pit while he went forward to assess the situation. When he found out everything was under control he called his party forward. The group quickly got over the low barbed wire fence surrounding the installation. The firing from the direction of the villa had stopped, but now there appeared to be more firing coming from the area of Rectangle. Matters were not helped by Lieutenant Vernon doing as instructed and he started to use a flashlight camera taking a photograph of the aerial. This at once attracted incoming fire and so Frost, who by now had joined the party at Henry, ordered him to stop using the camera. Incidentally when the film was developed back in England it was found that the one exposure was a double exposure, the inside of the Würzburg bowl being superimposed over a view of some wooden huts presumably at Tilshead. One sapper had been detailed in England to start sawing off the aerial while the others went inside the installation. The sapper detailed was Stan Halliwell and he later commented:

> I stood on what I thought was a concrete foundation which seemed to be very solid about 4 or 5 feet high. I jumped up and stood on that. From this I could reach the antenna which was at least 5 feet long. The first thing I thought of was had the power been switched off, otherwise it might have been a shocking experience. Anyway, I just took a chance and I started sawing with my hacksaw and it flew through the metal. It was only an alloy when I thought it might have been steel, as it looked sturdy when I had briefly examined it. Then I jumped down and was instructed to guard it with my life.

Outside Private Newman, under instructions from Major Frost, was questioning the somewhat shaken German prisoner. He confirmed he was a member of a Luftwaffe Signals Regiment and that around 100 of his comrades were billeted in La Presbytère, they were armed with amongst other weapons some mortars, but didn't train with them much, their main role being signallers. Lieutenant Naoumoff and his group were doing their best to suppress the fire coming from La Presbytère, but it did cause the first fatal casualty. Private H McIntyre was killed whilst in a position near the door of the villa. One man present here was Private R Scott:

> We took up positions and I was placed with a Bren gun on the left of the section facing the German camp. We were about 150 yards out and quite near to the radar post. There was some gunfire and then a lull. On the east side of the camp we could hear the Germans going away from the camp and were in a laughing mood. Then on the cliff-side tracers were seen attacking the radar post. I spoke to Private Crutchley and said I was having a go, but I can't boast of the result. Later I noticed six men in single file coming between the camp and us. There was no order to challenge them so I fired a couple of short bursts and they went to ground. I thought if they were Germans we would get something in our backs when we withdrew.

Frost could also hear firing coming from where he thought Lieutenant Timothy's group were positioned and more ominously the sound of vehicles could be heard. Frost later commented:

These vehicles might contain far more dangerous elements and if the enemy began to mortar us in the open with no means of retaliating it would be difficult to get the equipment away. All our small wireless sets (Number 18s) failed to work so I had no idea how the other parties had fared and I began to feel the lack of a proper Company Headquarters organisation. We had under the imposed plan turned ourselves into an assault group for the attack on the villa and now, when I wanted some signallers, runners and my Sergeant-Major, they were all dispersed doing other tasks. I then decided to act as a further covering screen with my party together with as many men from the Young group as could be spared.

Meanwhile, back at the radar pit, according to Cox's report, he then entered the actual 'control room' of the Würzburg, going through a blackout curtain. Once inside he found that the set was still hot and shouted out to Private Newman to ask the prisoner if they had tracked the Whitleys on their flight in. The prisoner agreed that they had done so. He further added that the longer range Freya sets in the other installation had detected the Whitleys and the Würzburg had got them on their displays at around 20 miles. Whilst the range of the Freya had been suspected by the scientific intelligence community, confirmation of the range of the Würzburg was the first real bit of intelligence gained on the raid. The prisoner, although somewhat shocked, added that they had expected to be bombed as they tracked a number of relatively low-flying aircraft who were heading almost directly for their position. The decision was taken or

63. The double exposure picture from Operation Biting. As well as the huts some scale numbers from the aerial bowl can just be made out. (National Archives)

orders given for the set to be switched off and some personnel sent to take cover. Then using the light from a hooded torch Cox began to make notes and sketches. He wrote (amongst other things),

> Like a searchlight on a rotatable platform mounted on a flat four-wheeled truck. Truck had its wheels raised and is well sandbagged up to platform level. Paraboloid is ten feet diameter and hinged so that radio beam can be swung freely up or down or sideways. Small cabin to one side shelters set's display gear and operator's seat. At rear of paraboloid is container three feet wide, two feet deep, five feet high. This appears to hold all the works with the exception of display. Design very clean and straightforward. We found the set switched off but warm. The top of the compartment taken by the transmitter and what looks like first stage of receiver. Large power pack with finned metal rectifiers occupies bottom. Between the TX (Transmission) and the power unit is the pulse gear and the receiver IF (Intermediate Frequency). Everything solid and in good order. Telefunken labels everywhere which one sapper was removing with hammer and cold chisel. Just enough light to work by, with moon reflected off snow.

After a quick discussion between Cox and Vernon, it was decided that the more important items were probably in the console rather than the display unit so it was decided to concentrate on this. Using tools that they had brought with them, the pulse unit and the IF amplifier were removed, both coming out easily. However when they tried to remove the transmitter it was found they did not of have a screwdriver long enough to reach the screw heads. So in keeping with the usual Army solution to any technical problem they called 'for a heavier hammer', in this case a crowbar. So while Vernon and Cox pulled on the handles and body of the transmitter, another sapper provided leverage with the crowbar. The whole unit came away with most of the lightweight fixing frame with a tearing sound. It later turned out to be a good decision as Cox later reported:

> When this piece of equipment was examined it was found that the frame which we in that somewhat hasty moment regarded as no more than an encumbrance, something we had not the time to detach from the transmitter, contained the aerial switching unit that allowed both the transmitter and receiver to use the one aerial, a vital piece of the design of any radar set.

Major Frost was now becoming concerned at the amount of incoming fire and indeed the sound of activity from the German positions, and as he only had a small time window, he ordered the engineers to finish what they were doing and get going towards the beach. Even now he did not know if it had been cleared. The sappers used crowbars to rip out what items they felt were important and then reported they were ready to go.

Charles Cox had this to say about the last few minutes at the radar site:

> We were told that we didn't have much more time and then we were told only one more minute so we literally ripped out everything we could and prepared to leave for the beach.

At this moment Frost took a few seconds out to consider his options and the current position; he later stated that he felt it was one of almost total confusion. There was firing from nearly everywhere. He could hear heavy firing coming from the area of the evacuation beach together with the odd white flare lighting up the sky. He sensed the German fire from the area of Rectangle was increasing, they had probably been reinforced and it was only a matter of time before they moved forward. Finally to his consternation, there were sounds of heavy firing from Bruneval village. This was temporarily worrying unless as he put it himself that 'some of Timothy's men had gone berserk and fought their way into the centre of Bruneval?'

He had received a message by runner from Lieutenant Timothy some time earlier which had told Frost that everything was under control, except that his Number 38 radio wasn't working. This problem continued to dog the airborne forces for most of the war. In any case it was time to go, a message was sent to Lieutenant Naoumoff by runner telling him to withdraw to firstly the radar pit and then to pass through Frost's group and clear the way to the beach followed by the radar booty.

I feel this is an appropriate moment to leave the Frost, Naoumoff and Timothy groups and look at the actions of Captain Ross and his Nelson group. You will recall this party was to move from the rendezvous point in a south-westerly direction to clear the German positions on and around the evacuation beach known as Redoubt, Beach Fortress and Guard Room. As previously stated this group was to have consisted of four sections of ten men but two of them had been dropped away from the drop zone and we shall meet up with them shortly. So, soon after Frost's group had left the drop zone, Captain Ross was left with ten men. Remember here that one section (commanded by Sergeant Tasker) had already gone to occupy the pillbox codenamed Redoubt which was intended to be a firm base upon which to launch the attack on the beach defences. Ross had to assume that it had been occupied as he heard no firing from that direction. The plan thrashed out in England envisaged that two sections led by Lieutenant Charteris would attack from the south-east, by this was meant going south from the drop zone and then swinging round to the east. Captain Ross was meant to be in reserve with what was known as the support section. However as the Airborne version of Murphy's Law had been proved for the second time, in that nothing ever goes to plan, Ross only had ten men to do the intended role of thirty. However, he had no option but to get on with it and he and his men headed off towards the evacuation beach. He recognised the ground they travelled across from the model, towards the road which was in a gully as it headed towards the beach. As they neared the approaches to the beach a white flare rose, fired by a German at the location known as Guard Room. This was otherwise known as the Villa Stella Maris, which was situated on some high ground on the south side of the beach entry road. They were instantly spotted and a fusillade of fire from this position was directed at Ross's group. The Germans had dug a series of interconnecting slit trenches facing inland, which was unexpected, and it was from these that the fire was coming.

In spite of the Ross section being called a support group the heaviest weapon he possessed was one Bren gun, the rest being armed with rifles and Stens. He also had two sappers with mine detectors to check the beach and two signallers, one with a Number 18 set and the other with a Number 38 set. It can be seen his resources were limited and Ross later commented he wished he had brought a 2 inch mortar with him. For the time being the Ross section was pinned down, we will return to his group soon.

The two missing sections from Nelson led by Second Lieutenant Charteris were as previously stated dropped away from the intended spot, making landfall near the village of L'Enfer just over one mile south of the intended drop zone. Pickard and the aircraft following him had been apparently caught in some accurately-aimed flak which helped to put the navigators and pilots off track and therefore in an attempt to get back on track they mistook landmarks and so dropped their loads in the wrong place. Second Lieutenant Charteris later commented:

> When we arrived over France, somewhere near Le Havre, we opened the hole and as I was the first to jump, I was sitting next to it. Everything was very clear; you could see the coast and every house, tree and fence. It was all black and white, clear-cut in the moonlight. I remember some flak which came up; it sounded as though a man was hammering a piece of tin below us. The aircraft took evasive action. Then the red light went on. I sat on the edge of the hole. I jumped immediately the light turned green. It was a lovely drop, there was no wind and I came down like a feather in about 10 seconds. I could see the rest of the stick landing. The plan was for them to form up round the containers while I moved south-west, meeting my batman who was to drop from another aircraft and wait for the rest to come along to me when we should all proceed together in a direction which I had previously reconnoitered. As soon as I was free of my parachute I put this plan into operation. I moved south-west, where I soon perceived that we had dropped in the wrong valley. The valley into which we had fallen looked very like the right one but there was no row of trees at the bottom of it as there should have been and it was not deep enough. I don't mind saying that this was a nasty moment.

Fortunately Second Lieutenant Charteris was able to work out their rough position when he heard and saw the remaining ten Whitleys heading further north. They were able to quickly find their containers and suitably armed they formed up and two of the men were sent ahead as scouts, who reported that they were close to a narrow road, which Charteris was able to work out led to Bruneval village. They jogged their way along the side of this road, hearing the sounds of gunfire in the distance to the north. The old maxim of 'marching to the sound of gunfire' is seldom proved wrong. On the way they were joined by a German soldier who mistook the patrol for one of his own side, when it was discovered he was with them, he was killed.

Second Lieutenant Charteris again:

> My men had got to the containers, opened them and formed up; they were coming towards me and at that moment other aircraft passed overhead. They seemed to me to be flying steadily and therefore had not yet dropped their parachutists. I knew then that we had dropped on the right line but I could not determine whether we had been dropped too soon or too late. The aircraft were flying steadily in a northerly direction. I, therefore went north and as soon as I picked up the section, I explained to them that we had been dropped in the wrong place but that I thought we could get to the proper spot by moving in the direction I was taking. As we moved off, another stick dropped from No 11, the last aircraft but one. Their number 1 dropped quite close to me and I told him that we were moving due north

and he had better follow us. We pushed off in diamond formation, myself in the lead moving at a rapid walk or kind of lope, about 6 miles per hour. Presently I saw the lighthouse on the Cap d'Antifer and knew where I was. We had then covered about ¾ of a mile. Soon afterwards I picked out the wood of the La Presbytère. Across the field I could see the dark edge of a wood. We were then fired on or maybe the Germans were firing at another stick. We had, however, then a casualty, Private Sutherland, who was hit in the shoulder and subsequently captured. He did his best to follow us but could not manage to keep up. We dodged into the side of the wood and I got the Bren gun to cover us while we turned at right angles and moved along the wood to its end with the intention of turning to the left and rushing up its other side. I was about to move off when I heard a screech or a scream and saw a Jerry about 4 or 5 yards from us. I tried to fire my Colt but I had forgotten to take off one of the two safety catches. Sergeant Gibbons, however, let him have the whole of a Sten gun magazine and he dropped. As a matter of fact the Hun had come up with us and had walked beside one of my men for some time thinking that we were Germans. When he discovered his error he fired once and then was killed.

Along the way one or two men became detached but the party reached the outskirts of Bruneval village, meeting some German resistance which had to be overcome. This came from a platoon of the 1st Company of the 685th Infantry Regiment.

These are the recollections of Second Lieutenant Charteris:

We went through some scrubby and difficult country and presently reached the edge of Bruneval village into which we plunged making a lot of noise. I was sure, however, that speed was more important than silence. At the bottom of the valley there was a road with some open ground on each side. I put a Bren gun team to cover us while we doubled across the open ground. While climbing up the other side of the valley we were again fired on. This was a great nuisance because we were then swarming up the hillside which was covered with bushes and we were not therefore together. I was on ahead leading the men and then I found some cover. The rear half of the section turned left into some woods when the firing began and I lost touch with them. The next thing we heard was Bren gun fire and deduced from this that the radio location station was being attacked according to the plan. This heartened us a lot.

By one of those lucky accidents all the various elements of C Company were now converging on the same small area from various different directions and it would be best to look at the actions as a whole.

We had left Lieutenant Naoumoff's section after they had withdrawn to the area of the villa, then leading the group to the beach. On his way through Frost's group he was told by Frost that he would probably have to try and contact Captain Ross and also to clear the beach area so the radar booty and men could get clear. Following him with most of the remaining group (less a small rearguard) was Major Frost and the radar group with the captured equipment. It is recorded that it was not easy to manhandle the trolley with its heavy load down the somewhat steep slope towards the beach. The Naoumoff party got to the area of the beach without being spotted and prepared to launch an assault on the German positions. However, when the 'radar party' got to the area of Redoubt they were spotted by some Germans, probably in the defensive position known as Beach Fort, and opened fire on with a machine gun.

Charles Cox again:

> We got about halfway down and all carrying the radar stuff when the Germans started firing at us from the pillboxes on the other side of the ravine. We then realised that the beach wasn't clear at that moment and bullets were cracking past us. We all laid down and I got a bullet hole in my shoe but I wasn't hurt.

Around this time Company Sergeant Major Strachan was hit and fell to the ground with three bullets in his stomach. It would probably be best to tidy up the next few minutes using Frost's own words:

> When we reached a pillbox on the shoulder of the cliff a machine gun opened up on us from the other shoulder and we suffered casualties. Sergeant Major Strachan was badly wounded in the stomach. We pulled him into cover and gave him some morphine. The machine gun opened up each time we moved, but it was possible to make contact with the Rodney party who were further inland. At this stage some confusion was caused by shouting from below. "Come on down! Everything is all right and the boats are here." This was immediately contradicted by John Ross who was nearer the beach. "Do not come down. The beach defences have not been taken yet."
>
> Obviously something was seriously wrong with this part of the plan and just as I was going across to see John Timothy of Rodney to order him to put in an immediate attack from his positions, a man came from behind to say that the Germans had reoccupied the villa and were advancing against us from that direction. Here again we were at a disadvantage as my men were armed only with Sten guns and grenades and the unorthodox formations we had adopted meant I personally had to lead the party back to deal with this new threat, while I had many other things to think of.
>
> Fortunately this threat did not amount to very much, for the Germans were still very confused and were up against they knew not what. They hesitated and withdrew. As we returned to the pillbox, we found that the sappers were on the move again, skidding and sliding with their heavily laden trolleys down the steep frozen path to the beach. The Sergeant Major was being dragged down at the same time. The troublesome machine gun was silent now, so one could presume that the beach defences had been taken. All the main features showed up well in the moonlight, but one could see men and movement only when close at hand.

At what can only be described at the opportune moment Second Lieutenant Charteris and his two sections arrived in the area and together with Captain Ross's and Lieutenant Naoumoff's groups proceeded to overwhelm the German defensive positions. Some of Ross's men found a joint in the wire defences and were able to pull it aside to make an opening. As they were joined by Naoumoff's men and started to go through the gap, shouts and firing could be heard from the south east. It was the Charteris group also attacking.

We left the Charteris group on the outskirts on Bruneval so let me finish their actions now:

I waited under cover and sent Corporal Hill to find the remainder of the section who had gone into the wood on the left. He came back presently having been unable to do so, but I found out later they reached the beach independently. They consisted of four men under the command of Private Matkin, and to reach the beach, they went round the edge of the village. There they saw a crowd, almost certainly composed of Germans, and so sheered off and reached the beach eventually, being guided by the sound of firing.

While this was happening to Private Matkin and his men, I had pushed on with the remainder of the men moving still at a fast lollop and meeting with no opposition. I kept hearing firing from the beach, which was then on our left hand side. My object was to reach the Rodney group, which was the covering party. Presently I fell in with Lieutenant Timothy commanding them. He told me that the Germans still held the beach and that one of my sections was held up at the bottom of the valley approaching the beach. He also said that the Hardy and Jellicoe groups, whose duty it had been to assault the house and radio location station, were now in a position in a dip on the edge of the valley. I went forward a little with my men and met Major Frost. He was surprised to see me because I should have, by then, been on the beach. I explained that we had been dropped in the wrong place. He was somewhat worried because he did not know what was happening in the valley. Major Frost decided to attack downhill and he gave me orders to do so. I had three men with me at that time – Sergeant Gibbons, Corporal Hill and Private Laughland. They were all very tired because of the speed of our march. The worst was Corporal Hill, as he had been carrying a lot of ammunition. I gave him my pistol and took his rifle in exchange.

By then all the parties were getting a bit mixed up so we all advanced together to take the beach and I found myself going down a gully. I felt as naked as a baby because I was only about 70 yards from the house on the beach, which I knew to be held by the enemy. I had thought for about a month how best to attack this house, I had examined all the photographs and worked out all possible plans but when I came to do so the reality was quite different from the expectation.

Between my men, myself and the house was a sunken road and some wire. We lay down as close as we could to the wire and then flung two volleys of hand grenades into the balcony of the house. Then we charged in the sunken road, crossed it and entered the house.

After that, things got somewhat confused. There were some Jerries in a dugout further on our side of the road. I flung some grenades into the cellar of the house from a small door which opened onto the sunken road. We charged into the house shouting "Hande Hoch." I then went round to the front and got on to the wooden terrace which was empty. I could not find the front door at all. I ran most of the way round the house until I discovered that it was at the back. When I got to it I found it was open and further on there was a lighted passage.

Faced with the prospect of being attacked from two directions at once, the German defenders around the Villa Stella Maris decided discretion was the better part of valour and slipped away in a southerly direction. One German, not moving quickly enough, was caught coming out of the Stella Maris and taken prisoner by Sergeant Jimmy Sharp, the second prisoner of the operation. The time was now around 2.15 a.m. and the way to the beach was clear. As Frost later commented:

> There was now time to take stock. So far the object had been achieved. We had very few casualties. We knew roughly where everybody was. We had given the enemy a good hammering and so far they had produced no effective counter-measures. All we wanted now was the Royal Navy to pick us up.

So waiting on the beach was the majority of those who had landed, the vital captured radar equipment and two prisoners. So where were the landing craft? Major Frost spoke to the various signallers, but none of them had been able to make contact with their Number 18 and 38 wireless sets. Not for the last time in the war would the airborne forces be frustrated by a failure in radio communications. Even more serious was the increasing fire coming from the cliffs on either side of the beach, and it was around this time that Private A Scott was shot and fatally wounded. Frost told the signallers to go to the second method of calling the Navy in and to try using a signalling torch showing a white light. They still got no reply. Frost commented that…

64. A view from the German positions on the southern cliffs looking down towards the beach and gully. Note the memorial to the raid on the right, which is built on the top of a German pillbox. (R Voskuil)

... there was a slight mist out to sea and visibility was no more than half a mile. We had arranged one last emergency means of communication, which was a green Verey light fired first to the north and then to the south along the beach. Even after this had been fired several times there was no sign of recognition from the sea. With a sinking heart I moved off the beach with my officers to rearrange our defences in the entrance to the village and on the shoulders of the cliff. It looked as though we were going to be left high and dry once more and the thought was hard to bear. The prisoners were questioned as to the whereabouts of the enemy reserves, but they were too frightened to be coherent, and the great cliffs each side of the little beach seemed to lean over and dominate us with ever-growing menace.

A very (at that time) secret piece of equipment had been brought with the party, which was the Rebecca radio beacon. This sent out a signal on a pre-determined frequency to be picked up by its companion set known as a Eureka, which was in one of the ALCs. This was the last roll of the dice, the sappers stated it was working correctly and all they could do was hope. Meanwhile as Major Frost was checking the defensive positions, Captain Ross was carrying out some badly needed administration at the hastily set-up control centre. Here it was confirmed that so far, they had suffered two killed, six wounded had been placed in relative shelter on the beach and six men missing. One of the wounded was the lucky winner of the card school in his Whitley on the flight out, Corporal Stewart. He felt he was a goner and as he had promised, handed over his wallet to his friend L/Corporal Freeman. L/Corporal Freeman examined Stewart's head and told him it was only a bit of a gash, upon which Stewart demanded his wallet back.

Here is a comment from Private R Scott about the withdrawal back to the beach:

> After the withdrawal from the radar post, I knew that CSM Strachan was wounded by his behaviour, Private Grant was also in great pain and I was forced to shout at him to get moving towards the beach.

Second Lieutenant Charteris was on the edge of the beach and instructed one of his Bren gunners to take up a position in an abandoned German weapons pit and gave him instructions to cover the woods further inland. Then Corporal Campbell appeared on his own, stating he had been sent forward to find out what was happening by Sergeant Lumb (they were part of the Rodney group) and had been dropped away from the correct place. Out of this group of ten, five had landed south of Bruneval, together with a wireless set and some weapons. The remainder had not landed with them as apparently the sixth man in the stick had got stuck in the exit and the Whitley had to make a second run. They were dropped on the correct DZ but had no weapons with them, so they were allocated to the 'engineer party' and helped with removal of equipment. Corporal Campbell was quickly told, with many deleted words, to get his group up here 'as quickly as possible'. Charteris was aware that the wireless set was urgently wanted by Captain Ross. The rest of the men were placed in defensive positions facing inland but about 50 yards from the beach. The thought in many men's minds was one of anxiety. Second Lieutenant Charteris later recalled:

65. Looking up from the evacuation beach towards the headland where the radar station was located at Bruneval, down which the men of C Company had to scramble. (N Cherry)

I remember wondering where the Navy was and looking out to sea. There was no sign of them and I then began to think that we would not get back but I was too busy to bother much at the time and I seemed to look at the situation quite impersonally. By then, of course, the position was fairly serious because we were an hour behind schedule.

The Navy was now well overdue, and Lieutenant Timothy reported that vehicle lights could be seen approaching the area from the east and south-east. Things were not looking good. It now feels appropriate to look at the actions of the Royal Navy.

Around 5.00 p.m. on 27th February the *Prins Albert*, carrying the 8 landing craft together with the 5 MGBs from the 14th Flotilla, weighed anchor and started out on their voyage across the Channel. Commander Cook started the trip on the *Prins Albert* but joined LSC2 for the latter part of the crossing. Taking their last bearing off the Isle of Wight, they steamed by dead reckoning to EA5 rescue float then to the dispersal point known as W, which was 12 miles short of the French coast, hopefully off Bruneval. This was reached at 10.00 p.m. on the 27th February. Here are some more words from Commander Cook:

We could expect no help from French lighthouses so borrowed taut-wire measuring gear from the navy hydrographers. Over the stern of *Prins Albert* we dropped a weight which was attached to a drum of piano-wire. As the wire ran out we read off the distance travelled in nautical miles. This certainly helped. The lowering of the 8 landing craft from the *Prins Albert* was carried out in the moonlight in record time – 2½ minutes – and then we set off in them for a 10 mile run to point X, 2 miles short of the beach. We were escorted by the 5 MGBs. Meanwhile the *Prins Albert* had left us for Portsmouth anchoring there at 3.00 a.m. on the following morning, but to fox the Huns if she was being plotted, she made a few dummy runs up and down as though she were laying mines.

At about 1.30 a.m. we arrived at point X. Things seemed to be fairly quiet so we sneaked in a little closer to Y, about a mile off the 300 feet cliffs. Suddenly the Cap d'Antifer lighthouse gave a few flashes (it was about 2 miles north of our target) and we got quick confirmatory bearings. We could not believe our good luck, but not for long.

The Navy had managed to get to the correct area by their appointed time but as the operation was taking place beyond the ideal window of opportunity, there was an added problem. This was that if things ashore did not run to the proposed timetable the ALCs would have to approach the beach on a falling tide. This could have been a repeat of the exercise in Southampton Water when the ALCs were left beached high and dry. The plan called for a somewhat orderly evacuation of the troops from the beach with the radar equipment taking priority, with the ALCs approaching in relays. The gunboats and landing craft were waiting anxiously offshore when just after 2.00 a.m. two German destroyers and two E-Boats were spotted steaming parallel to the coast but further out to sea than the British ships. Fortunately they were not spotted and soon afterwards some white flares fired by the Germans at Bruneval were seen, followed by the signalling light and green flares previously mentioned.

This is what Commander Cook later commented:

The Huns hadn't switched the lighthouse on for us but for 2 German destroyers and 2 E-Boats moving slowly a mile or so to seaward of us, just where we should have been! We had no torpedoes and could not hazard our main objective – the embarkation of the paratroopers. We held our breath. I ordered all 13 vessels to cut engines and for complete silence. We just rolled and prayed. Why we were not discovered I shall never know – perhaps the background of the cliffs, or the firing on shore, or the bombing of Le Havre might have distracted the German ships.

At 2.35 a.m. two of the ALCs were ordered inshore and shortly afterwards one of the signallers ashore got through on a 38 set and requested, without authority, that all the landing craft come in at once. On the beach someone saw the approaching landing craft and shouted out "Sir, the boats are coming in! The boats are here! God bless the ruddy Navy!"

Accompanying the six ALCs were two LSCs and each of these had four soldiers split into two two-man Bren gun teams and these sixteen Brens started pouring fire on the cliffs as they neared the shore. These few moments were summed up by Major Frost:

A sense of relief unbounded now spread amongst us all as we saw several dark shapes gliding in across the water towards us and we began to assemble in our various parties to embark. The men who manned the landing craft opened fire on the cliffs when they were about fifty yards from the beach. The noise was terrific as the echoes ran from cliff to cliff. We shouted and screamed at them to stop as some of our men were still in position to defend the beach from a landward attack. We had planned that only two boats would come in at a time, so that we could make an orderly withdrawal in three phases, but now all six landing craft came in together and some looked as though they might be beached, as the sea was beginning to run fairly high. Amidst the noise and confusion it was impossible to control the embarkation.

Fortunately we were able to get the wounded and the enemy radar equipment on to one of the landing craft very quickly, but the rest of my evacuation plan went by the board, and it was a case of getting as many men as possible to each boat in turn. The Germans began to emerge from some of their hiding places when they saw we were going and lobbed grenades and mortar bombs on to the beach. As far as we could tell, eventually all our men were away. Most of us were soaked to the skin, for we had had to wade and scramble through the waves to reach the landing craft. I was not too pleased with this finale as it had not been as I had hoped.

Commander Cook commented that the first two landing craft hit the beach at 2.40 a.m. and were initially rushed by paratroopers. He stated that they were hopelessly overcrowded – one actually had 68 men on board until some were transferred to another craft. Later two of the six ALCs had to be towed as their engines had burnt out due to the excessive strain imposed on them by being overloaded.

Flight Sergeant Cox later recounted:

The wait on the beach was very demoralising. A bloke near me was very morbid, kept moaning we were going to be captured. I replied there was still plenty of time, I don't know how long exactly we waited, but finally the boats did come in. We rushed for them and the water was really cold. The boat I got on had a boffin aboard and he collared me; "Now, Flight Sergeant, have you got what I wanted?" I answered "I think so, Sir." We started talking about what I had seen.

Private Scott again:

I was the last to get aboard my particular landing craft and it sped off much too quickly before the ramp was closed and we were in water nearly to our knees. There was a hand pump and we used our helmets to help bale out. On reaching the MGB our next predicament was to get the wounded CSM on to it safely for the boats kept parting until they were properly tethered. CSM Strachan kept calling for a drink, Corporal Fleming and I were left to manhandle him into the boat. When we got to sea I could see a flashing light from the shore, it could have been an SOS from the person whose duty it was to guide latecomers to the beach, but we didn't go back to find out.

Obviously it was impracticable to land the Noah party waiting, probably impatiently, on one of the ALCs, but they did not have to wait long to see the German radar equipment as it had been loaded into the first ALC to leave the beach. Preist became aware of this and he quickly got the skipper of his ALC to go to the allotted MGB. Upon rendezvousing with MGB 312 the booty, wounded and Flight Lieutenant Preist, Lieutenant Vernon and Flight Sergeant Cox were transferred to it and they then left at around twenty knots for England. By around 3.30 a.m. the remaining gunboats were under way towing the landing craft. It was about this time that a message was received that two men who had been trained as signallers had just reached the beach. Quite correctly they were told that it was impossible to come back for them and they would have to do their best to reach Switzerland or Spain. They were Privates Cornell and Embury, both from Rodney section. With the help of French patriots they had a good run for their money, being captured on 9th March when attempting to cross the Demarcation Line into Vichy France at Blére in the region of Indre-et-Loire. However, back in the Channel it was hard work making progress against a heavy sea and the best speed the convoy was making was about seven knots, not much more than a slow bicycle ride. By dawn the convoy was about 15 miles from the French coast with about 70 miles still to go. In spite of this slow progress things were looking up as before dawn six warships had found them and were providing an escort. Of these six ships, two were

66. Mr Preist, the radar expert, talking to Lieutenant-Commander Peate on the *Prins Albert* on the morning after the Bruneval raid. In the middle background wearing the helmet Lieutenant Vernon and just visible behind Preist, Flight Sergeant Cox. (ABF Museum)

Royal Navy (HMS *Blencartha* and HMS *Fernie*) and four were from the Free French Navy (*Calais, Bayonne, Larmor* and *Le Lavandou*). Additionally, soon after dawn, some Spitfires from Fighter Command provided aerial cover and this was maintained all the way back to England. Also a message was received from MGB 312 which arrived back in Portsmouth around 9.00 a.m. from Mr. Preist which stated, "Samples complete and perfect."

The scientist had wasted no time in examining the bits and pieces and questioning Vernon and Cox should anything happen on the return journey. Post-war it has been discovered that should he have landed in France and there had been the possibility of him being captured by the Germans, orders had been given to his close protection party that he was not to be taken alive, this also applied to Cox although he didn't know it at the time. This might have made Mr. Preist feel a little seasick on the way back. He was not the only one suffering as Flight Sergeant Cox was also rather sick, and he later commented about the trip back the following:

> I told Mr. Preist that the German set was behind our own gear. However, I thought it was a beautiful job. I was particularly struck by the ingenious way in which it was boxed off in units for easy fault-finding and quick replacement. I said to Mr. Preist that the Jerries must have had RDF as long as we had. After several other questions and discussion when he had finished with me I managed to hold down a cup of good strong tea and I was allowed to go to sleep in the Captain's bunk. When I woke up the vibration had stopped and we were alongside the *Prins Albert* in Portsmouth harbour.

Once the landing craft were clear of the beach, most of the soldiers and the German prisoners were transferred to the four remaining MGBs, who then took two landing craft in tow. The wind increased to Force 5, which made the 100 mile or so tow pretty nasty for the crews of them. According to Commander Cook the best speed obtained was only about 6 knots and two wire towing ropes parted and time had to be spent repairing or replacing them. Commander Cook commented later:

> I remember one small incident on the trip back. The rough weather conditions made a lot of people very seasick including a tall German prisoner who was doubled up like a hairpin over the guard rail of my MGB vomiting his heart out, or so it seemed to me. A little Scots paratrooper was sitting on the deck clamped to the German's leg. I asked him what he was doing and he replied; "Sir, I've come all this way to get a Hun prisoner and I'm damned if I'm going to let this bastard get away now!" Anyway we eventually arrived to the smoother waters inside the Isle of Wight and most people started to feel better. Later that day I managed to find the time to send a signal to Combined Operations which said:
>
> To Commodore Combined Operations
>
> From Tormentor
>
> Your inspiring message received P.M. Friday 27th February 1942 was much appreciated by all Boche Bitten.

67. The two German prisoners taken on the Bruneval raid being brought ashore at Portsmouth.
68. Note that in the picture below of the prisoners being searched, Private Eric
Freeman on the left still carries a captured German rifle. (ABF Museum)

Eventually the slow-moving convoy made its way back to England. The wounded had been treated by the medics of 181 AFA on the ALCs and MGBs, so it was probably a good decision to take them. See Appendix XIX for the post-action report compiled by Lieutenant A Baker of this unit.

By around 4.30 p.m. the entire party was back in England and soon after nearly everyone was reunited on the *Prins Albert*, where many propaganda photographs were taken. Also present was Wing Commander Pickard and his crews to join in the celebrations. This did not include most of the wounded, who had been taken to the Haslar Naval Hospital in Portsmouth. So what were the pluses and the minuses for Operation Biting?

On the minus side two men had been killed, six missing (one of whom had been seriously wounded and left at a French farmhouse) and six wounded who had been brought back to the UK. I suppose this was an acceptable casualty figure for a somewhat risky 'one-off' operation of 11.76%. Nevertheless, if repeated on subsequent operations such casualties could not be sustained for long periods. Apart from the Army casualties there were no real other negative points.

On the positive side, the operation had virtually achieved all its other objectives Most of the equipment from the Würzburg set had been taken together with two prisoners, one a radar operator. An interesting comment came out from the interrogation of the two prisoners, although regretfully it is not recorded which of the two had been on leave to Germany in January 1942. He had mentioned to his wife that his post was very isolated and perhaps an ideal target for a commando type raid and so he wondered was his wife a British agent?

69. Men from 181 Airborne Field Ambulance RAMC pictured at Bulford after their return from Operation Bruneval. From left to right: George Rose, Fred Cousins, Doug Kiddell, Dave Pusser, Jimmy Newman, Bill Hoath (below Jimmy Newman with headgear sideways), Bill Scott, Taffy Grinsberg, unknown, John Devitt, unknown, Joe Waters, Bernard Tuson, Johnny Griggs, Reg Maltby, Eddie England and Jack Stanton. Sitting Eddie Freer and Wilf Elliott. (N Cherry)

The radar party had obtained virtually everything that had been requested. Items that had been brought back included the receiver, the receiver amplifier, the transmitter and the modulated, this latter controlled the timing within the radar set. Additionally, the sawn-off aerial had been brought back. The only item missing off Dr Jones's shopping list was what he called the 'presentation unit'. There had not been time to get this item from its mountings before the order to withdraw came from Major Frost.

Perhaps of equal value were the labels that Dr Jones had specifically requested be brought back. These, amongst other things, showed that the manufacturer was Telefunken, which had most of its factories in the Berlin area. The works labels were examined and from his previous experience of equipment labels, mainly from crashed aircraft, Dr Jones deduced that the numbers allocated to the first production model of each component was 40,000. The earliest number he found in the captured units was 40,144 and the latest was 41,093, this suggested that the total number of sets of components manufactured by the date of the assembly of the last item was 1,093. The earliest inspection date, November 1940, was found stamped on part of the transmitter, while the last date of 19th August 1941 was found on the sawn-off aerial. Eventually the scientists at the TRE got their hands on the captured equipment to carry out 'a thorough examination.' Dr Jones was told that the equipment was relatively straight-forward and in no respect was it brilliant. On the other hand it must be remembered that the equipment was made in 1940 and designed in 1939 or earlier. Perhaps more importantly it was found that the Würzburg did not have any inbuilt anti-jamming capability. But

70. Men from C Company discuss the raid with RAF aircrews on their return to England. The RAF officer second from the left at the rear is Wing Commander Pickard. (IWM H17351)

71. The paraboloidal aerial from the Würzburg radar brought back
to England on Operation Biting. (National Archives)

as it could be used over a wide frequency, it would be a difficult job for the British to effectively jam it. However, due to this a significant amount of energy was then put into their efforts to 'spoof' this particular set. The British boffins did however agree and report that the German units were engineered far better than their British counterparts.

Some assistance was given by the German radar operator in the London PoW cage at Cockfosters, where the equipment was taken, so he could provide some details. It was reported that the boffins spent most of an afternoon sitting with him on the floor of an office, fitting the various pieces together and listening to his comments. It was discovered that his technical ability left something to be desired and was lower than that of the British radar operators. It turned out the high quality of the components and the low technical ability went hand-in-hand. This was discovered post-war when Dr Jones met General Martini, who had been the Head of German Air Signals and Radar. Jones stated that those two previously mentioned factors had surprised the British boffins, and Martini gave a very interesting reason for the low technical ability. It turned out the Luftwaffe radar branch was pretty well down the priority list for job selection and often had to accept men unsuitable for other more 'technically demanding' branches. The Luftwaffe had also been handicapped by the pre-war decision of the Nazi Party to ban the use of amateur radios. This particular hobby had been a rich source of radar technicians for the RAF and indeed Flight Sergeant Cox had been a 'radio ham' before joining the forces. The reason for the banning of amateur radio networks and enthusiasts was that Hitler felt it might be used as a means of secret communication by those opposed to him. Martini had therefore made sure that in the design of the equipment it was well made and easily replaceable if any part blew up, so that it could be maintained and operated by relatively unskilled men.

Dr Jones commented in his report that as well as having a good idea of the monthly production rate of Würzburgs (around 100 a month), that the captured example was an early type with a simple aerial, while later ones had a spinning version which enabled more accurate target finding. The boffins now knew the extreme limits of wavelength to which the Würzburg could be tuned. It also became clear that some of the Würzburg components were used in other equipment such as the 'Giant Würzburg' which an American Embassy official had managed to photograph in Berlin whilst still neutral. As Jones put it, the raid had helped give an estimate of the German rate of production together with a sample of the design and manufacturing quality – all in all 'the equivalent of a navigational fix in confirming the dead reckoning in the intelligence voyage into the German defences.'

Across in France, the Germans quickly decided that measures needed to be taken against a repetition of Operation Biting and the 'Würzburg pit' was relocated to the Freya compound slightly to the north. Although quickly searched by C Company and found to contain very little, the villa on the cliff top was demolished by the Germans, with the cellar being turned into a shelter. They had decided that it was the presence of the villa that had given away the position. As Dr Jones commented:

Apart from shutting the stable door after the horse had bolted, the action was ironic because it was the presence of the villa that very nearly caused us to overlook the Würzburg, and only Charles Frank's astute observation saved us from thinking that the path from the Freyas had no object than to go to the villa.

Another delicious consequence was that orders were issued that henceforth all German radar equipment were to be protected by barbed wire; since this soon shows up strongly on aerial photographs, because the grass grows longer underneath it or catches rubbish blown by the wind, the enclosing circles of barbed wire enabled us to confirm several objects that we had previously suspected of being Würzburg but where the photographs had been insufficiently clear.

Perhaps the final advantage gained from Operation Biting, certainly in Dr Jones's eyes, came a few months later, when the decision was taken to move the TRE from its Dorset base near Swanage. Many people had been thinking that the Germans might plan a retaliatory raid and where better than on the TRE? Things were not helped when it was discovered that a German parachute unit had moved to a location near Cherbourg, although it was not known for what reason. Also, even if the Germans didn't mount a raid, it was entirely possible for them to hear transmissions from new radar sets under development. So at pretty short notice the whole organisation was lifted and moved to Malvern in Worcestershire, where it still is although under a different name. Someone who was at the TRE during this period commented:

When it was known that the German paratroopers were just across the Channel, every night the trailers that held the centimetric equipment that was being developed were driven out at night to a secure location and brought back the next morning. Then at the end of April 1942 the team leaders were called together and told we had to leave before the next full moon. Malvern had been chosen for our new home. Pickfords arrived in force and we packed up and left in early May.

About 200 people were at the TRE in May 1940 and around 2,000 left in May 1942. At its peak Malvern employed nearly 4,000.

Within a couple of days Major Frost had been called up to London to explain the raid to the War Cabinet, Mountbatten was also present and this meeting probably did more to put the airborne forces on the map and guaranteed their future. Major Frost himself commented:

> The Bruneval raid came at a time when our country's fortunes were at a low ebb. Singapore had recently fallen and the German battleships had escaped up the Channel from Brest in the very teeth of everything that could be brought against them. Many people were disgruntled after a long catalogue of failures, and the success of our venture, although it was a mere flea-bite, did have the effect of making people feel that we could succeed after all.
>
> One very beneficial result from our own point of view was that it put airborne forces on the map. General Browning had been having difficulty in persuading people that the airborne forces could play a really useful part in the war. Despite the successes of the German airborne troops, the traditional conservatism of many Service chiefs stood in the way of experiment, very largely because our more conventional resources were already strained. Now our General was able to get some degree of priority and the Prime Minister, who had initiated the formation of our parachute arm, was encouraged to ensure that we had the necessary support. It was also a feather in the cap for HQ Combined Operations.

One member ended up with mixed feelings after the raid, as Lance-Corporal Bob Dobson recalls:

> Sergeant Gregor McKenzie and his section cleared the chateau of the enemy for Flight Sergeant Cox to dismantle the enemy radar equipment. One of the operators in his rush to escape, fell over the cliff edge. Sergeant McKenzie went after him and pulled him back to make him a prisoner. The orders had been no prisoners except those working radar equipment. The German was so grateful at being spared that he gave his wristwatch to the Sergeant as a thank-you present. Sergeant McKenzie took the watch home on leave with him, had it cleaned and a new glass fitted, on return to the unit he was told to report to the Company Office and told it had been reported stolen by the German and it must be returned. Sergeant McKenzie was not amused, it had cost him 5 shillings to be repaired. He would have liked to have found that German!

Chapter 12

The End of the Beginning

1942 was probably the high point for the relatively small-scale airborne and commando raids during the Second World War. After Bruneval (with a few exceptions which I will deal with shortly), the small raiding parties started to get larger and larger and the mantle for the smaller raids passed to other troops (such as the Special Air Service and the Special Boat Squadron). Following close on the heels of the success of the Bruneval raid was a commando attack on the French port of St Nazaire. This port lies around six miles upstream from the mouth of the river Loire on the western Atlantic coast of France. The most important military aspect of this port was that, in 1942, it had the world's largest dry dock measuring 1,500 feet long by 165 feet wide. The original port facilities were, in 1941 and early 1942, in the process of being enlarged to create a 'super port' from which the Germans could carry out large-scale attacks on the vital Atlantic shipping route. At this stage in the war it is probably fair to say that Britain relied to a great extent on imports of every kind, mainly coming from America. One of the greatest threats to the British during the entire war was if the German capital ships got out into the Atlantic shipping lanes and wreaked havoc amongst the supply convoys. In early 1942 intelligence reports suggested that the *Tirpitz*, a German battleship, although then in Norwegian waters, was planning a sweep of the Atlantic. It was entirely feasible that at the end of the voyage she could head for St Nazaire, as this port had the only dry dock outside Germany that was capable of accommodating her should she require repairs of any kind. If the dry dock could be put out of action, it was highly likely the *Tirpitz* would be forced to stay relatively out of harm's way in Norway.

The task of causing damage to the port facilities at St Nazaire was again handed over to HQ Combined Operations. The code name for the raid was Operation Chariot and was destined to take place on 27th/28th March 1942. The forces selected for the raid consisted of men from No 2 Commando supplemented by 'demolition parties' from nearly every other commando – Nos. 1,3,4,5, 9 and 12. The total force numbered around 620 commandos. A major part of the demolition plan was to sacrifice an old American lease-lend destroyer by ramming her into the dry dock gates. Originally called the USS *Buchanan* when she was launched in 1919, she had been renamed HMS *Campbeltown* on her transfer to the Royal Navy. She underwent some modifications prior to the operation, her exterior appearance was altered to give the impression of being a German *Möwe* class destroyer. Two of her four funnels were cut off and extra Oerlikon cannons added together with a 12 pdr gun on the forward deck. Sensibly, extra steel plate was added around the bridge and wheelhouse to protect the crew. An additional simple but effective idea was to weld a low 'fence' of steel plate along the deck to provide cover for the commandos carried on the *Campbeltown* on the run-in. It was felt there was a serious danger of vessels (especially the *Campbeltown*) running aground on the relatively shallow Loire estuary, so the *Campbeltown* had been stripped of all unnecessary equipment. Amongst other items removed were the torpedo tubes and the majority of the ammunition. The oil and water tanks were pumped out leaving only just about enough to last the one-way journey. To make the operation go with a bang, 24 Mark VII depth charges containing around 5 tons of explosives were placed in various locations on the *Campbeltown*. They were 'sealed in steel and concrete' to help withstand the shock of ramming the dock gates. They were set to explode eight hours after ramming. A subsidiary but no less important aim of the raid was to destroy some of the vital dock facilities. The demolition parties received special training under the leadership of a Royal Engineer officer, Captain W Pritchard, who had been making studies of possible targets ashore and the best ways to render them inoperable.

As well as the *Campbeltown*, the commandos were taken across in several MGBs, which would bring the survivors back. The force left Falmouth in Cornwall on the afternoon of 26th March with the intention of undertaking the raid the following night. This is precisely what happened and the raid was another success for Combined Operations, which, following close on the heels on the Bruneval raid, must have been a great fillip. Many words have already been written about Operation Chariot, suffice to say that the *Campbeltown* did in fact blow up around 10.35 a.m. on the morning of 28th March 1942. This explosion severely damaged the dry dock gates, which, together with the other equipment destroyed, meant it was not operational again until 1948. Casualties were quite high – as well as a large number of commandos taken prisoner (around 200), 169 out of a total force of 611 commandos were killed. It is probably fair to say that this was one of the first uses of the 'special service' troops in a major operation against a relatively well-defended and difficult target rather than the previous 'pinprick raids'.

It will probably come as no surprise to hear that five Victoria Crosses were awarded to men who took part in Operation Chariot and out of the 611 commandos who took part 135 or 22% received some sort of decoration, possibly a record for a large-scale operation. Two of the five VCs went to commandos and these are their citations:

The first VC went to the commanding officer of No 2 Commando, Lieutenant Colonel A C Newman, originally from the Essex Regiment:

On the night of 27th/28th March 1942, Lieutenant Colonel Newman was in command of the military force detailed to land on enemy occupied territory and destroy the dock installations of the German controlled naval base at St Nazaire. This important base was known to be heavily defended and bomber support had to be abandoned due to bad weather. The operation was therefore bound to be exceedingly hazardous, but Lieutenant Colonel Newman, although empowered to call off the assault at any stage, was determined to carry to a successful conclusion the important task which had been assigned to him.

Coolly and calmly he stood on the bridge of the leading craft, as the small force steamed up the estuary of the River Loire, although the ships had been caught in the enemy searchlights and a murderous crossfire from both banks, causing heavy casualties. Although Lieutenant Colonel Newman need not have landed himself, he was one of the first ashore and during the next five hours of bitter fighting, he personally entered several houses and shot up the occupants and supervised the

72. One of the aerial planning photographs for the St Nazaire raid. (National Archives)

73. Modifications being carried out to HMS *Campbeltown* in England prior to the St Nazaire raid. Note the extra steel plates around the bridge. (National Archives)

operations in the town, utterly regardless of his own safety, and he never wavered in his resolution to carry through the operation upon which so much depended.

An enemy gun position on the roof of a U-boat pen had been causing heavy casualties to the landing craft and Lieutenant Colonel Newman directed the fire of a mortar against this position to such effect that the gun was silenced. Still fully exposed, he then brought machine gun fire to bear on an armed trawler in the harbour, compelling it to withdraw and thus preventing many casualties in the main demolition area.

Under the brilliant leadership of this officer the troops fought magnificently and held vastly superior enemy forces at bay, until the demolition parties had successfully completed their work of destruction.

By this time, however, most of the landing craft had been sunk or set on fire and evacuation by sea was no longer possible. Although the main objective had been achieved, Lieutenant Colonel Newman nevertheless was now determined to try and fight his way out into open country and so give the survivors a chance to escape. The only way out of the harbour area lay across a narrow iron bridge covered by enemy machine guns and although severely shaken by a German hand grenade, which had burst at his feet, Lieutenant Colonel Newman personally led the charge which stormed the position and under his inspiring leadership the small force fought its way through the streets to a point near the open country, when, all ammunition expended, he and his men were finally overpowered by the enemy.

The outstanding gallantry and devotion to duty of this fearless officer, his brilliant leadership and initiative, were largely responsible for the success of this perilous operation, which resulted in heavy damage to the important naval base of St Nazaire.

The other award was to a commando who never even got ashore, Sergeant T F Durrant, who had originally been in the Royal Engineers:

For great gallantry, skill and devotion to duty when in charge of a Lewis gun in H.M. Motor Launch 306 in the St Nazaire raid on the 28th March 1942. Motor Launch 306 came under heavy fire while proceeding up the river Loire towards the port. Sergeant Durrant in his position abaft the bridge, where he had no cover or protection, engaged enemy gun positions and searchlights on shore. During this engagement he was severely wounded in the arm but refused to leave his gun.

The Motor Launch subsequently went down the river and was attacked by a German destroyer at 50–60 yards range, and often closer. In this action Sergeant Durrant continued to fire at the destroyer's bridge with the greatest coolness and with complete disregard of the enemy's fire. The Motor Launch was illuminated by the enemy searchlights and Sergeant Durrant drew on himself the individual attention of the enemy guns, and was again wounded, in many places. Despite these further wounds he stayed in his exposed position, still firing his gun, although after a time only able to support himself by holding on to the gun mounting. After a running fight, the commander of the German destroyer called on the Motor Launch to surrender.

Sergeant Durrant's answer was a further burst of fire at the destroyer's bridge. Although now very weak he went on firing, using drums of ammunition as fast as they could be replaced. A renewed attack by the enemy vessel eventually silenced the fire of the Motor Launch, but Sergeant Durrant refused to give up until the destroyer came alongside, grappled the Motor Launch and took prisoner those who remained alive.

Sergeant Durrant's gallant fight was commended by the German officers on boarding the Motor Launch. This very gallant Non Commissioned Officer later died of the many wounds received in action.

Sergeant Thomas Frank Durrant died aged 23 years old and now lies in the Escoublac-La-Baule CWGC Cemetery at St Nazaire.

By the middle of 1942 things were still not going too well for the Allies, the majority of the top brass agreed that if Germany was to be beaten, mainland Europe would have to be invaded at some time in the future. Admittedly this did seem a somewhat distant prospect as this brief overview shows.

Some of Britain's most important bases in the Far East, Hong Kong and Singapore, had fallen, Burma had been overrun by the Japanese Army and was pressing at the borders of India. In the Middle East in the campaign in the 'Western Desert', Tobruk had fallen to the Germans and Italians. They had followed this up with a massive advance against an almost-beaten and demoralised British 8th Army, so that they had their 'backs to the wall' only 80 miles from Cairo. It seemed one big push might send the British out of Egypt and all of the ramifications this would cause, such as the collapse of the Empire. On the Eastern Front the German Army was treating the Russian Army with contempt, taking many prisoners in a seemingly unstoppable advance south towards the Caucasus region with its precious oil fields. On top of all of this Churchill often berated the service chiefs by asking; 'Why won't our soldiers fight?'

However, there was at least one group of soldiers in England in 1942 who seemed quite willing to fight. This group was the Canadians, some of whom had been in England since 1940 and apart from mainly watching beaches for an invasion that never came had done very little in the way of action. This boredom, as usual with any group of young fit men, reared its ugly head in an ever-increasing spiral of indiscipline. They got drunk, stole, fought amongst each other and anyone else who got in their way and chased young women. It was reported by Lord Haw Haw, the German propagandist, that by midway through 1942 3,238 Canadians had been in front of a court martial. Not bad going for a Corps of three divisions (say 36,000 men) by my reckoning! He apparently stated in one of his broadcasts: "If you really want to take Berlin, why don't you give each Canadian soldier a bottle of whisky and a motor cycle. Then declare Berlin is out of bounds. The Canadians will be there within 48 hours."

Meanwhile, after the successes of the two smaller raids earlier in the year, the planners at Combined Operations thought about mounting a much larger raid. Not only would this continue to harass the Germans and perhaps divert attention from the Russian Front, but it was anticipated that, one day in the future an army of invasion would cross the Channel and information on what they could expect to encounter was needed. In early April 1942, it was suggested that a large-scale raid be undertaken to assess the possibility of taking a port, which would be vital in any full-blown invasion plan. Aerial photographs of several ports were examined before Dieppe was chosen. All of the ports were well-defended but it was a risk worth taking as it would give an idea of what might be facing the attackers at any point along the northern coast of France. Dieppe had the additional benefits that (even at this early stage) it was unlikely to be the actual place of the invasion and was within fighter range of bases in southern England. An added benefit was that a large-scale raid in daylight might provoke the Luftwaffe into a major pitched battle, which it had been unwilling to do for some months. If heavy losses could be inflicted on them it might well force the Germans to move aircraft from the East and so give a double benefit to the beleaguered Russians. It may also have been that there was a political motive in trying to show that Britain was trying to take some pressure off the Russians.

It seems that the first plan, called Operation Rutter, was intended to take place in early July 1942, and perhaps as a result of the difficulties with the Canadians, Mountbatten was 'invited' to ask the Canadians to participate. It is recorded that when he offered Lieutenant-General Crerar, who commanded the 1st Canadian Corps, the chance to take part in a large-scale raid on Dieppe, his reply was 'You bet!'

The coast of France around Dieppe has high chalk cliffs similar to that on the south coast of England, these being natural defences. The task of attacking Dieppe itself was given to six battalions and an armoured unit from the 2nd Canadian Division. Either side of Dieppe were two German artillery positions at Berneval and Varengeville, their guns could bring down a murderous crossfire on any approaching boats and so would have to be knocked out otherwise the landings had the makings of a massacre. Each gun position had ten 150 mm artillery pieces with a range of ten miles. The shell fired by these guns weighed around 90 lbs, so this was a large lump of steel.

The job of knocking out these two artillery positions was initially given to the 1st Parachute Battalion, who trained hard for the task. This however, was not the first operation to be planned for the 1st Battalion in 1942 as their then CO, Lieutenant Colonel J Hill recalled:

> First we were going to capture Alderney and hold it for a short time. That was cancelled. Then we trained for the Dieppe raid with the Canadians on the Isle of Wight. We were going to drop on each flank and take out some German artillery positions and then be evacuated by sea, pretty similar to the Bruneval raid. Security though was abysmal; several Canadians told my chaps that the objective was Dieppe. We got as far as being loaded in the aircraft when a weather front came in and the operation was postponed for a month. In that time Mountbatten decided to simplify the operation by eliminating one of the weather-dependent factors, so we were out and the commandos were given our task. I nearly had a mutiny on my hands; it was a hell of a job keeping the men happy. Our next job was to capture Ushant [Author's note: off the western Atlantic coast of France] and hold it for 48 hours, being taken off by Hunt Class destroyers. Again, we were in the aircraft at Hurn airport, with engines ticking over, when that one was cancelled! The reason, a group of American Flying Fortresses, despatched to bomb airfields supporting Ushant, got caught in a weather front, losing their way and formation. They were escorted by a squadron of Spitfires who were ordered to tail them. The Fortresses had the fuel capacity to find their way back, the Spitfires did not and were forced to

74. Memorial to No 3 Commando at Yellow Beach 1 Dieppe. (K Harris)

75. Looking down at Yellow Beach 2 Dieppe where part of
No 3 Commando landed in 1942. (K Harris)

land in France and as far away as Spain. I then took the battalion to Exmoor and we did an exercise with live ammunition. I then marched them back to Bulford, saying that anyone who fell out would not go on the next operation. We did the 112 miles in two and a half days, carrying sixty pounds per man. Some people failed to make it. They had to pay the price.

So taking the place of the 1st Parachute Battalion were to be Nos. 3 and 4 Commandos. No 3 Commando was given the job at the Berneval location while No 4 was to go to Varengeville. No 3 Commando was still under the command of Lieutenant Colonel Durnford-Slater. His plan consisted of splitting the troops into two parties, one commanded by him and the other by Major Young. This is the same officer who had been on most of the previous commando raids in an ever-increasing rank. They were to land at two different beaches and assemble at the rear of the position and take it from the rear. No 4 Commando, now commanded by Lieutenant Colonel The Lord Lovat, had a similar plan, in that they also split into two parties. The first and larger one of about 170 men was commanded by Lovat and was to assault the gun battery, while the other of about 90 led by his second-in-command, Major D Mills-Roberts, was to provide covering fire. In the middle were the (augmented) 2nd Canadian Division, the attacking troops came from the following units:

- Essex Scottish
- Fusiliers de Mont Royal
- Royal Hamilton Light Infantry
- Queen's Own Cameron Highlanders
- Royal Regiment of Canada
- South Saskatchewan Regiment

Supported by armoured vehicles from the Calgary Tank Regiment and No 40 Commando Royal Marines.

In spite of the fact that many people now knew that a raid had been planned against Dieppe in July, the somewhat regrettable decision was taken to go again in August. It is asserted that Mountbatten was not liked by the rest of the service chiefs, many feeling he was ambitious, vain and by his own admission consumed by desire for even higher command and greater glory. After the cancellation of Rutter he began using a few trusted staff who were literally sworn to secrecy to continue planning the raid against Dieppe. In July he asked the Chiefs of Staff to approve 'planning for a future raiding operation'. He was refused permission, but perhaps mindful that a success for him might make him the natural choice to command the real invasion pressed his case. The Chiefs of Staff authorised him to carry out 'small-scale minor raiding and outline planning for future operations.' He turned this round and reinstated Operation Rutter as Operation Jubilee with the same aims.

With the benefit of hindsight the plan of attack was little better than a 'Great War' assault. Instead of it being acted out in northern France it was on the channel coast with a frontal infantry attack in broad daylight against well-sited defensive positions, barbed wire and a ferocious enemy artillery barrage. The attackers were also denied any real fire support as the Royal Navy refused to risk any battleships and as it turned out the RAF bombing in support of the Canadians and Commandos was ineffective.

Again many words have been written about Dieppe and I feel all that is necessary is to give a brief summary of the raid. In spite of the cancellation of Operation Rutter the Germans were unaware that another raid was coming, that is until some of the assault force were spotted by an unreported German coastal convoy, who did send a warning ashore. No 3 Commando on the left flank had had a bad crossing as some of their craft had been attacked by Germans in the Channel and never made it ashore.

Out of 23 landing craft carrying men from No 3 Commando it is believed only seven made it ashore. From one of these seven craft, 19 men led by Major Young managed to at least reach the German artillery positions at Berneval. However they were unable to stop the artillery pieces firing both at them and shipping offshore. For a time it was a bit of a 'Mexican Stand-Off' with neither side making much headway in dislodging the other from their positions. Eventually Major Young decided, as ammunition was running low, fearful of a German counter-attack and with only a small number of men present, that discretion was the better part of valour and headed back towards their evacuation beach. This party only suffered a few men wounded. But overall No 3 Commando suffered around 120 men killed, wounded and missing.

The group led by Lord Lovat from No 4 Commando had better luck and they got ashore unscathed around 4.30 a.m. and proceeded in the next hour or so to demolish the gun position. However, at some cost, as from the 260 men or so who went ashore there were 45 casualties, including 16 killed and four missing. However, these flanking attacks did alert the Germans in Dieppe to the possibility of an assault aimed directly at them. When the Canadians did come in, it was purely and simply a disaster. Of the 4,400 Canadians that landed at Dieppe, only around 1,000 got back to England. The total number of dead was put at 1,027 and around 2,400 were taken prisoner. This represented a casualty loss rate of over 78%, even worse than the first day on the Somme in July 1916.

The Royal Navy lost a destroyer plus a number of landing craft together with around 550 casualties. The RAF lost 106 aircraft and 153 aircrew. All in all not a very good return. The comments about the raid at least privately did not make easy reading; the Army Liaison Officer at HQ Fighter Command stated: "Nothing was learnt except how not to do it: a little late in the war to be learning that lesson." Churchill tried to spin it and cabled back from Moscow where he was in talks with Stalin, "We must make this look as good as possible. Let us call it a reconnaissance in force."

Perhaps the only success that day was at Varengeville where No 4 Commando had at least inflicted some material damage on the Germans. It was also here that the commandos gained another Victoria Cross. This was awarded to Captain (temporary Major) P Porteous from the Royal Artillery. His citation read:

> At Dieppe on the 19th August 1942, Major Porteous was detailed to act as Liaison Officer between the two detachments whose task was to assault the heavy coast defence guns.
>
> In the initial assault Major Porteous, working with the smaller of the two detachments, was shot at close range through the hand, the bullet passing through his palm and entering his upper arm. Undaunted, Major Porteous closed with his assailant, succeeded in disarming him, and killed him with his own bayonet thereby saving the life of a British Sergeant on whom the German had turned his

76. Present day remains of the Command Post at Battery Hess blown up by men of No 4 Commando in the Dieppe raid. (N Cherry)

aim. In the meantime the larger detachment was held up, and the officer leading this detachment was killed and the Troop Sergeant Major fell seriously wounded. Almost immediately afterwards the only other officer of the detachment was also killed.

Major Porteous, without hesitation and in the face of a withering fire, dashed across the open ground to take over command of this detachment. Rallying them, he led them in a charge, which carried the German position at the point of the bayonet, and was severely wounded for the second time. Though shot through the thigh he continued to the final objective where he eventually collapsed from loss of blood after the last of the guns had been destroyed.

Major Porteous's most gallant conduct, his brilliant leadership and tenacious devotion to duty which was supplementary to the role originally assigned to him, was an inspiration to the whole detachment.

Here is the citation for the Distinguished Conduct Medal awarded to the Troop Sergeant Major mentioned in the previous citation:

Sergeant Major Stockdale took command of the troop after all his officers had been killed or had become casualties. Sergeant Stockdale, while leading a bayonet charge, had part of his foot blown away by an enemy stick-bomb. Although in very great pain, Sergeant Stockdale continued to engage the enemy. He set a splendid example and was an inspiration to his men.

It is probably fair to say that for a while Mountbatten decided to keep a low profile and concentrate on small-scale specialised raids, indeed some of these had started being planned and a few carried out between the St Nazaire and Dieppe excursions. One of the smallest commando raids of the war was carried out on the night of 11th/12th April 1942 when just two commandos took part in a small act of sabotage. Captain G Montanaro from the Royal Engineers accompanied by Trooper F Preece, were taken most of the way across the Channel before transferring into a canoe. The pair of them then proceeded to paddle their way into Boulogne harbour and managed to place a limpet mine on a German tanker and withdraw without detection. Their canoe had by now sprung several leaks and they were picked up by their motor launch just in the nick of time. An aerial reconnaissance photograph taken the next morning showed that the tanker had indeed been sunk. Both were awarded decorations for their exploits and the loss of a tanker in such circumstances must have been of some concern to the Germans. Captain Montanaro was awarded a Distinguished Service Order while Trooper Preece received a Distinguished Conduct Medal. Their citations read:

On the night of 11th/12th April 1942, Captain Montanaro, accompanied by Trooper Preece, entered Boulogne harbour in a canoe which had been taken by a Motor Launch to about 1½ miles from the harbour entrance. Successfully avoiding detection by the breakwater forts, and a number of vessels which were active in the harbour, they manoeuvred the canoe alongside an enemy tanker to which eight explosive charges were attached below water. They withdrew still undetected and commenced their return across the Channel without great expectation of being picked up until daylight some four hours later. Their canoe had suffered some damage during the operation and the sea conditions were deteriorating so that it was fortunate that as planned the Motor Launch was able to make contact and pick them up an hour after they had left Boulogne harbour by which time they were 2 to 3 miles clear of the enemy coast.

Subsequent air reconnaissance has established that the tanker was damaged and beached.

Trooper Preece contributed his share in the success of the operation by carrying out implicitly the orders of Captain Montanaro and by showing courage and endurance over a long period spent in imminent danger of discovery by the enemy.

Around this time, perhaps mindful of the ever-changing plans for the commandos (by this I mean being used in larger and larger numbers), a small unit was formed called the Small-Scale Raiding Force (SSRF). It was felt that the commandos had probably outgrown their original aims and that there was a need to get back to harassing Germans wherever they were by 'pinprick' raids. The SSRF was small, around 30 officers and men, led by Major G March-Phillipps assisted by Captain J Appleyard and Captain G

77. Captain G Montanaro pictured during a training exercise, armed with a captured Luger pistol with the unusual trommel or saddle magazine which held 32 rounds. Perhaps the other soldier is Trooper Preece. (IWM H14599)

Hayes. A suitable base was found at Anderson Manor near Blandford Forum in Dorset, close to various ports which could be used for raids. Their first excursion across the Channel was on the night of 14th/15th August 1942 to the area of Cape Barfleur on the Hague peninsula in Normandy. The objective was to destroy an anti-aircraft gun. They paddled their way ashore after travelling most of the way in a Motor Torpedo Boat, but landed in the wrong place and failed to find the gun position. They did, however, kill three Germans before successfully withdrawing back to England. The next raid was a return to the Channel Islands with the plan of capturing a complete German lighthouse crew. The raid was given the name of Operation Dryad and took place on the 2nd/3rd September 1942.

Situated eight miles north-west of Alderney, across a main (peace-time at least) shipping route are a series of rocks called the Casquets. Over the years these rocks have been the downfall of many a ship and in 1724 a 'lighthouse' started operating on the rocks, although this did not stop ships still running aground. As technology improved by 1940 the lighthouse had a light that was visible for nearly seventeen miles and a candlepower of 184,000. The British military decided to abandon the Channel Islands in 1940 and also Trinity House (who were responsible for the lighthouse) evacuated its personnel on 22nd June 1940.

When the Germans invaded the Channel Islands they eventually put a crew on the Casquets to man the lighthouse. It was not exactly an enviable posting, as all supplies including fresh water had to be brought by boat from Alderney. Obviously in bad weather, especially during the winter months, the sea conditions can make it impossible to reach the lighthouse. Even though the light was only switched on when requested (at reduced power) for friendly shipping, the Germans felt obliged to keep a garrison on this and a few other lighthouses in the area and so became an easy target for the SSRF. The raid was a complete success, all the Germans in the lighthouse being taken prisoner. They probably had no idea what had happened, being completely surprised and with the mentality that they were in a safe location. Captain Appleyard later commented on the initial landing:

> I navigated again for the whole job. It was pretty nerve-racking as it's a notoriously evil place and you get a tremendous tide race round the rocks. However, all went well and we found the place all right, and pushed in our landing craft. My job in the landing and embarkation was bow-man.
>
> I was the first to leap for the rock, taking a light line with me, and then had to hold the landing craft up to the rock on the bowline, whilst Graham Hayes, in the stern, held the boat off the rock with a stern-line and kedge-anchor he had dropped on the approach, so as to prevent her being dashed on the rock by the swell. There was quite a hefty swell surging up the rocks, and it felt pretty weird in the dark, but we got the whole party ashore safely. The boat was then hauled off the rock on the stern-line by Graham, who remained in her, and I handed over the bowline to the other man who was staying with the boat, and then she rode quite happily until our return.

Captain Appleyard and Sergeant Winter then went up to the light room in the lighthouse, to find it empty. Elsewhere in the lighthouse seven Germans were taken prisoner, three were found in their beds, two were off-duty and on the verge of undressing for bed and the two on duty were found doing odd jobs. Not a shot was fired, the Germans had a box of grenades and also an Oerlikon cannon for their defence but it did not do them much good. The German equipment was destroyed and with their prisoners in tow all got aboard the landing craft and set off back to England. The only casualty was Captain Appleyard who injured his leg getting back on board the landing craft.

The following is taken from Major March-Phillipps' report on Operation Dryad:

After innumerable fruitless attempts, this operation took place in spite of what has come to be called Dryad weather, wind force 3 rising to 4 and sometimes 5. MTB 344 and ten Officers and two ORs of SSRF personnel took part. The MTB sailed from Portland Bill at 2100 hours. In spite of a very careful overhaul, the port engine again gave trouble and the passage had to be made at a reduced speed of some 25 knots for the first 25 miles. It was then possible to increase the engine revolutions, and the normal cruising speed of 33 knots was maintained until within five miles of the objective.

At 2210 hours a white light flashing every five seconds was seen, bearing 20 degrees on the port bow. This light only showed for five minutes and then went out. It was probably Alderney at its maximum visibility. Two very bright light beams then appeared on the starboard bow, which might possibly have been a searchlight on Guernsey, and one on the starboard quarter which must have been on a ship. A vertical red beacon was also just visible well on the port bow. This was thought to be on the mainland at Cape de la Hague.

At 2230 hours speed was reduced to 15 knots, and a red light flashing once every fifteen seconds was seen very fine on the port bow. This was at first believed to be Casquets but at 2245 hours a rock was reported on the port beam at about one mile rise, and course was altered to close it. This turned out to be the Casquets and a course was laid to approach it from the northward against the tide. The MTB's main engines were then cut off and the silent auxiliary used. The red light was identified as Sark.

The MTB was manoeuvred to within 800 yards of the rock, where she was anchored with a 45 lb Admiralty-pattern anchor and 50 fathoms of 2½ inch rope, and the landing party went ashore in a Goatley-pattern assault craft, paddling four aside, leaving the MTB at 0005 hours. Many and conflicting eddies of tide were experienced on the approach, which took considerably longer than was anticipated, probably because the approach was later than had been calculated and the NE-going flood tide was by then running hard. In fact the landing was not made until 0025 hours.

Unlike plans made for previous occasions the landing was made, not at any recognised landing point, but on the face of the rock immediately under the engine house tower. This was done partly because of the difficulty of finding holding ground for the kedge anchor on the recognised north landing, and partly because it was feared that the landing points might be guarded or be set with booby traps. There was a fairly heavy run on the rocks from the south-westerly swell but the kedge anchor held well and the landing was made without mishap or any harm being done to the boat. A way was then found up the 80 feet cliff and any noise made by the party was drowned by the rumble of the surf and the heavy booming of the sea in the chasms and gulleys.

Meanwhile the boat had been pulled off the rock by the kedge anchor and was held riding the swell between the bow and stern lines about 20 feet off the rock. One officer, Captain Graham Hayes, MC, whose seamanship on landing and the much more difficult operation of re-embarking was admirable, was left in the boat in charge, and another officer minded the bowline and kept watch through the infrared receiving set on the MTB.

Coiled dannert wire was met and climbed through on the way up the cliff and the gateway was found to be blocked by a heavy knife-rest barbed wire entanglement, but a way was found over the western wall and the whole party made the courtyard unchallenged. At this point, the order was given for independent action and the party was split up and rushed the buildings and towers according to a pre-arranged plan. Complete surprise was obtained and all resistance was overcome without a shot being fired. Seven prisoners, all of them Germans, including two leading telegraphists, were taken in the bedrooms and living rooms. The light tower, wireless tower and engine room were all found to be empty, although the generating plant in the engine house was running, and the watch, consisting of two men was in the living room. The rest were in bed, with the exception of two telegraphists who were just turning in. A characteristic of those in bed was the wearing of hair-nets which caused the commander of the party to mistake one of them for a woman.

The prisoners were re-embarked immediately and taken down over the rocks by the way the raiding party had come up, some of them still in their pyjamas, as time was getting short and it was expected that the operation of embarkation would take some time. Re-embarkation commenced at 0100 hours. The wireless was then broken with axes and the buildings and offices searched for papers, documents and code books. The light and the engine room were left intact. The following papers were removed:

Code book for Harbour Defence Vessels FO (Flag Officer) i/c France, signal books, records, W/T diary, procedure signals, personal letters and photographs, identity books and passes, ration cards, Station Log, Ration Log, Light Log and a gas mask and gas cape. (These papers were handed over to the military authorities at Portland on return.)

A thorough search of the buildings revealed the presence of a quantity of arms and ammunition. Each man was equipped with a rifle of the old Steyr pattern and there were two large cases of stick grenades, one of them open. There was also an Oerlikon cannon gun, loaded and placed against the wall in the living room. If a good watch had been kept, or if any loud noises had been made on the approach or on landing, the rock could have been rendered pretty well impregnable by seven determined men.

Particular attention is called to the presence of stick grenades in such outposts for they are formidable weapons. The Oerlikon gun and the rifles were removed by the raiding party but the stick grenades and ammunition store were left untouched. It was not possible to remove them in time and no attempt was made to blow them up as it was considered most important to make no noise that might reveal the presence of a raiding party to the mainland. Meanwhile the embarkation of the prisoners was proceeding under the direction of Captain Burton and Captain Hayes. This was a particularly difficult and hazardous operation as the slope of the rock at this point was at least 45 degrees and the prisoners had to slide down and be hauled into the boat by Mr Warren, the bowman, as she rose on the swell. Great credit is due to all concerned that this operation was successful for one mistake might have meant the swamping of the boat which might have brought disaster on the party. When the search party arrived with the papers and arms, the prisoners had all been embarked and it was then decided by the commander and Captain Hayes not to send for the small emergency dory on the MTB but to load all personnel into the Goatley which was standing up well to the weight. It was decided, however, to jettison the arms and they were accordingly thrown into the sea. (The emergency dory was not sent for because of the distance it would have had to come and the inevitable delay which would have been caused.)

When the search party was finally embarked at 0110 hours there were nineteen men in the Goatley, which rode the swell admirably, though dangerously low in the water. A tribute must be paid to the Goatley which comes from all members of SSRF. This boat which is entirely without lines or shape and designed on the principle of the flat iron, has behaved splendidly under all conditions. It has weathered moderate seas and stood up to pounding at rock landings in a way that entirely belies its looks and the natural reactions of any seaman when confronted with such a hull.

During the operation, the MTB had dragged her anchor to the northward, and Lieutenant Bourne, RNVR, wisely decided to weigh and close the Casquets before the signal was received. The Goatley was intercepted about 500 yards off the rock, at 0135 hours and the prisoners, who were very docile, were battened down in the forecastle with Captain Dudgeon and two others, where they gave no trouble. The voyage home in a rising sea, though desperately wet, was without mishap and the MTB docked at Portland at 0400 hours.

There were two small casualties, Captain Kemp was injured in the leg while embarking and Captain Appleyard, who was acting bowman and the last to leave the rock, sprained his ankle in the descent which had to be made without the assistance of the rope and with the boat well away from the rock. In most cases of difficult landings, bowman must swim out to the boat.

Great credit is due to Lieutenant Bourne for his handling of his ship in this and the previous operation, both of which were hazardous and difficult undertakings in close proximity to reefs and sunken rocks, and to Captain Appleyard, whose navigation made them possible. Also to Private Orr, a German speaker, who marshalled the prisoners and did much to make the search successful.

It did not take the Germans long to work out that something was wrong. It was part of the standing operating procedures that a regular check call by radio was carried out between the lighthouse and Alderney. Fortunately the last check call had been made roughly five minutes before the men of the SSRF arrived. Obviously some time later, Alderney had heard nothing from the lighthouse and they were unable to raise them by radio. A boat was sent to the rocks and it returned advising that everyone had disappeared and as the radio had been destroyed it was assumed they had been victims of a commando raid. When Hitler was informed of the raid he flew into one of his infamous rages and insisted that the lighthouse be abandoned. However, the German Navy insisted that a manned lighthouse was essential for navigation around the treacherous waters. An argument broke out between the Army and the Navy as to who was responsible for the lighthouse and the defence of it. At the time of the raid there was one officer in charge from the Army (*Obermaat* Mundt), with three soldiers (*Gefreiters* Abel, Kepp and Klatwitter) as guards. The radio operators and light operators (*Funkgefreiters* Dembowy, Kraemer and Reineck) came from the German Navy.

The defences around the Casquets were beefed up with more barbed wire and mines, the garrison was increased to 33 men (25 Army and 8 Navy) and they were given more powerful weapons including a 2.5 cm gun. As the Casquets was not visited again by the British until 17th May 1945 this was obviously a waste of German resources who could probably have been better employed elsewhere. It is just another example of a pinprick raid having long-lasting consequences.

The SSRF did not wait long to launch other excursions across the Channel and three raids were planned for September and October, one of which was to have far-reaching consequences. The first raid was known as Operation Branford and took place on the night of 7th/8th September when eleven men under the command of Captain C Ogden-Smith headed for a small remote island known as Burhou to the north-east of Alderney and about five miles due east of the Casquets. The aim of the operation was to establish 'the military potential' of this island which was only about half a mile long and 300 yards wide. The raid did not get off to a good start when soon after leaving Portland their transport MTB 344, started to suffer from engine problems. After the port engine completely stopped, it was decided to return to Portland. However, the mechanic managed to get it working again but Captain Ogden-Smith decided that if it packed up again they would go back to England. Eventually soon after midnight and following a few navigational difficulties they managed to get to the correct island. Again a Goatley boat was used to paddle ashore. The party consisted of six men, Captain Ogden-Smith, Second Lieutenant Anders Lassen (who had also been on Operation Dryad) and four other ranks. Ogden-Smith's post-operation report stated:

> Shore was reached at 0028 hours and the landing made on the reef at a place about 60 yards west of the southernmost point of the island. The rock here is steep and in steps. The boat was held off by kedge anchor. There was no noticeable tidal set and the sea was absolutely calm. The party, less cox and bow who remained with the Goatley, made its way for 60 yards over broken rock which was wet and slippery with seaweed to the rockline above high water. The only building on the island was a house about 400 yards NE of the landing place. This house had been partly demolished by artillery fire, the roof and the first floor having collapsed inwards, entirely filling the ground floor. There were several small shell craters round. The party divided here, Corporal Edgar taking two men to examine the westward end and myself going with two men to cover the central and eastern part. No sign of recent habitation or any defence works were encountered.
>
> The island is roughly 700 yards long and ranging from 300 yards at the east and west extremities to 150 yards in the centre. There is a broken central ridge of bare granite rock which at the highest point rises 8-15 feet above the ridge

line, below is soft grassy soil which is split up by irregular rainwater channels 4-6 inches wide and anything up to 12 inches deep which makes walking difficult and hazardous. The average slope is 20 to 30 degrees. The highwater line is bounded by a more or less continuous band about 15 feet wide of smooth flat granite boulders. There are frequent lengths of smooth granite rock outcrop throughout the island. The foreshore is made up of broken granite rock with pools and long narrow gulleys which can be identified from the air photographs.

Pack artillery or mortars or loads requiring two or three men are practicable. Wheeled or tracked guns would present great difficulties as there are no sandy beaches and all landings would have to be made over rock. There are a number of places where high-angle guns could be placed, though the ground is very soft except where the grass grows. There is sufficient crest clearance except immediately behind the rough ridge rocks.

Landings in similar weather would seem possible anywhere west of the southern reef and east as far as the gulley immediately below the house. Similar conditions exist on the north shore. The higher the state of the tide the better.

Whilst the party was ashore carrying out their survey various lights were seen including the new replacement crew from the Casquets lighthouse signalling Alderney, possibly because they did not have a replacement radio. After an hour on shore they returned unscathed to the MTB and were back in Portland around three hours later. The island of Burhou was used as a convenient firing range for German artillery based in other places in the Channel Islands, which accounts for the craters and the ruined house discovered. As it turned out no British troops landed here again until after the German surrender in 1945. I regret to say I have been unable to find any trace of plans to use Burhou as a 'support base' for any invasion of the Channel Islands, which were somewhat ignored in the Allied invasion of France in 1944 and were left almost to 'wither on the vine' until 1945, with many lives only being saved by the despatch of 'Red Cross' parcels to the beleaguered civilians literally starving to death there.

On the night of 12th/13th September Major March-Phillipps accompanied by Appleyard, Hayes and nine other commandos set off for a foray on the French coast around the Normandy village of St Honorine north of Bayeux. It was the intention for the men from the SSRF to land, record information about the area, if possible take a German or two prisoner and then return to England. Aerial photographic reconnaissance had shown a small group of houses on the coast which were thought to be occupied by the Germans and so ought to provide an ideal opportunity to take some prisoners.

As Appleyard was still recovering from his injury suffered at the Casquets he acted as the Navigation Officer. The party got ashore safely but once on the ground things started to go wrong. The defences ashore, probably as a result of recent excursions to the Channel Islands, seemed more alert and greater in number. March-Phillipps decided it was not worth arguing with an opponent who seemed more awake than usual, aborting the operation to hopefully return at a later date with a stronger force. On the way back to the boat and about 200 yards short of it, they ran into a patrol of Germans but were able to kill all seven soldiers in it. Whilst the bodies were being searched for intelligence material, another patrol could be heard approaching. The decision was taken to get out of there quickly and everyone got into the Goatley and started to paddle back to the

MTB. Suddenly, when they still had not got very far from the shore, the Germans sent up parachute flares and the boat was spotted. A torrent of fire was aimed at the boat and March-Phillipps and two others (Sergeant Williams and Private Leonard) were hit and killed, nearly everyone else was wounded and the Goatley was sunk.

All three of them were buried in the small churchyard in the village of St Laurent. Private Leonard's real name was Lehniger and he had been born in the Sudetenland, that part of Germany on the Czech/German border handed over to Czechoslovakia after the Great War. He had fled to Britain as a political refugee from the Nazis (his mother was Jewish), he eventually ended up in the SSRF and had previously taken part in the Dieppe raid.

Appleyard on the MTB clearly recalls a voice, possibly Captain Hayes, shouting out that it was no good and the MTB was to leave. To their credit, Appleyard and the crew of the MTB did linger around looking for survivors but the MTB was hit and one engine was put out of action. Captain Hayes, who was a strong swimmer, managed to get ashore away from where the Germans were concentrated and with the help of the French Resistance got all the way to Spain, where regretfully the Spanish authorities handed him over to the Germans. After nine months in the notorious Fresnes jail, he was executed by the Germans on 13th July 1943. He is now buried in Viroflay New Communal Cemetery near Versailles outside Paris.

Another member of the party, Sergeant Major T Winter, managed to get away from the wreckage of the Goatley and swim to within 50 yards of the MTB before it was, as mentioned above, hit by German fire and moved off in the dark. Undaunted he

78. A view from the Hog's Back on Sark towards the landing bay for the men of the SSRF on Operation Basalt. (National Archives)

swam back to shore where in company with another exhausted survivor both were taken prisoner.

Undaunted by this setback, the now Major Appleyard was quick to organise another trip across the Channel. Again this was aimed at the Channel Islands, the mission was given the name of Operation Basalt and it was intended that a landing should be made on the small island of Sark, taking some prisoners and gaining intelligence on the defences *in situ* on the island. It was planned to land on the night of 3rd/4th October 1942 and it was intended to land a party of twelve including Captain Ogden-Smith and Second Lieutenant Lassen amongst others. The party was again transported in MTB 344 which left Portland soon after 7.00 p.m. on the evening of 3rd October. There were around 40 Germans stationed on Sark, possessing a variety of relatively heavy weapons, including machine guns, mortars and anti-tank guns. They all came from Infantry Regiment 583 of the 319th Infantry Division under the command of *Oberleutnant* Herdt.

As MTB 344 approached Sark it was spotted by a German lookout post on Little Sark who signalled to it requesting identification. Under the instructions of Major Appleyard a message was flashed back stating they were Germans and seeking shelter in Dixcart Bay for the night. This apparently satisfied the lookout post as no further lights were flashed in their direction. By around 11.30 p.m. MTB 344 had reached the drop-off point. One of the party Bombardier Redborn later commented:

> Everything went according to plan, the navigation was excellent. We landed exactly at the right spot. We rowed in and the landing boat was made fast and left with a guard while the rest of us clambered up the steep path which led to the top of the cliff. The job of guarding the boat was not to be envied. Under no circumstances were they to leave their post before a definite time whereupon they had orders to row out to the MTB whether the landing party had come back or not.
>
> When we got to the top of the cliffs, we found barbed wire entanglements. The stillness of the night was only broken by the cry of a seagull or when the wire was snapped with cutters. We fumbled around the whole time in the dark. When we eventually got forward a little, I was in the centre of the file with Corporal Flint and Anders Lassen, with Captain Pinckney bringing up the rear, we heard a German patrol coming. We all dived off the path and the Germans went past without noticing anything. After this, although we did not run into any other patrols, there were many false alarms, when we heard sticks snapping and suchlike.
>
> Major Appleyard thought it best to go into a house and find out the local situation. The houses lay almost a mile inland. The first was empty so we scrambled down and up a little valley to the next one, a big lonely house on its own. We kept watch for a few minutes and everything was silent as a grave. We tried every door and window but all were locked so we smashed a window in the French doors, undid the latch and tumbled into the room.
>
> Downstairs was all empty but Major Appleyard and Corporal Flint who went upstairs were luckier. There they found an elderly lady. I did not see her myself because I and some of the others had to stay on watch downstairs. We had made a lot of noise breaking the window and, as there was always the possibility of an enemy patrol, we had to be prepared to shoot if surprised.

The elderly lady was wonderful. Although alone in the house and awakened by two men with blackened faces, she remained completely calm and was immediately aware of what it was all about. When the Major came down he said she had given him important information about the gun emplacements and defended positions and so on. She also said the Dixcart Hotel up the road was occupied and used as a headquarters. She understood that there were some Germans at the hotel with sentries in the annex next door. Captain Pinckney asked the lady if she would like to go back to England with us but she said she would not as she did not want to abandon her property. She begged us not to say she had given us information, that we obviously would not do, although the Germans found out about it nevertheless.

We had already been on the island an hour and we would have to hurry if we were not to go home with our job unfinished. The MTB had orders to leave to leave the island if we were not back within four hours. A corporal was therefore sent back to the boat with instructions to make them wait an extra half-hour.

We set off towards the town and when we neared what we believed to be the German quarters. Anders and I were chosen to deal with the sentry. We went ahead to see the lie of the land. A little later we came back to tell what we had found out. As we made some jokes about it. Anders said it would have been better if he had had his bow and arrow!

We returned to the spot where the sentry was on patrol. As there was only one man, Anders said he could manage him on his own. We lay down and watched him and calculated how long it took him to go back and forth. We could hear his footsteps when he came near, otherwise everything was still. By now the others had crept up so that all caught a glimpse of the German before Anders crept forward alone.

79. A pre-war postcard of the Dixcart Hotel Sark. (Ivy Lane Prints and Postcards)

The silence was broken by a muffled scream. We looked at each other and guessed what had happened. Then Anders came back and we could see everything was all right. The Major believed that the way was now clear for us to approach the annex. We had expected to find another sentry outside the hotel and because of this we went in formation but none was seen.

It was difficult to open the door and we made a great deal of noise before we rushed inside. We were very surprised not to find anyone in the first room, a kind of hallway, and we carefully approached the door on the far side. It was Anders who opened the door and we found it led to a passageway with about six doors on each side. The Major gave orders that each man should take a room and all go in at the same time.

I rushed into the room allotted to me and heard snoring. I switched on the light and saw a bed with a German asleep. The first thing I did was to draw the curtains and tear the bedclothes off him. Half-asleep he pulled them back again. I got the blankets off a second time and when he saw my blackened face he got a shock....I hit him under the chin with a knuckleduster and tied him up. Then I looked round the room for papers or cameras.

I got him to his feet still half-senseless and out into the corridor where Captain Pinckney, Andy and the others already stood; there were five prisoners all told. I covered them while the others searched the rooms once more and when this was done we took the prisoners outside.

When we were all outside, it happened. Until then, everything had gone fine but as soon as we were out in the moonlight they began to scream and shout, probably because they saw how few we were. All five of them had their hands tied behind their backs but they were not gagged. As soon as they started hollering we set about them with cuts and blows. Major Appleyard shouted "Shut the prisoners up!", and this began a regular fight.

I was not exactly clear over what happened next as I had so much trouble with my prisoner – he had got his hands free and we were fighting. He was just on the point of getting away so I gave him a rugger tackle and we both fell to the ground. He got free again as he was much bigger than me but I grabbed at him and we rolled about in a cabbage patch. One of the officers shouted above the noise: "If they try to get away, shoot them.

Captain Pinckney's prisoner got free and started towards the hotel shouting at the top of his voice. The Captain went after him and a shot rang out. I had just about had enough of my German; I couldn't manage him so I had to shoot him and found that the others were doing the same with their prisoners. All, that is, except Anders who stood still and held two Germans tightly.

More shots rang out with shouting and screaming. It was a hell of a rumpus and lights were coming on in the hotel. Anders, who had now freed himself of his prisoners, wanted to throw some grenades through the hotel windows but Major Appleyard said no, keep them, we may need them later. By now Germans were pouring out of the hotel and when we saw how many of them there were, we decided to get away. We still had one prisoner who had seen what we had done to the others and he was stiff with fright and did everything we told him.

The most important thing now was to get back to the boat as quickly as possible. The island was waking up and the German headquarters was like a wasps' nest. How we ran. We ran until every step hurt but not in a panic, still in open patrol formation.

This is Major Appleyard's account of the events after his party had reached the Dixcart Hotel:

The whole party then entered the annex and a thorough search revealed the presence of five Germans, all sleeping in separate rooms. Their clothes were searched for weapons, pay books, papers etc. likely to prove of value, and the prisoners were then taken out of the house to be assembled under cover of the trees nearby. In the darkness outside the house one of the prisoners, seeing an opportunity, suddenly attacked his guard and then shouting loudly for help and trying to raise an alarm, ran off in the direction in which it was known there were buildings containing a number of Germans. He was caught almost immediately by his guard, but after a scuffle again escaped, still shouting and was shot. Meanwhile, three of the other prisoners seizing the opportunity of the noise and confusion, also started shouting and attacking their guards. Two broke away and both were shot immediately. The third, although still held, was accidentally shot in an attempt to silence him with the butt of a revolver. The fifth prisoner remained quiet and did not struggle. There were answering shouts from the direction in which the prisoners had attempted to escape and sounds of a verbal alarm being given.

After a bit of a struggle with the exhausted German everyone reached the pick-up point and just in the nick of time reached MTB 344 before it was about to depart for England. The time was now around 3.45 a.m. on the morning of 4th October.

Meanwhile as the men of the SSRF slipped away from Sark, the Germans were learning of what had been happening. The commander of the Germans on Sark, *Oberleutnant* Herdt, was informed of an incident probably involving commandos around 4.00 a.m. (German time, this was one hour ahead of that used by the commandos), and a general alarm sounded about five minutes later. Soon afterwards one of the escaped prisoners, *Gefreiter* Klotz, was found completely naked and he was able to provide some detail on what had happened and how he had managed to escape.

Some troops were sent to the area of the Hog's Back which ran from near the Dixcart Hotel area to the coast and a bay called Dixcart Bay to look for the commandos. By the time they arrived, the trail had long gone cold, but they did find several items of equipment and weapons left behind. These included two Fairbairn-Sykes knives, a pistol, a magazine for a sub machine gun, a pair of wire cutters, a torch, a woollen cap and several toggle ropes. The news that German occupied territory had once again been 'invaded' went quickly up the chain of command, reaching Army Group D HQ in Paris before 7 o'clock the same day. Much attention was also focused on the inhabitants of Sark, particularly the two owners of the hotel, Misses Duckett and Page, who had slept through the whole night and were unaware that they had been visited.

Whilst the Germans were carrying out their investigation into what had happened, it became clear to them that some of the men at the Dixcart Hotel had been tied up before being shot. This seemed in their eyes to present them with a marvellous propaganda opportunity, following close behind the Dieppe raid when orders had been issued to the Canadians stating that prisoners' hands were to be secured to prevent them from destroying secret papers. Three days after the raid, the Germans issued a statement stating the men on Sark had been illegitimately bound and that it was while resisting that two men had been shot.

Normally the British Government did not comment on the raids, but on this occasion they got HQ Combined Operations to issue a press release, which was carefully worded to avoid any mention of tying up any prisoners. Their statement said:

> A small-scale raid was made last Saturday night on the island of Sark. It was one of many such operations which are successfully and frequently carried out about which nothing is normally said. But since the enemy have, from ulterior motives, announced the raid, with the addition of inaccurate details, the facts are now issued.
>
> The main purpose of this raid was to obtain first-hand information about suspected ill-treatment of British residents on the island. As a result of this, these suspicions have now been confirmed by the seizure of a proclamation signed "Knackfuss *Oberst Feldkommandant*".
>
> This states that all male civilians (a) not born in the Channel Islands or (b) not permanently resident there, between the ages of 16 and 70, have been deported to Germany, together with their families. This deportation took place last week at the shortest notice. Nine hundred men were conscripted from Guernsey, four hundred are still to go, and it is expected that there will be more from Jersey than there will be from Guernsey. Eleven men of Sark were warned to go last week, but two committed suicide and only nine left.
>
> The total British raiding force consisted of ten officers and men and there were no casualties. Five prisoners were taken, of whom four escaped after repeated struggles and were shot while doing so. One was brought back to this country. He has confirmed these deportations and has stated that they were for forced labour.

It had been intended before the men of the SSRF left England to take prisoners and indeed as one officer Captain Ogden-Smith recalled:

> We had taken a grey-coloured cord with us specifically to tie the Germans up as the purpose of the raid was to bring back prisoners. We were all armed with .45 Colts. In the fight my prisoner got away and when the Germans started pouring from the hotel we ran like hell back to the boat. The prisoner held us up; he was still in his pyjamas.

However, this seemingly innocuous point about the prisoners on Sark being tied (which strictly speaking is a contravention of the Geneva Convention), was seized upon by the Germans. Hitler is said to have been furious when he read of the fact in a report on yet another commando raid. The Germans threatened retaliation and as an extra measure announced that British prisoners of war taken at the Dieppe raid in August would be tied up and chained from noon on 8th October 1942. They would be kept like this "until the British War Ministry proves that it will in future make true statements

THE END OF THE BEGINNING 257

regarding the binding of German prisoners or that it has succeeded in getting its orders carried out by its troops."

The British Government responded by stating "if Germany carries out this threat, the Government will have to consider its future action."

Captain Ogden-Smith said later that after the raid they never thought any more about the significance of what they had done until articles started appearing in the newspapers. He also commented that he thought Major Appleyard had to report to Winston Churchill about what had happened, but after hearing from him the Prime Minister was not in the least worried.

Undeterred by any of this, on 9th October, Berlin announced that 1,376 British officers and men had been shackled. In a game of tit-for-tat the same number of German prisoners in Canada were put on 'the chain gang' the following day. At this point, with the possibility of the situation getting out of control, the Swiss Government stepped in as a peace-broker. They suggested that both sides should simultaneously release their chained-up prisoners. The British Government announced this had been done on the 12th October. The Germans stuck to their guns a little while longer, initially requesting a statement that "the British Government would give an assurance forbidding the binding or shackling of prisoners in any circumstances whatsoever." Both sides backed down but enough was enough for Hitler, probably infuriated at the number of small-scale commando raids, he secretly issued a few days later the infamous *Kommandobefehl* (Commando order). The text of this document was as follows:

The Fuhrer
SECRET
F.H. Qu 18.10
No 003830/42g.Kdos.OWK/Wst

12 copies
Copy No 12

1. For a long time now our opponents have been employing in their conduct of the war, methods which contravene the International Convention of Geneva. The members of the so-called commandos behave in a particularly brutal and underhand manner; and it has been established that those units recruit criminals not only from their own country but even former convicts set free in enemy territories. From captured orders it emerges that they are instructed not only to tie up prisoners, but also to kill out-of-hand unarmed captives who they think might prove an encumbrance to them, or hinder them in successfully carrying out their aims. Orders have indeed been found in which the killing of prisoners has positively been demanded of them.

2. In this connection it has already been notified in an Appendix to Army Orders of 7.10.1942 Germany will adopt the same methods against these sabotage units of the British and their Allies; i.e. that, whenever they appear, they shall be ruthlessly destroyed by the German troops.

3. I order, therefore:-
   From now on all men operating against German troops in so-called commando raids in Europe or in Africa, are to be annihilated to the last man. This is to be carried out whether they be soldiers in uniform, or saboteurs, with or without arms; and whether fighting or seeking to escape; and it is equally immaterial

whether they come into action from ships or aircraft, or whether they land by parachute. Even if these individuals on discovery make obvious their intention of giving themselves up as prisoners, no pardon is on any account to be given. On this matter a report is to be made on each case to Headquarters for the information of Higher Command.

4. Should individual members of these commandos, such as agents, saboteurs etc., fall into the hands of the Armed Forces through any means, as, for example, through the Police in one of the Occupied Territories, they are to be instantly handed over to the SD. To hold them in military custody, for example in PoW camps etc., even if only as a temporary measure, is strictly forbidden.

5. This order does not apply to the treatment of those enemy soldiers who are taken prisoner or give themselves up in open battle, in the course of normal operations, large scale attacks, or in major assault landings or airborne operations. Neither does it apply to those who fall into our hands after a sea fight, nor to those enemy soldiers who, after air battle, seek to save their lives by parachute.

6. I will hold all Commanders and Officers responsible under Military Law for any omission to carry out this order, whether by failure in their duty to instruct their units accordingly, or if they themselves act contrary to it.

Signed Adolf Hitler

As it was stated at the top of the order only 12 copies of this order were ever issued and just to follow this order up the Chief of Staff to the German Army followed it up with another 'limited distribution' message. This read as follows:

Headquarters of the Army
Secret
No 551781/42G.K. Chiefs W.F.St/Qu.
F.H. Qu. 19/10/42

22 Copies
Copy No 21

The enclosed order from the Fuhrer is forwarded in connection with destruction of enemy terror and sabotage troops.

This order is intended for Commanders only and is in no circumstances to fall into enemy hands.

Further distribution by receiving Headquarters is to be most strictly limited.

The Headquarters mentioned in the distribution list are responsible that all parts of the Order or extracts taken from it, which are issued are again withdrawn and, together with this copy, destroyed.

Chief of Staff of the Army
Signed Jodl

The final two operations I intend to look at in finishing off the year of 1942 were when HQ Combined Operations decided to return to their old area of operations, Norway, with two excursions being undertaken each with mixed results. The first, codenamed

Operation Musketoon, was an audacious attempt to stop production at an aluminum smelting plant located just north of the Arctic Circle at a place called Glomfjord not far south of Narvik. The intention was not to destroy the smelting plant but to blow up

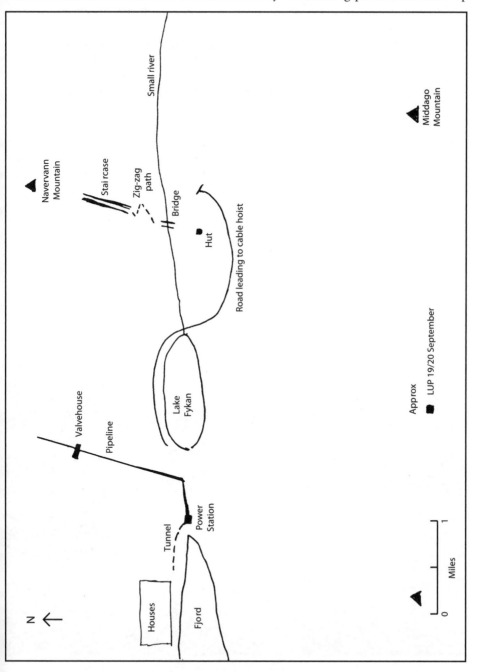

Map 10. Glomfjord Area

the power station that supplied it with electricity. The source of electricity generating was based upon the hydro-electric power (HEP) source, in which water is used to turn turbines which generate the electricity.

The men chosen to undertake this operation were two officers and eight men from No 2 Commando supplemented by two Free Norwegians who at the time worked for the Special Operations Executive. The commander of the raid was Captain G Black (he had been on the Vaagso raid and been awarded a Military Cross for his actions there), assisted by Captain J Houghton. The rest of the group was as follows:

CSM M Smith, Sergeant R O'Brien, L/Sergeant W Chudley, Corporal J Fairclough, Rifleman C Abram, Private E Curtis, Private R Makeham and Private F Trigg. The two Norwegians were Corporal E Djupdraet and Corporal S Granlund.

To transport the group to Norway a Free French submarine, the *Junon* was used. It was selected because it was thought she had a silhouette similar to that of a German U-boat. The group left the Orkney Islands in the morning of 11th September 1942. The escape plan called for the group to walk to Sweden although a flying boat would try and pick them up at one of two alternative locations even if they had not been in contact. They were provided with a special SOE radio to hopefully arrange this pick-up, but if not the fall back was to walk out.

The power station was located at the head of the fjord and it was felt that if the Germans did expect any attack it would come from the front, given the severity of the surrounding terrain. To hopefully catch the Germans unaware Black intended to

80. The HEP station at Glomfjord Norway. The target of Operation Musketoon in October 1942. (National Archives)

come over the mountains and approach from the rear. So whilst on the voyage across to Norway Captain Black asked the submarine commander, Commander Querville if he would be prepared to disembark the commandos at Bjaerangsfjord immediately south of Glomfjord and go cross-country to the target area. In spite of there being a shortage of information on the currents and depths of the fjord here Querville agreed to this last-minute change of plan. On their way up the fjord a small fishing boat was sighted whilst the periscope was up and a crash dive had to be carried out but it was hoped it was crewed by loyal Norwegians and they would keep their mouths shut.

This was indeed the case and after arrival on the afternoon of the 15th September they submerged all the way to the bottom of the Bjaerangsfjord where they spent the rest of the day in growing discomfort. Soon after 9.00 p.m. that night they blew the tanks and rose gently to the surface of the fjord. One of the two dinghies they had brought with them (one as a spare) was made ready and the 12 men silently rowed ashore. Once ashore, the dinghy was deflated and hidden under some stones and moss. They were only seen by one local an elderly lady, who claimed to have seen them coming ashore. Fortunately the other locals put it down to an over-active imagination or the first signs of senility. The group once ashore set a quick pace as they crossed over some open country between the coast and the mountains to the north. After a couple of brief rests to catch their breath the group safely reached the foot of the mountains containing a feature known as the Black Glacier which they would have to traverse to reach the power plant. Two of the group went ahead on an initial reconnaissance, these were Captain Houghton and one

81. A slightly closer-in photograph of the power station showing the pipes snaking up the hillside. The somewhat arduous terrain is all too obvious. (National Archives)

of the Norwegians, Corporal S Granlund, while the others rested up. They returned in an hour or so and then the whole group left to start the traverse of the Black Glacier. It was a difficult climb but they all made it successfully and it was easier than it could have been as they moved in daylight. However, their security had nearly been compromised by an almost unbelievable lapse in security. Unbeknown to the commandos, a party of German Army surveyors led by a *Leutnant* W Dehne, were in the area of the Glomfjord and they had been spotted close to the lake on one of the party's binoculars. Fortunately they were just too far away to make a positive identification, but later that day the Dehne group came across an 'abandoned camp' with some Players cigarette packets and other rubbish left lying around. Whilst confused about what he had found and how it came to be there Dehne did not report his findings at the time. Meanwhile the 12 commandos spent the night of 17th/18th September in a shelter which overlooked the power station at the head of the Glomfjord.

The rest of the next day was spent contemplating their options and discussing and finalising plans for the attack on the power station and the subsequent withdrawal. After dark on the evening of the 18th around 8.00 p.m. the group left their laying-up point and set off downhill towards the power station. After a dangerous journey of about 4 hours as they neared the bottom of the descent they heard the sounds of a small group of men singing and engine noises. Since Captain Black wanted complete surprise he decided to abort the attack that night and delay it for 24 hours. The group was now faced with an uncompromising climb back up to a position of safety. Whilst the decision to abort may have been the correct one, they had probably set off too late the previous night and when daylight came they had not reached their preferred hiding place. There was no option but to hide where they were, but fortunately they remained undiscovered during the daylight hours of the 19th. They were helped here by some atrocious weather, it rained heavily nearly all day. The commandos also spent a miserable day inside their supposedly waterproof sleeping bags which turned out to be nothing of the sort. In spite of their discomfort the group were probably glad to see the light fade so they could get moving again.

They had more luck on their second descent and as they neared the power station three men split off to carry out a secondary task. This gang of three, L/Sergeant W Chudley, Sergeant R O'Brien and Private E Curtis, were detailed to lay explosive charges on two high-pressure pipelines. Several plastic explosive collars were secured around the pipes with 30 minute pencil fuses but they were not to be activated until a signal was received from the main group.

This group now settled down to await developments. Their colleagues eventually arrived undiscovered at the rear of the power station and worked their way to the generating hall. Two of the group were left outside as guards while the other seven went inside. Initially taking cover behind some packing cases the situation inside the hall was assessed. After identifying that whilst a few Germans were in the control room, with the exception of one Norwegian technician the hall was empty. Then fortune smiled on the commandos as the Germans left the technician to apparently get on with his job. This solved what had felt to be one of the more riskier elements of the raid, that of overpowering any Germans in the generating hall. This made the job of collecting the Norwegians together easier, which the group then did. As well as the 'technician on duty', several others were found asleep in rooms at the top of the building. Somewhat shocked they were politely invited to get away from the power station going along the mile-long tunnel that was the main point of access to the outside world from the power station.

Once the Norwegians had disappeared a smoke bomb was placed in the tunnel to hopefully delay the process of any Germans sent to investigate. Then the first minor misfortune happened, some Germans appeared. Although one German soldier was shot and killed by Corporal Granlund, another managed to escape and disappear down the tunnel. Meanwhile whilst this was going on, explosive charges were being laid on the three turbines and generators, ten minute fuses being used to prevent the Germans having much opportunity to stop the explosions. At about this time sirens started sounding and so the commandos realised that their presence had been discovered. Their escape route was to climb up the mountain at the rear of the plant. Whilst the group of nine, now reunited, were starting on their ascent, the explosives on the turbines and generators went off, which was the signal for the group at the pipes to set their fuses. It was intended for the two groups to meet up and gain the high ground before the pipe explosives went off and millions of gallons of water started thundering down the hillside.

82. A post-raid photograph giving an idea of the amount of rubble brought down the mountainside by the water torrent. (National Archives)

Meanwhile further down the mountain at the tunnel, German soldiers were unwilling to enter the tunnel for fear of it also blowing up. It was decided to use boats to move to the power station but this of course led to delays. They were just too late to stop any of the two sets of charges going up and a torrent of water poured down the mountainside causing extensive secondary damage.

The two groups of commandos managed to meet up with each other and all headed for a mountain hut that was marked on their maps as Fykandalen. Once here they hoped to find some Norwegians to guide them to a staircase of steps that were cut into the mountainside nearby. This would make their progress easier as it was felt necessary to try and put as much distance between themselves and the power station as possible. Corporal Granlund, who was easily the best climber in the party, made it to the hut first and it was indeed occupied by two Norwegians who worked on a conveyor belt moving materials to a dam further up the Navervann and a young female Norwegian cook. Despite appeals to be shown the location of the suspension bridge that led to the staircase the best assistance he got was a hastily drawn map with some vague directions. Granlund bravely tried to find the bridge but was unsuccessful and when he returned to the hut area he found Captain Houghton and Corporal Djupdraet also blundering around in the dark. The rest of the group had found some cover a short distance away and were leaving it to the others to hopefully establish the route. After a brief search and a discussion the three of them returned to the hut, not being aware that in the time since Corporal Granlund had visited it, two German soldiers had also arrived.

When the Germans entered the hut they questioned the occupants as to whether they had seen any British soldiers around the area, which were answered in the negative. As Captain Houghton and Corporal Djupdraet entered the hut there was a few moments of almost 'slow-motion' action before the two sides leapt at each other. The outcome was that one of the Germans was killed and the other wounded, however, during the scuffle Corporal Djupdraet was badly wounded by a bayonet in the stomach.

The main party then converged on the hut and after giving what first aid they could to Corporal Djupdraet, the decision was taken to split up into groups of two and three and travel independently. The ominous sights and sounds of a search party could be seen heading up the mountain so there was little time to spare. It is believed two groups consisting of Sergeant O'Brien, Corporal Fairclough, Corporal Granlund and Private Trigg were on a more northern route climbing up a mountain known as Navervann. The others, consisting of Captain Black, Captain Houghton, CSM Smith, L/Sergeant Chudley, Rifleman Abram, Private Curtis and Private Makeham were to the south heading towards the almost impossible climb of the Middago Mountain. For this larger group their luck suddenly ran out and a German search party appeared close by and opened fire. They were only armed with a silenced Sten gun and pistols. Captain Houghton sniped at them with his silenced Sten and the Germans kept their distance. It was now growing lighter by the minute and as the others hurried up the steep slopes Captain Houghton did his best to gain them some time. Then at last a German spotted him and fired, wounding him in the forearm but he continued to snipe until his ammunition ran out. Still carrying his Sten he then withdrew and hurried after the others. They reached the crest of the mountain and unexpectedly found themselves in a shallow crater. This was partly covered with earth and a few large rocks and about 150 yards across. There was very little cover. The rocks they could see were about 50 yards into the crater and after that nothing till the far side of the crater. Indeed the far side of the crater appeared to be too steep to easily climb. However, before they could really decide what to do a large number of Germans appeared in a rapidly widening arc around the crater. Behind what limited cover they had found I feel every man knew the game was up and they started to dismantle and hide their weapons. Eventually a German called on them to surrender, but no one moved. Then a hand grenade was lobbed in their general direction giving an idea of what might happen next. The commander of the group, Captain Black was the first to rise with his hands up in the air followed by the others.

If they had known what was to happen to them they might have fought on.

The other four men had better luck, evading German search parties and with the help of many loyal Norwegians they managed to reach neutral Sweden and were eventually flown to Scotland and then to London for a meeting with Mountbatten. They were able to report that as far as they had seen the raid had achieved all its objectives, certainly severely damaging the water pipes, turbines and generators of the HEP station. In fact the damage caused by the explosions and the tidal wave of escaping water meant the power station did not come back on line until after the war. The raid was another good example of how a small group of men could cause an effect far greater than they should have done.

For the others it was not so good. Corporal Djupdraet died of his wounds three days later on 23rd September. Initially the other seven commandos were taken under heavy guard to Colditz Castle- the notorious 'special camp' for potentially dangerous prisoners in eastern Germany near Leipzig. Despite attempts by the Germans to isolate the group from contact with the regular inmates, communication was established between both sets of prisoners.

When he heard of the attack, Hitler flew into another rage and for a time there was confusion about what to do with the captured commandos. As previously stated Hitler's 'special treatment' orders for any captured commandos had been issued on the 18th October 1942, although the men had been captured before then. A decision was taken and they were removed from Colditz arriving at the Sachsenhausen concentration camp near Berlin on the 22nd October. Orders were issued by the SD that night that all seven were to be executed on the following day. Each man was killed by a single shot in the back of the neck and their bodies then burnt.

The Germans responsible for the actual executions were not traced after the war and I suppose the war-crime is still, in theory, open. Most of the victims are commemorated on the Brookwood Memorial to the Missing in Surrey.

Personnel taking part in Operation Musketoon
- Captain G Black executed Sachsenhausen 23rd October 1942
- Captain J Houghton executed Sachsenhausen 23rd October 1942
- CSM M Smith executed Sachsenhausen 23rd October 1942
- Sergeant R O'Brien returned to England via Sweden
- L/Sergeant W Chudley executed Sachsenhausen 23rd October 1942
- Corporal J Fairclough returned to England via Sweden
- Rifleman C Abram executed Sachsenhausen 23rd October 1942
- Private E Curtis executed Sachsenhausen 23rd October 1942

In memory of those brave members of the British and Commonwealth forces, many still unknown, who were interned in Sachsenhausen and perished here or elsewhere at the hands of their captors:

In Erinnerung an die tapferen Mitglieder der britischen und Commonwealth Streitkräfte, viele noch heute unbekannt, die im KZ Sachsenhausen gefangen gehalten und hier oder an anderen Orten getötet wurden:

Pte Cyril Abram
Capt Graeme Black DSO MC
OS Neville Burgess RN
LSgt William Chudley
Sgt Jack Cox
Lt Cdr Claude Cumberledge RNVR
Pte Eric Curtis
Sub Lt John Godwin RNVR
Capt W Grover-Williams Fr CdG
Sgt Thomas Handley MM

PO Harold Hiscock RN
Capt Joseph Houghton MC
Cpl Jan Kotbra
Pte Reginald Makeham
OS Keith Mayor RN
PO Alfred Roe RN
CSM Miller Smith
CSM James Steele MM
Maj Francis Suttill DSO
OS Andrew West RN

"Greater love hath no man than this, that a man lay down his life for his friends."

"Niemand hat grössere Liebe denn die, dass er sein Leben lässt für seine Freunde."

83. The memorial tablet at Sachsenhausen concentration camp with the names of those men from Operation Musketoon executed there by the Germans on it. (N Cherry)

- Private R Makeham executed Sachsenhausen 23rd October 1942
- Private F Trigg returned to England via Sweden
- Corporal E Djupdraet died of wounds
- Corporal S Granlund returned to England via Sweden

After a brief period of debriefing and leave the survivors of the raid were sent back to the war. Each of them was however, decorated for their exploits, Sergeant R O'Brien being awarded a Distinguished Conduct Medal which was announced in the *London Gazette* of 19th February 1943. His citation read:

Sergeant O'Brien was one of the detachment of 2 Commando on Operation Musketoon. This highly successful operation resulted in the destruction of the important electric power plant at Glomfjord in Norway on the night of 20th September 1942. Sergeant O'Brien throughout showed great skill and resolution. He helped reconnoitre the difficult mountain crossing from the landing place to the objective and personally laid the charge which destroyed the pipeline. He then made his escape, spending, in all, twelve days in enemy-occupied country. When suffering from sickness, privation and exhaustion he showed remarkable endurance and determination.

84. The Brookwood Memorial to the Missing in Surrey. Many of the men with no known graves mentioned in the text are commemorated here. (N Cherry)

The other two, Corporal J Fairclough and Private F Trigg, both received a Military Medal. Somewhat unusually the *London Gazette* of 7th January 1943 published a longish report about these awards which read as follows:

We left our home port on 11th September 1942 and disembarked four days later. After the operation, which took place successfully on the night of 20th September, we climbed up to the huts behind Glomfjord power station. Captain Black then told the rest of us to climb the hill as best we could and get away. We divided into two parties, Smith, O'Brien, Christiansen (Granlund), Fairclough and Trigg going up to the right and the others to the left. However Captain Black called Smith back to administer morphia to a man who had been wounded.

The four of us carried on for four hours up the mountain till 0600 hours 21st September when we reached the south side of a valley leading to Storglomvatnet Lake. We had abandoned our haversacks and everything but two Colts and our emergency rations. We had two compasses apart from the small compasses in the aid boxes. Christiansen had a large-scale map.

The river was deep and rapid and we were on the wrong side of it as the Storglomvatnet Lake blocked our way east. Christiansen managed to cross with difficulty but shouted to us not to follow him. He was in much stronger form than we were, he was as agile as a goat and was going strong when last we saw him. He still had the map. We now had a compass between three of us, Christiansen having taken one with him. We were very tired and hungry and ate all our emergency rations in twenty minutes.

We went on down the south side of a valley and during the afternoon had to lie low because four Messerschmitts and a Heinkel came to look for us. In the evening we were able to cross the river where it reaches the lake and skirted round the north of the lake.

We walked all night and by Tuesday morning 22nd September we reached a road going north and south just to the south of South Bjeliaa Lake. It was an appalling journey through snow and blizzard 5,000 feet up. On the road O'Brien approached a farmhouse and came out again with a parcel of food, bread, butter cheese. After eating this we waded across the stream and up into the woods. O'Brien thought he saw four Germans and we hid in some rocks for an hour. We then marched up the hill (385417 GSGS 4090 K.14) and Sergeant O'Brien lost the remaining compass. We continued but the following evening we found we had gone round in a circle and dropped with exhaustion. We made a big fire and slept there all that night. O'Brien went down to a valley thinking we were going east. We followed him the next day 23rd September but never saw him again. We went to a second farmhouse at 1200 hours, where they fed us and gave us sandwiches for the journey. They pointed at the valley down which we had come as being the way to Sweden. We had, in fact, come down the valley we had previously gone up. We set off again up the same valley and climbed all that night. At the top we passed a woodman's hut. We climbed over to the other side of the mountain, but we were so exhausted that we went back to the hut which we reached at dawn 24th September. We found some stale cheese, coffee and flour in it. Trigg made some doughnuts, fried the cheese and made some coffee. We slept until midday.

Despairing of getting to Sweden without help, we returned once more to the road intending to go to the farm again but got lost. We decided to follow the road north and came to another farm near South Bjeliaa Lake. The man who opened the door spoke English but was very frightened and said there was a German patrol on the road to the south. We carried on north along the road and after a few minutes the farmer followed us on a bicycle and told us to go to his parent's house which he pointed out east of the road. We went there and though they could not understand us, they fed us well and gave us some socks. Then the son arrived and said he would find a guide for next morning. He gave us a haversack each full of food and a bottle of milk. He took us a mile further up to another farm from where bedding, pillow and blankets were provided for us in a loft.

At 0500 hours 25th September he took us to the top of a hill, gave us a small compass on top of a pen and told us to march east. He drew a rough map showing the route to the north of a lake where we should see some telegraph poles. We were told to follow the line of these, but not too closely as there was a hut nearby where there was thought to be a Quisling. When we got near the poles, we saw in the snow some tracks of commando boots which we followed but these came to an end and we never picked them up again.

When we got to the Mo-Bod road we had some trouble crossing the river. A motorcyclist passed by on the road, we ducked and were not seen. We eventually found a boat and crossed the river. We made a fire on top of the hill that night. It was very cold indeed with snow about six inches deep. We went to sleep but kept waking up with cold and making the fire up. The following dawn 26th September we again set out climbing a very high peak about 5,000 feet. It was sheer rock and we were scared, sometimes snow up to our chests. We eventually got down into a valley intending to keep to valleys in future. We followed this valley down to the Junkerdal-Craddis road. There we found a farm and they gave us food. It was at this farm that we met a man who was to guide us over the frontier. He took us to a friend's house a mile along the stream. There we had another feed and went to bed at 1500 hours. The guide went out to make arrangements to get us across that night.

He woke us up at 1800 hours giving us another meal and sandwiches. We left at 1900 hours and went up to his sister's house at Skiati. We had more food there at 2200 hours, and left at 2300 hours. The guide and his brother-in-law then accompanied us over the frontier and left us three hundred yards the other side. This was at 0230 hours, 27th September. They told us to follow the telegraph poles for eight miles to some friends of theirs at Merkenes. The country here is very wooded and we could not have found this house unless we had been directed. We met nine Norwegian refugees here.

We were taken down the lakes by motor boat and rowing boats to Jackvik where we stayed two days and were disinfected. This consisted of a Turkish bath, having our hair closely cropped, the hair scrapped off our bodies and our clothes fumigated. Then we were taken to Jokkmokk where we were interrogated by a Swedish Intelligence Officer Lieutenant Levi. We said we had escaped from a prisoner of war camp in Norway. We afterwards discovered that there was no such camp for British prisoners of war but the Swedes did not ask too many questions. Orders then came through from Stockholm that we were to be passed through immediately. We were taken to the Legation there and left by plane on 6th October arriving at Leuchars 7th October 1942.

In early January 1943 citations were submitted for the award of a DSO to Captain Black and a MC for Captain Houghton. A reply was received in March 1943 which stated that as the officers were thought to be prisoners they would be considered for these awards at the end of the war. In September 1945, when it was learned that both had been executed, further representations were made for awards for them. The somewhat high handed official reply was "the ruling for citations in respect of personnel whose death takes place after the action for which recommendations are made is understood to be that such recommendations may only stand if they were submitted to higher authority before the death took place. It would appear, therefore, that the only award which can now be given is a Mention in Despatches."

In an appeal to the War Office from the Chief of Combined Operations again in September 1945 it was pointed out that the officers were shot on 23rd October 1942. The reasons for the delay in submitting the citations to the War Office were given as "the personnel taking part in this operation could only escape from Norway through Sweden and they therefore could not be expected back in the UK for several weeks. In fact, four men out of this force returned at intervals from three weeks to two months after the operation, and it was for some time hoped that others might be following. It is therefore strongly requested that the citations for the DSO and MC previously submitted on behalf of these officers may be allowed to stand, and that the date of award may read prior to 23rd October 1942." Fortunately the War Office showed some sympathy to this

85. An electrolysis cell used in the production of heavy water. An original from the Vermork plant, although it was a replacement for one of those destroyed by Norwegian members of SOE in February 1943. (ABF Museum)

86. The heavy water plant at Vermork, 60 miles west of Oslo. (ABF Museum)

appeal and allowed the names to go forward to the King for approval. On 9th November the Military Secretary at the War Office wrote to the Chief of Combined Operations stating that the King had given approval and both awards would be published in the *London Gazette* on 15th November 1945.

In a document at the National Archives is a report dated 20th November 1942 trying to assess the damage done to the power station. Also included is a translated report from a Swiss engineer from a firm called Brown Boveri who had machinery at Glomfjord. Without giving too much away the report states, "a report made by him to his firm, has reached this headquarters from Switzerland."

Selected comments from the report are as follows:

There are two separate reports regarding the quantity of rock, mud and rubble washed down by the temporary rush of water; one ungraded report mentions a figure of 15,000 cubic metres, and another report from Switzerland speaks of 20,000 cubic metres which covered the machines with a compact mass of rubble.

A representative of Brown Boveri happened to be at Glomfjord at the time of the attack making a survey with a view to further extensions, and a report made by him to his firm, has reached this headquarters from Switzerland.

The following are taken from the Swiss engineer's report:

As a result of certain happenings at 1.00 a.m. on the 21.9.42 the lower parts of the station were flooded with water and blocked by mud and rubble. The four stator halves were 1.7 metres deep in mud and water for the space of seven hours. Four machine poles, five main and auxiliary exciter armatures and seventeen stator coils are still buried under stones and rubble. Eight poles, which were still packed in their cases have been standing in water. Three current transformers for the neutral point of generator 5, all the stator connections for both generators, the lead-out conductors for the pole wheels, for tool boxes and special tools were partly stored in the hot air duct to dry, and all are covered with lumps of cement and rubble. Moreover, 93 generator coils have been in water and are still lying partly covered with mud and rubble. Since 1.00 a.m. on the 21.9 no machines have been in operation.

The final operation of 1942 I will be looking at was again intended to be undertaken in Norway and the codename given to it was Operation Freshman. Again intelligence reports from resistance workers in a German-occupied country led to an ambitious raid being planned. In this case reports were coming from Norway stating that a large hydro electric power complex in the Telemark region of southern Norway was being used for the production of deuterium oxide, more commonly known as heavy water. Heavy water was a vital component for the manufacture of an atomic bomb. Plutonium was an essential raw material for the manufacture of such a weapon. The electrolytic process for the division of water to obtain hydrogen for the manufacture of ammonia produced, as a byproduct, small quantities of heavy water. This is very similar to normal water except that the hydrogen atom is heavier than normal, which can then be used for the manufacture of plutonium.

Both sides in the Second World War were at this time working towards developing this powerful new weapon. The Allied one was being constructed in comparative safety in the USA, but it was thought that if the stocks of heavy water and manufacturing process at the Norsk Hydro plant at Vermork could be destroyed or damaged it would delay the German effort tremendously. It would however, not be an easy target – the plant was situated in a gorge close to the village of Vermork, about two miles west of Rjukan. This was about 80 miles from the coast and 60 miles due west of Oslo. To say it would be a difficult place to get to can be gauged by the fact that Rjukan was in a very isolated place, situated as it was in a deep valley, the sides of which were thickly covered in almost impenetrable forests which rose nearly vertically from the valley floor to over 3,000 feet. The valley itself was overlooked by Gaustal Fjell, a mountain rising to over 5,000 feet. The heavy water plant itself had been constructed on a broad shelf of rock which nature had forced out of the valley sides at about 1,000 feet high. Above the plant were again virtually vertical slopes covered with pine trees.

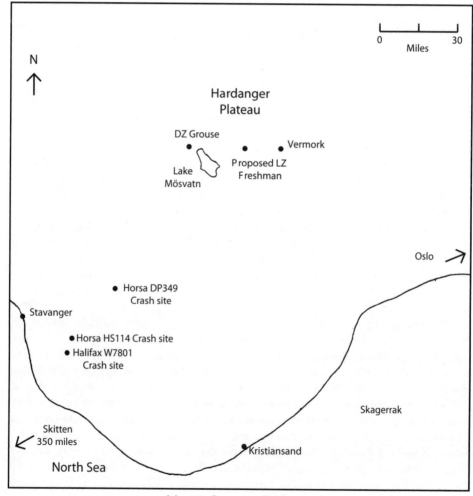

Map 11. Operation Freshman

Much valuable intelligence had been obtained from various Norwegian sources, indeed it is probably fair to say that as early as mid-1940, the intelligence community in Britain was aware of the activities at the Vermork plant. Soon after the German occupation of Norway in May 1940 British intelligence heard that the plant had been ordered to increase production of heavy water from around 3,000 lbs a year to over 10,000 by January 1942. Obviously in the background a watch was kept on the activities at Vermork, but a vital breakthrough came in March 1942 when a group of young Norwegians planned an escape to Britain aiming to join the Free Norwegian Forces. The plan was to hijack a coastal steamer and sail her to Britain. This is precisely what happened with the steamer *Galtesund* and she eventually arrived at Aberdeen in Scotland. Amongst the Norwegians aboard was an engineer from the Vermork plant, whose employers back in Norway believed was officially on his one month's annual holiday. His name was Einar Skinnarland. Some information had already been obtained about the layout of the plant from a Norwegian scientist, Professor Lief Tronstadt, who had escaped before the German occupation. Einar Skinnarland was able to provide much

87. Another view of the target of Operation Freshman. Note the large number of water pipes coming down the mountain side. (National Archives)

detailed information regarding the standard operating procedures of the local garrison and patrol patterns. After several debriefing sessions it was suggested to him that he offer his services as a guide for a future raid on the plant. He readily agreed to this and after a very basic parachute course at RAF Ringway found himself at action stations in an RAF aircraft over the Hardander Vidda mountains on the 28th March 1942. This was just 11 days after his arrival at Aberdeen, he would just be able to make it back to work in time. He also took a radio back to Norway with him. It was decided that the short Norwegian nights during the spring and summer would not provide enough hours of darkness to carry out a successful operation so the plan had been put on the back burner for a while. With the onset of autumn the hours of daylight were obviously getting shorter and so Operation Freshman was felt to have a better chance of success.

The military minds were assessing their options and eventually the idea for another Norwegian raid was passed to HQ Combined Operations to come up with a plan to cause damage to the plant. Various options were looked at, including a 'conventional' bombing raid by the RAF, a sabotage raid by Norwegians from SOE and lastly a raid using airborne troops. The first two options were ruled out, the RAF being hampered by their difficulties in finding targets especially a pinpoint one as small as the plant near Rjukan. For reasons that are not clear now, the use of Norwegians from SOE was also not selected. It is possible that Browning, perhaps basking in the glow of success from Bruneval, wanted to get his troops involved again and lobbied to get the operation. So, as it turned out, an airborne assault was considered to have the best chance of success. The initial thoughts were to land the men by Sunderland flying boats on Lake Tinnsjön, which was about 15 miles from the objective. There was a small problem, in that as a large quantity of explosives would have to be taken this virtually ruled the use of paratroopers out. The planners were also concerned about the scattering of the paratroopers in the rugged country. So in October 1942 it was thought that gliderborne troops would have the best chance of success. The decision was probably swayed by the discovery of a potential landing zone not too far from the objective which could probably be marked out by local Norwegian agents. However, just to be on the safe side, the party selected would also have to be parachute-trained.

This was the first proposed use of gliders. It would be useful to say a few words about the history of the types of gliders planned and used during the early years of the war. The Air Ministry and War Office drew up specifications for four military gliders. It was not long before bids came in and in the early days contracts were given to Airspeed Limited for a 28-seater operational glider and to the General Aircraft Company Limited for an 8-seater training glider. General Aircraft Company wasted no time in getting their prototype trainer built and the first flight took place on 5th November 1940. It was given the name Hotspur and so began the habit of calling British gliders after soldiers from history whose name began with the letter H. The first Hotspur arrived at the Central Landing Establishment at RAF Ringway near Manchester in February 1941. It could hold 8 troops or a cargo load of 1880 lbs. It had a wingspan of 45 feet and was 39 feet long. It was the glider that nearly all glider pilots learned to fly in and over 1000 were produced during the war. Airspeed's submission for a 28-seater glider (3 seats more than the Ministry specification) first took to the air in September 1941 and was accepted, with the first production aircraft being delivered in June 1942, the glider being named the Horsa after a 5th Century Saxon mercenary. It became the mainstay of the British glider force, with nearly 3,500 being manufactured during the war. With a wingspan of 88 feet and a length of 67 feet, a fully-laden Horsa weighed in at 15,250 lbs. It was built almost entirely of three-ply wood. As well as being a troop carrier, it could be used to carry various types of equipment. Perhaps it is most well known later in the war for carrying a load consisting of either a jeep and trailer, a 6 pdr anti-tank gun or a 75mm pack howitzer. At Arnhem in September 1944 other loads consisted of the Airborne Reconnaissance Squadron's Polsten guns and a Clarkair bulldozer.

In early 1941, as a safeguard against the Horsa glider proving unsuccessful, Slingsby Aviation Limited were given a contract to build another troop/load-carrying glider. This was called the Hengist but as the Horsa proved so successful, production was stopped after only 18 had been built. The other glider of the four was a large heavy lift glider, named the Hamilcar. This was able to carry bulk stores, light tanks, 17 pdr anti-tank guns or Bren gun carriers. In 1942 some of these were still on the drawing board.

Further thinking about the scale of the demolition task came to the conclusion that a minimum of 16 men would be required for the operation. The obvious thinking was they would need to be trained in handling explosives and demolition techniques, which obviously led the planners towards Royal Engineers. Additionally because of the inherent difficulties with a long glider tow, a relatively small landing zone and the importance of the target, it was decided to duplicate the party, each travelling in a separate Horsa glider. Initial thoughts went towards getting the troops from the 1st Parachute Squadron RE, who you will recall provided men for the Bruneval raid. However, around the time of the serious planning for the raid, the 1st Parachute Squadron had been warned for a move as part of the 1st Parachute Brigade to North Africa and did not really want to release men from the unit for this. Attention then turned to the 9th (Airborne) Field Company and the 261st (Airborne) Field Park Company, volunteers (who had been on the parachute course) were called for from both units using a subtle plan. Once the 1st Parachute Squadron had declined to take part, much of the detailed planning was done by the Commander RE of the 1st Airborne Division, Lieutenant Colonel M Henniker. He suggested that the parachute drop be replaced by a glider one using two Horsas carrying identical loads. They were big enough to carry the men and the required amount of stores and explosives. As might be imagined secrecy was the order of the day and a cover story was put forward asking for volunteers to take part in a competition called the Washington Cup. The competition was to be between an American combat engineer unit and a team drawn from the two airborne engineer units previously mentioned. The competition was sold to the men of consisting of either a parachute drop or glider landing, followed by a battle march across testing terrain culminating in a series of initiative tests coupled with a complex demolition task. There were a large number of volunteers and initially more than enough men to cover the two groups of 16 were selected and started training for the Washington Cup. This cover story explained away much of the influx of stores and new equipment and clothing. It also gave credence for much training at detached locations away from Bulford and the rest of the Airlanding Brigade. Some of the locations used were Capel Curig in Snowdonia in North Wales, where the terrain and climate were thought to be similar to Norway. A visit to a HEP station at Fort William in Scotland was also included to demonstrate to the group how and where to place explosives to cause maximum damage. Another visit was made to a Lever Brothers soap factory at Port Sunlight in the Wirral, to familiarise the engineers with machinery and castings, which were similar to those in the plant at Norway. It was likely that much of the intelligence came from Skinnarland in Norway, who had befriended the chief engineer of the plant and transmitted information gleaned from him back to London.

So the decision had been taken to try and land a party of Royal Engineers by glider and hope they could then escape overland to Sweden. The question now was to find some glider pilots and RAF crews for the tow to Norway. The job was given to No 38 Wing of the RAF, with Group Captain T Cooper being put in charge of the air side of the operation. He quickly realised that the only available aircraft in his inventory capable of towing a Horsa 400 miles or so to Norway and then being able to get back was the Handley Page Halifax. Several crews were selected and long distance practice flights with a Horsa in tow started around the end of October 1942. Time was certainly of the essence. The next part of the jigsaw was to find some glider pilots, two came from the newly formed Glider Pilot Regiment, Staff Sergeant M Strathdee assisted by Sergeant P Doig. The other two were provided by the Royal Australian Air Force, Pilot Officer N Davies and Sergeant H Fraser.

I received some information from another wartime glider pilot, Peter Aitken, on why Davies and Fraser were included in the operation. He told me:

> I was flying gliders in the RAF from January 1942 in close relationship with the early Army glider pilots. In many ways we were as one, flying together and attending lectures and so on together. The two Australians were part of our group and somehow or other two pilots were chosen from our group for the Washington Cup. I was close to Fraser but he would not divulge what he had got himself into but my opinion then has not changed now. They were chosen because it had to be seen that the Commonwealth contribution was recognized as important.
>
> There was no appeal for volunteers for the operation. The participants were approached and then clearly became uncommunicative. All I got from Fraser once was, "You are a reserve." I knew all four participants but Fraser was a buddy.

The landing zone was going to be marked out by agents from the Norwegian Section of SOE who would also guide the aircraft in using the Rebecca-Eureka homing system. A four-man team led by Lieutenant Jens Poulsson was dropped successfully into Norway on the night of 19th/20th October under the codename of Operation Grouse. The other three members were Arne Kjelstop, Claus Helberg and Knut Haugland. The weather in the area at this time of year can be best described as unfavourable, with sub-zero temperatures, high winds and drifting snow. They had been deliberately dropped quite a distance from Vermork in a remote part of the country and had been given several weeks to ski to the correct region. They were off net for quite a while and when they finally did make contact with London, they were asked a secret check question of "What did you see in the early morning of 5th November?" The answer came back correctly as "Three pink elephants."

This was, in theory, good news, as the local help was now in place and a suitable landing zone was found near Lake Mösvatn. Although this was about 5 or 6 hours hard marching from the plant it was felt to be an ideal choice and would hopefully give good reception and transmission for the homing beacons. All that was left now was to

88. A beehive explosive shaped charge, similar items were taken
on Operation Freshman. (National Archives)

89. A training aid from Operation Freshman showing the sappers where to place their
explosives on simulated electrolysis cells, possibly from Port Sunlight. (National Archives)

choose the men from the volunteers. The idea that all the training was culminating in a competition was wearing a bit thin amongst them but security was maintained. In the middle of November the group was briefed on the threat from the local garrison, which was known to number around 200 men, although it was felt they were not first class troops. The local HQ of the garrison was in the Kroman Hotel in Rjukan. Two fifteen-man teams were selected with one officer and nineteen men coming from the 9th (Airborne) Field Company and one officer and nine men coming from the 261st (Airborne) Field Park Company. There was a late change in the order of battle in that Lieutenant D Methven GM had replaced Lieutenant M Green, who had accidentally shot himself in the finger when cleaning his revolver. David Methven had won a George Medal for mine clearance work earlier in the war. On 17th November the group moved to RAF Skitten, a small airfield a few miles from Wick right up at the north-eastern corner of Scotland and about as close to Norway as one could get in mainland Britain. The men were fully briefed as to what was really happening and that once on the ground in Norway there would be a five or six hour march to the target with the warning that anyone who dropped out would be left to fend for himself. If the group was challenged by any German troops they were immediately to go into the assault and despatch them without hesitation and any forms of communication in the area were to be immediately put out of action. On reaching the objective the engineers would attack the power plant and heavy water equipment, while the four glider pilots would take care of any prisoners

90. A course photograph of early volunteers for the Glider Pilot Regiment.
Sergeant P Doig is second from the left in the front row. (ABF Museum)

and local workers and also try and destroy the telephone system and any other form of communication. They were also told that a reception party of the four Norwegian agents would mark out the landing zone and guide them to it with the Eureka-Rebecca system.

Here are some salient points from the planning for Operation Freshman and the kit that the men were to take with them. Perhaps the overriding consideration in the plan was the weight that could be safely carried in the two Horsas. Originally it was suggested that folding bicycles be taken so that the men could cycle to the plant, these also assisting in the escape leg to Sweden. This proposal had to be abandoned when it was realised that heavy snowfall would make it difficult to cycle and also the weight went over limits. Likewise, it was originally intended to take camouflage nets to hide the Horsas on landing but when it was worked out that the weight of these was between 500 and 600 lbs this was also shelved. However, a quantity of butter muslin was taken as it was felt to be a suitable snow colour and was relatively lightweight. It was discovered amongst documents found at the National Archives that prior to the operation a camouflage expert at the Royal Aircraft Establishment at Farnborough was asked for his opinion on camouflaging a Horsa in snow. His view was that to successfully hide it for a short time it would be necessary to remove the undercarriage, wings, fin and tail plane. This would virtually be a workshop job and not to be easily done in the dark and by inexperienced men. To achieve it much practice would need to be done and there was simply not the time available. He ended his summing up by pointing out that any attempt at camouflaging a Horsa with snow on the ground would be virtually useless. There would be the landing tracks and the footprints left in the snow during the dismantling that would be visible from the air. The size of the Horsa fuselage would also probably attract attention. He considered, therefore that the "chances of the operation being a success, were, in the circumstances, somewhat remote".

As previously stated the escape plan was for the men to travel in pairs overland to Sweden, and they were issued with maps and aerial photographs to assist them on this. To try and divert German attention from looking towards Sweden, it was intended for a 'deception wallet' to be left in the plant. This would apparently show on a map a pick-up point on the Norwegian coast together with other information that alluded to a submarine escape route. On the basis that two sections were being sent it is interesting to note on the stores list that only one deception wallet was provided and carried by Lieutenant Allen. The plan stated they were to remove their uniforms after the raid had been carried out and for this purpose had been issued with blue sweaters and civilian trousers. The intention was for the men to wear these under their uniforms, although they were told not to discard their uniforms or arms until at least five miles had been covered. It would still be a tough trek, in surviving records eight different routes lettered A to H are detailed, varying in distance from 190 to 250 miles.

It is also somewhat surprising to read of the relatively small amount of explosives taken for the demolition part of the operation. To destroy the electrolysis cells and other equipment 39 3 lb split sausage charges with magnets, 9 3 lb split sausage charges without magnets, 12 clam charges and 12 beehive-shaped explosive charges were taken. This is a total of only about 200 lbs of explosive in total. I am led to believe that the training had led to the sappers to concentrate on quality rather than quantity targets. The explosives were almost exactly spread between the two glider loads.

The weather for the coming days was forecast to be a relatively cloudless sky with a full moon, temperature to be just below zero and a two to three foot covering of snow on the ground. The camp was then sealed and all means of communicating with the outside world strictly monitored. It was now up to the senior RAF officer, Group Captain T Cooper, to decide when to go. The first available date was the night of 19th/20th November with back-up dates being any of the following nights during the full moon period. Cooper was advised by the meteorological experts that whilst the weather would not be ideal on the first available night in the window of opportunity, it was likely the weather may deteriorate over the subsequent few nights. The decision was taken to go on the night of 19th/20th November 1942. The war diary for the 9th (Airborne) Field Company simply recorded for this day: "Lieutenant Methven and 19 ORs of the Company proceeded on the operation known as the Washington Cup".

The first Halifax and Horsa combination took off just before 6.00 p.m. This was the aircraft flown by Squadron Leader A Wilkinson, with the glider being piloted by the two men from the Glider Pilot Regiment, Staff Sergeant M Strathdee and Sergeant P Doig. It was around a three and a half hour flight to Norway and the men settled down to consider their task and in keeping with other operations either to read, talk or sing. The other combination carrying Lieutenant Allen's party was due to leave about fifteen minutes after Methven's departure. The towing Halifax was flown by Flight Lieutenant A Parkinson of the RCAF, with the glider being flown by the two pilots from the RAAF.

It had been stated neither party was to wait on the LZ for more than thirty minutes for the other party to arrive. However, when the first aircraft neared the Norwegian coast the weather started to deteriorate and a sudden snow storm severely restricted visibility. Worse than this, the tow-rope between the Halifax and Horsa was starting to ice up. This also contained the radio communications between the two aircraft and it is reported that the icy conditions made contact between them difficult. An additional problem was that the Eureka-Rebecca homing equipment failed. The first combination did make it inland but it was difficult to pinpoint their position and suddenly the tow-rope broke under the weight of the ice and the Horsa crash-landed. I will return to this first Horsa shortly.

Back at Skitten, the ground staff were waiting anxiously for news and the first report was a faint signal at 11.41 p.m. which was believed to come from the second aircraft (Parkinson's aircraft B-Baker) asking for a course to bring it back to base. By quickly using intersecting bearings from another base which had also heard the request, it put the aircraft's position as over the North Sea. At 11.55 p.m. another message was heard, this time from the first aircraft (Wilkinson's aircraft A-Apple) reporting that they had to release their glider in the sea. By again using intersecting bearings it was worked out the aircraft was then over the mountains of southern Norway.

Nothing more was heard was heard until Wilkinson's aircraft arrived back at Skitten, the other aircraft failing to return. He reported that they had reached the coast of Norway safely but the Rebecca set was not working and so the run in to the LZ had to be made using a combination of dead reckoning and by aerial observation against any landmarks they were able to see. During a second attempt to find Lake Mösvatn their aircraft flew into a thick bank of cloud which led to a build up of ice on both glider and tug. Unable to climb due to this, they slowly lost height. Back on the coast in the area around Stavanger, the tow-rope snapped. The rear gunner of the Halifax saw it gliding slowly downwards to the ground. His name was Sergeant Tom Conacher and he later commented:

> The weather was just getting worse and worse and so the skipper told us he was aborting the mission. So we turned round and set course for home, we had nearly reached the coast when it started to really ice up. Then I noticed that the rope itself was starting to ice up and I reported it at the time. Suddenly the glider started getting out of line, it went away to starboard and then the rope just snapped. I only saw it peeling away and I was the last person to see the glider slowly disappearing into the darkness.

The Germans issued a communication on 21st November 1942, which was also picked up and printed in the British press:

> On the night of 19th/20th November, two British bombers, each towing a glider, penetrated southern Norway. One bomber and both gliders were forced down. The airborne sabotage troops were put to battle and wiped out to the last man.

Apart from this no news was immediately forthcoming about the fate of the men sent on Operation Freshman. The following day Lieutenant Colonel Henniker spoke to the assembled ranks from both units to try and stop the rumours flying round about the true purpose of the Washington Cup. There was really little constructive he could do. It would take another three years to find out what really happened, however the actual location of the target was still kept secret, as it was later successfully attacked by Norwegians in Operation Gunnerside.

We now need to fast forward to the spring and summer of 1945 when elements of the 1st Airborne Division were sent to Norway to assist in the disarming of the German Forces stationed there after their surrender in May 1945. The British had felt that something suspicious had happened to the two glider loads of Royal Engineers and a team from the war crimes investigation branch were sent to try and find out what had happened to them. The most important leads came from several Norwegians, one of them being a Corporal E Dahle, who stated that he had been arrested in July 1942 and been incarcerated in the Grini prison camp. He recalled that on an evening in early December of that year, a prisoner was put into the next-door cell, he heard him speak and felt he was English. He opened up dialogue with the prisoner and he told Dahle that he was a survivor from a crashed glider. He further added that there had been a violent snow storm and they had crashed into the side of a mountain. Eight men had been killed, four had been badly injured and the remaining five were all at Grini. His new English friend initially told Dahle that his name was Paddy Farrell, perhaps as a cover story. Dahle related all of this in a signed statement to a Flying Officer Straw of the war crimes team. This probably caused some confusion and in a subsequent statement Dahle changed his story slightly in that he now related that the soldier in the next cell was Sapper Frank Bonner and he had also had contact with a Sapper Tommy White. Dahle said he had obtained White's address in Gilfach Goch in Glamorgan, Wales and promised to write when the war was over. Dahle did write, but received a reply from Tommy's father saying that he had still not heard any news about his missing son. However, Dahle was able to provide some names of the guards and prison officials who had been there at the time.

Meanwhile more information had been received about the three aircraft crashes and visits were arranged to the sites of them. From the wreckage and local inhabitants a best guess was made as to what had happened. As stated before, the glider piloted by Strathdee and Doig had suffered a broken tow-rope and was last seen gliding towards (at the time) an unknown fate. We can only guess that the two pilots were desperately looking out into the darkness trying to spot a suitable landing spot or crash site. They were unable to do this and their Horsa DP349 crashed on the top of a snow-covered mountain at Fylgjesdal, about 30 miles east of Stavanger and about 70 miles from the intended LZ. The other combination fared no better. Because of bad weather over the LZ, the Halifax still towing the Horsa turned back heading towards Skitten. During the flight towards the Norwegian coast it is believed the tow-rope also broke and a similar scenario would have been repeated. The two glider pilots, Davies and Fraser, probably looking in vain for a suitable spot to crash-land. Their Horsa HS114 flew into the side of a mountain near Egersund. While the Halifax was circling the area it apparently suddenly banked heavily and the pilots lost control and crashed into a mountain range about 2 miles or so from the Horsa crash site, near a village called Heeleland. These locations are about 15 miles south east of Stavanger.

As stated before no definite news of any of the Royal Engineers or RAF personnel had been heard of since that fateful night in November 1942 and what happened after the crashes did not bring good news to their friends and relatives. The two Horsas both held fifteen men from the airborne engineers together with the two glider pilots. The crashed Halifax had had a crew of seven. This made a total of forty-one men unaccounted for. Slowly the story came out. The crew of the Halifax W7801 piloted by Flight Lieutenant Parkinson had all died in the initial crash. Germans from the local garrison were quickly on the scene and the spot was later cleared by Polish and Russian prisoners of war. The crew of seven were buried in the area by locals and in May 1945 the remains were exhumed by British troops and reburied in Helleland churchyard.

Crew of Halifax W7801 B-Baker
- Flight Lieutenant A Parkinson pilot
- Pilot Officer G Sewell de Gency co-pilot
- Flight Lieutenant A Thomas navigator
- Flying Officer A Haward navigator
- Sergeant J Falconer flight engineer
- Flight Sergeant A Buckton wireless operator/air gunner
- Flight Sergeant G Edwards air gunner

We can now turn to the fate of the two Horsas. First DP349, flown by the two men from the Glider Pilot Regiment. Out of the seventeen men aboard, eight were killed outright, probably on impact. The remaining nine all survived the landing although four had been seriously injured, the remaining five men all escaped unscathed and tried to get away from the area but were soon captured by the Germans.

The eight who were killed outright were as follows:
- Lieutenant D Methven GM 9th (Airborne) Field Company
- Staff Sergeant M Strathdee GPR

- Sergeant P Doig GPR
- L/Sergeant F Healey 9th (Airborne) Field Company
- Sapper J Hunter 9th (Airborne) Field Company
- Sapper W Jacques 261st (Airborne) Field Park Company
- Sapper R Norman 9th (Airborne) Field Company
- Driver G Simkins 261st (Airborne) Field Park Company

These men now all lie in Eiganes churchyard in Stavanger

Four seriously injured men were taken to a hospital in Stavanger after the discovery of the crashed glider. They were all very weak and unable to answer any sort of questions. I would ask the reader to remember that these men (and the other survivors) came under the jurisdiction of the Hitler Commando Order referred to earlier. So they were in practice under the jurisdiction of the Gestapo. Once the Gestapo had realised they were too ill to be interrogated, lethal injections of either poison or air bubbles were given. The head of the Gestapo in the area, *Obersturmbannführer* Wilkens instructed a Luftwaffe doctor, *Stabsarzt* Seeling, to poison them. Also present was a local Norwegian police collaborator, Inspector O Petersen. Apparently Seeling initially refused to do the dirty deed but later administered lethal injections. It is said that the four did not die immediately and Seeling and another man stood on the necks and chests of the four to try and hasten their end. Eventually they all succumbed and the bodies were loaded onto a truck and driven to the harbour at Stavanger where a boat was waiting. The bodies

91. Airborne Sappers carry coffins to the final resting place for some of the men of Operation Freshman at Eiganes Churchyard, Stavanger on 21st November 1945. (ABF Museum)

were loaded aboard and the boat sailed out into the open sea, after about an hour's sailing the four corpses were weighed down and thrown over the side.

These four men were:

- Corporal J Cairncross 9th (Airborne) Field Company
- L/Corporal T Masters 9th (Airborne) Field Company
- Driver P Farrell 9th (Airborne) Field Company
- Sapper E Smith 9th (Airborne) Field Company

These men have no known grave and are all commemorated on the Brookwood Memorial to the Missing in Surrey.

This leaves the five men who escaped relatively unscathed from the glider landing, after capture they were taken to the Grini concentration camp some thirty miles outside of Oslo. This is where they were kept in captivity for several weeks. This is where Dahle had managed to snatch a few words with the engineers. It is said that the Gestapo subjected them to a great deal of interrogation and Wilkens advised them they would at some stage be shot as spies and saboteurs. They also were questioned by a Luftwaffe officer, who perhaps gave them some false hope by telling them that they were looked on as soldiers and not spies or saboteurs, and would be treated in line with the Geneva Convention. However, on 18th January 1943, without having revealed anything useful to the Germans, orders were given to a *Hauptmann* Hans to get together a special detachment of men and escort the engineers to Trandum Wood just outside Oslo. The Germans had in the past used this wood as an execution site.

The five engineers were told that they were going to meet a special German delegation to discuss their prisoner of war status but for security reasons they would have to be blindfolded. They were then loaded into a covered truck and taken on the

92. The graves and memorial to Operation Freshman at Stavanger. (ABF Museum)

short journey to Trandum. Upon arrival, still blindfolded, they were helped from the truck and stood in a line. Hans called out the order 'Achtung', which was a signal for the special detachment to open fire. It is only hoped that all five died instantly.

These five men were:

- L/Corporal W Jackson 9th (Airborne) Field Company
- Sapper J Blackburn 9th (Airborne) Field Company
- Sapper F Bonner 9th (Airborne) Field Company
- Sapper J Walsh 9th (Airborne) Field Company
- Sapper T White 9th (Airborne) Field Company

The five were all first buried in a mass grave in the wood but after the war the spot was traced and the bodies were exhumed, one of those involved in the work being Vidkun Quisling. They were all later reburied in the Commonwealth War Graves Commission plot in Oslo Western Civil Cemetery at Vestre Gravlund.

This means attention can now be turned to the second Horsa HS114 flown by the two Australians and with fifteen sappers under the command of Lieutenant A Allen. This glider had crashed a short distance from the Halifax and it is said that the two pilots plus one other man, Driver Pendlebury, were killed on impact. Of the other fourteen, six had been badly injured whilst the other eight suffered minor cuts and bruises. Two parties, one of three men and the other two, set off down the mountainside hopefully looking for some friendly help. One of the groups reached a small farm and managed to get the owner to telephone for help. But it was not long before some Germans arrived on the scene and all the survivors were taken prisoner. They were initially taken to a German Army barracks at Slettebo, near Egersund. Shortly after their arrival here (including the bodies of those who died in the crash), the local commander *Hauptmann* Schottberger, received orders that they came under the Hitler Commando Order of the previous October and were to receive immediate special treatment. So within hours of the crash the survivors were taken to a small clearing just outside the camp and every one of them was shot, one by one. That evening the bodies of all seventeen were taken to the coast near Egersund, where they were all buried in sand dunes there. Although the Germans had tried to do their dirty work under the cover of darkness they were witnessed by a local, who returned several days later to discover the graves. This was later reported to British troops after the war had ended.

The occupants of Horsa HS114

- Pilot Officer N Davies RAAF
- Sergeant H Fraser RAAF
- Lieutenant A Allen 261st (Airborne) Field Park Company
- L/Sergeant G Knowles 9th (Airborne) Field Park Company
- Corporal J Thomas 261st (Airborne) Field Park Company
- L/Corporal F Bray 261st (Airborne) Field Park Company
- L/Corporal A Campbell 261st (Airborne) Field Park Company
- Sapper E Bailey 9th (Airborne) Field Park Company
- Driver J Belfield 261st (Airborne) Field Park Company
- Sapper H Bevan 9th (Airborne) Field Park Company
- Sapper T Faulkner 9th (Airborne) Field Park Company
- Sapper C Grundy 9th (Airborne) Field Park Company
- Sapper H Legate 9th (Airborne) Field Park Company

- Driver E Pendlebury 261st (Airborne) Field Park Company
- Sapper L Smallman 261st (Airborne) Field Park Company
- Sapper J Stephen 261st (Airborne) Field Park Company
- Sapper G Williams 9th (Airborne) Field Park Company

Close to the spot where the fourteen engineers were murdered a plaque has been erected recording that 'Here 11 British soldiers 20 November 1942 were executed by the German occupation force'. We can perhaps forgive the discrepancy in numbers. After the war the bodies were exhumed from the sand dunes and now all lie in Eiganes churchyard in Stavanger with their eight comrades from the other glider who died in the initial landing.

As the story was gradually pieced together certain names were mentioned as being involved in these unsavory incidents. As one of the jobs in Norway of the 1st Airborne Division was to screen all the 330,000 or so Germans stationed in Norway several suspects were found and placed in detention. However, some of the main suspects had already managed to evade any searching questions. Wilkens, the Gestapo chief for the Stavanger area, was shot dead on 4th of April 1945, during a skirmish with the Norwegian Underground. His boss, a German called Fehlis, who was head of the Gestapo for Norway, had committed suicide shortly after the arrival of British troops. Petersen was captured but committed suicide in Akershus prison while awaiting trial. Five names were put in the frame for at least the murders of four engineers and three of them were found during the screening of the Germans.

93. The memorial near Egersund close to the spot where fourteen engineers from Freshman were murdered. The plaque records that 'Here 11 British soldiers 20 November 1942 were executed by the German occupation force.' (ABF Museum)

A trial of these three was held in Oslo starting on the 10th December 1945. These three – *Stabsarzt* Seeling, *Hauptscharführer* Hoffmann and *Unterscharführer* Feuerlein, were all charged with "committing a war crime in that they at Stavanger, on a date unknown in or about November 1942, in violation of the laws and usage's of war, were concerned in the killing of four identified British prisoners of war". Two other Germans, Sachse and Kuhn, were also charged with these three, but although they were not in custody it was decided to proceed with the trial of the three who were present. Some of the evidence that came out in the trial does not make for pleasant reading. The three accused all pleaded not guilty to the charges.

During their time whilst they had been held in custody prior to the trial, all three had made statements. Werner Seeling, the Luftwaffe doctor, had given a statement at Trandum camp on the 6th November 1945. In this he admitted he had given the four prisoners morphine injections but only to help relieve the pain caused by injuries sustained in the crash. He stated that that the dosage given was not lethal, and that he had better poisons available should he have wished to kill the prisoners. He added that he saw Hoffmann repeatedly stamp on the throat of one of the prisoners, breaking his Adam's Apple. Seeling and Hoffmann then collected the prisoner who had recovered from the morphine, he was not greatly injured. He was then driven to the local Gestapo Headquarters. Once here the prisoner was then told to walk down the stairs towards a cellar. He was followed by Hoffmann. Seeling then stated that he heard a shot. When he entered the corridor, he said that he saw the prisoner on the floor with a bullet hole in his head, just behind his right ear. The other two prisoners had been strangled with a rope and a leather strap. One had been killed by Hoffmann and the other, Seeling thought,

94. The memorial to the men of Operation Freshman in
Eiganes Churchyard, Stavanger. (ABF Museum)

by Sachse. Each of the four prisoners had received three equal doses of morphine. He heard from Kuhn that all four men were going to be dumped in the sea. He ended his statement by saying that he regretted most deeply being unable to save the four wounded men.

In his statement dated 28th September 1945, made at Akershus Prison, Feuerlein stated that he saw Seeling and Sachse strangle one of the prisoners by hanging him from a radiator in an office. They then lifted the upper part of the prisoner's body off the floor. The Norwegian policeman called Petersen then asked Seeling to kill the other wounded prisoner by injecting air into a blood vessel. Feuerlein also stated that three of the group of four were carried into this office and killed, the fourth being taken away and later was shot by Hoffmann.

In his statement from 12th September 1945, later amended on 23rd October, Hoffmann stated that he drove Seeling to the Gestapo Headquarters and there Seeling gave all four men injections of morphine. He went on to add that it was Seeling who had stood on the throat of one of the prisoners. He denied murdering any of the four prisoners. He did add however that he had loaded the dead bodies onto a lorry and had heard they were to be dumped at sea. His final comment was that he neither saw nor heard that one of the victims had been throttled with a rope or leather strap.

These, then, were the pre-trial statements and more detail was to come out in court. On the second day of the trial Stabsarzt Seeling took the stand. His testimony closely followed his original statement and when asked a question by his defence counsel commented that he did not do anything to bring about the deaths of the prisoners and that the quantity of morphine injected was too small to kill and he did not strangle anyone. He denied giving air injections.

On the third day, it was Hoffmann's turn. He reiterated his statement that it was Seeling who had stood on the prisoner's throat and he had not strangled anybody but only helped to load corpses onto a lorry. He stated that Petersen had told him to shoot the fourth, but as he was so excited his shot missed. Petersen then went forward to do the job in his place and shot the prisoner in the head.

On the afternoon of the third day (12th December 1945) it was the third defendant's turn, Feuerlein. He admitted he had been working at the prison but had remained in an office at the time of the murders. He said he saw Seeling take syringes and bottles of medicine upstairs to where the prisoners were quartered. He claimed he later saw them all lying dead on the floor of the office where they had been killed as part of one of his patrols. He did admit to placing his foot on the chest of one of the victims but only when ordered to do so by Petersen. He also said he saw Seeling and Sachse lift one of the prisoners and hang him with some cord around his neck from one of the office radiators. Feuerlein also demonstrated to the court via one of the interpreters, how he had seen Seeling inject air into a vein on the inner aspect of the elbow of one of the prisoners.

This virtually closed both sides presentation of evidence and the court was adjourned until the following morning, the 14th December. On this morning the Judge Advocate summed up the evidence presented by both sides and the legal aspects of the case. The court then closed around 11.30 a.m. to consider their verdict. After about an hour the Court President announced that all three defendants had been found guilty as charged. Seeling then stated, in mitigation, that he did what he thought was best for the prisoners. He then again repeated that he neither gave lethal injections to nor did he strangle any of the prisoners. The other two defendants, Hoffmann and Feuerlein, left their pleas for mitigation in the hands of their defending officer, a Captain F Miller. His plea was based on the premise that his defendants were junior soldiers who formed part of a wider plan and were obeying orders.

The Court closed for consideration of the sentences to be imposed at 1.00 p.m. and ten minutes later returned with the sentences. Seeling was sentenced to death by firing squad, Hoffmann death by hanging and Feuerlein to life imprisonment. All three appealed against their sentences, with Feuerlein additionally appealing against the court's findings. Probably with no great surprise to the reader, all the various appeals failed and all the verdicts and sentences were confirmed on 26th December 1945.

Seeling was the first to die, being executed by firing squad in the morning of 10th January 1946 in the grounds of Akershus Prison in Oslo. Hoffmann, who had also been convicted of the illegal execution of seven Norwegians was taken to Germany to die. He was hanged in the afternoon of 15th May 1946 at Hameln Prison. The final defendant, Feuerlein, although facing life imprisonment, was handed over to the Russian authorities to be 'interviewed without coffee' for allegations of atrocities perpetrated on Russian prisoners of war. His fate remains unknown but I am making an educated guess that he failed to return from Russia alive.

This effectively draws a line under the fate of the personnel involved in Operation Freshman. Several perpetrators got away with their involvement in the murders and I suppose in theory the files are still open. Several memorials to those involved in Operation Freshman have been unveiled in both Scotland and Norway. The plan for the operation may have worked, given a bit of luck, and it is said that the follow-up operation by the Norwegians slowed the German production of an atomic bomb, so for these reasons their sacrifice was not in vain.

Most of the airborne and commando raids up to the end of 1942 have now been covered and at this point the use of these troops as 'raiders' virtually stopped. They were now looked upon as having a more strategic role, being involved with more conventional troops – one only has to look at the airborne and commandos role in the invasion of Sicily in 1943, Normandy in 1944 and the Rhine Crossing in 1945. Their place was taken on a more tactical level by such units as the Special Air Service, Special Boat Service and the Royal Marine Boom Patrol Detachment (the 'Cockleshell Heroes', who attacked shipping by canoe). However, this is not to overlook the important successes, hard won by the airborne and commando forces, that came in the early years of the war when good news was hard to come by. It is I feel, important that the contribution of the men who volunteered for 'special service', early on, should not be overlooked. I hope the reader will spare a thought for these brave men before they gradually fade away.

Appendix I

Documents relating to the creation of the Commandos

The following letter was sent from the War Office on 9th June 1940 to the GOC's Northern and Southern Commands.

Volunteers for Special Service.

1. It is proposed to raise and train a special force of volunteers for independent mobile operations.
2. You are requested to collect the names of up to 40 officers and 1,000 other ranks in your Command, who volunteer for this special service and whom you consider suitable for it.

   Volunteers will be employed on fighting duties only, and Commanding Officers should be assured that these duties will require only the best type of officers and men. All ranks will continue to wear their own uniforms but the question of awarding some special distinguishing badge is under consideration.

   Officers and men who have been approved for the force will be taken off the strength of their units and trained in the United Kingdom. Individuals are not likely to remain in the Force for more than a few months.
3. In compiling the list of volunteers, the following qualifications, shown in the order of their importance, must be borne in mind:-
   (a) General.

   All officers and men must be volunteers. They should be young and must be absolutely fit. They should be able to swim and be immune from sea sickness. Those who have already seen active service and are able to drive a motor vehicle are particularly valuable.
   (b) Officers.

   Personality, tactical ability and imagination.
   (c) Other Ranks.

   A good standard of general intelligence and independence. Character must be such that a man can be relied upon to behave himself without supervision (i.e. there must be no risk of looting etc. by men operating independently).
4. It is initially proposed to organise one 'Commando' from each of the Northern and Southern Commands. Each Commando will be led by a selected officer, and will consist of a number of 'Troops'. Each troop will be commanded by an officer (or a specially selected warrant officer or NCO), and will have a strength approximating that of an infantry platoon.

The officers selected as Commando leaders should be capable of planning and personally leading operations carried out by parties chosen from their own Commandos. These officers should be selected entirely for their operational abilities; they will be relieved of all administrative detail by the appointment of an officer of sufficient administrative experience who will be attached to each Commando.

Other ranks selected should, if possible, include a number of light tank drivers and sappers who are well trained in demolition work. A high proportion of NCO's will be allowed on the establishment of the Commandos.

5. All volunteers selected should be informed that they are liable to be returned to their units at the discretion of their leaders. The volunteers may also request to be returned to their units after the completion of any operation.

   The same personnel will not be continuously employed over long periods on operations of this special nature.

   Before joining the Force each volunteer will be interviewed by an officer and told of the sort of duties he will be required to perform. He will then have the option of withdrawing his name should he wish to do so.

6. Commando leaders will be officers below the rank of Lieutenant Colonel. The selection of these officers is a matter of urgency, as candidates will have to be interviewed at the War Office before final selection is made. You are therefore requested to forward to the Under Secretary of State for War (MO8) as soon as possible and under secret cover, the names of 6 or 8 officers selected from your Command who are recommended to lead Commandos.

Then this letter was followed by a further letter dated 23rd June 1940. This was sent to all the GOC's of Home Commands and also The GOC of Northern Ireland District.

Formation of Irregular Commandos.

1. I am directed to refer to War Office letter 20/Misc/1786 (AG 1a) dated 9th June 1940 regarding volunteers for a special force for mobile operations, and to inform you that the force will be organised as follows.

2. Organisation of a Commando.

   Each commando will consist of up to ten troops. The war establishments of a Commando and of a Troop are attached.

   Commandos and Troops will have no unit equipment. Each officer and other rank will hold the normal scale of personal arms and equipment. Other arms and equipment for training and operations will be issued from a Central Depot as and when required.

3. Allotment of Commandos.

COMMAND RESPONSIBLE	COMMANDO	LOCATION	REMARKS
War Office	No 1	Southampton	Already formed under direct orders from WO from personnel of Independent Companies.
War Office	No 2	Manchester	Parachute Commando
Southern	No 3	To be notified later	

COMMAND RESPONSIBLE	COMMANDO	LOCATION	REMARKS
Southern	No 4	To be notified later	
Northern	No 5	To be notified later	
Northern	No 6	To be notified later	
Eastern	No 7	To be notified later	
Eastern	No 8	To be notified later	
Western	No 9	To be notified later	
Western	No 10	To be notified later	
Scottish	No 11	To be notified later	
Northern Ireland	No 12	To be notified later	

No 2 Commando (Parachute) will initially consist of two troops from Northern and two troops from Southern Command. It will later be expanded to ten troops as under:-

A and B Northern Command

C and D Southern Command

E and F Eastern Command

G and H Western Command

J Scottish Command

H Northern Ireland District

Commandos will be formed by Commands responsible under detailed orders to be issued by the War Office (AG17) and each troop will be moved to the locations shown above as soon as it has formed.

General Officers Commanding-in-Chief, Commands, will decide the number of troops in each commando in their command, as the strength must depend on the number of volunteers available. No commando will consist of more than ten troops.

4.   Employment of Commandos.

The main characteristics required of a commando are:-

(a)   Capability to operate independently for 24 hours.

(b)   Capability to disperse widely and effect its aim by individual action. A commando is not expected to resist an attack or to overcome a defence by formed bodies of troops, but its success must depend on speed, individual ingenuity and dispersion.

A commando will be detailed by the War Office for a specific operation. Arms and equipment will then be issued as necessary, and the commando will be moved, probably by separate troops, to the starting point of the operation. After completion of the operation, which would normally be a matter of a few days, the commando would return to is normal location in this country and continue training for several weeks before being detailed for another operation.

5.   Conditions of Service.

Instructions regarding conditions of service are being issued separately.

6.   Reinforcements.

The administrative officer of each commando will deal direct with the headquarters of the affiliated Command as shown in paragraph 3 on the supply of reinforcements.

7.   Administration.

Each Commando will be administered direct by the headquarters of the Command in which it is located.

8. All Commandos will be under the direct operational control of the War Office.

Headquarters of a Commando
Consisting of a fighting portion and an administrative portion and designed to control up to 10 irregular Troops.
War Establishment

(i)   Personnel

DETAIL	FIGHTING	ADMINISTRATIVE	TOTAL HQ OF A COMMANDO
Lieutenant Colonel	1		1
Major	1		1
Major or Captain		1	1
Subaltern		1	1
Liaison Officers (Subalterns)	3		3
Total, Officers	5	2	7
Company Sergeant Major	1		1
Total, Warrant Officers	1		1
Company Quartermaster Sergeant		1	1
Pay Sergeant		1	1
Sergeant		1	1
Total Staff-Sergeants and Sergeants		3	3
Batmen Runners	5	2	7
Clerks		5	5
Drivers		2	2
Equipment repairer		1	1
Liaison personnel	6		6
Storemen		2	2
Total, rank and file	11	12	23
Total, other ranks	12	15	27
Total HQ of a Commando	17	17	34
Attached			
RAMC – Medical Officer	1		1
Nursing Orderlies	5		5
RAOC- Armourers		2	2
Total HQ including attached	23	19	42

(ii)   Transport
Car, 4 seater, 4 wheeled 1
Lorry, 30 cwt., 4 wheeled, GS 1

(iii)   Table of weapons and ammunition

DETAIL	NUMBER	AMMUNITION ON MAN OR WITH GUN	RESERVE	TOTAL
Pistols, .38 inch	15	24	540	900
Rifles, .303 inch	22	100	3,000	5,200
Light machine guns, .303 inch	10			
Machine carbines	20			

An Irregular Troop
War Establishment

(i)   Personnel
Note there were two sections in a troop

DETAIL	HQ	SECTION HQ	2 SUB-SECTIONS (EACH)	TOTAL, EACH SECTION	TOTAL
Captain	1				1
Subalterns		1		1	2
Total, Officers	1	1		1	3
Sergeants			1	2	4
Total Sergeants			1	2	4
Corporals			2	4	8
Lance-Corporals			3	6	12
Privates	1	1	5	11	23
Total, rank and file	1	1	10	21	43
Total, other ranks	1	1	11	23	47
Total, all ranks	2	2	11	24	50

(ii)   Table of weapons and ammunition

DETAIL	NUMBER	AMMUNITION ON MAN OR WITH GUN	RESERVE	
Pistols, .38 inch	3	24	144	216
Rifles, .303 inch	45	100	5,000	9,500
AT rifles	2	40	400	480
Pistols, signal	3		150	150

Appendix II

Personnel involved in Operation Colossus

Major Pritchard, Captain Lea, Captain Daly, Lieutenant Deane-Drummond, Second Lieutenant Jowett, Second Lieutenant Paterson and Flight Lieutenant Lucky.

Sergeant Clements, Sergeant Durie, Sergeant Lawley, Sergeant Shutt and Sergeant Walker.

Corporal Fletcher, Corporal Grice, Corporal Julian and Corporal O'Brien.

L/Corporal Boulter, L/Corporal Henderson, L/Corporal Jones, L/Corporal Maher, L/Corporal Pexton, L/Corporal Tomlin and L/Corporal Watson.

Private Humphrey, Private Nastri/Tristan, Private Parker and Private Samuels.

Sapper Davidson, Sapper Parker, Sapper Phillips, Sapper Pryor, Sapper Ross and Sapper Struthers.

Driver Crawford.

Fortunato Picchi.

Appendix III

Decorations Awarded to The Men of X Troop

Distinguished Service Order

25th November 1941 Captain (temporary Major) T A G Pritchard Royal Welch Fusiliers

Military Cross

29th September 1942 Lieutenant A J Deane-Drummond Royal Corps of Signals
Date unknown Captain C Lea Lancashire Fusiliers
Date unknown Second Lieutenant G R Paterson Royal Corps of Engineers
Date unknown Second Lieutenant A G Jowett Highland Light Infantry

Military Medal

20th June 1946 Sergeant P P Clements Leicestershire Regiment
20th June 1946 WOII A W A Lawley 11th SAS Regiment AAC
Date unknown Sergeant E W Durie
Date unknown L/Corporal R B Watson
Date unknown L/Corporal H Boulter North Staffordshire Regiment (this award was for actions with the partisans after his escape from Italian captivity in 1943)

Mentioned in despatches

Date unknown but probably 1946
Captain G F K Daly
L/Corporal J E Maher
Private N Nastri

Appendix IV

The Experiences of a RAF aircrew on Operation Colossus

N orman Kershaw's interest in aviation had begun in the early 1930s as a member of the Boy Scouts, learning airmanship. He had an ex-Royal Flying Corps pilot as his group's instructor and he never forgot the following words of wisdom from this Great War veteran: To survive in aerial combat, one must train to the peak of efficiency in all your skills. The following are some of Norman's exploits:

My first flight was in an old biplane of Sir Alan Cobham's flying circus from a field at Blackmoor near Blackburn. The mid-thirties saw the setting for the Second World War which was made inevitable by the pacifists' fear of standing up to a bully. One may get hurt in the process but the bully thinks twice if he is going to be hurt as well. It was to this background that I volunteered for aircrew as a wireless operator during the Munich crisis in September 1938. As a trainee for aircrew my feet never touched the ground until I was on the wireless course at Cranwell. As well as the peacetime day classes, night lectures were started and we also worked Saturday mornings. It was eat, sleep and studies. Anyway, we made it for September 1939 and with the outbreak of hostilities, I was sent to Linton on Ouse, Yorkshire. When the anticipated losses in aircrew did not materialise I was sent to the Gunnery School at Pwllheli in north Wales. From there I went to No 10 Operational Training Unit at Abingdon and was screened off the course as an instructor. This was where I teamed up with Walter, then Flight Lieutenant Williams training navigators on the Anson flight. We stayed here right into the Battle of Britain flying mostly twice a day or night.

I recall seeing German fighters attacking Harwell and then Abingdon, on a return training flight with the opposition amongst us. The speed of landing broke all records that day. There is an entry in my flying log that the two of us took an Anson with all the floor burnt out, except for the main spars to the Avro works at Woodford in Cheshire, and bringing back a replacement. I had done over 160 hours flying before leaving Abingdon for 78 Squadron at Dishforth in December 1940.

Then on the morning of 11th January 1941, Walter called me into the flight office, and said did we want to volunteer for a special operation, which would entail us having to leave the country for some time and to get our equipment absolutely spot on. So it was, that six Whitleys from No 4 Group Bomber Command flew to Ringway in January 1941, one of the pilots being Lieutenant Hoad of the Fleet Air Arm. We first trained dropping rubber dummies that looked for all the world like a tailor's dummy with a hook at the top to which a parachute was attached. Afterwards X Troop comprising 36 men and reserves were used as a live cargo.

There are many tales from that training. We did a night drop on Ringway and as there had been bombing raids, one of the lads recalls seeing a bomb crater beneath him. In the part moonlight he pulled his rigging lines to side-slip and avoid the crater. The crater then moved with him. A few moments of panic and then came the realisation that it was the shadow of his own parachute on the ground. We were on a tight schedule, so risks were taken with the wind strength that would not normally have been taken. One of the lads dropped into the lake by accident in Tatton Park and although a strong swimmer was drowned. One of the other lads with a strong sense of humour said the wind was so strong on the last dress rehearsal drop on a dummy aqueduct at Tatton, that he had to push the aircraft away with his feet in order to break the static line, and so open his chute. The drop was to be at about 500 feet at night. Two other Whitleys joined us during the last week. These were to act solely as diversion bombers on a nearby target whilst we dropped the paras. So on the 2nd February 1941 we all flew down to Mildenhall where our ground crews did a complete overhaul and fitted extra tanks in the fuselage. I remember asking our fitters why our plane was jigged up off the ground. It was to find out what weight of bomb had to be fitted in the front bomb bay in order to keep the planes nose down. This in spite of an engine block fitted in the front well of the plane.

Besides the paras, we had to carry every type of spare for our aircraft, as there were none in the Middle East. We also took two observers from the parachute school at Ringway and an engine fitter from Group, as there were none trained on Malta familiar with the Rolls Royce engines we used. Admiral Keyes came to Mildenhall to see us off on the night of the 7th February. We only knew we were going to fly direct to Malta, still ignorant of our ultimate target. We carried four paras in sleeping bags in the fuselage and Wing Commander Sir Nigel Norman from the parachute school, had to stay in the front turret until we had gained height, which was gradual due to the weight. It was intended for the trip to be ten hours but was actually twelve. We had a good navigator on this trip and we picked up reservoirs north of Marseilles, then blind over the sea, till we picked up Tabarka on the African coast, then to pick up the lighthouse on Cape Bon, then Luqa, Malta. We had flown between 1600 and 1700 miles. On Malta we were all billeted with the submarine crew of HMS *Triumph*, which was detailed to pick up the paras after the drop. We still have many a good laugh over the antics we got up to. Imagine our attempts to get into hammocks after a night on the beer. A photo recce plane on the morning of the 10th February showed that there were two aqueducts. But it was decided to still go for the original one, the largest. We were told then where the target was and that the raid was on for that night. So ended the guesses – Abyssinia for the paras and Yugoslavia for the aircrew.

The submarine lads laid on a hearty meal for the paras whilst we were going over the flight plan and last minute checks of equipment. The planes had been housed in sandstone walls to minimise bomb blast from the frequent air raids and were not brought out until the last minute. There were a few minutes between each planes departure, with two planes to act solely as bombers that night, being interspersed between the six carrying the SAS lads, one of the latter being delayed on take off with a problem. There was no spare plane to transfer to, as would have been the case on normal ops. This was to affect the dropping of those paras later that night. There was some flak over Sicily, but of little effect to us. It was an uneventful flight over the sea and with the glow from Vesuvius to our north, we turned over the river Sele inland for our target area. We were flying between two to three thousand feet as the valley of the Tragino was surrounded by hills two thousand feet above sea level and as we were to drop the lads about five hundred feet above the target we needed to see the area in detail as the tops of the hills would be above us. Back at Ringway we had studied a plaster cast model of the target and surrounding area and today I can still visualise it. We approached the valley through a fold in the hills turning into it for a flatter approach to the aqueduct. I had a brief look, with the farmhouse to our right, as I ducked through the wing under the emergency tank to get into the fuselage in order to pull the static lines in after the lads had gone out. The pilot switched a red light on in the fuselage on the approach to the target and then a green one for them to go. Four went out like shelling peas. Then the officer pressed the button to operate the release of the container from the rear bomb bay, followed by the fifth para and then himself. I remember clearly looking at the floor of the valley watching each detail becoming clearer each second as the Rolls Royce Merlin engines fought to climb above the approaching hilltop. Walter had his hand holding the throttles hard against the gates. Everyone held their breath as the mountain top slid past. We threaded our way through the mountains to the marshalling yards at Foggia, where Sergeant Ennis had religiously gone in and out of the target and surrounding hills dropping a single bomb on each approach in order to confuse how many planes were attacking the yards. A fuel train had been set alight and we could see them trying to push the rolling stock out of the path of the blazing fuel. Our rear gunner opened up with his Brownings, and they lost interest on the ground. We then had an uneventful return to Malta.

I was told in later years that Clem's expressions were superb as he was dangling with his feet through the floor of the Whitley, wondering when the lads holding him by the shoulders would let him go, and all the time watching the rocks slide underneath him. The pilot had pressed the green light, then back to red, not being satisfied with his approach causing Clem to start his exit. I think we landed back at Malta about half past two in the morning only to be wakened about nine, as we were to prepare to fly either to the Middle East to start a school there, or back to Britain as there was a build up of possible invasion craft in the channel.

Our plane was loaded as much returning as it had been coming out. Although we had no aircraft spares, men or equipment, all the mail from the island had been packed in the fuselage. Walter thoroughly checked the controls to ensure freedom of movement before take-off. The runway on Luqa had been refilled after every bombing raid and the take-off was a bit bumpy to say the least. Our flight plan was the reverse of coming out. Quite uneventful until half way up the Med when we ran into a violent storm making us fly blind until breaking cloud over the UK and eventually we made it back to Mildenhall. We were delayed at Mildenhall and didn't get back to Dishforth until the 18th because of the weather. Walter's logbook shows we were over the channel on the night of the 23rd February and the marshalling yards of Mannheim on the 26th.

Appendix V

Harry Pexton recalls some of the training in late 1940 with No 2 Commando before volunteering for Operation Colossus

Sometime towards the end of November 1940, it was decreed by the powers that be, that the few Airborne troops we had in training then, should be put to the test – and at the same time – let the public know we had such troops. So 16 or 20 of us were picked for an exercise on Salisbury Plain. The objective of the exercise was a village called Shrewton, it was to be defended by troops from Southern Command. It was our job to infiltrate and take the village, which would be signified by placing a flag on the high point in the village, namely the flagpole on the church tower.

We travelled down from Ringway by bus to RAF Old Sarum and the next day we flew in Whitleys and jumped onto the Plain. I had never seen such a reception committee. We gathered together and ran between an avenue of brass hats. It seemed like all the top brass in England were there and they were all applauding as we ran between them. Naturally with such a gathering of senior officers, there was a good selection of vehicles and as part of our training, taking a vehicle was quite easy. Trouble was they were all pointing the wrong way except one rather large estate type car, complete with driver. Our CO put a .45 automatic in the driver's neck and calmly told him to drive us away. He was only too willing to do so. We all piled in or on the car and drove away. Eventually we stopped and pushed the car into a ditch. We then stopped a lorry with a trailer and we all laid on the floor of the truck and trailer ordering the driver towards Shrewton. The defending troops never even stopped and searched the truck and we were inside the village. We got the driver to stop near the church and soon our flag was flying from the top of the flagpole. The essence of surprise and the inefficient defending troops made our job easier, the whole exercise taking only about 45 minutes from jumping to hoisting.

The outcome of the exercise was when the OC of the defenders accepted defeat. We took up defensive positions and I was lucky enough to be given the job with one mate of defending the village pub. Whilst in position there a car drew up and out stepped a splendid looking General complete with much scrambled egg and gongs. He came over to me and for several minutes questioned me about our training and the exercise. He was soon joined by another General who also asked several questions. They then went into the pub after wishing me good luck for the future. Their car driver shortly afterwards told me that one was General Sir Alan Brooke, C-in-C Home Forces and the other was Crown Prince Olaf of Norway, whose car we had stolen. However I guess they took it all in good heart as soon afterwards the landlady of the pub came out with 3 pints of beer on a tray, one for the driver and one each for me and my mate, courtesy of the Generals.

Our CO Colonel Jackson, complimented us on an excellent exercise, surpassing all expectations, proud of us and so on. He told us he was so pleased that he was going to give each man a pound to spend in Salisbury that night, which he then did. We certainly had a good night in Salisbury but the sting in the tail came on the next pay parade. The first of our exercise heroes when collecting his pay noticed he was one pound short and on remarking about this he was told by the Colonel, "Of course you are a pound short. You don't think I would give you all a pound out of my own bloody pocket, do you!"

Miscellaneous reports on Operation Colossus

Report Colossus Operation

Clothing and Equipment of X Troops in Aircraft
Clothing to be worn by men on flight out to operational base:-
Sidcot suit (inner lining only)
Battledress
Gabardine jacket
Mae Wests
Balaclava helmet
Flying helmet (with intercom for officers)
Silk gloves
Woollen gloves
Three pairs socks and no boots when in sleeping bag

Other items of equipment for flight out:-
Sleeping bag
Everhot bag
Lilo
Thermos flask
2 paper bags (for being sick in)
Food for flight and chewing gum
Ear-plugs
Statichute
Hot water bottle (for urination)

The statichute was to be taken off under orders of the Captain of the Aircraft and used as a pillow. As well as the above each man would have 2 haversacks, steel helmet and respirator, which would be taken off on entering the aircraft.

For the operational flight differences to the above were to be:-
1. No Sidcot suit or Mae West.
2. Statichute kept on, but harness straps between legs unfastened.
3. Boots kept on, one pair socks only.
4. Haversacks kept on, under gabardine jacket.
5. Kneepads and elastic anklets to be worn.
6. Steel helmet and respirator left at operational base.

Clothing and Equipment of X Troop (Operational)

1. All ranks were to wear the following:-
Battledress (special trousers and less parachute badge)
Pair Boots
Pair Socks
Braces or Belt
Underclothing
Shirt
2 Haversacks with slings special
Waist belt with Colt in holster and 18 rounds ammunition in pouch
Helmets, balaclava and flying
Gloves woollen
Gabardine jacket
Anklets and kneepads
Identity discs
Pullover

2. All ranks were to carry in pockets:-
Field dressing
AB 64
Clasp Knife GS
2 Grenades
1 box matches in tin container and waterproof
Plaster and iodine pencil
Chewing gum
A little toilet paper
4 ORs only, a pair of pliers in pocket
No letters or diaries were to be carried

3. Each man was to carry in 2 haversacks:-
Groundsheet
1 spare pair of socks
Mess tin and 4 days special rations
Small enamel mug
Torch
Nothing else was to be put in these haversacks

In addition 12 waterbottles (empty), 12 filled stoves and 12 filled petrol containers were to be carried in haversacks, divided among the 36 personnel of the party. Every officer and man would therefore have one of these, under arrangements made of OC X Troop. All officers and NCOs were to wear compasses and watches and carry field message forms and pencil with rubber.
Officers to wear field glasses and carry maps.
Each of the three escaping parties was to carry in addition to their weapons:-
1 Sextant and tables
60 feet of rope

2 elastic bandages, 2 pairs of spare bootlaces
1 razor, blades, brush, soap and comb

Containers

TYPE	QUANTITY	CONTENTS
Charge	20	2 Charge boards, made up.
Ladder	5	1 pair of Slingsby modified ladders, 1 set of four angle plates, 2 windlassing sticks, 1 50 ft strop of balloon cable with tensioner and handle attached, 2 50 ft alpine rope strops, 2 50 ft alpine rope lashings, 1 ball of kite cord, 1 ball of spun yarn. 1 parachute and webbing strops. Note. To this will be added in Malta, one entrenching tool, 1 26" saw, 1 mash hammer, 2 cold chisel, 1 drum of cordtex.
Bren	2	1 Bren Gun 1 Hat Box of 12 magazines each.
Thompson Gun (4)	1	4 Thompson Guns 4 Thompson Gun bandoliers of 16 magazines each.
Thompson Gun (3)	4	3 Thompson Guns 3 Thompson Gun bandoliers of 16 magazines each.
Food	1	9 Haversacks of food 3 Sextants 3 Air Almanacs 3 Astronomical Navigation Tables 3 Protractors.

Instructions for Air Crews and Special Service Troops on Colossus Operation
1.   Flight to Advanced Base
Each aircraft loaded with air crew and five special service troops.
(a) Take Off.

All Air crew in normal positions.

1 S.S. Trooper lying on floor beneath fuselage tank.

2 S.S. Troops sitting immediately behind overload tanks, facing aft with backs against tanks and knees up.

2 S.S. Troops immediately behind the above.

(b) In Flight.

When the aircraft has reached operational height, and at the captain's discretion it is safe to do so, the S.S troops will be instructed to stand down. Positions will then be taken up as follows:

1 S.S. Trooper on floor beneath fuselage tank.

2 S.S. Troops lying along fuselage between overload tanks and trap door.

2 S.S. Troops lying along fuselage behind the above.

Troops will remove parachutes and use as pillows.

(c) For Landing.
- • When aircraft is approaching destination captain will order troops to 'Prepare for Landing'.
- • 1 S.S. Trooper on floor beneath fuselage tank.
- • 2 S.S. Troops on overload tanks.
- • 2 S.S. Troops immediately behind overload tanks.
- • If captain wishes to move weight further forward, rear gunner should be withdrawn from turret to position in fuselage.

Aircraft/Loads on Flight to Malta:

Aircraft N1525 E-Edward
Air Crew:
Pilot Officer Robinson, Sergeant Hatcher, Sergeant Nolan, Sergeant Diamond and Sergeant Gurmon.
Passengers:
Second Lieutenant Paterson, Sergeant Shutt, Corporal Rowe, Sapper Pryor and Corporal Gray (RAF fitter).

Aircraft T4215 J-Johnnie
Air Crew:
Lieutenant Hoad, Sergeant Smith, Pilot Officer Houghton, Sergeant Markland and Pilot Officer Webb.
Passengers:
Flight Lieutenant Lucky, Corporal Grice, L/Corporal Tomlin, Sapper Ross and Private Samuels.

Aircraft T4235 W-Willie
Air Crew:
Flight Lieutenant Williams, Sergeant Hornsey, Sergeant Walker, Sergeant Kershaw and Pilot Officer McLeod.
Passengers:
Major Pritchard, Sergeant Clements, Corporal O'Brien, Sapper Parker, Private Parker and Wing Commander Norman.

Aircraft T4236 D-Don
Air Crew:
Sergeant Holden, Sergeant Williams, Sergeant Stevens, Sergeant Barton and Sergeant Balcombe.
Passengers:
Second Lieutenant Jowett, Sergeant Durie, L/Corporal Watson, L/Corporal Henderson and Driver Crawford.

Aircraft P5015 K -King
Air Crew:
Wing Commander Tait, Pilot Officer Purley, Sergeant Sharp, Pilot Officer Alabaster, Sergeant Patterson and Pilot Officer Careless.
Passengers:
Captain Lea, Corporal Chapman, Corporal Fletcher and Mr. Dupont.

Aircraft T4165 N-Nuts
Air Crew:
Sergeant Lashbrook, Pilot Officer Howley, Pilot Officer Way, Sergeant Green, Flight Lieutenant Williams.
Passengers:
Captain Daly, Corporal Julian, L/Corporal Boulter, Private Humphrey and Sapper Struthers.

Aircraft T4166 R-Roger
Air Crew:
Sergeant Ennis, Pilot Officer Stubbs, Sergeant Edgar, Sergeant Graham, Sergeant Billing.
Passengers:
Sergeant Lawley, L/Corporal Pexton, L/Corporal Maher, Sapper Phillips and Sapper Davidson.

Aircraft T4167 S-Sugar
Air Crew:
Pilot Officer Watherspoon, Sergeant Southern, Sergeant Meddings, Sergeant Albon and Sergeant Hodges.
Passengers:
Lieutenant Davies, Sergeant Walker, L/Corporal Jones, Private Humphries and Private Nastri.

Instructions to Personnel on Operation.
Each aircraft loaded with air crew, six special service troops and equipment.
  (a) Take Off.
   Air crew in normal positions.
   1 S.S. Trooper lying on floor beneath fuselage tank.
   2 S.S. Troops sitting on overload tanks, as far forward as possible.
   2 S.S. Troops sitting on floor facing aft with backs against overload tanks, and knees up.
   1 S.S. Troop immediately aft of above pair.

  (b) During Flight to Objective.
   When the aircraft has reached operational height and at the captain's discretion it is safe to do so, the S.S. Troops will be instructed to sit easy. Positions will then be:-
   3 S.S. Troops forward of the aperture.
   3 S.S. Troops aft of the aperture.

(c) Action Stations.

Twenty minutes before reaching the objective the captain of the aircraft will give the order 'Action Stations'.

S.S Troops distribute themselves, three forward and three aft of the aperture, hook up static lines and open the trap doors.

Article from the Royal Engineers Journal June 1942

The Italian Parachute Raid
Planning a Rapid Demolition
By T/Lieutenant Colonel J F Rock RE

Problem

To destroy an aqueduct bridge, of four 70 ft spans, carried on three masonry piers, so that its repair would take at least a month.

The demolition must be quickly prepared and the stores such as could be carried in bomb-call containers. As the dimensions of the bridge were only known approximately, the method must not be too rigid. The explosive must be such as could be obtained at a particular base.

Solution

To blow all three piers with gun cotton charges. Should insufficient stores or men arrive at the site, only two piers would be blown. No attempt would be made to blow only one pier, for the effort would not be worth while.

The details of this bridge were obtained from a photograph, drawings and short description in the Engineering Journal of 1928. In this description the piers were said to be masonry. In the photograph they appeared to be concrete and they appeared to be only 3 ft 6 inches thick, though of 24 ft height. Should they prove to be of reinforced concrete, no attempt would be made to blow them, but the R.C. girders of the aqueduct were to be blown at midspan on two adjacent spans on either side of an end pier, these piers having roller bearings.

Calculations

The length of a pier was thought to be 19 ft and its thickness 3 ft 6 inches to 4 ft. It was to be cut by two horizontal charges, one at the base and one 3 ft higher, so as to blow out three feet of each pier.

Using the formula $2/3\ BT^2$, each charge is $2/3 \times 19 \times 4^2 = 203$ lb.

But the gun cotton tins are 11 inches long by 6 ½ inches by 6 ½ inches.

Therefore it takes 19 x 12 divided by 11 = 20 tins to cover the length of a pier.

Therefore 20 tins will be used in each row. This presents 20 x 17 = 340 lb, nearly twice as much as is needed.

[*Author's note: I hope the reader understands this. I believe Rock was saying that the sapper logic was that a pier could be blown with 203 lbs of gun cotton. But because it was necessary to cover the length of a pier (20 tins) and gun cotton came in 17 lb tins, one ended up using 340 lbs.*]

Method

After some little experiment, a rapid method of fixing charges was evolved, which involved the use of the minimum of stores and was noiseless. The top row of charges was hung from a steel wire strop, pulled tight by a ratchet tensioner, and passing, at the four corners of the pier, over grooves in an angle plate. This angle plate had toothed claws to grip the stonework. It was found that the tension in the cable was equalized round the pier. The bottom row of charges was hung from the top row.

Each row of charges was bound together and to the pier by a 50 ft length of alpine cord, passed right round the pier and charges, and windlassed tight. Each row of charges was split into units of four tins, held on a board of 1 5/8 inch pine. These boards had sheet steel brackets at each end and a small loop of webbing riveted to the bracket both above and below the board. To the webbing was tied a length of cord, attached to a small hook and eye and adjustable by means of a sheepshank. The hooks were then dropped over the SWR (Steel Wire Rope) strop and each board could be adjusted to the right height with the sheepshanks. The lower board was hooked to the web loops of the one above it by small hooks held by a cord of fixed length. Each board was provided with both rope, sheepshank and hook and also short cord and hook, so that it could be used as top or bottom board.

Ladders were used to fit the SWR strop and hang the charges. Two were provided for each pier. They were 5 ft 9 inch long and extended to 11 ft, the height of the plinth being uncertain. All hooks were taped to avoid noise. The sag in the SWR strop with all charges in position was about 9 inches.

Detonating Agents

It was decided to fire all charges simultaneously, owing to the risk of the explosion of one charge dislodging another. One slab of the centre tin on each charge board was provided with a primer and 3 ft length of cordtex. A main ring of cordtex was then taken round both rows of charge boards on each pier and to a junction box at the foot of each pier. The cordtex lead from each charge board was then taped to the ring-main with insulating tape.

The three junction boxes, at the foot of each pier, were then connected in series with cordtex and a cordtex lead taken from each junction box to a firing-point fifty yards from the bridge, where a detonator and six feet of safety fuze were used. A duplicate firing system was created by taping a detonator and 2 feet of safety fuze to the ring-main on each pier. The firing system was tested and every length of cordtex detonated completely. The usual precautions were taken to prevent whip in the cordtex.

Packing in Containers

The standard arms container was modified slightly to hold two loaded charge boards. The lids were removed from each tin of gun cotton before loading and a primer and 3 ft of cordtex inserted in a vertical slab in one tin of each charge board. Thus each pier required ten charge boards and five containers.

The two ladders were lashed together and fitted with a harness and parachute to hang in a bomb cell. Between the rungs of the ladders were lashed all the small stores considered necessary for the job.

These were:-

SWR Strop
Ratchet tensioner
Two cordtex strops
Two cordage lashings
Four angle plates
Ball kite cord
Ball spun yarn
Mash hammer
Two cold chisels
26 inch saw
Entrenching tool.

Each Sapper carried a roll of insulating tape and a tin holding one detonator fitted with 2 ft safety fuze.

Drill

The party for each pier was an officer or sergeant and five men.

The total demolition party was two RE officers and 16 RE other ranks. It was anticipated that one man per pier might be injured on landing and the stores might have to be carried as much as half-a-mile to the pier. On landing Numbers 1 and 2 (one of whom was the officer or NCO i/c pier party) carried the ladder assembly to the pier, unpacked it, laid out the stores and erected the SWR strop. Meanwhile Numbers 3 to 6 carried charges and laid them out near the pier. A container load of two charge boards weighed 176 pounds and was a two-man load.

Procedure after this depended on the length of carry. Normally, as soon as the SWR strop was fixed, Numbers 3 and 4 remained at the pier and assisted Numbers 1 and 2 to fix the charge boards. Numbers 5 and 6, having fetched all the charge boards, ran out and fixed the cordtex in the firing circuit.

As soon as each pier was complete the officer or NCO i/c inspected the charges and firing circuits, sent his men to the RV and reported to the officer i/c at the central pier. When all piers were ready, the RE officer i/c and one man remained and fired a gun cotton slab as warning signal to the covering party to go to the RV. As the gun cotton slab detonated he lit a length of safety fuze timed to burn three minutes and retired to a discrete distance to observe results. If time allowed and there was no enemy interference, all parachutes and containers were to be collected and dumped on top of the charges.

Aircraft Loading

This was worked out for the journey out to the base, so that if as many as two of the aircraft failed to arrive there would still be sufficient stores to blow three piers. For the operational trip from the base, three alternative loadings were worked out, according to the different number of aircraft which might be serviceable to do the operation. If all the aircraft were available, the party of six Sappers and all the stores for one pier were to be carried in one aircraft. Three aircraft would carry the whole demolition party.

One set of complete stores for a pier was also to be carried distributed among the remaining aircraft carrying the covering party and one extra ladder assembly over and above these spare stores was to be carried. Thus, if only two RE aircraft landed their loads at the right spot, the two pier parties then available could, after completing their piers, collect the stores dropped with the covering party and prepare the third pier for demolition.

If one aircraft was unserviceable, the covering party was to be reduced by one aircraft load and the operation would proceed as before. Were two aircraft unserviceable, only two pier parties were to be taken. The stores for the third pier were to be carried on the covering party aircraft.

All men of the covering party were taught the demolition drill, so that, if no opposition were met, they could be used as Sappers. Every Sapper was armed with a .32 Colt automatic.

Landings

If all aircraft were available, the covering party detachments were to land first, at five minute intervals, in a valley leading towards the bridge. Ten minutes after the last covering detachment landed the first demolition party was to land and the other two were to land at five minute intervals. These rather long time intervals were prescribed by the RAF to avoid risk of collision in the rather narrow valley. The first RE party to land was to tackle the central pier. All containers were to be dropped between the 5th and 6th men to jump, so as to be as near the bridge as possible. Difficulty was anticipated in finding the ladder assembly, which, being much lighter than the other containers, would drift further.

Aircraft Details Operation Colossus

AIRCRAFT	PILOT	PASSENGERS	LOAD
K-King	Wing Commander Tait	Major Pritchard Captain Lea Flight Lieutenant Lucky Sergeant Walker L/Corporal Pexton Private Parker	Charge Ladder Food Arms TMG 3 x 2 (one failed to drop) 250 lb bomb
D-Don	Sergeant Holden	Sergeant Durie Corporal Julian Private Humphrey Driver Crawford Sapper Ross Sapper Phillips	Charge x 5 Ladder 250 lb bomb
E-Edward	Pilot Officer Robinson	Lieutenant Paterson Corporal O'Brien L/Corporal Maher L/Corporal Jones L/Corporal Watson Sapper Struthers	Charge x 5 Ladder 250 lb bomb

AIRCRAFT	PILOT	PASSENGERS	LOAD
J-Juliet	Lieutenant Hoad	Captain Daly L/Corporal Tomlin Sapper Davidson Sapper Parker Sapper Pryor	Charge x 5 (failed to drop) Ladder (failed to drop) 250 lb bomb
N-Nuts	Sergeant Lashbrook	Lieutenant Deane- Drummond Sergeant Lawley Sergeant Shutt L/Corporal Henderson L/Corporal Boulter Private Dupont	Charge x 2 Arms Bren Gun Arms TMG 3 x 2 250 lb bomb
W-Willie	Flight Lieutenant Williams	Lieutenant Jowett Sergeant Clements Corporal Fletcher Corporal Grice Private Samuels Private Tristan	Charge x 2 Ladder Arms Bren Arms TMG 4 (failed to drop) 250 lb bomb
R-Roger	Sergeant Ennis	None	500 lb bomb x 2 250 bomb x 6
S-Sugar	Pilot Officer Watherspoon	None	500 lb bomb x 2 250 lb bomb x 6

Narrative of the Air Phase submitted by Wing Commander N Norman on 13th February 1941

[Author's note – it should be noted this report was written very soon after the raid and it was at that point not exactly clear what had actually happened in Italy.]

(A) Loading of the Aircraft.
Eight aircraft were available for the operation. These were allocated as follows:
Covering Party 3 K, W, N.
Demolition Party 3 J, E, D.
Diversion Attack 2 S, R.

Details of crews and loads are given in Aircraft Loading Schedules at Appendix 1
[Author's note – not included but details given of crews/loads etc. above.]

These are in accordance with the plans made in England, with the exception of the two diversion aircraft, S and R. The containers were better packed than in previous trials, and nearly all bomb doors were completely shut.

(B) Take-Off.

The take-off was timed to allow assembly of the sub-flights in daylight, and climbing over the sea to the south of Malta, no aircraft being permitted to cross the coast northwards until after dark. The take-off times ordered were:-

Covering Party   17.40 hours.

Diversion Attack 17.50 hours.

Demolition Party 18.00 hours.

At the time of take-off a defect developed in J Aircraft. The Demolition Party therefore took off two strong. Assembly of each sub-flight was successfully carried out, and aircraft flew to the target area in formation, maintaining touch by R/T. Aircraft J took off about 18.17 hours and followed the others but did not join formation.

(C) Flight to Objective.

The course selected was from Malta to the Sicilian coast near Agrigento, to near Palermo and then direct to the mouth of the Sele River. There was some cloud over the sea, and fog over parts of Sicily. Flak was seen over Palermo. The landfalls made on the Italian coast were not all accurate but the River Sele was easily identifiable. All aircraft with the exception of J arrived in the target area at approximately 21.30 hours. J made a bad landfall on the Italian coast, and followed a river partially obscured by mist inland until the Adriatic coast was reached. It then returned to the west coast at Scalea, flew up to the Sele and reached the objective area at 23.15.

(D) Control System.

It was important that the dropping should be synchronised, that all or none of the aircraft should drop in the event of doubtful weather, and that risk of collision between aircraft operating in the small space of the target area should be slight. The following system of W/T control by the Air Attack Commander was instituted. The Air Attack Commander in the first aircraft arrived at the target leading the first sub-flight, broke formation and did a preliminary reconnaissance. A Zero Hour was then selected and transmitted to all aircraft. Each aircraft had allotted a period of five minutes for dropping, the first run being at Z plus 0 to Zero plus 5, the second being Z plus 5 to Zero plus 10, and so on. After completing the dropping each aircraft was to transmit 'operations completed' to the Air Attack Commander, who was then able to delay, if necessary, the dropping of the second sub-flight until the first had completed.

The first sub-flight arrived at the target at 21.25 BST and the Air Attack Commander broadcast Zero Hour to be at 21.35. At 21.35 however, wishing to confirm that other aircraft had located the target, he called for W and N to give this information, and broadcast a new Zero Hour of 22.00. This was received by the second sub-flight, and the dropping was carried out in the order N, W, K, E, D, J, N and W dropping at their first allotted time and reporting 'operations completed' to the Air Attack Commander.

After dropping at 22.00, the Air Attack Commander waited at Vulture for visual report of operations completed by any aircraft which had W/T failure. In fact no aircraft had W/T failure and with the exception of J all aircraft had left the area by 22.45.

(E) Rendezvous.

The rendezvous was Mount Vulture, and aircraft assembled there or in the vicinity, stepped off in height, awaiting final Zero. This was given at 21.25 as Zero 21.35. It was then found that some aircraft could not work to this Zero and the time was changed to 22.00. Two aircraft failed to receive the new Zero and dropped on the first one.

(F) Weather Conditions.

Cloud which had been seen over Sicily was entirely dispersed before the Italian coast, but some banks of ground fog lay in valleys. A thick bank filled the pass between the Sele and Alfonto valleys. Apart from this the weather was absolutely perfect and visibility was comparable with early dusk on a fine day. Detail on the ground stood out, and the snow covered peaks, rocky valleys and clustered mountain towns and villages made a beautiful scene. No difficulty was experienced in identifying the objective and surrounding landmarks.

(G) The Attack.

Although five of the six aircraft were in the area they only occasionally saw each other after stepping off preparatory to the attack. There was very little wind in the valleys and no difficulty was experienced in making steep turns low down well below the level of the hills on each side of the valley. Dropping was carried out approximately according to plan. The dropping ground appeared smooth, cultivated, mostly newly sown fields with some bushes. A schedule setting out the times and results of dropping is attached at Appendix II, and a diagram illustrating the estimated position of parachutes dropped is at Appendix III [*Author's note – these appendices have not been reproduced*]. In four cases the containers did not go with the troops. The explanation appears to be that the five-pin plug was not correctly fitted, although great care was taken by the Captains to see that selection and setting of bomb release gear was correct, and to remind Section Commanders regarding action in the fuselage. Several aircraft had to make three or four runs up and down the valley to get their containers off. One full load (ladders and 5 charges), and two other single containers (Arms TG) were not dropped but were carried back to Malta. It appeared that the troops would have little difficulty in finding the containers in the brilliant moonlight. Five aircraft completed dropping 21.45 and 22.30 hours. The sixth dropped troops but no containers at 23.00 hours. It was unfortunate that this machine carried Captain Daly, RE.

(H) Local Activity.

Very little sign of local activity in the vicinity of the objective was seen. A light was observed in one signal box north of the dropping area. The lights of a car were seen approaching the bridge opposite Calitri from the south. At that point the car apparently stopped, for the lights went out. No other vehicles were observed on any roads and apart, from occasional lights from Calitri and other towns and villages, no other lights. Our own troops were seen moving on the ground. Several times they flashed up their torches to aircraft as they passed over – probably to show that they had landed successfully.

(I) Diversion Action.

One aircraft of the Diversion sub-flight – S – apparently had failure of port engine and the crew signalled in Syko that they would land or abandon aircraft in the vicinity of the mouth of the Sele River. The other aircraft proceeded to Foggia and successfully bombed the railway station and yard, setting fire to a petrol train, the trucks of which exploded successfully and started large fires. Two other trains standing in the station were probably damaged. One which attempted to leave the station was machine gunned, and MG fire was also directed on to the area amid the burning train to prevent it being put out. Two craters were observed in the station buildings and one bomb was seen to fall on the junction of lines and points leading into the station and goods yard. One bomb was dropped on the buildings of Foggia aerodrome.

Smoke from the station was very black and reached over 2,000 ft indicated height, and the fires were observed by another aircraft thirty miles away. No Flak or defence was observed. Two aircraft of the other two sub-flights dropped their bombs on the railway yard at Rochetta Scalo. One bomb was dropped on the village of Montiverdi, one on a railway junction near the mouth of the River Sele and one, on the return journey, in Sicily.

(J) Return Flight.

This was uneventful, except that low cloud obscured and hid Malta, and W/T guidance was required by all aircraft before a landfall was made. One aircraft, J arrived about one hour later than the others at 02.00 hours.

Conclusion.

The failure of the operation cannot yet be explained. Although the order and times of dropping were not exactly as planned, the whole of the 'X' troop's force was dropped, apparently under good conditions, in the vicinity of the objective. The charges, ladders, and equipment dropped were the full amount required for execution of the complete demolition plan. The arms containers dropped contained 3 Bren Guns and 7 Tommy Guns and ammunition. While the lack of 7 further Tommy Guns may have been serious, nevertheless the force could probably give a good account of itself with the arms available and their personal weapons – and, in any case, no sign of opposition was observed from the air. The late arrival of Captain Daly was no doubt a serious handicap, but every member of the demolition party was familiar with the objective as it was thought to exist. If it was in fact the western bridge and not that on the main stream, the party could not have failed to recognise it, since in attacking the adjacent farm, many must have passed close to it, and their rendezvous was in fact within 100 yards of it. It seems impossible that some vital piece of equipment necessary for the demolition was lost or not taken on the operation. The only possibilities that seem to remain are that:

- (i)   The details of the operation were known to the enemy, and the party was captured immediately on landing.
- Or
- (ii)   That the objective was entirely different in construction from anticipated design, and the equipment available was insufficient for its destruction.

It is a significant fact that up to 19.30 hours on the night prior to the operation no-one concerned had any knowledge of a second bridge within about 230 yards of that over the Tragino.

A number of points have emerged having a bearing upon future operations of a similar nature.

1. It is clear that up to date intelligence supported by air photographs is absolutely essential at the time of planning the operation, and that the parachute party and the captains and crews of aircraft must have more time to study and memorise the details of the terrain.

2. The time required for dropping at night on an objective not previously known, even in ideal conditions, is much longer than was thought necessary. After arrival at the rendezvous the Air Attack Commander requires 10 minutes for reconnaissance and to confirm the arrival of other aircraft. Each aircraft should be allowed at least 10 minutes for general reconnaissance of the area before dropping. Approximately 10 minutes is required from giving Zero Hour until dropping begins. 5 minutes must be allowed to each aircraft for making runs over the target. In these circumstances considerable disturbance in the target area seems unavoidable when parachute troops are employed at night.

3. For the actual dropping all available eyes must be employed. In a Whitley, it is desirable that the navigator, in the front turret, should direct the run up. The second pilot, looking downwards, should work the red and green signal lights, the captain should concern himself primarily with the flying of the aircraft, and the rear gunner must observe the dropping and report to the captain immediately the last man has gone, so that he can put on engine and get clear, and if necessary, make a second run to release containers that have not fallen. Moreover, up to the time of the first drop, it is essential that the Attack Commander Ground and the Attack Commander Air, be in personal contact, so that decisions regarding the sufficiency of the available forces, the timing of the operation and details of the attack can be taken together. It is thought that the Attack Commander Ground should not be a Section Commander, but should drop separately on a second run.

4. The present arrangement for container release is not satisfactory. The five-pin plug should be put in and fixed before the flight begins. The container cells should be selected, the distributor timing set and the distributor then set to 'safe'. When 'prepare for action' is given the navigator will then turn the distributor to 'distributor' and confirm to the Section Commander that the tell-tale light in the fuselage is on. Alternatively, it is thought that when containers are dropped last, the navigator could very well release them on a signal from the rear gunner that the last man has gone.

5. The present design of container must be entirely revised, and the bomb release gear studied to ascertain that it will function properly with large containers. The new design should incorporate a rigid harness that can be fixed to the bomb rack and firmly stabilised before the container is raised into position. A mechanical means of raising the container to the harness should be provided so that one to two men can fix or lower containers. The dimension of the container must be such that there is no possibility of jamming in the bomb cell.

6. Army personnel should be given opportunity to become completely familiar with the aircraft used and their bomb release equipment and should have more air experience under operational conditions than was possible in the case of the present operation.

Appendix VII

Royal Navy reports regarding Operation Claymore

Report from the Commander-in-Chief of the Home Fleet Admiral Sir John C Tovey on the raid on military and economic objectives in the Lofoten Islands dated 4th April 1941 to the Lords Commissioners of the Admiralty

Raid on Military and Economic Objectives in the Lofoten Islands

1. Be pleased to lay before Their Lordships the enclosed report of Operation Claymore*, prepared by the Captain (D), 6th Destroyer Flotilla, HMS *Somali*, in command of the operation. I concur fully in the report and in the remarks of the Rear Admiral (D), Home Fleet, in his Minute II, particularly in paragraph 2.

   [*Operation Claymore – the destruction of fish oil plants in the ports of Stamsund, Henningsvaer, Svolvaer and Brettesnes in the Lofoten Islands, the arrest of local supporters of the Quisling party, the capture of enemy personnel in the ports, the evacuation of recruits for the Free Norwegian Forces, and the destruction or capture of enemy ships and of Norwegian vessels found to be working for the Germans.]

2. Among the factors which contributed to the success of this small combined operation I would draw attention to the following: -

   (a) The excellent co-operation between all ranks and ratings of the Navy and Army taking part. Each single phase required a joint decision to be taken, and in each phase Naval units and Army units were working side by side in complete agreement and harmony. It is appropriate to record the appreciation of the Naval officers and ratings who took part for the qualities of their soldier opposite numbers.

   (b) The weather. It had not been practicable to carry out more than elementary drills in the short time at Scapa, and it was a great relief to me that the landing craft did not have to contend with swell, strong wind or tide. I would stress moreover that any less time than was allowed for rehearsal and planning, and it was two days less than originally planned, would have been quite unacceptable.

3. I would mention the valuable part played by the submarine *Sunfish* in her role as a D/F beacon. This scheme worked well, and although in the event the force was able to fix by sights, had this not been possible they would have been in an uncomfortable position without the *Sunfish's* aid.

4. With reference to paragraph 29 of Captain D6's report, I laid particular emphasis in my verbal instructions on the importance of punctuality in withdrawing the forces at the end of the agreed time, and I endorse the opinion that it was necessary to sink the *Hamburg* rather than to attempt to steam her down the Vestfjord and then some

750 miles to the Faroes with the resources available, but she should have first been boarded and searched for papers or other material likely to be useful.
Signed Jack C Tovey,
Admiral,
Commander-in-Chief, Home Fleet.

Minute II
HMS *Tyne*
15th March 1941.

Forwarded.

2. Great credit is due to Captain C Caslon, Royal Navy, for his part in the efficient planning and execution of this operation.

3. It was fortunate that the conditions were ideal. The weather throughout the passage could not have been better, and the opposition was negligible.

4. It is thought that future operations of this nature will not only need equally efficient and careful preparation and execution, but also adequate air support, if the geographical position is not so favourable to us.

Signed L H K Hamilton,
Rear Admiral (D),
Home Fleet.

HMS *Somali*
8th March 1941

Operation Claymore – Report of Proceedings

I have the honour to forward the following report of the proceedings of Force Rebel in Operation Claymore.

2. Force Rebel consisted of the following ships:-
Destroyers
Somali – Captain C Caslon (Captain (D), 6th DF).
Bedouin – Commander J A McCoy, DSO.
Tartar – Commander L P Skipwith.
Legion – Commander R F Jessel.
Eskimo – Commander E G Le Geyt.
Troop Carriers
Queen Emma – Commander C A Kershaw.
Princess Beatrix – Commander T B Brunton.

3. During the afternoon of Friday, 28th February, Brigadier J C Haydon, DSO, OBE, embarked in *Somali* with his headquarters staff which consisted of Major A R Aslett

(Brigade Major), and Lieutenant L M Harper-Gow (interpreter in Norwegian) and four other ranks.

4. Force Rebel sailed from Scapa Flow at 0001 on 1st March 1941, and proceeded to Skaalefjord, Faroes, arriving there at 1900 on the same day. Destroyers refuelled there from Warpindari and the force sailed at 0001 on 2nd March. Course was set for position L (64° 00′ N 03° 00′ W) and thence for position P (67° 12′ N 02° 00′ W).

5. After clearing the Faroes a speed of 20 knots was maintained until 1100 on 2nd March in order to be as far northward as possible by that time. It was hoped that, by so doing, the force would evade detection by the Zenit* flight. No aircraft was in fact sighted.
[*Zenit flight – a daily meteorological flight flown by the Germans.]

6. After passing through position P at 0130 on 3rd March course was shaped for position Q (67° 09′ N 11° 55′ E) which was reached as planned at 0001 on 4th March, speed having been adjusted as necessary.

7. Up to this time the passage had been uneventful and the weather conditions very favourable. These were particularly so while making the approach to position Q from the westward. The sky was, for the most part overcast with low cloud and frequent snow showers were experienced which tended to reduce the chances of detection. The weather cleared sufficiently at intervals, however, for navigational observations to be taken to fix the position of the force.

8. During the passage from P to Q the wind was from ENE, force 3 and the state of the sea 24.* It was unnecessary, therefore, even to consider postponing the operation as conditions promised to be excellent. Special weather reports made by the Admiralty were received, also reports of air reconnaissance patrols from the Commander-in-Chief, Rosyth.
[*Wind force 3- gentle breeze of 7-10 knots; sea 24- slight sea, moderate average length swell.]

9. During the approach to position Q, D/F bearings were obtained of *Sunfish* at the expected times and these bearings confirmed the position obtained by astronomical observations. It is estimated that the force passed 2 miles south of *Sunfish* at 2335. This method of checking the position was most valuable in making the landfall. Had no sights been obtained, it would have been the only means of fixing the position of the force at this critical stage of the approach.

10. From position Q the force moved up Vestfjord towards position C (68° 05′ N 14° 29′ E) continuing in night cruising order until 0300 when ships formed into single line ahead. Position C was reached without incident at 0430 when the force split. *Somali*, *Bedouin*, *Tartar* and *Queen Emma* proceeding to position D (68° 14′ N 14° 42′ E) and *Legion*, *Eskimo* and *Princess Beatrix* to position E (68° 08′ N 14° 01′ E). It is believed that the force was observed by coastwatchers during this passage, but that no reporting message got through to the mainland. This point may be mentioned by the military who gave me the information after our return to Scapa.

11. Passage up the Vestfjord was much simplified by the fact that all lights were burning at full brilliancy and with normal characteristics, with the following exceptions: Skomvaer, Tennholm, Grytoy. By 0445 the outline of the coast could be distinguished.

12. After the splitting of the force, *Somali*, with *Bedouin*, *Tartar* and *Queen Emma* in company, moved towards position D where the landing craft for X landing were lowered by 0508. These were taken in charge by *Tartar* while *Somali*, *Bedouin* and *Queen Emma* proceeded to position F (68° 12′ N 14° 52′ E).

13. The weather conditions now were – wind ENE, force 3, sea 10 to 20*. It was intensely cold, the temperature being between 20° and 25° F. The weather continued to be fine, and very clear throughout the day, with brilliant sunshine.
    [*Sea 10 to 20 – smooth to slight sea with no swell.]

14. By this time it had become apparent that, in view of the lightness of the dawn and the perfect visibility, the landing of troops could, with advantage, have been made earlier than at 0645, the projected time. No alteration, except in the case of X landing, was however possible owing to the distances to be covered by landing craft after having been lowered.

15. Craft for X landing, covered by *Tartar*, were comparatively close to their objective on being lowered and must have been clearly visible to those ashore. To avoid the loss of the element of surprise, therefore, they moved off to Port X* at 0530 and arrived there approximately half an hour before the planned time.
    [* Port A (Stamsund), Port B (Henningsvaer), Port X (Svolvaer) and Port Y (Brettesnes).]

16. In the meantime *Legion*, *Eskimo* and *Princess Beatrix* had reached position E at 0540. Landing craft were lowered and led inshore to Ports A and B by *Legion* and *Eskimo* respectively. Disembarkation proceeded in accordance with the timetable and landings were made at 0645.

17. At 0610, shortly before the arrival of *Bedouin* and *Queen Emma* at position F, *Somali* parted company to proceed to Ports A and B to see if the landings were being effected satisfactorily there. On passage, an armed trawler, later found to be the *Krebbs*, was sighted steering away from Port X. Fire was opened at a range of 3,000 yards at 0620 and the enemy very quickly hit. Our fire was returned by three rounds fired from a small gun in the bows of the trawler, but no hits were obtained on *Somali*. Immediately afterwards three shells were observed to be effective, one apparently exploding the ready-use ammunition, another bursting in the wheelhouse and the third in the boiler room. A considerable volume of smoke was seen to be coming from the trawler which was clearly out of control. Fire was accordingly checked. Five survivors were then seen to be swimming in the water; they were picked up by 0655.

18. At this time gunfire could be heard at Port X. As W/T communication with the landing places had not yet been established and the Brigadier was anxious to find out if any landings had been opposed, *Somali* left the now helpless trawler, which had run aground on a small island, and proceeded to ascertain the state of affairs at Ports X, B and A.

19. At 0710 *Somali* made the negative W/T silence sign and from then on, throughout the operation, satisfactory W/T communications were maintained with all landing places. Visual Signal communication was also established at each landing place.

20. At each port, operations were proceeding according to plan and by 0735 reports had been received that at all four ports landings had been effected successfully without opposition and that relations with the Norwegian population were most cordial.

From this time onwards, reports came in from all military landing parties that allotted tasks were being carried out successfully and the Brigadier from his position on *Somali's* bridge, was kept in continual touch with the progress of operations.

21. By now the local Norwegian fishing fleet had put to sea; there were literally hundreds of little fishing smacks and small puffers beginning to fish in the adjacent waters. It quickly became clear to them that our operations were directed against the Germans and that they were not to be molested. They showed their friendliness and enthusiasm by cheering and waving and hoisting Norwegian flags.

22. From Port A *Somali* then proceeded back to Port X. During the passage the trawler *Krebbs*, still burning, was seen to have refloated and to be drifting towards the centre of the fjord. As *Somali* closed, a white flag was seen being waved and at 0910 a boarding party was sent over in a Norwegian fishing boat who volunteered their services. The survivors consisted of five ratings, all of whom were wounded by gunfire, two seriously. The balance of the crew, consisting of the captain and thirteen ratings, had been killed in the action.

23. The boarding officers, Major A R Aslett, Lieutenant Sir Marshall G C Warmington RN, the signal officer on my staff and 2nd Lieutenant L M Harper-Gow, searched the ship as far as was possible.

24. The wheelhouse was found to have received a direct hit and nothing could be recovered from there, other than a number of charts. The captain and one rating were found dead by the wheel; one or two bodies which could not be identified were also in the wheelhouse.

25. The ship was still on fire below and no entry could be made into the fore-peak or the engine room.

26. The search of the *Krebbs* occupied three quarters of an hour and while *Somali* was stopped numbers of fishing craft took the opportunity to come alongside and throw their fish on board as gifts to the ship's company. The fishing boat which took the boarding party was rewarded with gifts of food and cigarettes.

27. At 1015 the *Krebbs* was sunk by gunfire after an unsuccessful attempt had been made to destroy her by depth charge fired from the port thrower. She finally disappeared at 1030. Her armament consisted of a 3 or 6-pdr gun forward, a 2-cm Madsen machine gun aft and eight depth charges in two chutes.

28. A summary of the happenings at the various ports is given in the ensuing paragraphs.

29. At Port X an important success was the destruction of the *Hamburg* by gunfire from *Tartar*. This was a ship of 9780 tons which had been specially converted into a fish-refrigerating and factory ship. From the report of the officer in charge of the naval demolition party at Port X it appears that a plan was made to take possession of this ship and to steam her as a prize to England and that this plan was frustrated by *Tartar* opening fire and destroying her. I consider that the Commanding Officer HMS *Tartar*, was justified in the action he took, having regard to the general instructions for the conduct of the operation and to the fact that no information of the plan to seize the ship had been communicated to him. Nor was I, myself, aware of it.

30. In addition, *Tartar* sunk the *Pasajes*, 1966 tons and completed the destruction of the *Felix Heumann*, 2468 tons, which was still floating after partial destruction by the naval demolition party. The latter, from HMS *Nelson*, under the command

of Lieutenant D D Bone RN, sunk the *Eilenau*, 1404 tons, the trawler *Rissen* and, as stated above, commenced the destruction of the *Felix Heumann*. The work performed by this party was most creditable. It is believed that the large majority of the crews of all these ships were made prisoners by the military landing parties and brought back in *Queen Emma*.

31. At 1035 the Norwegian trawler *Myrland*, whose crew wished to proceed to England and asked for instructions was directed by *Tartar* to proceed independently to Skaalefjord in the Faroes. This was reported in my signal timed 1444 of 6th March 1941. She arrived safely today, 8th March.

32. At Port Y, *Bedouin* at 0626, while leading the landing craft in towards the shore, intercepted the Norwegian ferry steamer *Mira* flying the Norwegian flag and endeavoured to stop her by firing a shot across her bows. As this had no effect a second shot was fired into the fore part of the ship, but as the ship still did not stop effective fire was opened. One shot entered the ship below the funnel, steam poured from her and she lost way. *Bedouin* then left her to see the landing parties safely ashore. This done, *Bedouin*, acting in accordance with my instructions, returned to sink the *Mira*. It was seen that she was being abandoned and, when this was completed and the rafts were clear, fire was opened. Mira was very soon severely damaged and started to sink slowly.

33. I was subsequently informed by a military officer of one of the landing parties that the captain of the *Mira* was forced at the pistol point by a German officer on board to continue on his course, despite *Bedouin's* warning shots. It is believed that this officer and 12 German soldiers who were also on board were later taken prisoner and brought back in *Queen Emma*. It is feared that there were some casualties to Norwegian civilians as a result of *Bedouin's* gunfire.

34. By 0840 it had become evident that the work of the landing parties at Port Y would shortly be completed. *Queen Emma*, who had been lying off Port X, was accordingly directed to proceed to Port Y to commence re-embarkation of ALCs. This was completed at 1024 when *Queen Emma*, with *Bedouin*, returned to Port X who had reported all tasks completed at 1011 and parties ready to re-embark.

35. By 1030 *Somali* was proceeding to cover the landing parties at Port A as *Legion* had moved southward to investigate two trawlers which subsequently proved to be Norwegian puffers. During this passage, dense columns of heavy black smoke could be seen at Ports X and A rising to the tops of the surrounding mountains, a height of several thousand feet, sure evidence of the thoroughness with which the landing parties were carrying out their tasks of destruction.

36. At Port A the military completed their tasks successfully and *Legion* was not called upon to give any support. Two German trawlers, the *Ando*, 300 tons and the *Grotto*, 200 tons which were the only enemy ships in the harbour, were sunk by the naval demolition party from HMS *Rodney* under the command of Lieutenant C P N Wells-Cole RN. By the time *Somali* had arrived at 1100 re-embarkation of troops had already commenced.

37. At Port B, as at Port A, *Eskimo* was not called upon to give any support to the landing parties, who completed their tasks successfully, nor was there any enemy shipping present against which she could take action.

38. *Somali* returned to Port X at 1200 to find re-embarkation in progress. The time required for this was increased by the large number of prisoners and volunteers to be embarked in *Queen Emma* who sailed with 852 persons on board. By 1230, however, the last landing craft had left the shore and at 1255 *Queen Emma* reported that she was ready to proceed. At 1256 *Princess Beatrix* made a similar report from Port B.

39. *Somali*, *Bedouin*, *Tartar* and *Queen Emma* proceeded to position C at 20 knots. *Legion*, *Eskimo* and *Princess Beatrix* joined company at 1330 and the whole force in day cruising order, set course at best speed down Vestfjord. Columns of smoke were still rising from the burning oil tanks and plant and a heavy pall lay over the scene of the day's operations.

40. At 1530 as the force was passing Vaeroy, a German reconnaissance aircraft was sighted by *Bedouin* and was heard by the same ship to make a W/T report: *Bedouin* accordingly carried out jamming procedure. The aircraft flew at about 6,000 feet making full use of cloud cover and was engaged by ships' guns as opportunity offered. Although conditions appeared very favourable for a bombing attack none was made and the aircraft disappeared shortly after 1600. In view of the sighting, I made a W/T report of the successful completion of the operation at once, without waiting until the force was clear of the area.

41. At 1700 course was altered to the westward for position P which was reached at 0900 on 5th March, after which course was altered to the southward. Vice Admiral Commanding 18th Cruiser Squadron, in Edinburgh, with *Nigeria* in company, were sighted at 1020 on 5th March and provided escort for the remainder of the passage.

42. It was known on the morning of 5th March that the Germans had announced that a raid had been made and I therefore considered it desirable to signal a brief report of the success of the operation as early as could be done with safety. Accordingly when the force was in position of approximately 64° 00′ N 4° 00′ W and darkness was approaching W/T silence was broken for this purpose. Unfortunately signalling conditions were very unfavourable and it took much longer than had been anticipated to clear the message.

43. The wounded prisoners from the *Krebbs* were accommodated in the sick bay and my harbour cabin during the return passage. They received the greatest care and skillful attention from my Medical Officer, Surgeon Lieutenant M G Low RNVR, assisted by the sick bay staff, the Flotilla Chaplain and the canteen manager. The Army other ranks also assisted. Two of the men were very seriously wounded and owe their lives to the skilled nursing they received. Similar good arrangements for the wounded were made in *Queen Emma*.

44. The return passage was made without incident and Force Rebel arrived at Scapa Flow at 1300 on 6th March.

45. After arrival prisoners and volunteers were disembarked from all ships, the wounded being discharged to HMHS *Amarapoora*.

General Remarks

46. I was greatly impressed with the efficiency, handling and station-keeping of the troop carriers, particularly as they were both newly commissioned ships with no

previous experience of working in formation. The lowering and hoisting of the landing craft during the operation was carried out in a most efficient manner.

47. Owing to the troop carriers sailing for the Clyde a few hours after our return to Scapa it has not been possible for me to obtain details of the military operation with sufficient accuracy to make any but the most general reference to them in this report. It has, however, been arranged for copies of Brigadier Haydon's report to be forwarded to the Commander-in-Chief, Home Fleet, as soon as it has been prepared.

48. I should like to record with pleasure that throughout the planning and execution of this operation Brigadier Haydon cooperated wholeheartedly and at no time did we have the slightest difficulty in reaching mutually satisfactory conclusions. His presence on board *Somali*, with his staff was most welcome in every way.

Signed C Caslon.
Captain (D),
Sixth Destroyer Flotilla.

Appendix VIII

Report on Operation Claymore by Brigadier J C Haydon DSO OBE, Commanding Special Service Brigade

13th March 1941

Objects of the operation

1.(a) The Military objects of the operation were to destroy the facilities for producing herring and cod oil in the ports of Stamsund, Henningsvaer, Svolvaer and Brettesnes, all of which are situated in the Lofoten Islands; to arrest local supporters of the Quisling party; to capture any enemy personnel found in the ports, and to enlist recruits for the Free Norwegian Forces.

(b) The Naval objective at the ports was the destruction or capture of enemy ships and of Norwegian vessels found to be working for the Germans.

Forces taking part in the operation
2. Naval

(a) The 6th Destroyer Flotilla, under the command of Captain C Caslon, RN, and composed of:
HMS *Somali*, HMS *Bedouin*, HMS *Tartar*, HMS *Eskimo*, HMS *Legion*, formed the Naval escort and were responsible for the safety of the military forces during the approach to and return from the Lofoten Islands and for the provision of close support while the operations on shore were in progress.

(b) HMS *Queen Emma* (Commander C A Kershaw RN), carrying the troops destined for Svolvaer and Brettesnes.

(c) HMS *Princess Beatrice* (Commander T B Brunton RN), carrying the troops destined for Stamsund and Henningsvaer.

(d) Naval demolition parties carried in HMS *Queen Emma* and HMS *Princess Beatrice*.

3. Military

The Military forces taking part in the raid were:-

(a) Operational Headquarters Special Service Brigade in HMS *Somali*.

(b) 250 all ranks of No 4 Commando under the command of Lieutenant Colonel D S Lister MC (The Buffs) in HMS *Queen Emma*.

(c) 250 all ranks of No 3 Commando under the command of Lieutenant Colonel J F Durnford-Slater (Royal Artillery) in HMS *Princess Beatrice*.

(d)   One section of 55 Field Company Royal Engineers (2nd Lieutenant H M Turner Royal Engineers).

(e)   4 officers and 48 other ranks of the Norwegian Forces, under the command of Captain Martin Linge.

The detachments of Royal Engineers and of Norwegian troops were divided between HMS *Queen Emma* and HMS *Princess Beatrice* in accordance with the tasks to be carried out in each port.

Concentration of the force and preparatory work.

4.   Operational Headquarters Special Service Brigade, Nos. 3 and 4 Commando, the Royal Engineers detachment and the Norwegian troops embarked at Gourock in HMS *Queen Emma* and HMS *Princess Beatrice* during the afternoon of Friday, 21st February, 1941, and left for Scapa Flow on the evening of that day.

Scapa was reached at 1430 hours on the 22nd February and the ships were anchored between HMS *Nelson* and HMS *King George V.*

The troops remained at Scapa until the force sailed for the Lofoten Islands, at 0001 hours on Saturday, 1st March 1941. Thus, there intervened a period of almost a week during which all the final arrangements, plans and orders could be prepared, published and explained and during which those who were to operate together during the operation could meet and get to know one another.

There can be no doubt whatsoever regarding the essential nature of this comparatively short time of preparation. Though the nature of the raid precluded meticulous rehearsals of the tasks allotted to each troop or detachment, the week at Scapa was invaluable from the military point of view, in that it gave both officers and men time to accustom themselves to the ships from which they were to work; to get to know the officers and crews of the landing craft which were to take them inshore, and, in general, to make the personal contact which are so essential a preliminary to an enterprise of this kind.

5.   So far as the Naval and Military Commanders were concerned, the period at Scapa was filled by a series of conferences, at which all details and difficulties were examined and solutions reached. Several points of major importance emerged during these meetings. The first concerned the problem of supporting fire from the destroyers. Captain C Caslon, RN, the Senior Naval Officer, having studied the charts of the area of operations, reached the conclusion that, owing to navigational difficulties, the escorting destroyers would not be able to lie closer than approximately 1 mile from each port. This distance, taking into account the somewhat tortuous nature of the approaches, and the half-lights of early morning, made it unlikely that the destroyers would be in a position to afford support by direct fire or that they would even be able to keep the landing craft in view throughout the passage between the ships and the shore.

These were, of course, important considerations and changed somewhat drastically the military aspect of the operation, under which it had been envisaged that the landing craft would be able to move into each port with the escorting destroyers in the closest attendance and dominating any possible opposition with their guns.

However, in view of the information available concerning the enemy forces which were likely to be encountered, it was decided to accept the disadvantages and difficulties arising from the possible employment of indirect fire and to insert special instructions in the operation order concerning the use of this method of support. In this connection, it will be appreciated that the lack of gridded maps, the restricted size of each port, the danger areas which would have to be allowed for and the desire to avoid any unnecessary damage to Norwegian property, all tended to complicate the situation and to make it more and more apparent that there would probably be a period in each port during which the troops would have to rely only on their own weapons and on such covering fire as could be given by any detachments which had already been landed.

In these circumstances, Commanders were instructed to make their approach with caution and to use the landing craft at each port as a scout so that all would not be subjected to fire at one and the same time. Further, troops were to be prepared to open fire and mutually support each other from their landing craft should the need arise. The situation which might have arisen clearly called for the use of Support Landing Craft but there were none available.

6. A further decision arrived at after a study of the navigational difficulties, concerned the movement of HMS *Queen Emma* after the landing craft for Svolvaer had been launched. It was thought originally that the two ALCs required for Brettesnes could be dropped at the same time as those for Svolvaer and that they would then be able to proceed astern of their escorting destroyer through the narrow channel named on the chart as Holen Skjoldver. It was decided, however, that it would be both unsound and unwise to risk passing either a destroyer or unescorted landing craft through this passage. As a result of this decision, HMS *Queen Emma* was instructed that, having dropped the landing craft for Svolvaer, she was to proceed to Brettesnes in company with the escorting destroyer, passing to the south of Skravven.

As this route was appreciably longer than that through Holen Skjoldver and it was desirable that the concentration of the force after the conclusion of the shore operation should not be delayed, orders were issued that the troops landed at Brettesnes should be ready to re-embark at 1130 hours which was 1 hour earlier than the time limit fixed for the other three ports.

7. The third matter of importance from the military point of view was the possibility which was explained by the Commander-in-Chief, Home Fleet, that the escorting destroyers might be forced to leave the vicinity of the four ports should a naval action be precipitated by the move of the force to the Lofotens. The period during which the destroyers might be away could not, of course, be forecast with any accuracy but, as a precautionary measure, each man was ordered to take ashore with him rations sufficient for 48 hours.

8. It should be stressed that it was the few days spent at Scapa which gave each Commander ample opportunity to examine in the most complete detail the problems which faced him and to consult naval officers concerned on any points of difficulty arising out of them. It is also worthy of emphasis that, had the nature of the operation entailed a long approach in darkness for the landing craft, or had the tasks allotted to the various detachments been such as to require exact and repeated rehearsal, the preparatory period of six days would not have been long enough. In such circumstances 14 to 18 days might well have been required.

The approach to the Lofoten Islands

9. The force, which bore the code name Rebel, left Scapa Flow at 0001 hrs on the 1st March and proceeded first to Skaalefjord in the Faroes where the destroyers were to refuel. The fjord was reached at 1900 hrs on 1st March and the weather conditions had been such that it was hoped, with some degree of confidence, that Force Rebel had escaped enemy observation.

10. After a stay of about five hours, the force proceeded on its way routed through various points previously fixed by the Commander-in-Chief, Home Fleet.

11. During the night of Monday, 3rd March, Force Rebel entered the Vestfjord and shortly before 0400 hrs on the following morning, the many navigational lights in the neighbourhood of the Lofotens came into view. That these should have been burning at what appeared to be full brilliance was somewhat surprising but certainly gave good cause for the hope that the arrival of the force had been unheralded and that the complete effects of surprise might be obtained. Such indeed proved to be the case.

12. The exactness of the timing and the extreme accuracy of the naval approach, both of which were due to the careful arrangements and the untiring supervision of Captain C Caslon, RN, and of his Navigating Officer, Lieutenant Commander Shaw, RN, cannot be praised too highly. There is no doubt whatsoever that the accomplishment of the military tasks on shore was much facilitated thereby.

The operations on shore

13. The operations ashore proceeded according to plan and all tasks allotted to the force were carried out. The times of the initial landings at each port varied but troops were ashore at all of them by 0650 hours. By 1300 hours both HMS *Princess Beatrice* and HMS *Queen Emma* had re-embarked all their troops and were ready to sail.

Inter-communications

14. Owing to the excellence of the inter-communication arrangements made by Lieutenant Sir Marshall G C Warmington RN, of HMS *Somali*, it was possible to obtain at all times a most clear and accurate picture of the progress of the operations on shore. The personnel for the various signal detachments were all drawn from the Home Fleet. They were faced with the task of operating wireless sets to which they were not accustomed, and with but little time to practice with them. The ease with which they overcame this difficulty and the speed and accuracy with which the many signals were passed says much for their individual skill and for the instruction and training they were given by the naval officer to whom I have referred above.

State of the light at the time of the landings

15. The original intention was to make four simultaneous landings at 0630 hrs but, after further examination of the meteorological data, it was considered that such early landings would force the ALCs and MLCs* to make their difficult approaches in conditions of what may be termed 'dangerous' darkness. The time of landing was therefore put back to 0645 hrs. In the event the morning of 4th March was

exceptionally clear and calm. There was no fog, no sea mist, no rain or snow and what breeze there was blew from a favourable though unusual quarter. Thus the landing craft approached the shore under rather better light conditions than were required or were desirable. However, it is difficult to see how such rare conditions can be legislated for except by abandoning the idea of making the landings simultaneously and allowing instead a 30 or 45 minutes period during any part of which they may take place. The obvious danger of such a procedure is that the defences at the point where the earliest landing is made may be given time to warn other points at which landings are attempted 10 or 20 minutes later.

[*MLCs- Landing craft for mechanised vehicles.]

Effect of low temperatures

16. Even during the short passage between HMS *Queen Emma*, HMS *Princess Beatrix* and the various ports, it was found that weapons had a distinct tendency to freeze up and become hard to operate. Should such low temperatures be anticipated again in the future, some special arrangements would have to be made to guard against this danger.

Opposition

17. At no point on shore was any opposition encountered, though some of the enemy personnel, notably those at the air station outside Svolvaer who were armed with a machine gun and other weapons, might well have inflicted casualties and delayed progress. So far as is known, the only shots fired by the enemy were the three or four rounds aimed at HMS *Somali* by the armed trawler *Krebbs*. No casualties were incurred by our own troops.

Reception by the inhabitants

18. The reports received from the Military Commanders at each port show that in every case our troops were given a welcome, the genuine enthusiasm of which cannot be doubted. Although it must have been abundantly clear that the demolitions which were being carried through would inevitably have sad effects on the livelihood of many, there always seemed to be the over-riding realisation that they were well worth aiding and abetting so long as they were also the means of retarding and interfering with production urgently required by the enemy. In many instances, the gifts distributed by our troops were at once matched by presents given to them by the inhabitants. In short, they were welcomed by a people whose natural virility and inherent soundness of character had ridden safely over the many insidious dangers which must follow from months of enemy occupation.

Military actions at the four ports

19. The following were the Senior Military Officers at each port:-
     At Stamsund – Lieutenant Colonel J F Durnford-Slater, RA.
     At Henningsvaer – Captain A S Ronald, KRRC.
     At Svolvaer – Lieutenant Colonel D S Lister, MC, The Buffs.
     At Brettesnes – Major M E Kerr, The Rifle Brigade.

20. The characteristics which seem to stand out from the operations as a whole are the excellent and frequent reports rendered by the senior officers at each port; the speed with which the detachments carried out their allotted duties, and the initiative shown by junior commanders in seeking for and carrying through useful and important tasks in addition to those specifically mentioned in the operational orders. I would particularly bring to your notice Lieutenant Colonel D S Lister, MC, The Buffs, who was in command of the operations at Svolvaer and Brettesnes and Lieutenant Colonel J F Durnford-Slater, Royal Artillery, who commanded the troops at Stamsund and Henningsvaer.

21. Lieutenant H M Turner, Royal Engineers and his section of No 55 Field Company Royal Engineers accomplished excellent work and carried out their tasks in a most skilled and competent manner.

22. Consolidated results of the operation are given in the Annexure.

Assistance rendered by the Norwegian troops

23. It is not too much to say that the operations on shore could not have been carried through within the time limits laid down in the Operation Orders or with the ease or good relations and understanding that existed had it not been for the enthusiast help and co-operation of the Norwegian detachment commanded by Captain Martin Linge. This officer never spared himself for one moment either during the preparatory period or during the raid itself. His enthusiasm and personality were infectious and it is hoped that his most valuable services and those of his detachment may be brought to the notice of the Norwegian authorities.

Outline plan for the raid

24. The outline plan for the Military Operations, which dealt with the total force to be employed, the division of the force between the four ports and the main tasks to be accomplished at each was drawn up in the office of the Director of Combined Operations. This plan was not altered in any one of its essential features.

Naval assistance and co-operation

25. Nothing could have been more inspiring than the help and assistance given to the Military force by the Royal Navy. It is suffice to say that no officer, NCO or man left Scapa Flow without the deep seated and often expressed hope that it would be his privilege to co-operate again with the Royal Navy in the very near future.

26. It is hoped that it will not be considered out of place if in this, a Military Report, some tribute is paid to the Senior Naval Officer with Force Rebel. Captain C Caslon RN (HMS *Somali*) was responsible for carrying through the arrangements which resulted in the force arriving undetected and with absolute accuracy at the appointed destination, and for their safe return to this country.

Throughout the operation his bearing, skill and obvious ability could not but give confidence to all those who came in contact with him. So far as the Military Commanders were concerned there could not have been a more easy person to work with and this comment applies with equal force to the captains of the other destroyers forming the 6th Flotilla.

Signed J C Haydon,
Brigadier,
Commanding Special Service Brigade.

Annexure
Consolidated Reports of Operation Claymore
4th March, 1941

1. Shipping destroyed and sunk

SUNK BY	SHIP	TONNAGE	FLAG
HMS *Somali*	Armed Trawler *Krebbs*	300	German
HMS *Tartar*	*Hamburg*	9,780	German
HMS *Tartar*	*Pasajes*	1,996	German
HMS *Tartar*	*Felix Heumann*	2,468	German
HMS *Bedouin* (after partial destruction by naval demolition party)	*Mira*	1,152	Norwegian
Naval Demolition Parties	*Eilenau*	1,404	German
Naval Demolition Parties	*Rissen*	250	German
Naval Demolition Parties	*Ando*	300	German
Naval Demolition Parties	*Grotto*	200	German
RE Demolition Parties	*Bernhardt Schultze*	1,500	German

19,350 tons

2. Factories Destroyed.

Stamsund
Lofotens Cod Boiling Plant
Møller Medicinal Oil
Yttervicks Cod Meal
Blix Cod Oil
Vagle Cod Oil
Henningsvaer
Allen & Hanbury*
Johannes Malnes*
Aarseather Bros.*
Renneberg*
Christiansen*
Linon Seleskap*
Clement Johnson*
Electric Light Plant
Henningsvaer Oil Feeding Stuffs
[*Boiling Plant]

Svolvaer
Cuba*

Silda *
[*Herring oil]

Brettesnes
Oil and fish meal factory
Cod meal factory

3. Oil Tanks and approximate total of oil destroyed.

Stamsund
Kerosene Tanks
Oil Tanks

Henningsvaer
Hendriksen Paraffin Tank
S Bang Oil Tanks

Svolvaer
Oil Tanks
Oil Tanks at Klofterhl

Brettesnes
Oil Tanks

Approximate total = 800,000 gallons.

4. Quisling supporters captured   12

5. Enemy subjects captured:

(a)	Naval	7
(b)	Army	3
(c)	Air Force	15
(d)	Merchant Navy	172
(e)	Civilians	14
(f)	SS Police	2
		= <u>213</u>
	Total Prisoners	225

Appendix IX

Report from No 4 Commando Operation Claymore

Report on operations at Port X on 4.3.41

1. At 0500 hrs, 4 ALCs and 2 MLCs were lowered to the water and proceeded under the stern of HMS *Tartar* to Port X. All details of embarkation and approach to the objective went smoothly, but it is considered that if there had been resistance the time of landing was late.

2. ALC Q2 landed its party at quay near Customs House at 0615 hrs. The scaling ladders taken with this party, and other parties were invaluable. The first party to land secured the quay and approached without any difficulty. A party also took control of the Post Office leaving a Norwegian Officer in charge of the operation room where several calls for Narvik were intercepted and stopped. The Hotel was also taken over and several German prisoners taken, including the Director of the newly established Fishery Control, whose office produced valuable documents. Documents were also taken from the Harbour Master's office.

3. ALC Q4 landed at 0625 hrs. A post was established immediately at road fork north of the word yards on Plan X, and the Norwegian personnel under the command of Captain Linge with Captain the Lord Lovat, as Liaison Officer proceeded through the town gathering information and arresting quislings and Germans. Unfortunately the Harbour Master and the Mayor had escaped before this party arrived, presumably owing to the gun fire. The Naval Signal Personnel in this landing craft immediately established a Signal Station on the top of a building on the quay.

4. 2 MLCs landed at the quay at 0630 hrs, with local and general reserve and comforts, which were immediately unloaded. The Royal Naval demolition party were also in these landing craft, and proceeded to transfer on arrival to ALC Q4. A sub-section of the local reserve established a post on bridge across the Storo Valen, and the remainder manned anti-aircraft positions and supplied guard over comforts. The general reserve under Captain Montgomerie remained concentrated under the hand of the commander at Force HQ. At 0830 hrs, on information received a party from the general reserve under Captain the Lord Lovat with Captain Linge, proceeded in commandeered cars and buses to an Air Force barracks situated in a village about 10 kilometres away. The barracks were captured without difficulty in spite of the fact that a machine gun was mounted on the premises. 15 German Air Force signallers were captured and a large wireless transmitting set was destroyed. Papers, arms and equipment were taken. The Officer in charge of the post on the bridge across the Storo Valen, patrolled forward from his post to investigate the

Shell tankage marked F on plan, which had been reported destroyed. One oil tank was found half full of diesel oil. This was set on fire and completely destroyed.

Captain Pettiward assisted by Lieutenant Strachan, had by this time established a Prisoner of War concentration camp on the quay, into which many enemy personnel and quisling supporters were taken and searched.

A recruiting post had also been set up on the quay in charge of a Norwegian Officer where recruits were being mustered.

The comforts, by 1030 hrs, had been handed over to the local Welfare Society for distribution.

5. The Royal Naval demolition party had proceeded in ALC Q4 and boarded and destroyed the following German vessels:-

SS *Felix Heumann*, cargo vessel of approximately 3000 tons.

Cargo vessel SS *Eilenau* of Bremerhaven of approximately 3000 tons.

Trawler *F.D. Rissen* of approximately 1000 tons.

Crew and papers were taken.

The mail steamer was boarded and searched, but after a consultation with the Captain and the Norwegian Harbour Master it was decided to leave it unmolested. Inspection of the ship's log book showed that it only plied within the Lofoten Islands, and its destruction would be an unnecessary hardship on the Norwegians.

6. SS *Hamburg* approximately 8000 tons, a factory and refrigerator ship, was set on fire by HMS *Tartar*. The crew and ship's papers were captured later on shore.

7. At 0615 hrs, ALC Q1 landed near Cuba Factory . The machinery was completely destroyed and the building in flames by 0950 hrs. Documents were taken form the office. A depot with stocks of filled barrels situated nearby was also set on fire.

8. At 0620 hrs, ALC Q3 landed at Klofterhal. Three oil tanks and a store of crude oil was set on fire and destroyed. The new Silda factory, was located nearby, was destroyed and set on fire and documents taken. A German timber ship of about 1500 tons, *Bernhardt Schultze* lying alongside the Silda quay was also captured, blown up and papers taken from it.

Withdrawal from the raiding area

All troops, equipment, volunteers, prisoners, captured documents and equipment were evacuated on time and without incident. The last ALC with the Commanding Officer left the main quay at 1230 hrs.

General

Altogether 8 German civilians, 1 German Police official, 11 quislings, 23 captured German Military ORs, some German officers and 152 German merchant seamen were captured and transferred to HMS *Queen Emma*.

85 volunteers for the Norwegian Army and Navy were recruited and 8 Norwegian ladies were recruited for nursing and clerical duties.

Documents and equipment captured

Documents other than personal papers include secret documents from the wireless station mentioned in paragraph 4. This wireless station has subsequently been established at being at Kabelvog. Uncensored reports by a Military propaganda correspondent who was himself captured, and a GAF mail bag was being taken by hand from Tromso to Trondheim. Ship's papers included confidential documents and secret codes. All personal papers, passports etc., were taken from prisoners.

Enemy clothing and equipment

A quantity of enemy uniform and equipment was taken and transferred to HMS *Queen Emma*. This included 1 light machine gun and approximately a dozen rifles, together with small arms ammunition and bombs. All the above papers and equipment have been placed in charge of Lieutenant Strachan.

Conclusion

I wish to place on record the valuable assistance given to me throughout the raid by Captain Martin Linge of the Norwegian Army. Thanks to his energetic assistance in getting information, arranging transport, organising guides and local knowledge, the results set out above were accomplished. I would also like to make special mention of the communications established by the Royal Navy signallers. They were excellent throughout. All Royal Naval officers i/c landing craft and Lieutenant Bone, RN, i/c the Royal Naval demolition party, carried out their duties in an exemplary manner. Second Lieutenant Turner and his detachment of Royal Engineers carried out their tasks thoroughly. All ranks of No 4 Commando carried out their tasks in a satisfactory manner and the reception accorded by the populace was overwhelming in its enthusiasm.

D S Lister
Lieutenant Colonel
Commanding No 4 Commando
At sea HMS *Queen Emma*
6.3.41.

Appendix X

Naval & Military Reports relating to Operation Archery

Report from the Commander-in-Chief of the Home Fleet Admiral Sir John C Tovey on the raid on military and economic objectives in the vicinity of Vaagso Island dated 7th January 1942 to the Lords Commissioners of the Admiralty

Raid on Military and Economic Objectives in the vicinity of Vaagso Island

The following despatch was submitted to the Lords Commissioners of the Admiralty on the 7th January 1942, by Admiral Sir John C Tovey KCB, DSO, Commander-in-Chief, Home Fleet.

Be pleased to lay before Their Lordships the attached report on Operation Archery.

2. The operation was well conceived, planned and rehearsed with skill and thoroughness, and executed with great efficiency, precision and boldness. Though a minor operation, it affords a fine example of smooth and effective co-operation between the three Services and reflects great credit on Rear-Admiral H M Burrough, CB, Brigadier J C Haydon, DSO, OBE, and all officers, ratings and ranks taking part.

3. The co-operation of the aircraft of Coastal and Bomber Commands was most effective. The operation could not have proceeded without it.

Signed Jack C Tovey,
Admiral,
Commander-in-Chief

From: The Naval and Military Commanders, Operation Archery
Date: 2nd January 1942

To: The Commander-in-Chief, Home Fleet

The following report by the Naval and Military Commanders, on Operation Archery which was carried out on Saturday, 27th December 1941, is forwarded.

2. The intention of Operation Archery was to carry out a raid on military and economic objectives in the vicinity of Vaagso Island with the object of harassing the coastal defences of SW Norway and diverting the attention of the enemy naval and air forces from Operation Anklet.

Planning

3. The Naval and Military Commanders were appointed on 6th December 1941, which gave three weeks to plan and rehearse the operation. This is considered to be the absolute minimum time required. At least two full rehearsals should take place to allow timing and communications to be perfected. Weather conditions frequently make rehearsals impossible for days on end and this must be allowed for in the programme.

4. After the preliminary meeting between Force Commanders and the Air Adviser to the Chief of Combined Operations, the plan was drawn up in London. It is strongly recommended that this procedure be followed in future as the facilities for obtaining the latest intelligence and information of all kinds are so much better than those elsewhere.

Composition of the Force

5. (a) Naval

HMS *Kenya* (Rear Admiral Commanding 10th Cruiser Squadron-Naval Commander)

HMS *Onslow* (Captain (D), 17th Destroyer Flotilla)

HMS *Oribi*

HMS *Offa*

HMS *Chiddingfold*

HMS *Prince Charles*

HMS *Prince Leopold*

HM Submarine *Tuna* *

* *Kenya* acted as HQ ship and carried Brigade Operational HQ

Onslow, Oribi, Offa and *Chiddingford* Destroyers

Prince Charles and *Prince Leopold* – Infantry Assault Ships, later known as Landing Ships, Infantry (Small).

(b) Military

Operational Headquarters, Special Service Brigade

Detachment of the Special Service Brigade Signal Section

All ranks of No 3 Commando

Two Troops (less one Section) of No 2 Commando

An RAMC detachment from No 6 Commando

An RE detachment from No 6 Commando

Troops of the Royal Norwegian Army

Officers from the War Office (M.I.9)

A Press Unit of correspondents and photographers

Total Military Personnel: 51 Officers 525 Other Ranks

(c) Air Force

Ten Hampdens of 50 Squadron (for smoke laying and bombing)

Blenheims-fighter protection

Beaufighters-fighter protection

19 Blenheims of Bomber Command (for bombing diversion)

6. The Naval Force with the exception of *Onslow* and *Chiddingfold*, assembled at Scapa Flow by 15th December, when embarkation of the Military was completed. A programme of rehearsals followed.

7. The Force proceeded from Scapa at 2215 24th December arriving at Sollum Voe at 1330 25th December. Heavy weather was encountered on passage and on arrival both *Prince Charles* and *Prince Leopold* discovered and reported various defects including compartments forward flooded to a depth of about fourteen feet.

8. In order to allow time to make *Prince Charles* and *Prince Leopold* as seaworthy as possible, and in view of the latest meteorological reports it was decided at 1615 to postpone the operation for 24 hours.

9. All ships had topped up with fuel and all repairs had been completed by 1400 26th December. The weather forecast was far more promising and it was therefore decided to sail the Force at 1600 that day to carry out Operation Archery at dawn, 27th December 1941.

The Naval Approach

10. The passage across the North Sea commenced in bad weather but, as anticipated, the weather rapidly improved as the Force proceeded to the eastward and conditions were perfect on arrival off the Norwegian coast.

11. Position by the landfall, which was made exactly as planned, was confirmed on sighting the mark submarine *Tuna* in the position ordered. She was passed at 0730, one minute late on planned time.

12. The Force entered Vaagsfjord* on time apparently unobserved and it seems possible the look-out post at Hovdenoes was not manned. *Kenya* moved over to the southern side of the fjord while *Chiddingfold* led *Prince Charles* and *Prince Leopold* to the bay south of Hollevik as planned. *Onslow* closed on *Kenya*'s starboard quarter and *Offa* closed astern of *Kenya*. *Oribi* remained near the entrance of the entrance of the fjord to cover the Force from the west.
    [*Vaagso is less than 2½ miles up this fjord, whose entrance is less than half a mile wide.]

The Bombardment

13. Hampden aircraft* timed their arrival in the area perfectly, keeping all the attention well up-fjord and drawing the fire of four or five light AA guns.
    [*The aircraft operated from bases on the NE coast of Scotland, a distance of approximately 300 miles.]

14. At 0842 *Prince Charles* made the signal indicating that the Assault Landing Craft were formed up and moving ahead. *Kenya* was moving ahead slowly and at 0848, just before the line of fire opened, starshells were fired to burst over Maaloy Island. These were bursting and illuminating the point of aim on the island when, half a minute later, the line of fire opened and the bombardment commenced, *Onslow* and *Offa* joining in as soon as clear.

15. The battery on Rugsundo, which had already been bombed by Hampden aircraft. opened fire on *Kenya* at 0856. It was erratic and the rate of fire low, but nevertheless proved a great nuisance throughout our stay. The guns were thought to be smaller

than 5.1 inch and were more probably about 4.7 inch. On bursting, the shells gave off a purple smoke.

16. At 0857¾ the cease bombardment signal was made by the Military in the Assault Landing Craft now rapidly approaching their objectives. The Naval bombardment of Maaloy Island thus came to an end and from reports received from the Military who landed on the island, there is no doubt whatsoever that it had been completely successful.

17. At 0858 *Kenya* having changed over to full charges, opened fire on Rugsundo. After 2½ minutes the enemy guns were silenced. The smoke bombs, dropped by the Hampdens near Rugsundo, were by now effective and gave cover to our ships in the fjord.

Smoke Laying by Aircraft

18. At 0858½ on a signal from the *Kenya*, seven Hampden aircraft, showing great skill and dash, came in at very low altitudes to drop their smoke bombs. These were placed on Maaloy Island, and as a result the landing there was unopposed. The bombs were dropped on a front of approximately 250 yards, and as there was practically no wind, gave a screen of ideal density in which visibility was some 15-20 yards.

19. The smoke bombs dropped at the landing place at South Vaagso were only 50 yards away from the desired position, but one of them most unfortunately struck a landing craft setting it alight and causing some 20 casualties from burns.

20. Despite this serious accident it is considered that these bombs were of great value, for they enabled the troops to be put ashore with few casualties from the automatic weapons which were bringing fire to bear on the landing place, and which might have inflicted even heavier losses had they been given a clear and unimpeded view of their targets.

21. It must here be noted that the aircraft which dropped the bombs at South Vaagso appeared to be on fire and not properly under control. It was almost certainly the Hampden bomber which later fell into the sea near the entrance to Vaagsfjord. If this was so, then the degree of accuracy in placing of the bombs must have been the result of a very gallant attempt on the part of the crew of the aircraft to carry out in full their allotted tasks. *Prince Leopold* proceeded to the rescue, but unfortunately only one of the three crew picked up, survived.

22. One Hampden bomber which overshot the target attacked and silenced positions in the area with machine gun fire.

23. It is regretted that one other Hampden failed to return from this operation.

24. Of the three Hampdens bombers detailed to attack the Rugsundo battery, one had to return with engine trouble, but the other two carried out an attack, the results of which could not be observed from Kenya but which were apparently very successful.

Military Operations

25. For the purpose of the operation, the Military Forces set out in paragraph 5 (b) were organised into the Operational Headquarters which remained throughout in the Flagship *Kenya*, with the Brigade Commander in close touch with the Naval

Commander on the bridge, and the troops who were put ashore in Assault Landing Craft from *Kenya*, *Prince Charles* and *Prince Leopold* and in the ship's boats from *Oribi*.

The Forces ashore were divided into five groups for purposes which will become clear in the course of this report.

General Tasks of each Group

26. The purpose of Group 1 was to land near Hollevik and clear the Halnoesvik area where a German gun had been reported. Having accomplished this task Group 1 was to move along the coastal road to South Vaagso and form a reserve for Group 2 unless given other orders.

    Group 2 which was to be put ashore immediately south west of South Vaagso, was to attack the town itself and carry out a number of military and industrial tasks.

    Group 3 was to assault the island of Maaloy.

    Group 4 was retained as a floating reserve in the hands of the Military Commander of the Force.

    Group 5 was to be landed from a destroyer on the western shore of Ulvesund in order to cut communications between North and South Vaagso and to send a fighting patrol into the latter village.

The Landings

27. At 0839 *Prince Charles* and *Prince Leopold* lowered all landing craft which moved off in formation about three minutes later. In little more than five minutes No 1 Group was ashore at Halnoesvik and landing craft of Nos. 2 and 3 Groups were moving towards the headland just south of Halnoesvik village.

28. Just before the landing craft came into view of the enemy defences in South Vaagso and Maaloy Island, *Kenya* opened fire. The Naval bombardment was extremely accurate and most effective, and Lieutenant Colonel J F Durnford-Slater, who was in command of Group 2 and the senior officer proceeding ashore, was able to let the landing craft of Group 2 and 3 approach to within 100 yards of their landing places before sending up the cease bombardment signal. *Kenya* signalled the Hampden aircraft who then came in at very low altitudes to drop their smoke bombs. As a result of these bombs Group 3 completed their landing unopposed and the volume of fire brought to bear on Group 2 was considerably reduced.

The Operations Ashore

29. Groups Nos. 2 and 3 landed almost simultaneously, and from that time onwards the sequence of events was as follows:-

30. Group 1 cleared the area and village of Halnoesvik very rapidly and signalled the Headquarters ships for instructions. They were at once ordered to move along the coastal road and to come into reserve at Lieutenant Colonel J F Durnford-Slater's Headquarters which were situated near Group 2's landing place, this signal was made at 0950.

31. Group 3 very quickly gained control of Maaloy Island, where those enemy troops who had not been killed by the enemy bombardment were for the most part demoralised and dazed by its effect, and quickly surrendered. At 0920 Major J M T

F Churchill was able to signal that all guns on the island were in our hands and four minutes later he reported that the whole area was under control. *Oribi* carrying Group 5 and following *Onslow*, moved past Maaloy some ten minutes later, as soon as the smoke had cleared sufficiently for them to do so, and entered Ulvesund.

32. Group 2 from the start, encountered very stiff opposition, both from German infantry who fought to the last man in the buildings in which they were established, and from snipers, armed often with automatic rifles, who took up positions on the hillside west of the town where they were very difficult to locate owing to the excellent natural cover. It must be emphasised that the opposition in South Vaagso was severe in degree and skillful in quality. It appears from the interrogation of prisoners that the garrison had been fortuitously augmented by a detachment who had been moved into the town for Christmas but, however that may be, there is no doubt that the fighting spirit, marksmanship and efficiency of the enemy in this area was of a high order.

33. At 1020 Group 5 were landed just south of the village of North Vaagso. They cratered the coast road between North and South Vaagso and were able to capture a number of prisoners who had escaped ashore from ships attacked by Oribi and Onslow. A fighting patrol which was sent forward into North Vaagso directly the Group had landed, collected the chief Quisling, took over the telephone exchange and, before leaving, wrecked the instruments.

34. In the meantime Group 3 had been instructed (0925) to send a party by landing craft to destroy the herring oil factory at Mortenes, and at 1015 Captain A S Ronald landed with his troops in the area of the factory and completed its destruction without meeting opposition.

35. From 1000 hours onwards, the situation became confused in South Vaagso, where Group 2 were encountering strong opposition in the northern end of the town. The destruction of communications with the forward troops rendered control by the Flagship difficult.

36. By 1020 hours the whole of Group 4 had been despatched to the assistance of Group 2, and were committed on the left flank.

37. By 1030 hours house-to-house fighting in the centre and northern end of the town had become bitter, resulting in severe casualties, especially in officers and senior NCO's. Group 1 arrived from Halnoesvik and was committed in support of No 4 Troop in the centre. With the authority of Force HQ, Group 3 on Maaloy Island contacted Group 2, and on request No 6 Troop was despatched.

38. No 5 Group at North Vaagso were ordered to move south and close on the rear of the enemy in South Vaagso.

39. No 1 Troop (Group 2) secured the landing place, cleared the southern end of the town, capturing a prominent Quisling, and prepared the main demolitions.

40. At 1230 hours Lieutenant Colonel Durnford-Slater, after personally directing operations in the town, reported to Force Headquarters that resistance was nearly overcome and that demolitions were in progress.

41. As the majority of the industrial targets had been destroyed and as landing craft were becoming dispersed in ferrying wounded and Norwegian volunteers out to the ships and might take some time to reorganise for withdrawal purposes, the

Military Commander, in agreement with the Naval Commander, ordered re-embarkation at 1250 hours.

42. The withdrawal of all groups was carried out without opposition. The Firda factory, which was the last of the industrial targets, and the Sternes lighthouse were demolished before the troops re-embarked.

43. Group 5, who had been delayed in their southward move along the coast road by the shelling from beached merchant shipping in Ulvesund, were ordered to re-embark in Oribi to the north of South Vaagso.

44. At 1408 hours Lieutenant Colonel Durnford-Slater reported that all troops had left the shore, and returned himself in the last landing craft.

45. The re-embarkation had been completed and all landing craft hoisted by 1434.

46. In considering the course of the operation particular attention is drawn to the following factors which both had important bearings on the course of the fighting: in the first place, the hampering effect of the desire to comply strictly with orders which had been issued to avoid all possible damage to Norwegian property; and in the second place, the conflicting claims of the comparatively short time limit imposed by the whole nature of the operation, and of the restrictions on speed which are inherent in all street fighting but particularly when it is conducted against determined opposition.

47. It here requires mention that the opposition was overcome, and all the demolition tasks completed, often under heavy fire, well within the time limits laid down that such results could not possibly have been obtained had it not been for the personal leadership of Lieutenant Colonel Durnford-Slater, and for the sense of discipline, the initiative and courage that was shown time and again by junior leaders, both officers and NCOs.

Task Completed

48. One hundred and two prisoners were captured, comprising seven officers (1 Army and 6 Merchant Navy), 91 ratings and other ranks (40 Army, 15 Navy and 36 Merchant Seamen), and 4 Norwegian quislings. In addition 77 Norwegian volunteers were embarked. It is estimated that at least 150 Germans were killed in South Vaagso and Maaloy by Naval, Army and RAF Forces in the course of the operation.

49. The tasks executed on shore were as follows:-
    i. All German offices were burnt or demolished.
    ii. The W/T station and mast were destroyed.
    iii. The German car and lorry garage were destroyed.
    iv. One German tank of 10 to 15 tons was destroyed.
    v. Four coast defence guns and one anti-aircraft gun on Maaloy Island were blown up.
    vi. The petrol tanks on Maaloy Island were cut by explosives.
    vii. The ammunition store on Maaloy Island was demolished.
    viii. The German barracks and headquarters on Maaloy Island were burnt out by the initial Naval bombardment.
    ix. A searchlight and generator were blown up on Maaloy Island.
    x. A beach mine store was destroyed.

xi. A telephone cable hut was destroyed.

xii. All huts used as billets by German soldiers, both in South Vaagso and Maaloy were burnt down.

xiii. The Ulvesund Hotel, entirely occupied by German soldiers and held as a strong point, was burnt down.

xiv. The mechanism of Sternes lighthouse was destroyed.

xv. The road was cratered between North and South Vaagso.

xvi. The telephone exchange at Rodberg was taken over and apparatus smashed.

xvii. The building and plant of the main canning factory in South Vaagso were entirely destroyed by explosives.

xviii. The herring oil factory at Mortenes was entirely destroyed by explosives and fire.

xix. The Firda factory was set on fire and left blazing.

xx. A smaller canning factory and herring oil factory were set on fire, and the plant damaged by explosives.

Naval and Air Operations – 0900-1445.

50. During this period *Prince Charles*, *Prince Leopold* and *Chiddingfold* had moved across to Slaaken Bay on the south side of the fjord to obtain cover in accordance with the prearranged plan.

51. The first sortie of Blenheims arrived shortly before 0930 while *Oribi* and *Onslow* were taking up position to enter Ulvesund but it was not possible to establish reliable R/T communication with them. (Maaloy Island was now in our hands but the smoke was still too thick for the destroyers to pass through Maaloysund.)

52. Two minutes later at 0932, Rugsundo Battery reopened fire on *Kenya* who hotly engaged with A and B Turrets and again silenced the guns which did not reopen fire until 1308.

53. By 0930 the smoke screen across the Rugsundo line of fire was thinning and *Chiddingfold* was ordered to reinforce with smoke floats and funnel smoke, while moving fast. She did this well and also engaged the battery with a few salvoes.

54. At 0945 Maaloysund was sufficiently clear for the destroyers to proceed. *Oribi* followed by *Onslow* entered Ulvesund.

55. The first enemy aircraft appeared at 1005, when two Me 109s came in and immediately engaged two of our Blenheims, one of which was shot down two minutes later. The Blenheim would possibly not have been lost and the mortality among German aircraft later in the day, would probably have been higher, if efficient R/T communication between ship and aircraft could have been established and maintained.

56. Quite apart from the need for efficient communication it was apparent that two RAF officers should be carried in the Headquarters ship with the sole duties of concentrating on the air situation and directing the fighters. The ideal would be to have officers personally known to the fighter pilots and for those officers to have carried out rehearsals from the Headquarters ship.

57. *Kenya* fired occasional salvoes at Rugsundo Battery, to check gun range and to discourage any attempt to get their guns functioning again.

58. The second sortie (Beaufighters) arrived at 1015 and about 25 minutes later was in pursuit of the first two enemy bombers - two Ju 88s - to put in an appearance. These two aircraft never got within range of *Kenya*'s guns. Only intermittent R/T communication could be established with the Beaufighters.

59. At 1100 *Kenya* opened fire at long range on two Me 109s who quickly turned away and disappeared to the south.

60. During this period the position regarding merchant shipping in Ulvesund had not been clarified so it was decided to send in *Kenya*'s motor dinghy, with Lieutenant J N Kempton, RN, in charge, to investigate and report. After entering Maaloy Sound this boat was heavily fired upon, caught fire and burnt out. The crew were rescued by a Support Landing Craft.

61. About noon, a small number of enemy bombers were sighted to the northwards but no attack developed at this stage.

62. During the period since the bombardment of Maaloy Island had been completed, *Offa* had been protecting the Force from the west, and shortly after noon reported a merchant ship and armed trawler escort proceeding to Vaagsfjord from the north. She was ordered to capture if possible and *Chiddingfold* ordered to support her. Unfortunately, in spite of all efforts, the merchant ship, SS Anhalt, beached herself and the escort vessel endeavoured to escape.

63. *Offa* proceeded to chase and engage the armed trawler *Donner*, securing several hits. The crew abandoned ship but the vessel continued to steam out to sea at 10 knots. *Offa* proceeded alongside the trawler and, finding that she had insufficient fuel for the return passage to the UK under a prize crew, destroyed her and then picked up survivors from her crew.

64. During this period *Chiddingfold* had closed on the merchant ship *Anhalt* and, using a loud hailer, ordered the crew, in German, to bring their boats alongside. They were told that if the order was disobeyed they would be fired upon. The boats disregarded the warning and pulled for the shore, only a few yards distant. *Chiddingfold* immediately opened fire and sank one boat. The other, although hit, succeeded in escaping inshore while *Chiddingfold* was engaging some enemy aircraft.

65. It was at this time, 1236, that all ships became engaged with enemy bombers. Several formations, generally consisting of two or three Heinkels, were driven off and their bombs dropped wide. One He 111 was destroyed.

66. These raids continued until 1300 and shortly afterwards Rugsundo Battery reopened fire. *Kenya* immediately replied from X and Y turrets and with 4 inch. *Kenya* was hit by one round on the armour belt and a few minutes later a near miss abreast the port torpedo tubes slightly wounded one rating. At 1317 *Kenya* received a hit which burst and holed her about ten feet above the waterline abreast the bridge. Rugsundo Battery was then finally silenced.

Onslow and *Oribi* in Ulvesund.

67. Having received the signal that Maaloy Island was in our hands and Maaloysund clear, the destroyers passed through the narrows and entered Ulvesund at 0941. A good deal of light fire was directed at the ships and *Oribi* sustained three minor casualties.

68. When clear of the smoke, the German SS *Regmar Edzard Fritzen*, SS *Normar* and armed trawler *Föhn* were observed proceeding so as to beach themselves in the small bay immediately to the north of Brandhaevnes Point. Shots were fired across their bows and their upper decks were swept with Oerlikon fire but they had gained sufficient time to succeed in their project.

69. *Oribi* proceeded up Ulvesund and landed Group 5 at 1007. Two Me 109s were in the vicinity one of which attacked *Oribi* with cannon fire but obtained no hits.

70. *Oribi* and *Onslow* then proceeded to destroy the three ships referred to in paragraph 68, the Dutch schuyt *Eismeer* which had also been abandoned and another German merchant ship, the *Anita L.M. Russ*, with a tug in company, which at this time had entered Ulvesund apparently unaware that a raid was in progress.

71. *Oribi* after an engagement with two low-flying Me 109s re-embarked the remainder of Group 5 with their prisoners, while both destroyers gave supporting fire and dealt with snipers who were troublesome during the re-embarkation. On completion of their task they rejoined the Force at Vaagsfjord at 1356 and then engaged Rugsundo to keep that Battery quiet while *Kenya* was re-embarking her troops. *Chiddingfold* also laid a smoke screen to mask it. All troops having been re-embarked the Force commenced to withdraw at 1445.

Bombing Diversions

72. At 1202 13 Blenheims from No 114 Squadron, each carrying four 250lb GP bombs and some 4-lb incendiaries attacked from a height of 250 feet the aerodrome at Herdla*. Many hits were observed on the timber runways and an enemy fighter was seen to turn over while taxiing. PRU photographs taken immediately after the attack confirmed that there were at least 20 new bomb craters on the aerodrome. [*Herdla, the nearest enemy aerodrome, some 80 miles south of Vaagso.]

73. It is to be regretted that two Blenheims were lost from this squadron due to a collision after bombing; both aircraft fell into the sea. It is probable that this happened because one of them was hit by flak.

74. Six Blenheims from No 110 Squadron, each armed with two 500lb bombs left Lossiemouth at 0850 to patrol off the Norwegian coast southwards from Obrestad. After keeping together to a point two miles south west of Eigore the leader and one aircraft carried out an apparently successful attack on a single ship of 1,500 tons, while the remaining four proceeded towards a convoy observed four miles further south.

75. None of the four aircraft which turned south to attack the convoy have returned to base, but a number of explosions were seen round the convoy and one ship was observed to be sinking rapidly with her stern well out of the water. There is no evidence to show how these four aircraft became casualties, but one was seen to make a good landing in the sea with the port engine on fire, while another crashed into the sea after being attacked by a fighter.

Fighter protection

76. Fighter protection over the Force was provided from 0928 until 1615 by Blenheim and Beaufighter aircraft of 404, 254, 235, 236 and 248 Squadrons operating from Wick and Sumburgh aerodromes. Five sorties were made, and with the exception

of the fourth, enemy aircraft were encountered by each sortie and a satisfactory toll taken of them, for the loss of 2 Blenheims and 2 Beaufighters.

The Naval Withdrawal

77. The destroyers were ordered to proceed out of the fjord and form a screen for the assault ships and *Kenya*, who left last. *Kenya* stopped off Hovdenoes Point and fired 15 rounds of 6-inch, at point blank range, at the merchant ship Anhalt and she was left aground and burning fiercely.

78. A few minutes later, at about 1500, when ships had just cleared the fjord, a formation of Heinkel bombers came in to attack. These aircraft were hotly engaged by *Kenya* and the destroyers with the result that the formation broke up and their sticks of bombs fell wide.

79. After the escort of Beaufighters had had to return to base at 1600 single aircraft attacks were driven off by the Force in the dusk and bright moonlight. When darkness fell a large alteration of course was made and the Force arrived at Scapa, without further incident, at 1600, 28th December 1941.

Signed   J C Haydon Brigadier.
            H M Burrough Rear Admiral.

Appendix XI

Selected Medal Citations for Operation Archery

Brigadier J C Haydon DSO OBE, Special Service Brigade
Bar to the Distinguished Service Order

Brigadier J C Haydon was the military force commander for the combined operations against Vaagso, Norway on 27th December 1941. This operation turned out to be the perfect example of the success that can be achieved by a perfectly planned coordinated and executed operation. The credit for the military side must fall entirely to Brigadier Haydon since not only did he plan and execute the operation, but as commander of the Special Service Brigade, was responsible for the training and state of efficiency of the SS Troops, without which this complete success could not have been achieved.

He remained on board the Naval Force Commanders Flagship, under fire, throughout the whole operation and was in the words of the sailors who took part 'an inspiration to all.'

Lieutenant Colonel J F Durnford-Slater Number 3 Commando
Distinguished Service Order

Lieutenant Colonel J F Durnford-Slater was the senior officer ashore during the operations at Vaagso in Southern Norway on 27th December 1941. He was in command of the assaults on the Isle of Maaloy at the town of South Vaagso, and was in immediate charge of the operations ashore following the landing on the latter objective. The task with which he faced was not easy, the opposition was unexpectedly heavy, and at once developed into house-to-house fighting. Under such conditions, when it was extremely difficult to maintain effective command over the independent actions, which were being fought, to gain control of the town in time for the various tasks to be completed.

Lieutenant Colonel Durnford-Slater on two occasions went forward to take charge of the situation, only returning to his HQ in order to report progress to the flagship at one period when the street fighting had become very bitter in character, and when the two leading troops had lost five out of six officers and nearly 40% of their effectiveness, he immediately took personal command of the leading troops, reorganised his forces, set the attack in motion again and completed the capture of the town. At this time, any delay or hesitation might have had the most serious results. He was constantly under fire, and both his orderlies were wounded beside him. His personal courage, complete coolness, and quick grasp of the situation were outstanding throughout the day and rightly inspired complete confidence. As a result all his allotted tasks were completed and the casualties inflicted on the enemy at least double those suffered by his own troops from enemy action. He left South Vaagso in the last craft to put off from any landing place.

Sergeant R G Herbert MM, The Northamptonshire Regiment attached Number 3 Commando
Distinguished Conduct Medal

During the operations at Vaagso in South Norway on 27th December 1941, L/Sergeant Herbert saw one of the enemy run into a dugout. He placed his men to cover the entrance and followed the man in alone. He found the German Battery Commander inside with some fifteen of his men whom he captured.

Later he personally bombed the enemy out of the front room of a warehouse, enabling his men to get forward without casualties. Throughout the operation he showed great determination, initiative, organising ability and powers of leadership. His personal gallantry and drive set an inspiring example to those under him.

Corporal E G White Number 3 Commando
Distinguished Conduct Medal

Throughout the operations at Vaagso in South Norway on 27th December 1941, Corporal White displayed leadership of a very high order coupled with a remarkable spirit. When his Troop Commander had been shot, the other officers in his troop put out of action and the Troop Sergeant Major delayed, Corporal White took command of the remnants of the troop. He carried out a series of assaults and proceeded in destroying a hotel which was manned as a strong point and continued in charge until the end of the operation. He personally accounted for some fourteen of the enemy. His gallantry and leadership were of a high order, and had a direct bearing on the allotted tasks being carried out, within the time limit which had been laid down.

Corporal M B Fitzpatrick RAC attached Number 3 Commando
Military Medal

Almost immediately after landing at Vaagso in South Norway, Corporal Fitzpatrick was acting as lead scout to his section. The advance was held up by a wire obstacle covered by heavy enemy fire. Corporal Fitzpatrick without hesitation moved forward alone and cut a gap through the wire, thus allowing the advance to continue without loss of time.

The moment was somewhat critical as a hold up in the early stages might have had serious delaying affects on the operation as a whole. Corporal Fitzpatrick's coolness and presence of mind quite definitely prevented any such delays occurring.

Appendix XII

RAF losses on Operation Archery

The RAF losses on this raid, which was the first time it had really committed a sizeable force to a Combined Operation were quite high - 11 aircraft were lost with only one man from any of these crews surviving. The complete list is as follows:

50 Squadron
Ten Hampdens from this Squadron were given the task of close air support to the Commando Force in the Vaagsfjord by bombing and dropping smoke.

Handley Page Hampden AE 369 VN
This was shot down in the vicinity of the Vaagsfjord while dropping smoke bombs. Of the four crew members lost only one body was recovered.
- Sergeant L F Redfern buried at Trondheim
- Sergeant D K Roberts
- Sergeant L R Brockett
- Sergeant A V W Sherwin

The last three aircrew mentioned have no known grave and are commemorated on the RAF Memorial to the Missing at Runnymede.

Handley Page Hampden AE 428 VN
This was also shot down by flak off Maaloy Island. Crew as follows:
- Sergeant R N Smith rescued from the sea but later killed in action on 7th February 1942.
- Sergeant D Bell
- Pilot Officer R Watson
- Sergeant J D Williams

The body of the last mentioned member of this crew was recovered and buried at sea. The other two were not recovered and all three are commemorated on the RAF Memorial to the Missing at Runnymede.

110 Squadron
Six aircraft from this Squadron flying Blenheims from RAF Lossiemouth were tasked with patrolling the Norwegian coast each armed with two 500 lb bombs. Four aircraft were lost as follows either by flak or enemy aircraft while attacking a convoy south of Egerøy:

Bristol Blenheim V 6429 VE
- Pilot Officer J B MacLeod
- Pilot Officer H G Harris
- Sergeant T E Anstey

All have no known grave and are commemorated on the RAF Memorial to the Missing at Runnymede.

Bristol Blenheim V 6448 VE

Apparently reported as crashing into the sea with one engine on fire. Nothing more ever heard of the crew and all commemorated on the Memorial to the Missing. The first two were RCAF.

- Pilot Officer D M Jenkinson
- Pilot Officer R J McLachlan
- Sergeant R C Hawkes

Bristol Blenheim Z 7317 VE

- Flight Lieutenant R T Blewett
- Pilot Officer M Murphy
- Sergeant J L Bell

Blewett's body was later recovered from the sea and is now buried at Sola churchyard, he was from the RNZAF. The other two commemorated at Runnymede.

Bristol Blenheim Z 7442 VE

- Sergeant N Kaby
- Sergeant R C Davis
- Sergeant N Coatesworth

Kaby's body was later recovered from the sea and is now buried in Trondheim, with the other two commemorated at Runnymede.

114 Squadron

Aircraft from this squadron flying from Lossiemouth in northern Scotland had been given the role of attacking Herdla airfield.

Bristol Blenheim V 6227 RT-Z

- Flight Sergeant R W Fisher
- Sergeant J Williamson
- Sergeant W F G Fletcher

Bristol Blenheim Z 7500 RT-H

- Sergeant K A Davis
- Sergeant J J B Ward
- Sergeant J E Kitley

These two aircraft collided over Herdla airfield during the attack and there were no survivors. All six casualties were buried at Bergen. Fisher was from the RAAF.

254 Squadron

Bristol Blenheim Z 6081 QY

- Pilot Officer D A Halsall
- Flying Officer J W Roche

- Sergeant F H Silk

No details known except that Halsall is now buried at Trondheim, Roche was from the RAAF and he and Frederick Silk are commemorated at Runnymede.

235 Squadron

This squadron provided the fighter cover for Operation Archery in the form of somewhat unsuitable Beaufighters and lost an aircraft, it had taken off from Dyce and was shot down by a Me109.

Bristol Beaufighter IC T 4765 LA-T
- Pilot Officer W H Hughes
- Sergeant C F Myhill

236 Squadron

Again this squadron provided fighter cover in the form of Beaufighters, they also suffered one aircraft lost. It was last seen after breaking off from attacking a Heinkel 111. It had taken off from Sumburgh.

Bristol Beaufighter IC T 4825 ND-U
- Pilot Officer R A Baseby
- Sergeant S D Gummery

None of the crews from the two aircraft above were recovered and all four are commemorated at Runnymede.

Appendix XIII

Report on Operation Archery by Lieutenant-Commander A de Costabadie DSC RN

I went north on the 22nd December and eventually went on board HMS *Kenya* at Scapa. Here I received orders from Rear Admiral Burrough to remain on board until we reached Sullum Voe, where I was transferred to HMS *Onslow*, commanded by Captain D. I was to be in charge of the boarding parties. The Rear Admiral informed me that I should be responsible for bringing back any merchant ships captured back to England and that, for that purpose, I should be appointed Commodore of the Convoy while the merchant ships were being taken from Norway to England.

During the passage to Norway the weather steadily improved, though it was a bit rough to start with. On the way over, I inspected my boarding party and turned in early. The operation started at dawn on the 27th and I watched the Assault Landing Craft leave their parent ships and also the bombardment of Maaloy by HMS *Kenya*.

Frankly I was worried about the boarding parties, which were found for me by the First Lieutenant of HMS *Onslow*. I was more than worried, I was in fact horrified. They consisted to the best of my recollection of one Sub-Lieutenant, one Midshipman, one Petty Officer, one Leading Seaman, three seamen and two stokers. None of these men appeared trained. They turned up when paraded in any sort of rig, so I roared them up and sent them off to get into proper rig. My position was very invidious, because, although I was in charge of the boarding parties, they were being provided by someone else and I had no say in their composition nor armament. I felt I could not interfere in any way, but must just carry on with whatever men were provided. I should like to say that my remarks do not apply to the two officers, who did their best to improve matters.

On entering Vaagso Fjord we sighted a German ship, the *Föhn*. The Captain of that ship was certainly a very gallant man. He grasped the situation very quickly and, in the face of very heavy fire, he rounded up the other German ships, the *Regmar Edzard Fritzen* and the *Normar* and drove them ahead of him. At the same time he opened fire on our aircraft and I am under the impression he may have hit one of them and brought it down. He steamed up the Fjord with Vaagso Port and Maaloy Island astern. We steamed after him. I think the first lesson to be learnt was that we were too kind to him. In my opinion we should have plastered him with pom-pom and machine gun fire, for all the way up the Fjord he was engaged in ditching his confidential books.

All the enemy ships rounded Brandhaevnes Point to port and then ran aground. The *Normar* to the southward, the *R E Fritzen* in the middle and the *Föhn* to the northward. The *Föhn* was definitely ahead of the others.

The order was given "Away boarding parties" and off we went in the *Onslow*'s motor boat. The boarding party got away at about 1000 hours. They were wearing No 3 rig with webbing equipment over it and they were armed with rifles, their bayonets were in their scabbards. I was carrying a revolver. None of the party carried grenades or anything suitable for setting ships on fire.

The distance between the *Onslow* and the *Föhn* was about 300 yards. When we left the *Onslow*'s side there was a bit of rifle fire coming from the shore to port. It came I think from the *Föhn*'s crew who had got ashore and were firing over their own ship at us. With me in the motor boat was Lieutenant Bacon, RNVR, whose instructions were to get the code books and any other secrets he could find on any of the ships.

Bacon and I were standing amidships in the motor boat and we both took rifles from the men in order to return the enemy's fire. This was not at first very successful as we found that the rifles were bunged up with thick grease and had never been inspected. I should also mention that the boarding party went away with empty stomachs. If my First Lieutenant had let nay men go into action without a proper meal I should have dealt very harshly with him.

I must repeat, however, that my position was invidious; I could not give the order to the boarding party for inspection port arms before we left the *Onslow*, for though I was in command of them I was only a visitor on the ship and, therefore, a guest. I had to take the boarding party on trust; I shall never do that again. I have already said they had no grenades or Thermite bombs.

Eventually Bacon and I managed to fire about ten rounds apiece at a range of about 400 yards at the men on the road and I thought I hit one, but of this I am not sure. We went alongside the *Föhn* and I scrambled up on deck. To reach the deck I stood on the canopy of the motor boat and jumped for it. We also had no ladders with us. On reaching the deck of the *Föhn* I found a rope and dropped it immediately overboard for the others to use in getting up the ship's side. I took four men and Lieutenant Bacon, who at once began his search. The fire directed against us was becoming unpleasant, so I took two seamen on to the upper deck. I should explain that the *Föhn* had run aground on an even keel. About 200 yards away to the north a party of the ship's crew had taken up a position on the road and were firing at us. It would have been impossible for us to board the other ships without silencing this party of enemy on the road.

I found two rifles and a lot of ammunition lying on the deck together with a corpse or two, one of which was the Captain, who had been on the bridge and had been killed in the act of throwing over more of his confidential books.

For a minute or two the fire was very heavy. I stood for a moment at the top of the companion ladder, therefore in shelter with two seamen and I decided not to take them on deck with me. I then left the shelter of the companion way and walked four yards to where one of the ships boats was hanging. Resting my rifle across it, I opened fire on the enemy. After some minutes the Germans ran from the road, I called up my two seamen and we pursued them with shots, none of which I think took effect.

After the Germans had left the road, I sang out to Bacon "How's the search going?" He said it was going fine. I then returned with the men to the motor boat and went ashore at a point between the *Fritzen* and the shore.

I remained in the motor boat and ordered Sub-Lieutenant Vaux to go ashore with four men and capture a group of merchant seamen, who could be seen on the road. They had obviously got ashore from one of the grounded ships. I told him to be careful, as they would probably be armed. He left his men under cover in a ditch beside the road and walked off alone down the middle of the road, pointing his revolver at them an shouting, "come here you buggers." They did as requested. It was a grand thing to do, for if they had chosen to open fire, he hadn't a chance. Seventeen merchant seamen surrendered. As soon as Sub-Lieutenant Vaux had rounded them up I tried to get them across the deck of the *Föhn* to the motor boat. In doing so I made a mistake, because Bacon obviously did not want them to see what he was doing and I did not realise that until he sang out "Not over here, Commander, if you please. I am trying to search this ship for confidential papers."

Then I boarded the *Fritzen* with some of the boarding party and searched her. I sent one stoker to the engine room. I myself suffered a bitter disappointment. In the Captain's cabin I discovered a locked cupboard and nearly broke my foot trying to break it open. Then I remembered my revolver which was in its holster. I took it out and fired into the lock and broke three bottles of Courvoisier brandy! I found some papers which I took away. Then I dropped into the motor boat, went back to the shore and found Sub-Lieutenant Vaux with the prisoners on the rocks. I took them into the motor boat. One of them, a German, was badly wounded in the body, he subsequently died.

We headed back to the *Onslow* with the prisoners. Before we did so the Captain of the *Onslow* roared me up on the loudspeaker about taking too long in boarding. This irritated me at the time, but he obviously thought I was jeopardising his ship. He was a damned good chap, but when you send a boarding party away, it is in my opinion, essential to trust their leader and I was in fact doing the job as fast as I could.

I must now describe the boarding of the large Dutch-type schuyt, called the *Eismeer*. I should explain that while we were on the way up the fjord, chasing the *Föhn* and the other two ships, we passed the *Eismeer*, anchored close ashore north of Vaagso. As we steamed past here the crew came aft, waved the Dutch flag and cheered us. As a matter of fact it was a most successful *ruse de guerre*, for when we returned we found the *Eismeer* anchored against the Tröllebor light she was deserted. She was in fact a German ship.

The *Onslow* stopped and the boarding party went away again. This time in the whaler and with them went Midshipman Hayes, RN, instead of Sub-Lieutenant Vaux. When pulling away from the *Onslow* to the *Eismeer* we were sniped at by, I think, a single sniper. He was firing at anyone from the hills and his shooting was very accurate, though he did not in fact succeed in hitting anyone in the whaler in the passage from the *Onslow* to the *Eismeer*. When we reached the *Eismeer* we were under the lee, and, therefore, out of the line of fire.

The *Eismeer* was anchored with her bows pointing south. We got inboard over the port side of the vessel and I was handed a loaded rifle from the whaler.

I should explain that, as far as I can judge, the sniper was about 400 or 500 yards away on the side of the hill to starboard. I went over to the starboard side of the *Eismeer*, where there was a rope ladder hanging over the quarter. I tried to pull in the ladder, so as to take it over to the port side and there rig it for the use of the boarding party.

Midshipman Hayes went with me to get the ladder and while we were doing so the sniper fired two shots which hit the paint work just behind us. I handed Hayes the rifle and told him to lie down behind the bulwarks and return the fire of the sniper.

At this time when I was trying to get hold of the ladder I still did not realise how bad the firing was and I, therefore, made a mistake, for I ordered the whaler to drop away from the port side of the *Eismeer*. As soon as she got clear of the ship she came under the fire of the sniper, and the seaman at the stoke oar was hit and mortally wounded. Just before she got away I took a stoker and a seaman on board the *Eismeer*.

While the whaler was returning to the *Onslow* at my orders, I realised that the *Eismeer* was in splendid condition and quite undamaged. I, therefore, signalled to the *Onslow* to send a diesel engine room artificer back in the whaler, for I thought he would be able to get the *Eismeer's* engines started and that we should, therefore, get her under way.

With this object in view I took one of the seamen and we tried to get on to the fo'castle and tried to weigh anchor. Several times as we showed ourselves the sniper had a crack at us. As it was a bit rough here I sent the seaman down below to see if there was anyone still in the ship.

While he was below I tried to crawl to the cable and unshackle it. The sniper, however, made things too hot for me. If I went on I thought I should be hit. I therefore stopped and returned to the Captain's cabin, which I searched. I collected the ship's papers and took them back to the *Onslow* in the whaler, which had returned for us. We were sniped at all the way back. The boat was punctured and an oar broken. I should mention that throughout the proceedings on the *Eismeer*, the *Onslow* was directing machine gun fire against the sniper, but without effect, as his whereabouts on the mountainside could not be discovered.

We then re-embarked and the *Onslow* fired a couple of salvos at the *Eismeer* and then left the fjord. The *Oribi* who was behind us, further up the fjord, was also withdrawing and she finished off the *Eismeer* as she went by. We had also fired at, and sunk, the *Regmar Edzard Fritzen* and the *Oribi* sank the *Normar*. Between us we sank all four ships, including the *Föhn*. While I was on board the *Eismeer* an enemy trawler, escorting a cargo vessel called the *Anita M Russ*, came into the fjord, obviously knowing nothing about the show. She made her name and after doing so realised that something was up. She, therefore, immediately ran ashore on the east side of the fjord and was sunk by gunfire from the *Oribi*. The *A M Russ* ran ashore south of Brandhaevnes Point and was sunk by gunfire from *Onslow*. Survivors were picked up by the *Oribi*. This ended my part in the Operation and apart from being bombed a little on the way back the journey was uneventful.

Appendix XIV

Operation Anklet Report from No 12 Commando

Summary of Operations carried out by No 12 Commando on D1

1. General

No 12 Commando carried out unopposed landings at Napp, Suns, Andoy, Reine and Sörvaagen. Eight German prisoners, together with certain documents, were captured at Glaapen near Sörvaagen.The W/T station at Sörvaagen was destroyed. Telephone communications on Fladstadoy and Moskensoy and the telephone lines between Fladstadoy and Vest Vaago were cut.

2. Napp

0815 hrs – Off Napp in HMS *Bedouin*. Landed at Napp.

0900 hrs – Cut telephone cable and demolished control box. Fraternised with inhabitants and endeavoured to obtain information.

1000 hrs – Force aboard HMS *Bedouin*. HMS *Bedouin* then proceeded to Kirke Fjord, where personnel of No 12 Commando were transferred to HMS *Prins Albert* at 1930 D2.

3. Sund

0715 hrs – Off Reine in HMS *Prins Albert*.

0745 hrs – Left HMS *Prins Albert* in R Boats for Sund.

0830 hrs – Landed at Sund. Fraternised with inhabitants and distributed comforts and newspapers. Endeavoured to obtain information.

1230 hrs – Left Sund for Reine.

1315 hrs – Arrived Reine.

1600 hrs – Re-embarked on HMS *Prins Albert*.

4. Andoy Island

0715 hrs – Off Reine in HMS *Prins Albert*.

0745 hrs – Left HMS *Prins Albert* for Andoy.

0830 hrs – Landed on Andoy Island.

0840 hrs – Cut telephone cable and endeavoured to obtain information.

0905 hrs – Re-embarked in ALCs.

0930 hrs – Re-embarked on HMS *Prins Albert*.

5. Reine

0715 hrs – Off Reine in HMS *Prins Albert*.

0745 hrs – Left HMS *Prins Albert* for Reine.

0830 hrs – Landed at Reine. Took over telephone exchange and cut lines.

0830 hrs – Ascertained no Germans in area and numbers of Germans at Sörvaagen.

0930 hrs – Cut wires and removed telephone exchange at Hauno. Assisted Major Torrence in collection of information and distribution of comforts, newspapers, etc.

1430 hrs – Commenced re-embarking in R Boats.

1530 hrs – Arrested Quisling Alfred Pererson at Kirkefjord.

1730 hrs – All re-embarked on HMS *Prins Albert*.

6. Sörvaagen.

0950 hrs – Off Sörvaagen in HMS *Prins Albert*.

0955 hrs – Left HMS *Prins Albert* for Sörvaagen.

1010 hrs – Party landed north side of Sörvaagen Fjord. Cut telephone wires between Sörvaagen and Moskenes and advanced into Sörvaagen.

1020 hrs – Party landed south side of Sörvaagen Fjord. Ascertained that enemy were at Glaapen lighthouse.

1035 hrs – Glaapen lighthouse surrounded. Eight Germans surrendered and were taken prisoners. All documents, samples of food, soap, etc., were taken (also mail, equipment, arms and ammunition).

1045 hrs Fraternised with inhabitants and distributed comforts and newspapers.

1130 hrs – Commenced re-embarking in R Boats.

1145 hrs – W/T Station at Sörvaagen demolished.

1200 hrs – Re-embarked aboard HMS *Prins Albert*.

Appendix XV

Brief notes on Gee, Oboe and H2S

Gee arrived with the bomber squadrons at the end of 1941 but it had first been thought of in June 1940, after one of the top brass on the Air Staff complained at a meeting about the navigational difficulties causing poor bombing results. Present at this meeting was Sir Robert Watson-Watt and he suggested that people at TRE ought to be able to come up with a design based on the German Lorenz blind landing system. The development work was led by a team from the TRE under the wonderfully named Robert Dippy. He had first set his ideas down on paper for a navigational aid during 1937, but it was overlooked in the rush to throw resources at setting up the Chain Home system for air defence –not a bad policy at the time.

Designs were worked up in the winter of 1940/41 with the test flying programme beginning later that year and the first operational flight took place in August 1941. Gee transmitters located in various places on the east coast sent out precisely timed radio pulses. These were picked up by a receiver in the aircraft which displayed the time of arrival. If the pulses from two stations arrived at the same time, the aircraft was an equal distance from both, allowing the navigator to draw a line on his map of all the positions at that distance from both stations. Similarly, a difference in the times of arrival indicated that the aircraft was closer to one particular transmitter than another, the actual difference being a particular curve along which the aircraft must lie. By using similar measurements with a third station, an additional curve could be produced, leading to a fix at the intersection of the two lines.

Gee was stated to be accurate to about 160 yards at short ranges gradually decreasing in accuracy the further away from the transmitting stations. At extreme ranges of about 400 miles, it had an accuracy of around 2 miles. Unlike the German X-Gerät and Knickebein systems, in which the bombers flew along the beam to their targets, the Gee transmissions were not directional, so even when they were detected they did not reveal the bomber's likely target. Additionally, as the system was a passive one, there was the added benefit of no return signals, which could give away an aircraft's position to both airborne and ground receivers. However, the system was open to jamming which the Germans started doing after about six months uninterrupted use. However, the jamming was only really effective over Europe, so it was a great aid on the first part of the outward flight and also for finding the way home on the last leg.

Oboe was probably the best British blind bombing aid of the Second World War. It was based on radio transponder technology. The basic theory of Oboe originally came from Mr A Reeves of Standard Telephones and Cables Ltd, and worked up in conjunction with scientists from the TRE, notably Mr F Jones. Alec Reeves was apparently the pulse code modulation expert at Standard and it is said that the idea was worked out on the back of an envelope. Oboe used two transmitting stations at different and well-spaced locations in England (known as Cat and Mouse) to send a signal to a suitable aircraft carrying a radio transponder. The transponder was able to reflect the signals back to both

Cat and Mouse. The time taken for the signal to reach and return from the aircraft gave the distance to the aircraft.

The two Oboe stations used this radio ranging to define an invisible circle of a specific radius, with the two circles crossing in the air over the intended target. The theory and practice was that the aircraft flew along the circumference of one circle defined by one of the stations (usually the Cat) and dropped its load when it reached the intersection point with the other circle (the Mouse). Eventually a network of Oboe stations were set up all over southern and eastern England, and it was possible for these to operate as either a Cat or Mouse as circumstances dictated.

Without getting too technical, the two stations transmitted a series of pulses at 133 times per second. The pulse width could be varied so that it appeared as either short or long, when these were received in the aircraft they sounded like either a Morse code dot or dash. The Cat station sent continuous dots if the aircraft was too close and continuous dashes if the aircraft was too far away from the ideal path. The system was further refined in that various letters could be transmitted in Morse to indicate certain milestones on the path to the target. When the aircraft was over the target the Mouse station sent five dots and a dash to tell the crew to release their load.

The first operational use of Oboe was in December 1942 and because Oboe could only really handle one aircraft at a time it was decided to use aircraft equipped with it as marker aircraft only. Later on when more ground stations had been established 18 aircraft an hour could use it to mark or bomb. Another disadvantage was that an Oboe-controlled aircraft had to fly on an arching course for several minutes, not ideal conditions for trying to avoid German night fighters and flak. To compensate for this the newly-introduced Mosquitoes, which flew at a superior speed to a heavy bomber and at almost 30,000 feet, negated this disadvantage to a large extent. Oboe was a 'line of sight' device and therefore its range was limited by the curvature of the earth, enabling it to cover the Ruhr industrial area but not much further. Here is a comment from an Oboe operator from 109 Squadron, Flying Officer H Boyd:

> One had to navigate to an exact point in space and be there within about 30 seconds of a stated time. Then, on receiving your call sign, the Oboe set was switched on and the pilot flew straight and level for about 15 minutes and was directed by means of dots and dashes to the dropping point. The bombs or markers were dropped on receipt of a signal and when one returned home you were told how much off target you had been. We averaged about 100 yards error on Ruhr targets.

Used in this manner, the Mosquito was the perfect target illuminating aircraft, once they had dropped their target indicators other aircraft backed them up with additional markers. The main force would then bomb the markers (or try to!). When Oboe-equipped Mosquitoes were not required for marking they were often employed as individual precision bombers. Obviously provided the aircraft could take off and land, the weather over the intended target was immaterial. The Germans certainly tracked the Mosquitoes on their Oboe runs but found them difficult to shoot down and so never captured an Oboe set in good condition and thus found it difficult to jam the signals. It is recorded that the signals on the original wavelength of 1.5 metres were jammed to some extent but by the time this had been done, technology had moved Oboe on to a 10 cm wavelength and were using the old transmissions to fool the Germans.

One particularly successful Oboe-led operation was to Essen and the famous Krupps armament factory. With the Oboe beams crossing above the factory the target markers were accurately laid and the rest of the main force concentrated their bombs on them. More than 600 acres of Essen were destroyed or badly damaged, with the Krupps work being particularly badly hit, with only 14 aircraft lost from over 400 sent out (3.5%).

H2S was a variation on the Coastal Command radar set known as ASV (Air to Surface Vessel) and was a device carried in the aircraft. The advantage of this was that it would not be limited to a line of sight to any transmitters. One of the TRE scientists had noticed before the war during other experiments that radar returns from fields, cities and water were somewhat different from airborne ones and produced a form of map on the operator's display. Again, like Oboe, this was forgotten about until the call for help with navigation came from the RAF. In October 1941 one of the TRE scientists, Mr P Dee, attended a meeting with Bomber Command where the thorny question of finding targets was discussed. Soon afterwards an experiment was undertaken using an airborne interception set which was able to pick up the outline of a town flying in a Blenheim from around 40 miles away. The green light was given to the TRE to press on with all speed. It was intended to fit a transmitter/receiver in a blister fairing on the underside of the bomber. Originally it was intended to call it 'Blind Navigation' or BN, but the name eventually got changed to H2S. There are several explanations for this, with one being that it means 'Height to Slope', others suggesting it means 'Home Sweet Home'. Another reason put forward is that Churchill's scientific adviser did not think it would work and claimed it stank, hence the connection with hydrogen sulphide – rotten eggs. A final entirely plausible explanation was that it was intentionally named after this smelly compound, because the inventor realised that had he pointed the radar down instead of towards the sky, he would have found a new application for radar, the end idea being that he was simply rotten for not having thought of it sooner.

The first experimental flight took place in a Halifax in April 1942, and was not without problems over the coming months. In June the flying test bed crashed killing everyone on board and destroying the prototype set. The major reason why H2S was possible was the use of a device called a cavity magnetron which enabled the radar to be of the centimetric size rather than the longer radio waves used before. An example of the difficulties was that because the CH transmitters in 1940 did not have cavity magnetrons they required an antenna over 350 feet high. Such a structure would of course be impracticable in an aircraft. In order to make radar sets small enough the boffins needed a device that would produce microwaves, which is where the cavity magnetron came in. At the heart of a modern microwave oven is, in fact, a cavity magnetron.

Cherwell wanted the design team to build the set around an inferior device called a klystron rather than the cavity magnetron. The reason for this was that the cavity magnetron was a highly secret invention which it was thought that the Germans didn't have. To start putting it in aircraft that were highly prone to crashing in German territory was not on according to Cherwell. The klystron was not as powerful as a cavity magnetron, but it could be more easily destroyed in an emergency. However, the development team did not believe the klystron was up to the job and in a set built with them showed a drop in output power of between 20 and 30 times. It was also argued that even if the Germans did capture a cavity magnetron, it would take them two years or so to develop a centimetric radar. In both of the assumptions the scientists were correct, the Germans didn't have any cavity magnetrons and it did take them two years to develop a centimetric radar. As was Churchill's style he got to hear of these problems and in July 1942 called a meeting to 'bang heads together' and demanded that Bomber Command get 200 H2S sets by October that year. This deadline was not met but by 1st January over 20 Stirlings and Halifaxes had been fitted with sets. It is believed its first operational use was in January 1943 on a raid in Hamburg. This raid did have a measure of success. The Germans did not have to wait long to get their hands on a H2S set as a Stirling equipped with a set crashed landed near Rotterdam on 2nd February 1943. As the British had in 1940 they carefully searched the wreckage for any new electronic aids and discovered the set. Most of the set was recovered except for the navigator's display and they were initially puzzled as to what it was for. The Germans called it the 'Rotterdam Gerät'. Eventually other pieces were recovered from other crashed aircraft and a set cobbled together. On a test on one of Berlin's flak towers the onlookers to their amazement saw clearly displayed other flak towers and recognisable features. To combat H2S the Germans developed two tracking devices. One was ground-based and they were able to track aircraft using it, another receiver was fitted to some of their night fighters, which enabled them to home in on the aircraft using it. When bomber crews realised the Germans were homing in on H2S signals prolonged use was discouraged and morale suffered.

Appendix XVI

Memo calling for more volunteers for Air Service Battalions

Urgent Memorandum
Date 28th August 1941
Subject Formation of two additional Air Service Battalions.

1. It has been decided to form two additional Air Service battalions forthwith.
2. Volunteers are required.
   - Officers. Any infantry officers.
   - Other Ranks. From all field force infantry, rifle and machine gun battalions, in Great Britain.
3. Conditions of service are as follows:-
   (i) All personnel now volunteering will be normally rationed and accommodated and will not draw any special allowances.
   (ii) Personnel will volunteer on no fixed terms of service and without any right to return to their former units.
   (iii) Parachute Pay at the rate of 4/- per day for Officers; 2/- per day for Other Ranks; may be granted at the discretion of the Commanding Officer after the performance of a minimum of three drops.
   (iv) Personnel of Air Service Units may be returned to former units if found unsuitable under authority of the Brigade Commander.
   4. Physical standards required for parachutists are laid down in an A.C.I. which is in course of publication. Advanced copy is attached at Appendix A.
   No volunteers with glasses will be considered.
   5. Volunteers must be first class fighting soldiers and show keenness, intelligence and initiative and must be men of first class character only.
   A high standard of individual weapon training is essential. Men must be able to shoot off right shoulder.
   6. Return of volunteers as under to reach War Office (AG17) by 13th September 1941.

Officers' Nominal roll showing:-
   - Name, Substantive or war Substantive Rank. Any Acting or Temporary Rank. Age. Unit.
   - Officers of the rank of Captain to have qualified at a Company Commanders' Course.
   - Two Subaltern Officers required as Signalling Officers.
   - Two Subaltern Officers required as Mortar Officers.
   - Other Ranks. Numbers of volunteers by ranks and units.

Summary of WO and NCO ranks required for each battalion:-
- WO's 4
- Sergeants 47
- Corporals 39
- Lance-Corporals 27
- NCOs submitted must be recommended for promotion to next higher rank.
7. In order that no unit may be unduly depleted maximum of 10 Other Ranks only permitted to volunteer from any one unit.
8. Detailed instructions with regard to postings will be issued in due course.

Appendix A Standards of Fitness for SAS Training.

1. Personnel selected for parachute training will not be below 22 years nor more than 32 years of age and will be medically examined to ensure that they comply with the standards noted below.

   The age limit may be relaxed in exceptional circumstances, e.g. Officers and NCOs, but there must be no relaxation of the standards of physical fitness in these cases.
2. Height – any height applicable to the man's arm of the service.
3. Weight – without clothes is not to exceed 196 lbs and must correlate normally with the height.
4. Visual standards – the visual acuity must not be below 6/12 in each eye without glasses and personnel must have normal or colour defective safe colour vision.

   Visual acuity and colour vision will be tested at the nearest Military Ophthalmic Centre.
5. Hearing standards – the acuity of hearing must comply with Hearing Standard 2, i.e. The man standing with his back to the examiner and using both ears must be able to hear a forced whisper from 10 feet away.

   No man with otorrhoea or a perforation of an ear drum will be accepted and the eustachian tubes must be patent.
6. Dental standard – there must be eight sound or repairable teeth (including two molars) in the upper jaw, in good functional opposition to corresponding teeth in the lower jaw.
7. General – at the medical examination special care will be taken to ascertain that the circulatory system is normal; that there are no disabilities of limbs, especially of the bones and joints, present; and that in all other respects the man is fit for army medical category A1.

Appendix XVII

Operational Order for Operation Biting, Major J D Frost, Commanding C Company, 2nd Parachute Battalion

SECRET   **Not to be taken in aircraft**

OPERATIONAL ORDER 'BITING'
Major J D Frost, Commanding C Company, 2nd Parachute Battalion

From aerial photographs no sign of weapons heavier than MGs can be seen. Until recently these appeared to be sited for defence against seaborne invasion only, but in the last three months three blockhouses have been constructed on the north shoulder of the exit from the beach. These are all thought to cover the valley and are connected to each other by communication trenches, work on these still continues. This group will be called REDOUBT.

There appears to be a strong point at mount of the beach exit, consisting of two blockhouses, four LMG posts and a road block. This group is likely to be sited for all-round defence, it is connected to communication trenches to a further LMG post one hundred yards up the valley. This group will be called BEACH FORT, it is surrounded by wire two metres thick.

Further inland there is a house on the edge of a depression running north from the valley. This being the main perimeter of wire, is surrounded by wire ten metres thick. This house is believed to contain two MGs and is permanently manned. This will be known as GUARD ROOM.

There are more possible LMG posts as shown on the model.

The garrison consists of 30 men under an NCO, five sleep in the GUARD ROOM and the remainder in the village in a house some 500 yards from the beach.

To the north of the valley is a lone building which will be known as LONE HOUSE, 50 yards west of LONE HOUSE is the main objective which will be known as HENRY. LONE HOUSE is believed to contain 20 signallers.

North of LONE HOUSE is an enclosure of trees and buildings, believed to contain a number of signallers, this will be known as RECTANGLE.

OWN TROOPS. 120 all ranks.
OBJECT:-
1. To capture various parts of HENRY and bring them down to the boats.
2. To capture prisoners who have been in charge of HENRY.
3. To obtain all possible information about HENRY and any documents referring to him which may be in LONE HOUSE.

METHOD. The force will be divided into three main parties, each party to be allotted a definite task.

Number 1. NELSON.

(i)   Task – To capture and hold REDOUBT, BEACH FORTRESS and GUARD ROOM and to cover withdrawal of the remainder of the force for embarkation in ALCs.
(ii) DZ – NELSON will be dropped in the area due east of the track running north and south (model).
(iii) Direction- The aircraft will be flying from south to north.
(iv) FUP – The line of the track and the hedge running north and south in the re-entrant due east of the DZ.
(v)   Action – OC NELSON will detail three light sections to approach as near as possible to the three objectives enumerated in the task paragraph. The heavy sections will move to and take up a position on the spur due east of the REDOUBT so as to cover the road leading from the village and give support for the assault on the GUARD ROOM and BEACH FORTRESS.
(vi) Timing – First NELSON stick will be dropped at 0015 hrs. The whole party will move to their objectives as soon as possible after forming-up.
(vii) Co-ordination – It is of vital importance that the enemy at LONE HOUSE and HENRY should be taken by surprise. Therefore NELSON will take every precaution to make no noise of any kind until either:
      The attack on HENRY begins, or successive blasts on a whistle are heard, or it becomes absolutely necessary to fire on the enemy. However should any Section Commander find it possible to occupy any one of the objectives silently, he will at once do so.
(viii) RE – Immediately it is possible, Lieutenant Ross will move to the beach and RE personnel and stores to:-
(a)   Clear and mark a route through the minefield (if any).
(b)   Establish HQ and check point.

Number 2. JELLICOE, HARDY, DRAKE.

(i)   Task – Move to LONE HOUSE and deal with HENRY. Immediately all material has been taken, information and prisoners captured, to withdraw to the beach and prepare to embark.
(ii) DZ – As for NELSON.
(iii) Direction – As for NELSON.
(iv) FUP – As for NELSON.

(v)   Action – DRAKE will move towards and take up a position west of the RECTANGLE in order to prevent enemy movement towards LONE HOUSE.
      HARDY will move to and surround LONE HOUSE (less RE party).
      JELLICOE will move to and surround HENRY (less RE party).
      RE party will follow JELLICOE.
(vi) Timing – JELLICOE, HARDY and DRAKE will be dropped at 0020 hrs.
(vii) Co-ordination – On the sound of four blasts on the whistle, HARDY will force their way into LONE HOUSE, collect all enemy into a room on the ground floor and await further orders. RE party will commence their task with HENRY, JELLICOE will be responsible for their protection while doing so and will give any assistance they require.

Number 3. RODNEY.

(i)   Task – To prevent with two sections any attempt by the enemy to attack HARDY from RECTANGLE and to support with two sections, NELSON, in the event of an attack from the village.
(ii)   DZ – As for NELSON.
(iii) Direction – As for NELSON.
(iv)   FUP – As for NELSON.
(v)   Action – RODNEY will take up position on the ground to the west of the FUP so as to be able to carry out both tasks. He must be able to reinforce either detachment in case of emergency.
(vi)   Timing – RODNEY will begin dropping at 0025 hrs.
(vii) Co-ordination – No noise or firing until HENRY has been taken or the signal- four blasts on the whistle- is heard.
(viii) RE and Signals – OC RODNEY is responsible for ensuring that RE and Signal personnel are guided to area of BEACH FORT, where they will be met by Lieutenant Ross and will then carry out their duties (see Signal Instructions).

Withdrawal for Embarkation.

1.   Immediately HARDY have completed their task they will move to the beach by the most direct route.
2.   JELLICOE and DRAKE will follow at 50 yard intervals.
3.   However should OC RE have any doubts concerning HENRY, and should the situation warrant it, JELLICOE, HARDY and DRAKE will remain in position until a small party named NOAH arrive from the beach, inspect HENRY and complete their task. The withdrawal will then continue according to plan.
4.   RODNEY will receive orders to withdraw by W/T or runner when HARDY etc. have reached the beach. OC RODNEY will however prepare to withdraw as soon as he sees LONE HOUSE area evacuated.
5.   RODNEY will move by the most direct route.
6   NELSON will withdraw immediately RODNEY are clear of the beach.

Beach Control.

1. OC parties are responsible for the disposition of their parties on the beach.
2. RE personnel will lay tapes to guide parties through the minefield (if any), Lieutenant Ross to ensure that guides are in position when required.
3. Section Commanders will report their sections present or otherwise to Lieutenant Ross, at the check point (BEACH FORT).
4. Parties will embark under orders from the Beach Control Officer- appointed by Lieutenant Ross.
5. The Beach Control Officer will ensure that parties get to their boats as quickly and vigorously as possible. He will ensure that each boat takes its correct load, and will inform the Naval Officer in Command as soon as the boat is correctly loaded, and ready to leave. He will give the Naval Officer all possible assistance.

General.

1. No prisoners will be taken off, other than signallers.
2. Ammunition will be conserved as far as possible.
3. Sentries will be dealt with silently, whenever possible.
4. The password will be BITING.
5. It is emphasised that the whole operation fails unless HENRY is effectively dealt with and the parts required are captured. All ranks must be fully aware of this.
6. On the ALCs the senior officer or NCO is in command of all troops. He is responsible to the Naval Officer in Command of the ALC and will ensure that all orders given by the NO are implicitly obeyed.

Intercommunication.

1. Officers i/c. NELSON, HARDY, DRAKE and RODNEY will communicate with each other by:-
   (i)   Number 38 W/T set.
   (ii) Whistle.
2. Signallers with RODNEY will communicate with the Naval Force by:-
   (i)   D/F transmitter.
   (ii) Number 18 W/T set.
   (iii) Visual (torch).
   (iv) Verey pistol.
3. The senior signaller will decide which equipment is to be used where two similar equipment's are available.
4. Signals containers can be identified by a green light and will be painted with four black and white bands.
5. Signallers will RV with RODNEY in accordance with paragraph 3.
6. On orders being given by OC RODNEY to take up battle positions signallers will accompany RODNEY.
7. Communications will at once be established with the Naval Force by Number 18 W/T set.
8. As soon as notification has been received that the beach is clear, signallers will leave RODNEY and proceed to the beach. Number 18 W/T sets will be carried without being dismantled.

9. On arrival at the beach a REPORT CENTRE will be opened as near as possible to the check point at BEACH FORT.
10. D/F transmissions will begin immediately on taking up positions at check point. The drill for establishing D/F transmissions will be in accordance with Appendix.
11. As soon as Naval craft are heard to be approaching, D/F transmissions will cease and the signaller i/c D/F apparatus will signal in the direction of the craft with a signalling torch using the white light.
12. In the event of communications with the Naval Force failing, signals will be fired by Verey pistol but only under order of OC NELSON.

Verey light signals.
To indicate the direction of the beach to the Naval Force:-
> Two green lights will be fired one to the right and the other to the left along the base of and below the cliffs.

Administration.
1. Normal morning routine.
2. 1000 hrs. Pack containers- check weapons and ammunition.
3. 1400 hrs. Containers to Thruxton.
4. 1700 hrs. Tea.
5. 1930 hrs. Move to Thruxton by MT.
6. 2030 hrs. Arrive Thruxton.
7. 2100 hrs. Tea and refreshments.
8. 2115 hrs. Fit statichutes.
9. 2140 hrs. March to aircraft.
10. 2200 hrs. All troops emplaned by.
11. 2215 hrs. First aircraft takes off.

Appendix A.
The following objects and information are required:-

A. Objects required to be collected.
1. The box behind the paraboloid.
2. All panels, switchboards etc.
3. All spare parts – or samples of them, particularly values.
4. The safe, or its contents, if there is one.
5. The SCREEN on which grid squares or a map may be traced. Cathode Ray tubes. Take care to preserve fluorescent powder; water spoils it.
6. Any scales in miles or kms on the switches.
7. All diagrams – circuit diagrams especially and MANUALS.
8. Aerial complete (this is probably in the centre of the paraboloid).
9. The aerial probably connects to 'something'. Bring me the something.
10. Prisoners who have worked the apparatus to be captured alive.
11. All maps.

B. The following information is also required.

12. Does paraboloid tip up?

C. Larger Twin Station.

13. If possible, investigate the larger twin station on the cliffs 750 yards north of the house, and bring back any of a/m (above mentioned) equipment that is easily removable. Particular attention should be paid to the control post situated between the two 'emplacements'.

The investigation of the twin station must only be undertaken AFTER the successful removal of everything of any possible interest from the site near the house, and THEN ONLY if the Commander of the force is satisfied that this will not jeopardise the successful evacuation of the apparatus which he has already acquired.

It is emphasised that **the object of the raid lies in the plant situated near the house, and NOT in the plant on the cliffs 750 yards north of the house.**

Appendix XVIII

Operation Biting – composition of parachute parties

This is the make up of the parties by Whitleys together with the name of the pilot of the aircraft:

Hardy Section (19 men) carried in two Whitleys:
First Whitley
- Major Frost
- CSM Strachan
- Sergeant Fleming
- L/Cpl Dobson
- Private Hayhurst
- Private Taylor
- Private McLeod
- Sapper Halliwell
- Flight Sergeant Cox
- Pilot Sergeant Clow

Second Whitley
- Lieutenant Vernon (RE)
- Sergeant McFarlane
- Corporal Heslop
- Private Conroy
- Private Galey
- Private Gordon
- Private Keyes
- Private McIntyre
- Private Nagel/Newman
- Corporal Jones (RE)
- Pilot Sergeant Hughes

Jellicoe Section (10 men) carried in one Whitley:
- Lieutenant Young
- Sergeant McKenzie
- L/Corporal Burns
- L/Corporal Heard (RE)
- Private Addie
- Private Draper

- Private Flitcroft
- Private McAusland
- Private Wilson
- Sapper Manning
- Pilot Squadron Leader Peveler

Nelson Section (40 men) carried in four Whitleys:
First Whitley
- Captain Ross
- Sergeant Sunley
- Corporal McLennon
- L/Corporal Kerr
- Private Calderwood
- Private Ewing
- Private Grant
- Private Heron
- Private Shaw
- Private Thacker
- Pilot Flight Lieutenant Coates

Second Whitley
- Second Lieutenant Charteris
- Sergeant Gibbons
- Corporal Hill
- Private Branwhite
- Private Grafton
- Private Laughland
- Private Matkin
- Private McCormack
- Private Sutherland
- Private Venters
- Pilot Wing Commander Pickard

Third Whitley
- Sergeant Sharp
- Sergeant Tasker
- L/Corporal Dickie
- Private Barnett
- Private Coates
- Private Gould
- Private Henderson
- Private Sturgess
- Private Synyer
- Private Wood
- Pilot Flight Lieutenant Towsey

Fourth Whitley
- Sergeant Grieve
- Sergeant Ellis RE
- Corporal Stewart
- Private Creighton
- Private Fleming
- Private Freeman
- Private Horne
- Private Hughes
- Private Willoughby
- Sapper Mitchell
- Pilot Sergeant Pope

Drake Section (10 men) carried in one Whitley:
- Lieutenant Naoumoff
- Sergeant Boyd
- Sergeant Lutener APTC
- L/Corporal Webster
- Private Beattie
- Private Bond
- Private Herwood
- Private Murphy
- Private Welsh
- Private Williamson
- Pilot Sergeant Gray

Rodney Section (40 men) carried in four Whitleys:
First Whitley
- Lieutenant Timothy
- Sergeant Forsyth
- Corporal Walker
- L/Corporal Johnstone
- Private Crutchley
- Private Greenough
- Private Hutchinson
- Private Millington
- Private 335 Scott
- Private Stephenson
- Pilot Squadron Leader Meade

Second Whitley
- Sergeant Muir
- L/Corporal Fleming
- Private Cadden
- Private Collier
- Private Higgins

- Private Judge
- Private McCann
- Private Richardson
- Private Thomas
- Sapper Hornsby
- Pilot Pilot Officer Mair

Third Whitley
- Sergeant Reid
- Corporal Finney
- L/Corporal MacCallam
- Private Buchanan
- Private Flambart
- Private Graw
- Private Lough
- Private O'Neill
- Private Stirling
- Sapper Harris
- Pilot Pilot Officer Haydon

Fourth Whitley
- Sergeant Lumb
- Sergeant Bennett
- Corporal Campbell
- L/Corporal Finlay
- Private Cornell
- Private Eden
- Private Embury
- Private 681 Scott
- Private Stacey
- Private Ward
- Pilot Sergeant Cook

Appendix XIX

Reports from 181st (Airborne) Field Ambulance RAMC on Operation Biting

LSC1 – Private J Stanton

No casualties dealt with. Took aboard some paratroopers suffering from the overcrowding on ALC3 and later transferred them to the MGB. Whilst alongside transferred three casualties from ALC7 to the MGB. Private Stanton was slightly sick once after taking a tot of rum but remained fit throughout the journey except for cold wet hands and feet. His slight sickness was rapidly removed by eating butterscotch.

LSC2 – L/Cpl D Pusser

No casualties dealt with. Took aboard about 20 paratroopers from the ALC3 and gave them tea. Some wrapped in blankets. L/Cpl Pusser transferred with the paratroopers to an MGB and remained fit throughout the journey. Seasickness occurred amongst the paratroopers after a meal of corned beef sandwiches, cocoa and rum. L/Cpl Pusser sucked butterscotch and successfully treated cases of sickness with it. Chocolate ingestion also noted to precede sickness. He also suffered from cold wet feet and hands. These from wet woollen gloves. He also mentioned the necessity for a waterproof dressing haversack. Tea developed foul taste in the flasks, he suggests milk be added before ingestion.

ALC3 – S/Sgt J Griggs – Private E Freer

Under fire whilst on the beach, as they came in heard shouts that casualties were present. Upon landing about 50 or 60 paratroopers stormed aboard, trampling on one seaman who received abrasions. One paratrooper had abrasions on his hands and legs due to a fall down the cliff. First field dressing applied. Another seaman sustained friction burns of his fingers from pulling on the kedge rope. These were covered with gauze dressings. The trampled seaman and the paratroopers were transferred to an MGB. S/Sgt Griggs had rum and chocolate and was slightly sick twice. Private Freer who had the same remained well. Discussions with S/Sgt Griggs and Private Freer brought forward the following points:-

(a) A smaller pair of scissors in addition to the larger pair because of the danger of the latter when the craft was pitching and rolling.
(b) Difficulty in using compressed dressings because of cold, wet hands.
(c) Possibility of a waterproof cover to enclose the stretcher and patient for the journey and trans-shipping.

(d) The tea did not remain hot in the thermos flask.

(e) The feeding cup was of more value than the domestic type.

(f) Advantage of 1" and 2" bandages for finger injuries etc.

(g) Rum considered a major cause of seasickness. More hot sweet tea essential. Impossible to use a primus stove because of rolling.

(h) Dry towels can be kept in the engine room for use on men immersed in the sea.

(i) Sea boots essential. Duffle coats of immense value in keeping men warm.

(j) The medical water bottle was not used. Water carried in cans aboard the craft was made use of.

(k) Waterproof haversacks essential.

(l) Essential equipment consisted of dressings, morphia, scissors, stretchers and possibly tourniquets.

ALC4 – Private J Waters and Private B Tuson

15 paratroopers taken aboard including three casualties, one abdominal, one shoulder and one groin. The last casualty refused any treatment but he had been given morphia. With three feet of water in the craft they were immediately transferred to an MGB where wounds were dressed by the naval surgeon. The man with the injured groin still refusing any treatment. Privates Waters and Tuson had also transferred to the MGB and helped the naval surgeon. Crowding rendered treatment difficult and both RAMC personnel were sick.

ALC5 – Private W Elliott and Private J Devitt

12 paratroopers including three casualties, one abdominal, one thigh and one a minor wound was redressed. The abdominal was placed in a Neil Robertson stretcher but as difficulty in fastening was experienced because of the bent knees the patient was placed on a ordinary stretcher which was placed along the centre of the ALC. There was no room for two stretchers inside the boat because of the numbers aboard. The patients were later transferred to an MGB. Privates Elliot and Devitt remained on the ALC and stayed fit. The boat and gun crews were seasick. Difficulties in treating casualties were due to:-

(a) Crowding.

(b) Rocking of the boat.

(c) Water in the boat with immersion of dressings etc.

ALC6 – Cpl W Kiddell and Private W Scott

No paratroopers came on board until leaving the beach, one sergeant flung himself into the sea and was promptly hauled aboard by Cpl Kiddell who caught him by the shoulders. The ALC shipped a lot of water. The paratrooper was stripped, rubbed down with a blanket and wrapped in a duffle coat and blankets and then stowed under the deck. He was given tea and then transferred to an MGB. Cpl Kiddell showed slight sickness. Private Scott none at all. The boat and gun crews were sick, they were up to their knees in water and they suggest sea boots, waterproof haversacks and some type of thin, but waterproof glove. They state there was insufficient tea for the long journey, especially as the primus stove could not be used owing to the choppy sea. Other suggestions were similar to ones made by other personnel.

ALC7 – Private W Hoath and Private L Hatcher

About 50 to 60 paratroopers came aboard, three casualties already given morphia and wounds dressed. A head wound – shrapnel, an injured toe and prisoner with superficial wounds of neck and back. Transferred to MGB 316. Head wound excitable until taken aboard MGB where he slept. Hot sweet tea, soup etc. given. The injured toe and prisoners' wounds redressed. Privates Hoath and Hatcher also mentioned difficulty in working with the overcrowding. Neither was sick but stressed the importance of sea boots.

ALC8 – Private J Newman and Private G Rose

5 paratroopers aboard, no casualties. Transferred these to an MGB. Private Rose stayed aboard the ALC. Vomited once after drinking foul-tasting tea. This complaint of bad tea was made by all and all agreed it was due to the milk being added at the beginning of the operation and suggested that tinned milk be added before use. Neither Private Newman or Rose were seasick, both felt fit.

HMS *Prins Albert*

The thigh wound was admitted to the sick bay at 0930 28-2-42, but transferred almost immediately to the shore. The head wound and the toe injury admitted to the sick bay and later transferred to the shore at approx 1730 28-2-42. The PoW's injuries were dressed by Private Grinsberg in the ship's office. A piece of shell casing emerging from the wound was removed.

MGB 317 – Lt A S Baker

6 paratroopers were taken aboard from ALC6 and 8. No casualties. Slight seasickness amongst the paratroopers evident after food had been taken. Came aboard HMS *Prins Albert* at 1720 28-2-42, visited sick bay and saw the head and toe wounds. Detailed stretcher party to take these ashore.

Conclusions by Lt A S Baker

The following points emerge:-

(a) Wholesale administration of morphia even to head injuries, suggest that head wounds in relation to morphia be discussed with the paratroopers. To be treated in the recumbent position.

(b) Suggestions as to medical equipment.

(c) Suggestions as to comfort of RAMC orderlies whilst working.

(d) Relation or possible relation of seasickness to rum and large amounts of food after a long period of fasting and the often marked relief obtained from sucking glucose sweets.

(e) The addition of milk to the tea in the flasks only when about to be drunk.

Equipment taken on Operation Biting

ALC
- 2 Stretchers with Blankets
- 1 Neil Robertson Stretcher
- 1 Surgical Haversack
- Extra dressings including shell, first field, gauze, cotton wool, stomach and Moyes
- Medical Water Bottle
- Blankets – 8 Naval and 4 W.D.
- 2 Groundsheets
- 2 Thermos Flasks
- 2 Cups

LSC
- 1 Neil Robertson Stretcher
- 2 Haversacks and Dressings (as ALC)
- 1 Tube Morphia Tablets
- 2 Thermos Flasks
- 1 Water Bottle
- Blankets – 8 Naval and 4 W.D.

MGB
- Medical Companion Boxes
- 4 Neil Robertson Stretchers
- Cramer Splints
- Dressings as above but in greater amounts
- 2 Thermos Flasks
- 2 50cc Morphia solution for injections
- 2 x 5 Tubonic Morphia
- 5 x 30cc Anti-Tetanus serum
- 10cc Syringe
- Singer Tourniquet/Safety pins

Note. A Neil Robertson Stretcher would be used to transport a casualty from small spaces. It is made of split bamboo sewn onto canvas. Metal rings at the head and feet provide means of hoisting vertically. It has four hand grips to permit a horizontal carry. Four wrap around straps secure the casualty to the stretcher and a head strap prevents movement of the casualty's head.

Appendix XX

Miscellaneous Reports and Decorations Awarded from Operation Biting

British Report on Success of Raid

Certain specialist personnel were required to deal with the RDF Station. Flight Lieutenant Preist was given a temporary commission in the RAF so that he could accompany the force and provide expert scientific knowledge if required; he was taken over in an ALC and was not allowed to drop by parachute, as his capture by the enemy could not be risked. In fact he did not land but his knowledge was of great assistance.

Flight Sergeant Cox, RAF, a RDF specialist, was trained in parachute jumping at PTS Ringway, and actually dropped with C Company, to assist in dismantling the RDF apparatus. His work was excellent throughout.

Number 13801753 Private Nagel, 93 Pioneer Company, a German fighting against Hitler, also joined C Company and dropped with them. His knowledge of the German language and of the psychology of Germans proved of great assistance.

All the above specialists were obtained through HQ Combined Operations.

The take-off and flight went exactly according to plan. Some flak was met in the area of St. Jouin and some damage was done to aircraft but not to personnel. This has been reported in detail by the Air Force Commander.

Two aircraft dropped their parachutists south of the dropping zone. Estimates of how far south they were dropped vary between 1500 yards and 3 miles. One aircraft dropped 15 minutes late. The remaining aircraft dropped their parachutists according to plan. All containers were dropped successfully and were found quickly. There was no enemy AA fire on the dropping zone and none of the parachutists were fired at as they dropped.

NELSON (less that part which had been dropped short) moved off unopposed to attack the beach defences. They were partly successful but could not complete their task owing to shortage of personnel.

HARDY and JELLICOE formed up and moved off according to plan. During this time a few shots were heard and it appeared that some of the enemy were aware of the attack. HARDY surrounded and took the house and found it empty except for one German in the attic- he was killed.

JELLICOE surrounded the radio location set; the crew of 5 men offered little resistance with the exception of one Luftwaffe man who was taken prisoner. From him it was learnt that were 100 Germans in the RECTANGLE and approximately one company in the Bruneval area. The lighthouse at Cap d'Antifer had warned them that a parachutist raid was taking place.

In the meantime RODNEY and DRAKE had dropped. DRAKE moved to their positions near the RECTANGLE and when they received orders to withdraw threw grenades and opened fire on the enemy in the RECTANGLE.

Some of RODNEY were in the aircraft which dropped short and RODNEY were therefore slightly under strength. However, they took up their positions in reserve without difficulty.

After the RE and RAF RDF experts had taken what was required from the RDF set, HARDY, JELLICOE and DRAKE withdrew southwards about half way to the beach, when it was learnt that the beach defences had not yet been completely taken by NELSON.

The Company Commander detailed a party under Lieutenant Young from HARDY, JELLICOE and DRAKE to assist NELSON to take the remaining beach defences. This was done successfully and soon afterwards Second Lieutenant Charteris, who was in charge of that party of NELSON which had dropped short, arrived with 4 of his men and took over the beach according to plan.

RODNEY, who had been engaged with some enemy fire from the RECTANGLE, then moved back to the beach under orders of the Company Commander.

HARDY and all the technical experts, with the equipment which they had collected, also moved down to the beach. The remainder of the company was arranged in defensive positions near the beach while contact was made with the Navy. This was done by Number 38 wireless set and a Verey pistol, as the signallers with the Number 18 set were amongst those who had been dropped short.

As soon as the ALCs arrived, orders were given for the whole company to withdraw and embark. This was done successfully with the exception of a small party, including the signallers mentioned before who had not yet reported to the beach.

At about 0300 hours it appeared from various vehicle lights that were seen that reinforcements were arriving just north of the RECTANGLE and possibly a counter-attack might have been put in at about 0330 hours. The troops actually left the beach at 0315 hours.

At 0815 hours a wireless message was received from Commander Cook that the operation had been successful.

Return sea voyage

One MGB, with the RDF equipment and technical experts, returned independently at high speed and reached HMS *Prins Albert* off Spithead at 1000 hours 28th February.

The remainder of the force arrived at 1630 hours on 28th February, the sea being moderately rough most of that day. Number 11 Group Fighter Command had fighters protecting the returning boats from about 0815 hours 28th February until they were all back. In consequence no German aircraft interfered in any way.

Prisoners

Three German prisoners were brought back in the boats, including one of the Luftwaffe.

Casualties.

German casualties are estimated at a minimum of 40 killed.

Our own casualties were as follows. There were no casualties amongst V Corps troops in the boats, the Royal Navy or RAF.

Killed in action
- 3252284 Private McIntyre, H D McD.
- 5347681 Private Scott, A.

Wounded
- 2751640 CSM Strachan, G. Bullet wound in abdomen, may recover.
- 3195970 Sergeant Boyd, J. Bullet wound in foot, looks well.
- 2929915 Corporal Heslop, G. Bullet wound in thigh, feeling well.
- 2879337 Corporal Stewart, V. Bullet wound in scalp, feeling well.
- 2037582 L/Corporal Heard, R. Wound in hand, feeling well.
- 2928756 Private Grant, W. Bullet wound in abdomen, very seriously ill.
- 3058375 Private Shaw, H. Bullet wound in leg, not likely to continue.

Missing
- 2930416 L/Corporal MacCallum,J.
- 2879968 Private Sutherland, J. Badly wounded, left at farmhouse.
- 4745152 Private Willoughby, J.
- 5951642 Private Thomas, D.
- 4622613 Private Cornell, G.
- 5047949 Private Embury, E.

The operation was completely successful.

A preliminary report on the value of the RDF equipment captured is attached. Since that report was written, it has been ascertained definitely that all the equipment required was captured and brought in very good condition.

The prisoner of the Luftwaffe who was captured had spent some time previously in a German concentration camp and was willing to talk. As he is a RDF expert, the information he has given has been sufficient to complete the whole picture.

[Author's note: The two soldiers who were killed in the raid are now both buried in Ste. Marie Cemetery, Le Havre.]

German Report on the Bruneval Raid

At 0055 28.2.1942 the German Freya station reported aircraft NNE, range 29 km.

The parachutists were sighted by the Army and the Luftwaffe (ground and communications troops) at 0115. The landing was made south east of the farm and was carried out in complete silence. All Army and Luftwaffe posts in the area were at once alerted. Scouts sent from the Freya position (near Cap d'Antifer) and the Luftwaffe.

Communications Station (at Le Presbytère) returned with information that the enemy was on the move south of the farm (Le Presbytère) in the direction of the Château.

The parachutist commandos had split into several groups and were converging on the Würzburg position and the Château.

In La Poterie the reserve platoon of the 1st Company 685 Infantry Regiment had just finished an exercise shortly after 0100 when the parachutists were sighted. The officer commanding at once made contact with the Bruneval Guard; the sergeant there had already alerted his men. The platoon reserve in Bruneval was ordered to occupy Hill 102 to the south east of Bruneval. The officer commanding La Poterie platoon then led his men in a westerly direction towards the Château.

On reaching the farm buildings north east of the Château the German troops came under fire from the commando machine guns, and from the west end of the buildings they engaged the British, who were already in possession of the Würzburg : Luftwaffe station near the farm. Here one of the commandos fell. This German platoon encountered fire from the left flank, but the commandos were nevertheless prevented from proceeding with their attack on the Freya position. The remainder of the Luftwaffe Communications Station unit quartered in the farm buildings took part in this action.

In accordance with orders, the platoon from Bruneval village divided into two groups and advanced on Hill 102. Outside Bruneval they came under fire from the commandos who had landed north of L'Enfer.

Although this platoon was unable to prevent the commandos from infiltrating between Bruneval and Hill 102, it was because of this platoon's action that individual commandos did not reach the boats in time, and were later taken prisoner. One wounded commando was also captured. It was only because the British objective was not known that this Bruneval platoon did not take part in the action at the Château.

The Bruneval Guard, one sergeant and nine men, had meanwhile taken up prepared positions guarding the coast. These (main) defensive positions were so built that they were effective only against attacks through the ravine from seaward. The commandos, approaching from north and north east were able to get close to these strong points under cover of the woods. Thus the German guard positions were attacked from the high ground by heavy fire from three or four commando machine guns. After one German soldier had been killed and another wounded the sergeant was obliged to take up new positions. It was not until after one to one-and-a-half hours fighting that the commandos were able to get through the strong point and the ravine to the beach. With them the commandos took a wounded German soldier and also the soldier who had been on telephone watch at the post. Here another commando fell, and one was wounded. The latter was assisted to the boats, which had come close inshore on the exchange of signal flares.

The commandos embarked just as strong German reinforcements reached Bruneval.

The platoon from La Poterie fought their way to the Luftwaffe Communications Station Würzburg as the commandos withdrew. It was learned that the Luftwaffe personnel there had put up a stiff resistance and, only after some of them had exhausted their ammunition were the commandos able to break through to the Würzburg.

One of the crew had been killed by a British grenade as he tried to set off an explosive charge to destroy the Würzburg. The commandos then dismantled parts of the set and also took photographs. On conclusion of this task they obviously intended to attack the Freya station. The skillful intervention of the La Poterie platoon, however, prevented this.

The operation of the British commandos was well planned and was executed with great daring. During the operation the British displayed exemplary discipline when under fire. Although attacked by German soldiers they concentrated entirely on their primary task. For a full thirty minutes one group did not fire a shot, then suddenly at the sound of a whistle they went into action.

German losses: Army, two killed, one seriously wounded, two missing. Luftwaffe, three killed, one wounded, three missing.

British losses: two killed, one wounded (reached the boats), four captured.

Report from Flight Sergeant Cox

I met Mr. Vernon at the forming-up point at approx. 12.35. We proceeded under Mr. Vernon's directions to pull trolleys up towards house over various barbed wire defences and through snow, which was rather rough going.

In about 200 yards, Mr. Vernon went on to the house and said we must make our way to the left hand side of the house and conceal ourselves until he whistled or shouted for us. This we did, and lay in a small ridge for what seemed to be quite a long while, but was really a very short time. Then one of the sappers went over and said we must go through and meet up with the equipment immediately. Then we all went forward and through some more barbed wire to the equipment. I saw Mr. Vernon and he said 'This is it!'

The barbed wire was not more than 2 feet high, a criss-cross network about 10 feet thick. Range of distance round equipment about 50 yards radius.

In view of the obstacles, it would have been better to have made arrangements for carrying the equipment and tools etc. in haversacks rather than on trolleys. I surveyed the apparatus and found to my surprise it was just like the photograph. The first point of interest was the aerial, which I looked at, and one of the sappers proceeded to cut it from its centre. I went round the back tracing the aerial lead to the top box of the paraboloid. A compartment behind the paraboloid contained a big box, at the top; two smaller boxes underneath it; at the right hand side of the small boxes was a panel of push buttons, and in the base of the compartment was a thing which appeared to be a large metal rectifier, but this had round fins instead of square. I then proceeded to attack the equipment with the tools to try to get it out without damaging it. This proved unsuccessful except in one case, which came away easily, so we proceeded to rip the rest of the stuff out by sheer force.

By this time the soldiers were getting impatient, and we were told to withdraw. During the whole period of working at the equipment, bullets were flying much too close to be pleasant, but while we were working at the back of the paraboloid we were protected by the metal of the paraboloid itself.

I noticed on the paraboloid before the aerial was cut out, on the left hand side, slightly above centre, the letters WD, and a row of lines, horizontal lines arranged in a vertical scale, and against each line was a number about an inch apart. The whole equipment was very solidly made and turned on its base with the slightest pressure. All leads were sealed into it in concentric plugs and sockets. The aerial sockets ended in a type of attachment known to us as a Niphan plug.

The mounting was not on wheels, but looked as if it had been mounted on wheels and the wheels removed. There was no barbed wire on the boxes surrounding the equipment. We retired when the Army made us, and found that the equipment could be carried better on our shoulders than by the trolley, so the trolley was abandoned. On coming down the slope we were met by a hail of machine gun fire from the opposite side of the cliff and we tried to dig ourselves in. Mr. Vernon told me to take charge of the sappers while he went back with the rear guard. We lay on the bank for about 15 minutes and then received a call from the village that the beach defences had been taken. We made our way down the slope to the beach and found we had to wait, so we stowed the equipment in a safe position under the cliff and as there was nothing else we could do, we just sat down and waited.

After about half an hour the Navy came and we got the equipment aboard, with the wounded, and after the rearguard had time to make the beach and get into the boats, we pushed off. Slight enemy fire was directed against us from the cliff tops but was soon silenced by Bren guns on the boats.

Decorations awarded for Operation Biting

All gazetted in the *London Gazette* 15th May 1942 except the Pickard award which was 26th May 1942.

Royal Navy
Distinguished Service Cross
- Acting Commander F N Cook Royal Australian Navy
- Temporary Lieutenant D J Quick Royal Navy Volunteer Reserve
- Temporary Lieutenant (E) C W J Cloes Royal Navy Volunteer Reserve

Distinguished Service Medal
- Able Seaman J T Bland
- Stoker First Class C W Hurst

Mentioned in Despatches
- Lieutenant-Commander W G Everitt
- Lieutenant-Commander H B Peate Royal Navy Reserve
- Temporary Acting Lieutenant-Commander G H Garrard Royal Navy Volunteer Reserve
- Temporary Lieutenant P R MacKinnon Royal Navy Volunteer Reserve
- Chief Motor Mechanic B Barry
- Able Seaman W D Burns

Army
Military Cross
- Captain (Temporary Major) J D Frost Cameronians (Scottish Rifles)
- Second Lieutenant E B C Charteris King's Own Scottish Borderers

Military Medal
- Corporal (Acting Sergeant) G McKenzie Black Watch
- Sergeant D Grieve Seaforth Highlanders

Mentioned in Despatches
- Lieutenant P A Young East Surrey Regiment
- Corporal S Jones Corps of Royal Engineers

Royal Air Force
Distinguished Service Order
- Acting Wing Commander P C Pickard DSO, DFC

Military Medal
- Flight Sergeant C W H Cox

This is the citation for this somewhat rare award to a member of the RAF:

> This NCO volunteered to carry out a hazardous task in the parachute raid on Bruneval on the night of the 27th/28th February 1942. The success of the operation on the technical side depended largely on the performance of the duty allotted to him. After being dropped by parachute he had only a few minutes to complete a task which had previously been estimated to require half an hour and during this time he was continually under enemy fire. He displayed great courage, skill and devotion to duty in completing his task in spite of these difficulties, thereby contributing greatly to the successful execution of the raid.

Here is the citation for Pickard's DSO, which may appear strange as he managed to drop his parachutists in the wrong place. However, as he was already a relatively well-known name from the film 'Target for Tonight' and had been mentioned in the press as leading the RAF element, it was probably a more 'politically correct' award.

> This officer has made his Squadron an extremely efficient bombing force. He has extracted the maximum effort from all, at the same time promoting and fostering an excellent comradeship between flying personnel and ground staff, thus instilling the team spirit so necessary to achieve success. He has instituted a fine spirit among his flying crews for accurate bombing and in obtaining photographs.
>
> On 27th February 1942, he led the force of aircraft which carried the parachute troops who made the raid on Bruneval, thus again demonstrating his outstanding powers of leadership and organisation. By his courage, self-sacrifice and devotion to duty, this officer has set an example which, although attained by few, is admired by all.

Appendix XXI

Memories of the Bruneval Raid by Don Preist

One day I got another call from the Air Ministry in London and was told to report to the HQ of the 1st Airborne Division at Netheravon in Wiltshire. After lunch with several officers – including Major-General Browning and Major Bromley-Martin, I was taken upstairs to a room with a large table on which was a large aerial photograph. Bromley-Martin said to me "This was taken from a great height over the north coast of France." He then invited me to have a look at it in detail giving me a magnifying glass. The detail was amazingly good. He pointed to an object about the size of a pea. "Do you think that that could be a mobile radar? Could that round thing be a small antenna dish? Attached to a small cubicle, mounted on a rotatable pedestal?"

I stared at the photo for a long time using the magnifying glass. Finally I said to Major Bromley-Martin, "I think you are right. It could be a radar at a rather high frequency."

"I'll tell you why we're so interested," he said. "The Germans have been shooting down our bombers over the Ruhr Valley at night, when the sky is completely overcast there by anti-aircraft fire. Their accuracy is amazing. We know they have a radar for gunlaying called a Würzburg. This one across the Channel looks like a Würzburg. It may be a bit smaller. We intend to make a raid and bring it back here. By taking it apart we may learn something interesting, like how to jam it. Or something. Would you like to come along?"

I replied I certainly would and asked when do we start. He replied "Then come back here in a couple of days. We'll train you in parachute jumping. This is going to be a raid by paratroops. When they have taken the equipment and neutralised the Germans they will move it down the cliffs and the Navy will take it away in their boats."

I asked how high the cliffs were and was told they were about 300 feet high but they were not too steep.

On the way back to Swanage my feet were already a long way off the ground. This was to be a great adventure. The next day I got a telephone call from Bromley-Martin: "Sorry to disappoint you. Somebody pointed out you are a radar expert loaded with information, most of it secret. If you fell into the hands of the enemy it could be a bit awkward, possibly very unpleasant for you. So we want to cancel the paratroop training and have you go with the Navy, make a landing on the beach and make sure the radar gear is brought safely back."

I was disappointed and said so but said I would go along with whatever they wanted, I asked what the next move was and I was told to report at a certain time and date at Combined Operations HQ in London.

So I went up to London and met with a Wing Commander Casa-Maury, who explained to me my next three roles. He first explained about the plan for the forthcoming raid reminding me that it was most secret and that the raid had to take the enemy completely by surprise. Then we came to my three tasks, firstly I was to advise a Brigadier Schonland who was in charge of the detachment of Royal Engineers on how to dismantle a piece of delicate equipment without hopefully wrecking the contents. Secondly I was to operate a radio receiver that I was to take in a landing craft when we crossed the Channel and try to pick up the German radar signals. Lastly, I was instructed to report to Cowes on the Isle of Wight to take part in exercises in which we would all gain experience in making landings at night on a beach.

My next temporary home was a house in Cowes on the Isle of Wight taken over by the Government for billeting service personnel. I spent the nights there except when out in boats practicing landings.

We spent a lot of time on board our mother ship, an ex-cross channel passenger ferry boat. From the davits, normally used for lowering life boats in an emergency, our Assault Landing Craft could be lowered into the water. There was plenty of room on the mother ship. We used it for meetings and relaxation. There was a great deal of ribbing among the troops, mostly good natured. A certain Duke who had large ears and a rosy baby face was known as 'Trotters'. He really did resemble a piglet. The ship's bar was well-patronised in the evenings when we were not at sea. I do remember this well as I didn't often get on ships and so the customary excise duty on alcohol was waived. A gin cost 3 pence (just over 1p in today's currency) and a Drambuie 7 pence (3p). Because of this the amount of alcohol consumed was beyond the capacity of many of us. This made some of the daytime seagoing exercises colourful. One day we were far from shore. I heard the song of a meadowlark and looking round in astonishment I saw one of the paratroopers grinning at me mischievously. He had imitated the bird song perfectly. There was a lot of waiting. What we were waiting for was a favourable combination of moonlight, calm sea and favourable tides. Our ALCs were unseaworthy unless the sea was fairly calm. Rain would interfere with good visibility. In England in February this combination is somewhat rare.

Then one day we got the word- "Tonight's the night!" We put on our battle dress, warm clothing because at sea the nights were bitterly cold, blackened our faces with burnt cork because white faces would be too visible in the moonlight, and had our briefing about the plan of action. The paratroopers were being dropped by Whitley bombers together with some sappers to take care of the radar equipment. Our boats would arrive by sea at the appointed time. We had enough boats to hold all the paratroopers as well as our small force, including me, to ensure the safe removal of the radar gear. Three miles off the French coast a few Motor Gunboats would be ready to cover the withdrawal of the ALCs. One would pick up me and the radar gear. It was a good plan in my view, but as so often happens things did not go quite according to plan. About 20 miles from the French coast we got into the ALCs and were lowered into the water and proceeded under our own steam. It was very cold. I was suitably dressed in many layers of clothing and fur-lined flying boots. I had my little radio receiver, tuned to 550 MHz., the frequency of the radar.

I picked up the signal from the radar with no difficulty. It got louder and softer, rhythmically because it had a narrow beam and it was sweeping through an arc of about 180 degrees. I was not too concerned about our boats being detected because we were very close to the water and had no superstructure. A mile or so from the French coast we stopped and waited for the show to begin. For a long time nothing happened. It was a worry. We could not discuss it by radio between the boats, we had been told that radio silence was imperative until we were contacted by the paratroopers ashore. At last we saw signs of activity ashore. The signal from my receiver disappeared. We then moved into the shore, expecting to land peacefully on the beach. To our surprise we were being fired on from a machine gun post on the top of the cliff. Evidently it had not been put out of action as planned. We could see the tracer bullets. Obviously it was aiming at us. We were sitting ducks but most of the bullets went into the water. While this was going on the troops came down the cliffs. I spotted the radar gear and had it put into my boat. We tried to move out to sea but our boats were stuck in the sand.

Because of the delay the tide which had been fully in at the appointed hour was now ebbing fast. The water was shallow. A gallant RN Lieutenant jumped overboard and managed to attach a line between my boat and another boat that was about to move. With a lot of pushing and shoving, still under fire, we got under way. I heard later the Navy chap deservedly got a decoration.

Finally the machine gun stopped firing. We sailed away and soon found the MGBs. By now quite a sea was running. My job was to get the captured equipment onto a MGB. I climbed aboard one of the MGBs and told the chaps on the ALC to hand the gear up to me. I was leaning over the rail and it seemed like when the MGB went up on a wave, the ALC went down. It was therefore becoming a tricky operation and I still remember with horror the consequences after all the hard work, the preparations and the battle itself, of dropping the stuff in the drink. Luckily everything got safely passed up to me and it was all on board the MGB. Flight Sergeant Cox also came across and without delay I got Cox to come below. I was conscious that I wanted him to tell me what had happened before he forgot any details.

"Please, Sir," he begged, "I'm seasick. I want to be sick." I had visions of Cox, incapacitated for hours, exhausted and in a daze, unable to remember anything much, so I showed no mercy. "Sorry, old man. Come down below and tell me the story. Then you can be sick." He did as he was told, gave me his report very clearly, then went aloft, leaned over the rail and was very, very sick. He was a brave and extremely capable man.

By then the dawn had come and the daylight grew. The commander of the MGB, a young man dressed in flannel trousers and a sweater seemed quite upset, moaning at the lack of an RAF escort. To me this didn't seem to matter as I went below deck again as I'd been offered a tot of Navy rum which went down very well. Soon we were back in Portsmouth and I met Bromley-Martin and supervised the transport of the radar equipment ashore. The next day, tired but happy, I was taken by Bromley-Martin to the Air Ministry. I was introduced to the Assistant Chief of the Air Staff, Air Marshal Sir Charles Portal. He was terribly pleased by the success of the raid and shook my hand warmly. Over lunch with B-M at his club he told me that at one point a flotilla of German E-Boats had sailed along the coast between us and the shore, but fortunately they did not see us.

A day or so later at Worth Matravers I remember having a good look at the captured gear and admired the German craftsmanship and technology it revealed. Then it was whisked away to the Royal Aircraft Establishment at Farnborough for further study. I heard later what they did. It was very significant in terms of the radar war. They had found a weak spot in the design of the receiver. They then designed a very clever jammer which was installed in our bombers. This story should really be told by those who actually did it, at RAE Farnborough, but I will simply state what I was told about it.

The Würzburg designers apparently made one small mistake which had great consequences. The receiver was a superheterodyne with a front end tuned to about 550 MHz, a local oscillator and an intermediate frequency amplifier. The wire from the mixer to the intermediate frequency amplifier was unshielded, so that if a modulated signal at the intermediate frequency, for example a jamming signal, was introduced there it would appear at the output of the Würzburg receivers in Germany assuming that they were identical to the one we ran off with at Bruneval. The observed fact that the jamming was successful proved that this was indeed the case. Exactly how this was done at RAE I do not know but was told it was a great help to our bomber crews.

[*Author's note: In spite of asking several pertinent questions as regards what happened to the captured Würzburg equipment after the war, no answers have ever been received. I can only assume that with the end of the war there were more than enough Würzburgs left over for the Allies to play with and the captured equipment got sent to a scrap yard.*]

Appendix XXII

Reports from two Prisoners of War taken on the raid after interrogation back in England

P/W was a telephone orderly in the house, but was sleeping. At about 0115 hours he was awakened by the Uffz and told to go to the telephone which was ringing. The *Oberfeldwebel* ordered him to awaken the section as enemy parachute troops had landed. Grenades were issued and the MG was brought up from the forward to the rear position, in order to cover the hill opposite. The whole section took up position behind the house eight minutes after the first alarm. The Bn Cdr then rang up and asked what was the matter. The P/W reported the landing of parachute troops and said that the section was in position. The Bn Cdr asked for the *Feldwebel*. Firing then started which was heard by the Bn Cdr. The P/W called at the door for the *Feldwebel*, but came under fire. A runner then came back for tracer ammunition and magazines, and took them out to the section which was then using hand grenades. The P/W turned out the lights and went into an inner room as he could not get out. The enemy threw in hand grenades and P/W surrendered without firing his pistol.

When the raid was reported P/W was ordered to remain in the house used by the coast defence sector to which he belonged and to telephone to Bn HQ. He stayed there with hand grenades coming through the window and bursting all round him. Every few minutes he was called by a major who was in the last stages of agitation. The major told him not to make so much noise, and P/W explained that the noise was caused by hand grenades bursting in the room. The major thereupon told him to withdraw. Before he could do so, British troops burst in, firing tommy guns. P/W said that, as the room was in darkness, he could see them, but they were unable to see him. He wondered whether he should fire but could not bring himself to shoot into a man's body at a range of a few yards. He therefore surrendered.

Second Account

The following information has been obtained from an RDF operator brought back by the paratroopers who raided Cap d'Antifer on the night of 27th/28th February 1942.

P/W is very willing to impart all he knows, but is of limited intelligence. For instance, he was unable to cope with morse during his training and even after over two months practical experience of the Würzburg-Gerät, he still believes that the instrument 'sees' the aircraft in some way and is consequently less effective in bad than in good weather.

In view of P/W's lack of scientific knowledge, the present report confines itself to a faithful rendering of his descriptions and explanations and does not purport to draw conclusions of a technical nature.

P/W came off sentry duty at 2120 hours on the evening of 27th February and was resting in the empty house on the sea front which is used as a guard room and beach post HQ. He took off his equipment and boots, as he was permitted to so, and went to sleep. A man remained at the telephone to take any messages, to call the NCO, if necessary and to awaken in good time the sentries who were next to go on duty. P/W was awakened at about 0100 hours and told by the NCO in charge to dress and put on his equipment. The NCO was annoyed because the men were so slow in getting ready.

It was a brilliant moonlit night; there was no wind and visibility was very good. The weather was relatively mild and the sea was calm. The NCO hearing low-flying planes, went outside to look. Almost immediately afterwards the man on telephone duty called him in to speak to Company HQ, who told him that parachute troops had landed on the fairly high ground a little inland.

The man on telephone duty (Schmidt) was left to man the telephone. The NCO ordered the LMG from the post at C to be brought in and assembled the section in the first place at the house. One sentry was also recalled from the beach post, leaving only two on duty there. The NCO then went out at the back of the house and examined the high ground where the British troops were thought to be located. He could see men moving, and in order to satisfy himself that they were not Germans fired one white Verey light. As he received no answering signal he fired his machine pistol high into the air in that direction. He was then convinced that the men were enemy troops and ordered his section and the LMG into the disjointed trench system at H, the LMG being mounted first of all at point K behind the pillbox at point E.

The P/W was then ordered by the NCO to go to the sentry box (C) and fetch some Verey pistol ammunition. When the P/W returned, the fire of the attacking party was very heavy on the whole area covered by points B, C, D, E and H. P/W was then ordered to point K, to take the LMG to point marked MG and to assist in carrying SAA. He duly compiled with this order. Thereupon he was ordered to go to point B and fetch hand grenades. P/W attempted to do so in the face of heavy rifle and MG fire, but he was hit and took cover eventually reaching the empty pillbox at D where he was found and taken prisoner. Action was then finished in so far as the P/W was concerned. When he reached our boats he found that P/W Schmidt had also been taken at point B where he had remained at the telephone.

This prisoner's name was Tewes.

Appendix XXIII

Appendix to Report by Commander, The Airborne Division on 'Biting'

Training Programme as actually carried out by C Company 2nd Parachute Battalion

January 14th
First warning to 1st Parachute Brigade that one company with sappers and first reinforcements, would be required for training in combined operations.

January 24th
C Company 2nd Parachute Battalion and attached sappers, moved from Hardwick Camp to Tilshead Camp (Salisbury Plain). (Move had been postponed for 4 days owing to snow.)

January 25th to February 8th
Preliminary ground training, collection of stores and equipment, first meeting with 51 Squadron (about February 7th), decisions on weapons and equipment to be carried in containers and notification of those to AFEE (Airborne Forces Experimental Establishment). Training very severely restricted by heavy snow. Much equipment not yet available. Concentration on night training.

February 9th to 14th
Move to and return from Inveraray. Preliminary combined training with Royal Navy. Musketry.

February 15th
Aircraft drill practices with 51 Squadron RAF, followed by practice drop as a complete force on open ground just east of Divisional HQ. All containers also intended to drop under new system; nearly all did and final adjustments carried out as necessary.

February 16th
First practice with Royal Navy on south coast (Redcliffe Fort). No aircraft. ALCs to come inshore 2000 hours, but cancelled about that time owing to weather. Company returned to Tilshead.

February 17th
Should have been combined night rehearsal with Royal Navy and RAF in Arish Mell area, but weather turned very bad at last minute. Also ground frozen, with deep ruts and unsuitable for dropping. Aircraft therefore dropped containers only, but few were dropped in right place as visibility very bad. Company went to wrong place and took no part in practice. They stayed night with Gunnery Wing, AFV School, Lulworth Camp.

February 18th
Practice with Royal Navy in Arish Mell area. No aircraft. ALCs to come inshore 2000 hours but again cancelled at about 2015 hours, as weather unsuitable. Company carried

out their own part of the practice according to plan and stayed night with AFV School again.

February 19th

Company returned to Tilshead Camp. Sappers practiced with RDF set loaned by Colonel RJ Schonland. Lecture on escaping by MI9.

February 20th

Demonstration of how to cross wire obstacles, by troops of No 3 Commando. Practice with Royal Navy in Southampton Water. No aircraft. ALCs to come inshore 2015 hours. Practice successful except that troops could not actually embark in ALCs as falling tide beached some ALCs and prevented others closing shore. Company returned to Tilshead.

February 21st to 23rd

Final collecting of equipment, clothing, identity discs, weapons etc. Packing of containers. Training in attacking pillboxes and wire, by day and night. Final rehearsals by each party of own particular tasks. Thorough study by all ranks of models and photos. Liaison with 51 Squadron RAF.

February 24th to 27th

Standing by for the operation. Study of plan and all relevant information, all minor details of training and liaison with 51 Squadron RAF continued.

Appendix XXIV

Containers/Stores/Weapons Taken on Operation Biting

AIRCRAFT NUMBER	LOAD	WEAPONS	CONTAINERS
1 Nelson	2 i/c	Knife .45 pistol 3 square mags 3 HE grens	A1 RED
	1 Sgt	Knife Sten 8 spare mags 3 HE grens	1 Bren
	1 Cpl.	Knife Rifle Bayonet 50 rds 3 HE grens	1 Hatbox
	No 1 Bren Gun	Knife .45 pistol 3 spare mags 1 Bren Gun	6 Rifles & Bayonets
	No 2 Bren Gun	Knife .45 pistol 3 spare mags 3 HE grens	300 rds bandolier
	3 ORs	Knife Rifle Bayonet 50 rds 3 HE grens	3 Wire Cutters
			1 No 38 W/T set
2 Nelson	Sgt	Knife Sten 6 spare mags 3 HE grens	A2 RED
	Cpl	Knife Sten 6 spare mags 3 HE grens	1 Bren
	6 ORs	Knife Rifle Bayonet 50 rds	1 Hatbox
	No 1 Bren Gun	Knife 1 Bren Gun .45 pistol 3 spare mags	6 Rifle &
	No 2 Bren Gun	Knife .45 pistol 3 spare mags 3 HE grens	Bayonets
			300 rds bandolier
			3 Wire Cutters
3 Nelson	Sgt	Knife Sten 8 spare mags 3 HE grens	B1 & B2 RED
	Cpl	Knife Sten 8 spare mags 3 HE grens	1 Bren
	6 ORs	Knife Rifle Bayonet 3 HE grens	1 Hatbox
	2 Nos 1 Bren Gun	Knife Bren Gun each .45 pistol 3 spare mags	2 Rifles & Bayonets
	2 Nos 2 Bren Gun	Knife .45 pistol 3 spare mags 3 HE grens	100 rds bandolier
			1 Wire Cutter
4 Nelson	1 Sgt	Knife Sten 8 spare mags 3 HE grens	C RED
	1 Cpl	Knife Rifle Bayonet 50 rds 3 HE grens	1 Bren
	2 Sprs	Knife .45 pistol 3 spare mags 3 HE grens	1 Hatbox
	1 No 1 Bren Gun	Knife 1 Bren Gun .45 pistol 3 spare mags	5 Rifles & Bayonets
	1 No 2 Bren Gun	Knife .45 pistol 3 spare mags 3 HE grens	250 rds bandolier
	4 ORs	Knife Rifle Bayonet 50 rds 3 HE grens each	3 Wire Cutters
			B1 VIOLET
			Mine Detector
5 Jellicoe	1 Subaltern	Knife .45 pistol 3 spare mags 2 HE grens	E1 AMBER
	1 Sgt	Knife Sten 8 spare mags 2 HE grens	1 Trolley
	1 Cpl	Knife Sten 8 spare mags 2 HE grens	F1 VIOLET
	5 ORs	Knife Sten 8 spare mags 2 HE grens each	Explosives Tools packed in
	2 Sprs	Knife .45 pistol 3 spare mags	4 bags

AIRCRAFT NUMBER	LOAD	WEAPONS	CONTAINERS
6 Hardy	Coy Comd	Knife .45 pistol 3 spare mags 2 HE grens	E1 AMBER
	1 Sgt	Knife Sten 8 spare mags 2 HE grens	1 Trolley
	1 Cpl	Knife Sten 8 spare mags 2 HE grens	F1 VIOLET Explosives Tools
	5 Ors	Knife Sten 8 spare mags 2 HE grens each	packed in 4 bags
	1 Spr	Knife .45 pistol 3 spare mags	1 No 38 W/T set
	1 Specialist	Knife Sten 8 spare mags 2 HE grens	
7 Hardy	1 RE Officer	Knife .45 pistol 3 spare mags 2 HE grens	E3 AMBER
	1 Spr	Knife .45 pistol 3 spare mags 2 HE grens	1 Trolley
	1 Sgt	Knife Sten 8 spare mags 2 HE grens	F3 VIOLET Explosives Tools
	1 Cpl	Knife Sten 8 spare mags 2 HE grens	packed in 4 bags
	5 ORs	Knife Sten 8 spare mags 2 HE grens each	
	1 Specialist	Knife Sten 8 spare mags 2 HE grens	
8 Drake	1 Sgt	Knife Sten 8 spare mags 6 HE grens	G RED
	1 Cpl	Knife Sten 8 spare mags 6 HE grens	8 Rifles & Bayonets
	8 ORs	Knife Rifle and Bayonet each	400 rds bandolier
			2 Telegraph wire cutters
			(insulated) '
			1 No 38 W/T set
9 Rodney	1 Subaltern	Knife .45 pistol 3 spare mags 3 HE grens	B3 RED
	1 Sgt	Knife Rifle Bayonet 50 rds 3 HE grens	1 Bren
	1 Cpl	Knife Rifle Bayonet 50 rds 3 HE grens	1 Hatbox
	2 No 1 Bren Gun	Knife 1 Bren Gun .45 pistol 3 spare mags	2 Rifles & Bayonets
	2 No 2 Bren Gun	Knife .45 pistol 3 spare mags 3 HE grens	100 rds bandolier
	1 Signaller	Knife .45 pistol 3 spare mags 3 HE grens	1 No 38 W/T set
	2 ORs	Knife Rifle Bayonet 50 rds 3 HE grens	B4 RED
			1 Bren 1 Hatbox
			2 Rifles & Bayonets
			100 rds bandolier
			1 Verey Pistol
			1 Signal Torch
			2 Red & 2 Green Cartridges

AIRCRAFT NUMBER	LOAD	WEAPONS	CONTAINERS
10 Rodney	1 Sgt	Knife Rifle Bayonet 50 rds 3 HE grens	B5 RED
	1 Cpl	Knife Rifle Bayonet 50 rds 3 HE grens	1 Bren
	2 No 1 Bren Gun	Knife Bren Gun each .45 pistol 3 spare mags	1 Hatbox
	2 No 2 Bren Gun	Knife .45 pistol 3 spare mags 3 HE grens	2 Rifles & Bayonets
	1 Spr	Knife .45 pistol 3 spare mags 3 HE grens	100 rds bandolier
	2 ORs	Knife Rifle Bayonet 50 rds 3 HE grens	1 Signal Torch
	1 Signaller	Knife .45 pistol 3 spare mags 3 HE grens	B6 RED
			1 Bren
			1 Hatbox
			2 Rifles & Bayonets
			100 rds bandolier
			1 Verey Pistol
			4 Cartridges
			H2 GREEN
			D/F Set
			1 Signal Torch
			1 Verey Pistol 2 Red & 2
			Green Cartridges
			D2 VIOLET
			Mine Detector
11 Rodney	1 Sgt	Knife Rifle Bayonet 50 rds 3 HE grens	B7 RED
	1 Cpl	Knife Rifle Bayonet 50 rds 3 HE grens	1 Bren
	2 No 1 Bren Gun	Knife Bren Gun each .45 pistol 3 spare mags	1 Hatbox
	2 No 2 Bren Gun	Knife .45 pistol 3 spare mags 3 HE grens	2 Rifles & Bayonets
	1 Signaller	Knife .45 pistol 3 spare mags 3 HE grens	100 rds bandolier
	1 Spr	Knife .45 pistol 3 spare mags 3 HE grens	B8 RED
	2 ORs	Knife Rifle Bayonet 50 rds 3 HE grens	1 Bren
			1 Hatbox
			2 Rifles & Bayonets
			100 rds bandolier
			1 Verey Pistol
			4 Cartridges
			J1 GREEN
			18 W/T set
			1 Signal Torch

AIRCRAFT NUMBER	LOAD	WEAPONS	CONTAINERS
12 Rodney	1 Subaltern	Knife .45 pistol 3 spare mags 3 HE grens	A3 RED
	1 Sgt	Knife Rifle Bayonet 50 rds 3 HE grens	1 Bren
	1 Cpl	Knife Rifle Bayonet 50 rds 3 HE grens	1 Hatbox
	1 Signaller	Knife .45 pistol 3 spare mags 3 HE grens	6 Rifles & Bayonets
	1 No 1 Bren Gun	Knife 1 Bren Gun .45 pistol 3 spare mags	300 rds bandolier
	1 No 2 Bren Gun	Knife .45 pistol 3 spare mags 3 HE grens	J2 GREEN
	4 ORs	Knife Rifle Bayonet 50 rds 3 HE grens	18 W/T set
			1 Signal Torch
			1 Verey Pistol
			4 Cartridges

RE Containers

CONTAINER NUMBER	PURPOSE OF CONTENTS	DETAILS OF CONTENTS
D1 Nelson	Mine detection on the beach	Polish mine detector (a) Instrument (b) Search rod
	Taping a path through the minefield	4 rolls of white tape, each 50 yds long. 20 – 6" nails
	A/Tk mines on the road to the beach	
		5 A/Tk mines Mk IV.
	Wire cutting	1 box fuses.
		1 pr wire cutters RE pattern
D2 Rodney	Ditto	Ditto
E1 Jellicoe	Carrying away objects of interest	1 trolley
E2 Jellicoe	Ditto	Ditto
E3 Hardy	Ditto	Ditto
F1 Jellicoe	Tools and Explosives for opening windows and doors	1 No 1 bag
	Tools for opening set and removing parts	1 No 2 bag
	Wrecking set after work is done	
		1 No 3 bag
F2 Jellicoe	Tools and Explosives for opening windows and doors	1 No 1 bag
	Tools for opening set and removing parts	1 No 2 bag
	Photographic set	
		1 No 4 bag
F3 Hardy	Same as F2	Same as F2

Notes on Attached Tables
- D1 and D2 are exactly alike.
- E1, E2 and E3 are three folding trolleys.
- F1, F2 and F3 are very nearly similar; their contents are:-
- Bag of tools and explosives F1 F2 F3
- Bag of electricians tools F1 F2 F3
- Bag of incendiaries F1
- Photographic equipment F2 F3
- One man in each Jellicoe 5, Hardy 6 and Hardy 7 must carry a detonator magazine.

Details of bags.
No 1 bag
- 3 clams, magnet and screw
- 3 made up charges
- 8 short lengths of safety fuze
- 1 roll insulating tape
- 2 jemmies
- 2 axes insulating handles

No 2 bag
- 1 claw hammer
- 1 cold chisel
- 1 hacksaw and spare blade
- 1 large screwdriver
- 1 long thin screwdriver
- 1 comb spanner
- 1 pr end cutting pliers
- 1 pr side cutting pliers
- 2 prs rubber gloves
- 1 roll of copper wire
- 1 head torch
- 2 hand torches
- 1 shifting spanner 6" handle

No 3 bag
- 3 Tarbabies
- 2 tin boxes of tysules (incendiaries)
- 1 box of fuzees

No 4 bag
- 1 Leica camera with wide angle lens and film loaded
- 1 tin of spare bulbs
- 36 flash bulbs
- 1 hand torch

Appendix XXV

Attack plan and stores and equipment for Operation Musketoon

Demolition Orders

Plan 1. Target.

(a) Pipeline and Valve House.
(b) Power Station.

Target (a). Attacking party to consist of Force Commander, 4 ORs, No 2 Commando and 1 Norwegian wireless operator.

Valve House to be attacked by party of 2 ORs under Force Commander. Norwegian OR will assist with verbal and active disposal of possible Norwegian watchman, and will thereafter take up covering position.

Valve chains will be locked and valve arms wire bound. On completion of task, party will withdraw to pipeline demolition point and then to foot of cable railway.

Pipeline party consists of 2 ORs, each carrying 2 link charges in rucksack, to be worn on chest, while paying out on either side of pipe. No 1 mounts concrete block nearest to valve house, straddles pipe just below it, and pays out link charge on either side. Charge is bound at right angles to pipe by No 2.

No 1 supported by rope, slides about 10 feet lower, and pays out second charge, which is bound vertically below by No 2. This is repeated on second pipe.

No 1 stands by with fuses and time delays, ready to initiate on receipt of signal. No 2 takes up position halfway between demolition point and lower end of cable railway (where main change of pipe direction takes place) to pass on light signal relayed from power station. Norwegian wireless operator (valve house party) receives signal at change of direction point and passes it on to No 2 party.

Target (b). Attacking party to consist of Captain J B Houghton, 4 ORs No 2 Commando and 1 Norwegian OR.

Speed is essential in making an entry and a vigorous, quick assault is to be recommended whether the watchman is permanently on the spot or not. It might even be desirable to make entry through a window, though this is governed to some extent by the nature of the window frames (steel or wood).

1 OR takes up covering position outside power station southern entrance. Once in, Captain Houghton and the OR will go straight upstairs to the control room. The watchman will be assured that he will come to no harm if he does as he is told. He will be firmly bound and gagged, and put on one side until withdrawal time.

Procedure will then be as follows:-
1. Captain Houghton will supervise maximum damage to switch installations by Norwegian OR.
2. The British OR will force the ground floor door into the tunnel and start the two smoke bombs 200 yards and 100 yards along it. Returning forthwith to the station.
3. The two remaining British ORs will already have started on charge laying with twin cordtex leads in half herring-bone formation. Charges will be taped in angle between bearing pedestal and bearing support, with installation point near door at southern end of power house. Delay Timing 10 minutes, with time pencils and safety fuse.
4. Charge-laying completed, Captain Houghton will signal by torch to foot of cable railway. Signal will mean "Charge-laying completed, initiation takes place in three minutes." All but initiator will proceed forthwith to foot of cable railway preparatory to withdrawal.

Force Commander and 2 British ORs will cover withdrawal to foot of cable railway of both charge initiations. Captain Houghton will lead main body on first stretch of withdrawal route.

Plan 2 – In the event of pipeline attack proving impracticable, task will be restricted to power station. Extra explosives available will be used on switch installations, transformers, converters etc., and on generators. Pipe line demolition party will assist power house party. Remainder of party to provide covering fire between power house and assembly point at foot of cable railway.
Weight of charges: Pipeline charges- 4 link charges of 20 lbs each. Power station charges- 6 pedestal charges of 5 lbs each. Smoke bombs- 2 of 1 ½ lbs. Fuses etc. for pipeline about 2 lbs. Fuses etc. for power station- about 6 lbs.

Signal Plan
1. Norwegian signaller in party will carry a special signal set supplied by SOE.
2. Instructions as to how to work this set will be given to party.
3. This set is specially tuned to give low transmission which is unlikely to be picked up by the enemy, but arrangements will be made with SOE listening sets so that messages can be picked up satisfactorily.
4. Two messages at times to be fixed by SOE will be sent back by Force Commander in code to indicate to Officer Commander Flying Boat:-
A. (i) That he is come next day to Beach A Bremneset.
B. Beach B. SW corner of Tekamoma Island.
C. (ii) That he is not to come at all.

5. If no message is received, Officer Commanding Flying Boat will at first light on D15 and D 17 (i.e. September 25th and 27th) land his Flying Boat on Beach A to pick up party and, if party is not seen, proceed to Beach B before returning.
6. Military Force commander will include in his signal message a code letter to report:-
(a) If operation successful.
(b) If operation partially successful.
(c) If operation unsuccessful.
7. SOE will immediately report receipt of signal message to:-
(a) CCO HQ's.
(b) Officer Commanding Flying Boat.

Stores taken on Operation Musketoon
Arms
- 2 SMLE Mk III
- 2 Sten SMGs (silenced)
- All with 3 magazines.
- 8 .45 Colt automatic pistols
- All with 2 magazines

SAA
- .303 25 rounds per man = 50
- .45 28 rounds per man = 224
- 9 mm 90 rounds per man = 180

Clothing (per man)
1 suit BD, 3 pairs socks oil, 1 pair boots soulier vibram and four spare laces, 1 pair braces, 2 pairs underpants woollen long, 2 vests woollen, 1 shirt, 1 housewife, 1 gas cape practice, 1 balaclava, 1 roll neck jersey (blue), 1 towel, 2 handkerchiefs, 1 pair anklets web, tooth brush, soap and razor, 1 pair gloves 3 compartment wool and silk, 1 pair gym shoes white, 1 jerkin leather, 1 Mae West life jacket.

Equipment
1 rucksack British bergen large, steel frame, 1 belt WE, 1 knife fighting, 1 First FD, 1 togglerope, KFS, 1 torch hand, small waterproof and spare battery and bulb, 1 bag waterproof, Icelandic sleeping bag, toilet paper, clamp ons, spectacles, tinted.
All the above carried by each man.

The following to be carried by the party as a whole.
- 4 wire cutters, 6 compasses with pouch, 6 cooking containers with primus and petrol,
- 6 packets of spare prickers, 4 watches wrist waterproof, 6 protractors, 2 pairs binoculars, 1 telescope scout, 8 pistol pouches, 8 pouches ammunition, Alpine Rope 100 feet.

Food 10 days ration per man

- Pemmican 40 ozs per man
- Biscuit 90 ozs per man
- Cocoa and milk powder 10 ozs per man
- Chocolate 20 ozs per man
- Lump sugar 20 ozs per man
- Cheese 40 ozs per man
- Horlicks 10 ozs per man
- Oatmeal 40 ozs per man
- Dried Fruit 40 ozs per man
- Tea 10 ozs per man
- Halibut oil 10 capsules per man
- Salt 2 ½ ozs per man
- Tobacco, cigarettes and matches
- Weight approximately 2 lbs per man per day.

Escape kit: 10 days concentrated rations per man

- 1 handkerchief map (Norway and Sweden)
- 1 file rubber covered
- 1 compass
- 1 cap civilian
- 1 pair trousers blue (Naval PO)
- £12 Norwegian in purses
- Maps – 2 sets sectional map showing Glomfjord to Sweden.

Appendix XXVI

Kit List, Stores and Nominal Roll for Operation Freshman

Kit List

ITEM	RUCKSACK	WORN	REMARKS
Anorak jacket, white	1		
Anorak trousers, white	1		
Blue sweater		1	
Ski trousers		1	
Mittens		1	
Gloves, gauntlet		1	
Gloves, silk		1	
Gloves, woollen	1		
Helmets, balaclava	1		
Steel helmet		1	
Cap, FS	1		
Ski scarf	1		
Sleeping bag	1		
Rucksack straps	3		
Compass	1		
Special 48 hr rations	5		
Margarine, lbs	1		
Barley sugar, lbs	1		
Fruit bar, lbs	1		
Oxo cubes	20		
Horlicks, tablets	20		
Salt, ozs	2		
Spare tommy cookers	5		
Escape kit	1		Map, money and file
Sunglasses	1		
Wind cheater		1	
Frostbite ointment, tins	2		
BD coats		1	
BD trousers, pairs		1	
Boots		1	
Socks, prs	4	2	
Anklets, web, prs		1	
String vests		1	
GS vests	1	1	

ITEM	RUCKSACK	WORN	REMARKS
Pants	1	1	
Shirts	1	1	
Shaving kit	1		
Scissors, prs	1		
Housewife	1		
Towel	1		
Matches	2		
Gas capes	1		
Spare bootlaces, prs	3		
Mess tin	1		
Forks	1		
Spoon	1		
Handkerchiefs	4		
Dubbin, tins	1		
Foot powder	1		
2 Star red signal	1		
Torch	1		
First field dressing	1		
Shell dressing	1		
Medical pack	1		
Jack knife and lanyard		1	
Water bottle		1	

Stores List

ITEM	QUANTITY	ISSUED TO
Rifle	14	Bailey, Grundy, Faulkner, Bray, Belfield, Smallman, Stephens, White, Norman, Simkins, Farrell, Blackburn, Hunter and Smith
Rifle Ammunition	560	40 rounds per man with a rifle
Pistol	4	Allen, Methven, Healey and Knowles
Pistol Ammunition	200	50 rounds per man with a pistol
Sten	16	Thomas, Williams, Legate, Campbell, Bevan, Pendlebury, Cairncross, Bonner, Jacques, Jackson, Masters, Walsh, Strathdee, Doig, Davies and Fraser
Sten Ammunition	2,048	Sappers issued with 96 rounds each and glider pilots with 224
Day's rations	340	Ten per man
Rucksack filled	34	One per man
Torches	25	One per man except Faulkner, Stephen, Simkins, Smith, Walsh, Strathdee, Doig, Davies and Fraser
Wire Cutters, T6	2	Thomas and Bray
Wire Cutters, Two handles	2	Healey and Campbell

ITEM	QUANTITY	ISSUED TO
Wire Cutters, folding	2	Cairncross and Farrell
Fighting knives	2	Allen and Methven
Watches	11	Allen, Methven, Healey, Knowles, Thomas, Campbell, Jackson, Strathdee, Doig, Davies and Fraser
Maps A &B	7	Knowles, Williams, Bailey, Grundy, Legate, Faulkner and Campbell
Maps C&D	6	Bonner, White, Norman, Jacques, Simkins and Jackson
Maps E	3	Methven, Hunter and Walsh
Maps F, G & H	8	Healey, Farrell, Blackburn, Masters, Smith, Walsh, Strathdee and Doig
Maps I, J, K & L	1	Allen
Wallets	34	One per man
Binoculars	1	Allen
Deception wallets	1	Allen
Sets 9 – ½ lb	6	Bailey, Grundy, Faulkner, Norman, Jackson and Farrell
Double pull switch igniters	30	Williams (4), Bailey, Grundy, Legate, Faulkner, Campbell, Bray, Bevan (2), Belfield, Cairncross (3), Bonner (2), White (2), Norman (2), Simkins, Jackson, Farrell, Blackburn, Hunter, Masters, Smith and Walsh
Jemmy	7	Grundy, Legate, Faulkner, Campbell, Cairncross, Norman and Jacques,
Gloves rubber light	8	Grundy, Legate, Faulkner, Campbell, Cairncross, Bonner, White and Norman
Footprints 6"	6	Williams, Bailey, Bevan, Cairncross, Bonner and White
3 lb split sausage charge with magnets	39	Thomas, Williams, Grundy (2), Legate, Faulkner, Campbell (2), Bray (2), Bevan (2), Belfield (2), Smallman (2), Pendlebury (2), Stephen (2), Cairncross, White, Jacques, Simkins, Jackson (2), Farrell (2), Blackburn (3), Hunter (2), Masters (2), Smith (2) and Walsh (2)
3 lb split sausage charge	9	Allen (2), Methven (2), Healey (2), Knowles (2) and Thomas
Cordtex taped 200 ft double	1,600	200 ft each to Grundy, Bray, Bevan, Belfield, Cairncross, Farrell, Masters and Walsh
Tape adhesive 200 ft	6,000	200 ft per man except glider pilots
Tape adhesive 1" rolls	60	Two per man except glider pilots
Emergency igniters	30	One per man except glider pilots
¼ lb PHE	30	One per man except glider pilots
Primers ½ oz	60	Two per man except glider pilots
Clams ½ lb	12	Allen (2), Methven (2), Healey (2), Knowles (2), Thomas, Legate and Cairncross (2)
Axes fireman	8	Williams, Grundy, Smallman, Pendlebury, Bonner, White, Jackson and Smith
Pencil time fuzes	4	Allen, Methven, Healey and Knowles

ITEM	QUANTITY	ISSUED TO
Dets Mags	4	Allen, Methven, Healey and Knowles
Striker board	30	One per man except glider pilots
Cordtex 30 ft tin	15	Allen, Methven, Healey, Knowles, Thomas, Legate, Campbell, Smallman, Stephen, Cairncross, Norman, Jacques, Blackburn, Hunter and Smith
Beehives	12	Williams (2), Grundy (2), Legate (2), Bonner (3) and Norman (3)

Complete Nominal Roll for the 'Washington Cup'

Lieutenant Allen A C
Lieutenant Methven D A
L/Sgt Healey F
L/Sgt Knowles G
Cpl Thomas J G L
Sapper Williams G S
Sapper Bailey E W
Sapper Grundy C H
Sapper Legate H J
Sapper Faulkner T W
L/Cpl Campbell A
L/Cpl Bray F W
Sapper Bevan H
Driver Belfield J T V
Sapper Smallman L
Driver Pendlebury E
Sapper Stephen J M
Cpl Cairncross J D
Sapper Bonner F
Sapper White T W
Sapper Norman R
Sapper Jacques W
Driver Simkins G
L/Cpl Jackson W M
Driver Farrell P P
Sapper Blackburn J F
Sapper Hunter J G V
L/Cpl Masters T L
Sapper Smith E J
Sapper Walsh J W
S/Sgt Strathdee M F
Sgt Doig P
P/O Davies N A
Sgt Fraser H J

Appendix XXVIII

Report by Lieutenant Colonel M Henniker on Operation Freshman 23rd November 1942

Report on Operation Freshman.

1. Object
The object of Operation Freshman was to destroy the stocks of 'heavy water' and the apparatus for making it at Vermork in southern Norway about 80 miles due west from Oslo. The scientific significance of this is not material to this report.

2. Possible Methods
(a) Attack by bomber aircraft was ruled out because of the risk of killing large numbers of Norwegians and because it was a difficult target to find.
(b) Attack by Norwegian saboteurs was considered to be too difficult having in mind the technical training required and the quantity of explosive needed.
(c) Attack by airborne troops was decided upon and three possible methods of getting to the site were considered. By flying boat, to land on the lake, by parachute or by glider. Parachute would have entailed low flying in precipitous valleys and would have aroused the populace even if none of the aircraft crashed. Glider was decided upon.

3. Force Required
Technical considerations necessitated a minimum force of 12 to 15 men. To make sure of this two Horsa gliders each towed by a Halifax bomber and each carrying one RE officer and 14 ORs besides two glider pilots was considered necessary.

4. Dates
Airborne Division first considered the operation on the middle of October. By this time the lakes were too likely to be frozen to enable a flying boat to land, yet not sufficiently frozen for a glider to land on the ice. If the operation were delayed after the November moon, a skiing party would be necessary to cover the snow. The November moon period was therefore decided upon and the horoscope showed that the moon would only cast sufficient light into the valleys between 18th November and 26th November, both inclusive.

5. Landing Ground

There were two possible alternatives. Either the gliders must be landed sufficiently near to the objective to attack the same night, or the gliders might be landed at a considerable distance from the target in a desolate place where the approach could not be seen and an approach march of several days made to the objective. This latter was ruled out by the difficulty of concealing the glider.

6. Agents

Agents could be sent to any desired landing ground to place lights and a radio homing device for the aircraft – called Rebecca.

7. Outline Plan

The outline plan was to send the agents to recce and mark a landing ground on the marshy edge of the Mösvatn Lake Lat. 40° 50' N, Long 8° 10' E. By a system of code signals they were to be told of the date of the proposed attack and by contrary they were to send reports on enemy dispositions and met conditions.

The operation was to be sent off from Skitten aerodrome – a satellite of Wick in Scotland in two similarly loaded Horsas, each containing one RE officer, two glider pilots and 14 ORs. Each glider was to be towed by a Halifax bomber crewed by personnel of 38 Wing RAF.

On arrival the men from the first glider were to wait up to 30 minutes for the second and then if necessary proceed independently. The agents were to produce guides to lead the party to the target avoiding enemy sentries on the way.

The sappers were to enter the electrolysis plant and power station and (a) destroy any stocks of 'heavy water' (b) destroy the machinery for producing heavy water and (c) damage the power station.

When the demolitions were complete the party was to divide up into small groups and make their way to Sweden where they were to say that they had been captured on a raid and had escaped, thereby entitling themselves for repatriation. Enemy dispositions are in the operation order.

8. Training

The army training presented few difficulties. The men had to be very fit and able to carry 10 days rations each. They required technical training to enable them to recognise the pieces of machinery etc. to destroy and they had to have in a high degree the military qualities of any good troops.

The RAF side was more complicated. Air crews had to learn to fly the Halifax. A night tow of a glider of up to 800 miles (supposing they could not find the objective and had to tow home) is far in advance of anything so far attempted. The aircraft had to be fitted with towing devices and with Rebecca. The whole thing had to be done in about 8 weeks.

The RE party did one week's preliminary training on Salisbury Plain. This was mainly to weld the selected men into one unit and consisted of drill, weapon training, map reading and route marches. Particular attention was paid to observation. The men were posted to watch and report o sentries and guards of units in the district without themselves being seen. The second week was spent hardening them in the mountains of north Wales. They marched over the mountains with small-scale maps and lived on hard rations on the bleak mountain sides. The next week was devoted to technical training arranged by CO HQ. It included visits to plants similar to the objective in England and Scotland.

The fourth was spent on Salisbury Plain and included fitting out with their special equipment and a rehearsal. (Weather conditions prevented flying so the ground part only was rehearsed.)

They went to the base aerodrome arriving on the Monday of the fifth week and the operation took place on the Wednesday night 19th/20th November.

The only military difficulties in the training were (a) the difficulty of getting sufficient opportunities for the glider pilots to work with the RE as they were required for flying training and (b) the distances to be covered. From Bulford to north Wales takes 14 hours, from Bulford to the base aerodrome takes 30 hours and the plants in England visited took the best part of 4 days in the train.

9. Selection of Personnel

The decision to do the operation by glider and not parachute was not made until after the training had been started. At the time there was no RE parachute unit available. Consequently the men had to come from those of 9 Fd Coy and 261 Fd Coy who were trained as parachutists. Now men cannot be compelled to parachute who are not regular paid parachutists and 9 and 261 Coys are not paid parachutists, therefore the men had to be volunteers so that made it necessary to tell them very early in the training what they were training for.

10. Security

For the reasons given in the previous paragraphs the men selected had to be told from the start that they were required for an operation that might involve parachuting and all accepted the opportunity with alacrity. They were told nothing about the time, date or place of the operation and they were given a cast iron 'cover story' to tell when asked what they were training for.

The cover story was that they were training for the Washington Cup Competition. This (fictitious) competition is a RE competition between RE units and engineer units of the US Army. It involves an approach march by air either by glider or parachute and is then a demolition task followed by an endurance test.

Under this cover story all training and most of the equipment could be dealt with in the open. Storekeepers, quartermasters, cooks, cobblers and the unit workshops where much of the equipment was made, dealt with the problems that cropped up without need for being put into the true picture.

For the first two weeks I am certain that none but the men themselves knew that an operation was afoot.

For the third week the training establishment where the technical training was arranged by CO HQ insisted on the men bringing neither berets nor divisional signs. I protested at this but was overruled by CO HQ with the result that suspicions in Bulford were first aroused when the men went off to the station in FS caps and without divisional signs.

By the end of the third week, all the intelligent NCOs and men of the party had guessed that the operation was to take place in Norway and that the objective was a power station.

On arrival at Skitten there was another rather childish breach of security. CO HQ insisted on the aerodrome being 'sealed'. The intention being to confine everyone to barracks and to censor letters and telephone conversations. But as the glider floated in to land the squadron on the aerodrome took off to move to another station. This was an operational move and could not be avoided. But there is not the slightest doubt that most of the squadron saw the gliders and left the station with this knowledge.

A much more satisfactory plan would have been to put across the Washington Cup story before our arrival at Skitten. This could well have been made to convince the RAF and other personnel on the station. In spite of this, I never heard any breach of security and I think it reflects the greatest credit on the personnel at Skitten and on the party themselves.

11. The Operation.

The operation did not go according to plan. The weather forecast was reasonable though not ideal and events showed it to be accurate.

Aircraft A in which Group Captain Cooper DFC, RAF flew with Squadron Leader Wilkinson as captain, left Skitten with a glider in tow at 1750 hours on 19th November. The glider pilots were S/Sergeant M F C Strathdee, AAC and Sergeant P Doig, AAC and the half section RE under command of Lieutenant D Methven GM RE. On approaching the Norwegian coast the Rebecca in the aircraft went unserviceable. The failure of the raid is due to this. A landfall was made and the aircraft flew towards the target but could not find it. A second attempt to find the target was made. There was barely sufficient petrol to get the tug and glider home. The tug was unable to climb above a cloud and had to fly into it over an area about 40 miles NW of the target. Ice formed; both tug and glider lost height and at last the tow-rope broke. The wireless operator sent out a signal in clear at 2355 hrs; 'Glider released in sea.' This was picked up in Wick and at another RAF station and an intersection of the bearings showed the position as over the mountains in SW Norway. At 0151 hrs on 20th November the tug returned and a careful check of courses and times proved that the glider was in fact released over land.

Aircraft B captained by Flight Lieutenant Parkinson RCAF took off from Skitten with a glider in tow at 1810 hrs on 19th November. The glider pilots were Pilot Officer Davies RAAF and Sergeant Fraser RAAF. The RE half section in the glider was under the command of Lieutenant A Allen RE. Nothing further was heard of this till at 2341 hrs a signal was received believed to have been from the tug asking for a course to bring it back to base. The position at that time was found by intersection to be Lat. 58° 16' N Long 0° 17' W. Nothing more was heard and from first light on 20th November two squadrons of Coastal Command aircraft and a destroyer searched the area all day without finding any trace.

On 21st November the following announcement was made over the German wireless and repeated in the English papers: "On the night of 19th/20th November, two British bombers, each towing a glider, penetrated southern Norway. One bomber and both gliders were forced to land. The airborne sabotage troops in the gliders were engaged and killed to the last man."

From this, all that is certain is that two gliders and the missing tug actually landed in Norway. It is impossible to have a battle in which there are no wounded and it is possible, indeed probable, that a number of the men concerned are at large in Norway. The agents reported that no glider landed in the proper place.

12. Equipment.
A detail of the equipment is in an Appendix to the Operation Order. It consisted essentially of arms (rifles and Sten guns), demolition stores, 10 days rations, sleeping bags, escape kits and maps. The majority of the equipment was produced by CO HQ. The escape plan and maps were produced by the War Office MI9.

13. The Future.
It is essential to keep from the enemy the number of men who took part as that would prejudice the chances of escape of the survivors. It is also important to keep from the enemy the objective as that would prejudice any further attack. The factors liable to give away those secrets are the casualty return of the missing men and a deception map in Lieutenant Allen's pocket. This map had a false route marked on it leading from the objective to a point on the Norwegian coast to which no-one in the party intended to escape.

14. Nominal Rolls and Next of Kin.
The nominal rolls and next of kin of Army personnel are given in Appendix C to the Operation orders with the exception of No 320272 S/Sergeant M F C Strathdee AA Corps – next of kin, Mother, Mrs. A D Strathdee, 73 Grange Park Road, Thornton Heath, Surrey. No 3250420 Sergeant P Doig AA Corps – next of kin, Mother, Mrs. A Doig, 1172 Argyle Street, Glasgow.

It is not proposed to notify next of kin until some definite news is received.

15. Organisation of the Raid.
The help given by CO HQ, Major Rheam and MI9 was extremely efficient and I am most grateful to them for the trouble they took.

16. Morale.
The morale of the troops was extremely high and did them great credit. No praise could be too great for the RAF aircrews and the glider pilots in particular who perhaps understood better the hazards of the flying part of the operation.

One can only hope and pray that such splendid men have not been lost.

Bibliography and Sources

Unpublished material

The National Archives Kew
War Diary 1st Airborne Division
War Diary 1st Parachute Brigade HQ
War Diary 1st Parachute Battalion
War Diary 2nd Parachute Battalion
War Diary 3rd Parachute Battalion
War Diary No 2 Commando
War Diary No 3 Commando
War Diary No 4 Commando
War Diary No 6 Commando
War Diary No 12 Commando
War Dairy 9th Field Company RE
War Dairy 261st Field Company RE
War Diary 1st Parachute Squadron RE

From the Ministry of Defence files (DEFE/PREM series)
Operation Biting
Operation Basalt
Operation Colossus
Operation Flipper
Operation Freshman
Operation Musketoon
Operation Record Book Central Landing Establishment

From the WO series
WO32/4273 Volunteers for Special Service (deals with formation of commandos and parachute battalions)

Documents from the Parachute Regiment and Airborne Forces Museum Aldershot
Operation Biting files
Operation Colossus files
Operation Freshman files
War Diary 11th Special Air Service Battalion

Department of Documents Imperial War Museum
Captain F Cook
S Gordon

Major General J Haydon
Colonel Sir Thomas Macpherson
Captain J Nicholl
E Smith

Sound Archive Imperial War Museum
F Birch
E Chappell
J Dunning
W Etches
G Haines
T Hill
C Kennett
C Purdon
J Ramsden
B Rose
G Salisbury
J Smale
D Struthers
R Swayne
J Timothy
G Webb
unnamed commando in 2523/E/A

Published Works
Anon, *Combined Operations 1940-1942* (HMSO 1943)
Cherry, N., *Red Berets and Red Crosses: The Story of the Medical Services in the 1st Airborne Division in World War II* (RN Sigmond 1999)
Deane-Drummond, A., *Return Ticket* (Collins 1953)
Deeley, G., *Worst Fears Confirmed* (Barny Books 2005)
Frost, J., *A Drop Too Many* (Cassell 1980)
Otway, T., *Airborne Forces* (Imperial War Museum 1990)
Peatling, R., *Without Tradition: 2 Para 1941-1945* (privately published 1994)
Pronk, P. RN, *Airborne Engineers The Shiny 9th* (RN Sigmond 2001)
Purves, T., *The Ninth* (privately published 1988)

Articles from *After the Battle* magazine
'Operation Ambassador' issue 32
'The Tragino Aqueduct Raid' issue 81
'The Vaagso Raid' issue 109

Index

Note the rank given is at the first mention although some achieved higher ranks later.

Related titles published by Helion & Company

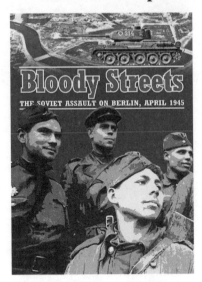

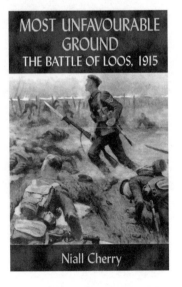

Bloody Streets: the Soviet
Assault on Berlin 1945
A. Stephan Hamilton
424pp   Hardback
ISBN 978-1-906033-12-5

Most Unfavourable Ground:
the Battle of Loos 1915
Niall Cherry
378pp   Paperback
ISBN 978-1-906033-21-7

A selection of forthcoming titles

Diary of a Red Devil: by Glider to Arnhem with the Seventh King's Own Scottish Borderers
A. Blockwell
ISBN 978-1-906033-20-0

Blood Clot: In Combat with the Patrols Platoon, 3 Para, Afghanistan 2006
J. Scott
ISBN 978-1-906033-31-6

*Bombs, Bullets and Cups of Tea. Further Voices of the
British Army in Northern Ireland 1969-98*
K. Wharton
ISBN 978-1-906033-34-7

HELION & COMPANY
26 Willow Road, Solihull, West Midlands B91 1UE, England
Telephone 0121 705 3393   Fax 0121 711 4075
Website: http://www.helion.co.uk